Baba
Symphony

Vinny Chitluri

STERLING PAPERBACKS
An imprint of
Sterling Publishers (P) Ltd.
A-59, Okhla Industrial Area, Phase-II,
New Delhi-110020.
Tel: 26387070, 26386209; Fax: 91-11-26383788
E-mail: mail@sterlingpublishers.com
www.sterlingpublishers.com

Baba's Divine Symphony
© 2014, Sterling Publishers Pvt. Ltd.
ISBN 978 81 207 8485 7
Reprint 2016

Cover designed by Mohit Suneja

Printed in India

Printed and Published by Sterling Publishers Pvt. Ltd.,
New Delhi-110 020.

PREFACE

A miracle or *leela* is defined as an extraordinary event believed to be the work of God or a saint. It is the manifestations of a living God and Baba is eternal. According to the definition, Baba performed miracles throughout the day and night then, and is doing so even now. Because, in every person's life some unbelievable, inscrutable event occurs that leaves an indelible impression on them. Thus, numerous sceptics became believers, and believers became ardent devotees.

Baba often asked his devotees to read religious texts and the lives of numerous saints, so that they could read and learn from their leelas and stories. Thus they could imbibe qualities that he liked, such as humility, devotion and complete surrender.

Leelas are like doing *japa* because you meditate while reading and are quite unaware of what is happening around you. Leelas enrich your spiritual life. It's a good way to start and end your day.

During my 60 years of devotion to Baba, I met numerous devotees who read one chapter of the *Shri Sai Satcharita* consecutively every day. I liked the idea very much, so I thought why shouldn't the devotee read a leela every day. I decided to date the leelas rather than give the days of the week; hence, this book can be read every year including the leap year. The leelas cover a wide range of issues that we face in our everyday lives.

Throughout the years many devotees have asked me to write about those people who were fortunate to have met Baba; hence, the first part of the book is dedicated to those devotees and their experience with Baba. The rest of the leelas cover a wide range of subjects, such as humour, compassion, stubbornness and empathy. This gives us a glimpse of the numerous facets of Baba's human side which is wrapped in divinity.

When I was writing this book I got a glimpse of how Shirdi was during the early 1900s and how Baba interacted with his devotees. And how no devotee was sent away empty handed. Even today, no devotee returns empty handed after visiting Shirdi. Finally, Baba has never failed to run to the aid of a devotee. Nor has a devotee ever been cast by the wayside after seeking refuge in him, and these leelas have gone to prove exactly this.

DEDICATION AND ACKNOWLEDGEMENTS

I would like to dedicate this book to Sandhya and Ajay Gupta from Agra. My *rinanubandhic* ties with them are deep and unfathomable; they stood by me and encouraged me to complete the book when I often wanted to give up. I owe them a debt of gratitude for all the help that they gave me, and thank them from the bottom of my heart.

I owe a debt of gratitude to Pawar Kaka from Pune who allowed me to take all the magazines that I wanted without hesitating for even a moment.

I would like to thank Manjula S. from Bangaluru for helping me in innumerable ways.

Last but not the least I would like to thank Mr. S. K. Ghai of Sterling Publishers for undertaking the publication of the book for the benefit of the devotees.

MAHLSAPATHY CHIMANAJI NAGRE

One day Mahlsapathy had gone on his *Madhukari* rounds (collecting alms). At that time Baba suddenly got up and resolutely left the Masjid and walked out of the village. As soon as Mahlsapathy returned home his mother informed him that Baba had left Shirdi. Immediately Mahlsapathy put his *bhiksha jholi* (bag used for collecting alms) down and said, "If Baba does return, I too will return; if not I don't know where I will go or what will happen to me," and saying this he left. He searched for Baba in all the usual places. There was a small river on the northern border of Shirdi (now Lakshmi Nager); Baba frequently went there. He had dug a deep hole in the sand. Sometimes he stood inside that hole and covered his whole body with sand. That day Baba was not there. Mahlsapathy walked further to Rui and finally found Baba at the Rui *Maruti Mandir*. Baba was sitting on the ground and pulling a thorn out of his foot.

Mahlsapathy entreated Baba to return to Shirdi. Baba said, "*Arre bhagat* you have come to fetch me, hence I will have to return," and thus Mahlsapathy averted a tragedy for Shirdi.

One day Baba said, "My devotee has developed an abscess and is writhing in pain. I too have developed an abscess on my buttock. But I will recover soon." Mahlsapathy saw that Baba had developed a painful abscess on his buttock. He was very concerned, but Baba said, "Bhagat don't worry, after two or three days it will heal and I will feel better." Mahlsapathy did not know at that time whose abscess Baba had taken upon himself. Two days later the abscess burst and Baba was relieved of the pain.

Three days later Mahlsapathy received a letter from his wife who was in Nandur Singota at that time. She wrote that she had had an abscess on her buttock. As the pain was unbearable, she prayed to Baba and immediately got relief when two days later the abscess

1

burst and she was all right. It was then that Mahlsapathy realised that Baba had taken his wife's abscess upon himself. Overwhelmed by Baba's love and compassion Mahlsapathy said, "Look Marthand, to give your mother relief, Baba took the abscess upon him. Hence your mother became all right and our God suffered so much." Only the Guru can take our *karma* on himself.

Aptly Baba called Mahlsapathy 'bhagat', that is, 'devotee' and he was a devotee par excellence. We too should strive to become a bhagat. Each devotee should search for the Sadguru to attain 'self-realization' but if he is not there what's the purpose. We have to find and merge in him that is the ultimate goal.

Ref: *Shri Sainath Maharajache Ek Mahan Eknist Sevak, Mahlsapathy Bhagat Hanche Charitra* and *Shri Sai Leela* Magazine; No. 4; 1952.

***

January 2

SHAMRAO RAMCHANDRA JAYKAR

Shamrao was born in 1865 in Mumbai and belonged to the *Pathare Prabhu* caste. His grandfather was a famous, highly educated *pundit* and so was his father. Unfortunately his father passed away when Shamrao was only 16 years old. Thus his mother along with her four sons and daughter sought shelter in her brother's home. His uncle Baba Sahib Ajankya owned half of the port and docks of Mumbai and even today they are known as '*Bhau ka Dhaka*'.

Shamrao studied in the Mission School and spoke English fluently but his passion was painting. From a very young age he had been interested in painting and although he didn't go to Art School and wasn't taught by anyone, he travelled to Rajkot and was commissioned by the king to make portraits of his entire royal family and that is where he became famous.

He also worked in Pune till 1916 and then returned to Mumbai. During that time his brother-in-law told him about Baba's divinity. Up until that time there was only the picture of Baba sitting on the stone. Then he met Moreshwar Pradhan who requested him to make a portrait of Baba. In 1917 Jaykar came to Shirdi and requested Baba's permission to make his portrait. Shama interceded on his behalf and finally Baba gave his permission. Thus the portrait of Baba seated in the *Dwarka Mai* pose and the *Chavadi* procession along with his devotees was also painted. The young lad in the picture, holding a plate of offerings in his hand, is Moreshwar Pradhan's son Chotta Sainath and the boy with the silver staff in his hand is Jaykar's son Surindra.

In 1917 Jaykar painted the portrait of Baba in the Dwarka Mai pose, as he wanted to take it home to be worshiped. After he had finished painting it he placed it in Baba's hand and Baba said, "This should be placed in the Chavadi." Somehow Jaykar didn't understand what Baba said, and he took the painting and touched it in the place where Baba used to sit. Then Baba took *Maha Samadhi* (casting away of the human body) in 1918. In 1925–26 Kaka Dixit and Pradhan requested him to give that portrait to be kept in the Dwarka Mai. He accepted with a great deal of joy, and got it framed and gave it to them. Thus that portrait came to be placed in the sanctum sanctorum in front of the *dhuni*. Later when the Museum was constructed, the original was set there, because the *Sansthan* was concerned that it would get damaged with the heat from the dhuni.

In 1917 Jaykar developed diabetes and returned to Mumbai. He passed away in 1938. Thus a very talented artist was lost forever, whose specialty was painting portraits and making sculptures. He also painted on ivory, and painted miniature portraits that were made with joining dots, on lockets and rings. Baba's devotees are however eternally grateful to him for giving us his masterpiece of Baba sitting in the Dwarka Mai.

Ref: *Shri Sai Sagar*; January–March 2011

***

January 3

JAYKAR'S SON RAGHUNANDAN DIES IN SHIRDI

When Shyamrao Jaykar painted the famous Dwarka Mai portrait of Baba, he stayed in Shirdi with his family for about 8 months. Two of his young sons were very dear to Baba, especially Raghunandan.

Baba would pamper him with sweets, seat him in his lap, and often times clean his nose. Unfortunately Raghunandan got small pox and died at the age of 5 years. His mother was overcome by intense grief. She ran to Baba and clasped his feet and said, "Baba, Raghu was your favourite, and you pampered him, yet you let him die." Then Baba said, "Raghu was your child and a favourite of mine, but he was highly spiritual. His spirituality was of the highest calibre; hence he would have been a misfit in this wicked world. However I shall bring him back as your son again." After Baba spoke to her in this manner she was consoled. His words gave her the inner strength to face any adversity calmly. Baba's words were so powerful — and even today if you read them and take time to understand them, you will perceive how powerful they are."

At that time Upasani Maharaj was staying in the Khandoba temple as ordered by Baba. Surinder and his mother often visited him and spent time with him. Once they visited him a short while after Raghu's death. Upasani Maharaj saw them and cried, "Raghunandan, Raghunandan," and shed tears. Surinder's mother consoled him saying, "my son Raghu has passed away so why are you mourning his loss? Whatever happened was my *prarabdha karma* (fruits of previous karma borne in this life) and it has happened that's all." Surinder states, "I was glad to know that my mother had accepted his death and was at peace."

Baba let Raghu pass away as his work was over. Although he was highly spiritual Baba told the mother he would bring Raghu back. Even liberated souls who merge in Baba will obey Baba's command and come back to earth as a detached soul, when Baba calls them.

Ref: Surinder Jaykar; *Saianubhav*

***

> ### *January 4*

JAYKAR'S CHILDREN AND NANAVALI

In Dixit *wada* behind the room that Bade Baba stayed in, there was another room in which a sadhu lived. He was known as Nana Baba (possibly Nanavali) and it is said he had been given some sort of

4

penance by Baba. He was unable to complete it and as a consequence he lost his mental balance and behaved like a mad man.

"Once he entered our room and asked me and my brothers to sing devotional songs and dance. We were frightened of him and did as we were told. While dancing my younger brother Dhirsen missed a step or two, and Nana Baba kicked him. My mother luckily had just entered the room and saw what was happening; she could not control her anger. She shouted at Nana Baba and pushed him out of the room. Then she comforted us and asked us to rest a while," states Surinder.

On another occasion he placed Shripad, Jaykar's youngest son on his shoulder and took him to the Dwarka Mai. At that time Shripad was about 2 years old. In the *Sabha Mandap* there was a wire strung across the room and Nana asked Shripad to hold on to it and he walked away. Jaykar was seated with Baba at that time and Surinder was seated on the platform below. He wondered if Shripad were to fall on the floor there would be a catastrophe. Simultaneously Baba said, "Don't you want your son to live? What are you waiting for? Go get your son who is hanging from that wire before he falls." Immediately Jaykar caught Shripad and he was safe. Then the entire family returned to Mumbai without any further problems.

Baba watches vigilantly over his disciples; both in their spiritual and worldly affairs, simultaneously.

Ref: *Shri Sadguru Sai Kripa* Magazine; 24 October 1993 (*Dussera* Issue)

***

January 5

THE THREAD CEREMONY OF SURINDER JAYKAR'S SON

In 1953 Surinder and his family lived in Mumbai; that year it was decided to perform the thread ceremony of his eldest son. The ceremony was to be celebrated in a grand manner as his son Vijay was the only male child in the entire family. The ceremony that was planned was very expensive and Surinder didn't have the money for it. The date was fixed and his relatives were invited, but how would he pay for the expenses.

Then he prayed to Baba and sought refuge in him. That night he had a vivid dream wherein he saw Baba seated in front of some people. He looked at Baba intently. Baba was clad in a snow-white *kafni* having a luminous aura around him. Then Baba got up and walked away. Surinder followed him and clasped his feet and sobbed while narrating his problem. Baba lifted him and placed his hand of benediction on his head and said in Marathi, "Distribute packets of salt." Surinder thought that that's what he heard. He narrated to his wife and mother, the entire dream but they could not decipher the meaning. He wondered why Baba would ask him to distribute salt.

He asked his colleague, Digaskar who was a wise and enlightened man, what could possibly be the meaning of his dream. Digaskar told him that Baba must have said, "Distribute sweets (confectionery) not salt." (In Marathi the word for salt is *meet* while the word for confectionery is *mithai* so the confusion) He said, "You get seven packets of confectionery and distribute it to seven ascetics *(fakirs)*."

Immediately Surinder got seven packets of confectionery and distributed them to the fakirs. Two days later he got 500 rupees from two separate individuals on loan. With the 1000 rupees he celebrated the ceremony in a grand manner.

Ref: Surinder Jaykar; *Saianubhav*

***

January 6

BABA GETS SURINDER A BUNGALOW TO LIVE IN

As Surinder worked for the Reserve Bank, he was allotted an apartment where he lived with his family. He was due for retirement in 1967 and would have to vacate that apartment. As retirement was approaching, he was worried where he would live in a city like Mumbai. His elder brother had built a bungalow in Vile Parle many years ago, and some years later he passed away. His sister-in-law was living alone in it. One day while visiting her, Surinder told her his problem of accommodation upon retirement.

She said, "There is no need to worry as my husband had asked me to transfer the house in your son's name. So why don't all of you come and stay with me and the transfer can also be done" Surinder moved in with his family, but for the transfer of the bungalow the documents were necessary, but they could not be found. They diligently searched the whole house but couldn't find them.

Surinder prayed to Baba and also completed one reading of the *Charita*. That night he had a strange dream wherein he saw Baba searching for something in a rusty box that was placed in the attic. He got up at once and looked for that box in his attic. He was surprised that such a box did exist. Immediately he opened it and found the documents. Thus Baba helped him to get a bungalow for himself to live in after his retirement.

Ref: Surinder Jaykar; *Saianubhav*

***

January 7

CHANDORKAR'S ABSCESS HEALED

Baba said, "I will willy-nilly drag anyone here who is mine even if he's hiding in the seventh nether world." Thus he brought Chandorkar to Shirdi in 1887. What a great devotee Chandorkar was that the creator of this universe called him to his feet.

Once Nana Sahib Chandorkar had a large painful carbuncle on his buttock, but he did not pray to Baba for relief. Nana knew that Baba would give him the relief by taking the carbuncle upon himself. And he could not bear the thought of seeing his Guru suffer, so he cancelled his trip to Shirdi.

He consulted a doctor who told him that it would require surgical intervention. But Nana was afraid of the procedure and decided to wait for some more time. When he couldn't endure the pain and discomfort any longer he visited the doctor again. The doctor told him that the surgery was the only treatment for it. He also warned him that it was difficult and dangerous to operate upon it. Then he scheduled the procedure for the next day.

Nana was panic stricken, so he placed a picture of Baba under his pillow and slept on his stomach. The next day a tile from the roof suddenly fell on his buttocks and the pus spluttered out. Nana was groaning with pain when the doctor entered the room. Upon examining him the doctor said that the procedure was not necessary, as the tile had done the job of expressing all the pus out.

After a few days Nana visited Shirdi and before he could sit Baba said, "I removed Nana's boil with my little finger." Nana was overcome with gratitude at Baba's compassion. With tears in his eyes he prostrated at Baba's feet.

Baba knows each and everything and allows Chandorkar to suffer the pain for a short while and effectively relieves it without surgery.

Ref: Acharya E. Bharadwaja; *Sai Baba the Master*

✱✱✱

January 8

HOW VYAS MEETS BABA

When Kaka Dixit went to Khandwa he met Puroshotam B. Vyas and told him about Baba's divinity and his wonderful experiences. Vyas yearned to visit Shirdi and seek Baba's blessings, but for some reason he was unable to make the pilgrimage. One night he had a dream wherein a man riding a white horse came up to him and said, "There is an order from the Government that you should go to Shirdi this *Gurupurnima*." Taking this to be an order given by Baba he visited Shirdi for the festival and had a wonderful experience.

He returned home that night and was surprised to see that the gate of his house had been left open for him. His daughter informed him that Baba told her in a dream to leave the gate open as Vyas was returning home that night. After his pilgrimage to Shirdi, Baba often appeared in his dreams and used him as a 'medium' to cure and help people in distress.

Once Vyas' neighbour's son was extremely ill and the parents despaired for his life. One night Baba appeared in his dream and asked him to tie his pendant around the child's neck and assured him that the child would recover. The next day Vyas went to their home and after taking permission from the parents tied the pendant around the child's neck and left. Three days later the ecstatic mother told him that the child had been cured and was on the way to recovery.

Vyas used to worship a picture of Baba that he had housed in the top floor of his home. Once when Shama visited his home, Vyas arranged for Shama to sleep in the hall of the ground floor. That night Shama had a vivid dream in which he saw Baba going up the stairs. Shama asked him, "*Deva* where are you going?" Baba stopped and answered, "Don't you know I am staying here on the top floor" and then vanished.

The brother-in-law of Vyas was upset that his cow didn't produce any milk, as her calf had not survived. Vyas prayed to Baba and meditated on him to help his brother-in-law. When he came out of meditation he received orders from Baba to tie a pendant of his around the cow's neck. He did as ordered and the pregnant cow delivered a healthy calf that survived and subsequently yielded plenty of milk. Thus Vyas helped various people and a cow through Baba's grace.

Baba is the Government and we have to obey his order and come to his feet. Once we come he is so merciful that he will be with us forever.

Ref: Ramalingaswami; *Ambrosia in Shirdi*

***

January 9

GOVIND G. PANSARE

In 1912 Govind G. Pansare was studying in class 7 in Marathi and his chances of passing the examinations were slim. During that time he frequented the home of Bhagwant R. Shirsagar who often visited Shirdi. Pansare told him that he was doubtful of passing the examinations. Pansare advised him to pray to Baba for his success and to take a vow that he would walk from Kopergaon to Shirdi and prostrate before Baba. Pansare gave the exam and did quite badly in Mathematics. He states, "Baba did something because not only did I pass but also got a job, and so I was eager to meet and thank him."

Finally he was able to go on 18 January 1914; he walked to Shirdi and entered the Dwarka Mai. Eagerly he walked up the steps and Baba looking at him said, "Why are you so restless to come here? Where are you from? What do you work as?" With devotion Pansare said, "I came from Sholapur, and I came to thank you for giving me the job as a teacher" Then Baba told him he had not given him the job, but God had given him the job.

Pansare again visited Shirdi in 1915. At that time, as *Dakshina* (offering of money), Baba took all the money Pansare had. He got on well with Jog who often asked him to sit a while and hear him read the religious text. But Pansare would go and sit near Baba. One day Baba gave Pansare five flowers and asked him to give them to Jog. Jog said, "The time has come for the goldsmith to pierce your ears. You will understand it when you receive *Udi* from Baba." That day when Baba distributed Udi he said, "You don't listen to the text being read, nor do you read it yourself. As soon as you wake up you will come and sit here." Since then Pansare sat with Jog and listened to the reading.

When Pansare was leaving Shirdi he didn't have any money and no one was willing to loan it to him. He travelled ticketless to Dhond without any problem. At Dhond he met a friend who gave him two rupees and so he bought a ticket and as soon as he got into the train his ticket was checked. Pansare was devoted to Baba and lived a spiritually rich life.

Ref: *Shri Sai Leela* Magazine; November 1930

***

January 10

B.V. DEO'S FIRST MEETING WITH BABA

In June of 1910 Deo had a vivid dream, in which he and his daughter Rangutai were walking together in the morning. The street was in a village but it was about 20 feet wide. As they walked, they saw two gentlemen approaching them in the opposite direction. The younger man was wearing a white *Angrakha* (a short Indian frock) over a white *dhothi*, a red turban with a white shawl over his shoulders. The older man had a white cloth tied around his head and was wearing a short *khaddar* (linen) coat over a white dhoti.

They stood in front of Deo and the younger man said, "Hey! Wait. Do you know who this person is?" Deo replied, "No." The younger person said, "He is Lord Datta Guru." Hearing this Deo and Rangutai prostrated before him. The younger man then asked them to give dakshina to his companion. Immediately Deo took out a coin from his pocket and gave it to Rangutai to offer it with prostrations. Then Deo took out another coin and was about to offer it when the younger man inquired why he was offering dakshina again. Deo told him that the first coin was offered by his daughter.

Then the older man asked Deo how many children he had, Deo told him he had two sons and this daughter. The older man said that he had no children. Deo said, "Maharaj why do you say you have no children; all the people in this world are your children." Then they proceeded and came to a wada that was not very tall and there the two men disappeared and the dream ended.

Later Deo met Chandorkar who spoke about Baba's divinity. Deo first visited Shirdi on 30 November 1910, and stayed at Sathe Wada. He recollected having seen this wada in his dream. Then he went to the Dwarka Mai, and prostrated at Baba's feet. He then realised that Baba was Lord Datta and the younger man was Chandorkar.

Ref: *Shri Sai Leela* Magazine; Vol. 3, No. 12, 2009

***

January 11

"I OFTEN SANG THESE *ABHANGS* BEFORE BABA" STATES MAI

Swami Sharananand states, "My room at Shirdi was adjacent to Radha Krishna Mai's home. Once I was reading aloud to her an Epic about various saints. The life of one of the saints had a tremendous effect on her and she could not hold back her tears, and soon she was sobbing uncontrollably. It was dark in her room at that time, when suddenly a beam of light akin to lightening flashed in front of her. Following this she became calm and fell asleep.

Mai was an avid reader and she borrowed books from me and other devotees and studied them thoroughly. Her favourite book was *Tukaram's Gatha* and she sang the *abhangs* (devotional songs in a

11

specified meter) from it in a sweet melodious voice. She said, "When I first arrived at Shirdi I often sang these abhang's before Baba. He was very fond of them." She knew a vast number of abhangs related to saints, and on compassion and peace. She sang many of them to the devotees when reading and explaining Tukaram's Gatha.

One evening Vamanrao Navarvekar brought Eknath's *Bhagvat* along with him. Radha Krishna Mai gave a long discourse on the *shloka* "*Kayena vaca manasendriyairva*", that is, the total surrender of my body, speech, mind, senses, intellect, and my innate being I offer to you Lord Naryana. She said, "The essence of the Gita lies in this *shloka* (verse). Remember this always." *Gopigeet* written by Jaydev was another favourite book of hers; she would sing the same verse in different *ragas*. In the evenings she would sing these verses, and Dr. Pillay would play the sitar in accompaniment. I was fortunate to sit before her while she read Ramdas Swami's *Das Bodh* aloud to him and she explained it in great detail. Another book that she liked was Ram Krishna's *Bodhamrit* that I would read aloud to her. After a few days Bapusahib Jog came there and said, "Reading all these great books before Mai will not give you any knowledge. What you need to do is to carefully listen to what she says," so I stopped reading aloud. Mai told me that the book was an excellent instrument for breaking the circle of *maya* (illusory). It teaches us to be content with life in whatever condition we are in."

Mai gives us the key to the treasury through the shloka on how to reach one's Sadguru.

Ref: Swami Sharananand; *Shri Sai Leela* Magazine;
Vol. 64, No. 12, March 1986

***

January 12

BABA CONCURS WITH MAI
REGARDING *ASSAN*

During Swami Sharananand's stay at Shirdi, Baba appeared in his dream, wherein Baba had Tukaram's Gatha in his hand. He opened it and said, "Page 104" and pointed to it. As soon as he awoke the next morning he checked page 104 and found that a Sufi Saint named Dervesh had written a *doha* (metered verse) where the first word is Allaha. The moral of the doha is that one should be content with one's lot in life and happily accept it. Not choosing the path to heaven or hell but choosing path of compassionate righteousness.

Swami Sharananand would sit in *Sidhasan* (a yogic posture) and meditate for a fixed period of time. Once Radha Krishna Mai saw this and advised him to sit in *Swastika Assan* or *Saheg Assan* posture, (both are yoga postures). She also went on to show him how to sit in those postures. That night when he went to meet Baba he was surprised to find him sitting in Swastika Assan instead of his usual way of sitting. Thus he got confirmation from Baba about the assan and started sitting in Swastika Assan.

Radha Krishna Mai had a small brass idol of Krishna that she carried with her everywhere she went. Whenever she had a meal she would offer the idol every morsel of food before putting it in her mouth. Swami Sharananand was intrigued by this and mentally he longed to possess an idol exactly like hers. He was always silent when he was with Mai, so he kept silent because he knew she could read his thoughts. But he persistently thought about owning an idol like hers. Finally one day she said, "You don't need an idol like mine as Baba has given you a picture of his."

Mai did not appreciate it when people talked, and if ever some devotee voiced his opinions on any religious subject she argued and tore his opinion to shreds. But Baba was unhappy with his silence and said, "I sent you there and yet you don't speak up. What am I to do?" Nonetheless he remained silent.

Ref: Swami Sharananand; Shri Sai Leela Magazine;
Vol. 64, No. 12, March 1986

***

January 13

MAI GIVES SHARANANAND A NEW LEASE OF LIFE

One evening around 4 p.m., Dixit and Swami Sharananand set out to the Dwarka Mai. Dixit took the path in front of the *Maruti Mandir* while Sharananand walked in front of Butti Wada. At that time it was being constructed and a huge stone fell on his head and bounced off his shoulder. Immediately he sat down and then lost consciousness. When he became conscious he heard Baba saying, "This is how people die." His head and shoulder hurt a little. Dixit said, "I asked you to walk in front of the Maruti Mandir but you didn't heed my warning"

A short while later Baba sent a mixture of Udi paste through some devotee, who carefully applied it on Swami Sharananand's head and shoulder. The mixture formed an airtight seal over the injured areas and the pain abated. A few days later without any other treatment the wounds healed completely.

Sharananand had gone to the Dwarka Mai prior to the accident. After he had prostrated, Baba lifted up his seat and showed him a huge hole about a few feet deep and quite wide. He wondered if Baba was warning him of his impending death. Sharananand then went back into the Butti Wada and sat against its southern wall and started reading the *Bhagvat Gita*. Dixit came and asked him how he felt and reported his well being to Baba. Baba advised Sharananand to keep quiet, and he obeyed.

At dusk Radhakrishna Mai gave Sharananand her woolen blanket to use. She came and glanced at him compassionately twice during the night and said, "Now it's clear why Baba was asking about you repeatedly before you arrived. He was in a terrible rage and even hit some of the devotees who came to see him. He was obviously turning away death and misfortune from affecting you."

"A few days later Radhakrishna Mai at dawn sat in front of me and taught me *Apanvayu Urdhva Pranayam* (the perfect breathing exercises that control the gastrointestinal tract and release and expel toxic substances) and thus both our life forces became one. For about 10 minutes she entwined her life force with mine till they became one, and bestowed part of her life force on me thus giving me a new lease of life."

Baba sometimes made *kada*. Kada is a sweetened brew made with ginger, black pepper, and numerous herbs and spices. After Sharananand's head injury Baba gave him kada made out of *Sona Mukhi* (Senna pod); he drank it and found it very invigorating. He didn't take any medicines orally or apply any ointment to his injuries and recovered completely.

Ref: *Shri Sai Leela* Magazine; Vol. 65, No. 8, October 1986

***

14

HIS *JEEV ATMA* HAD MERGED WITH THE *PARAMATMA*

One day at about 8 a.m. Sharananand went to the rear of Dixit Wada and was walking alongside it when he heard the most melodious *sitar* (string instrument) music. The door to the room was open and he peeped in and saw a beautiful lady playing the sitar. She beckoned to him to come in, so he went and sat down. Then the lady handed the sitar over to Sharananand and asked him to play it. He replied, "I can't play it as I have no knowledge of music." When he exited the room Nanavali walked towards him in a rage and picking up a marble slab hit him on the head saying, "If you cannot play the sitar why did you take it?" Sharananand though shaken, however, wasn't bleeding nor did he sustain any head injury.

The next day Nanavali came towards him screaming and wrote 14 letters on his chest in a childish scrawl that he couldn't decipher. As his finger had no charcoal or any dye on it, Sharananand couldn't read what was written. He guessed it must have been a blessing. He also realised that Baba wanted to convey through Nanavali the message, "Why did you ask me for the *mantra* (a sacred formula) on the formless if you didn't have the capacity to practice it."

Once at dusk Sharananand went and sat on the roadside leading to Kopergaon and started singing Baba's *Arati* loudly. He heard Baba say, "Why are you tearing the sky with this thunder?" Hearing this Sharananand silently completed the Arati, prayers and then he meditated. Sharananand states, "Suddenly there was a huge explosion of the mantra that I had been chanting continuously and ceaselessly. It exited my body through the *Bramharundra* (the soft spot on the head of a new born baby) and ascended up through the sky and merged with the sun. I had asked Baba to give me the mantra to enable me to achieve the grace of his formless divinity and I had failed miserably. And Nanavali had hit me on my head and made me aware of my failure that must be the reason of it exiting my being through the head. In turmoil I thought, 'Now which mantra should I chant? What does Baba wish me to do?' After a few hours Mai and

15

Kaka came searching for me and holding my hand took me back to Shirdi."

Now 43 years later I have understood that the magnificent mantra that exploded and finally merged with the sun was not a sign of my failure. Baba had opened my skull and allowed the mantra to reach its destination. By Baba's infinite grace my *jeev atma* (the soul) had merged with the *Paramatma* (God/Supreme being). And this had opened the seventh door on my journey as a Yogi and enveloped my entire being with his loving grace."

Ref: *Shri Sai Leela* Magazine; Vol. 65, No. 8, October 1986

***

January 15

DEBT OF KNOWLEDGE REPAID

One evening Swami Sharananand sat in blissful meditation on the roadside, when he saw Baba and Radhakrishna Mai traversing up to the sky leaving him alone on Earth. With a feeling of sadness he prostrated before them. Immediately he was seized by the thought that Baba had guided him and taught him so much. But he had never thanked him. Nor had he tried to repay the debt in any way. Baba had given him a vast ocean of spiritual knowledge but he hadn't showed his gratitude to Baba. Then he heard Baba saying, "Arre! I haven't taught you anything new. What you taught me in your previous life the same knowledge I am giving back to you in this life. I was indebted to you and I have only repaid that debt."

Swami Sharananand would wander about at night, and once he found a secluded spot on the way to Kopergaon and sat and meditated there. Suddenly he heard Radhakrishna Mai say, "Kaka and I will come to fetch you." He replied, "There's no need to bring Kaka along but you can come." After a few hours Mai and Kaka came searching for him with a lantern in their hand. Mai said, "Vamanya why do you do this? Why are you sitting here?" Sharananand replied, "Just as I was about to return it became bright day light, then I saw *Eknath Maharaj's* temple so I sat here." In fact there isn't any temple of Eknath Maharaj on the way to Kopergaon. After returning to Shirdi,

Mai said, "You are such an unusual person as you have brought my Guru Eknath Maharaj with you."

Ref: *Shri Sai Leela* Magazine; Vol. 65, No. 8, October 1986

***

January 16

SERVICE TO THE GURU IS IMPOSSIBLE WITHOUT HIS GRACE

During his numerous visits to Shirdi, Sharananand had many enlighting experiences. Once he went to Radhakrishna Mai's residence in the evening. She had a green chili that she asked him to eat. He ate it and was surprised that it was not pungent and hot. Radhakrishna Mai had cast a spell through that chili on him, but he couldn't decipher what its goal was. Following that he started seeing strange objects; and objects that were actually present in the room he couldn't see. Once she asked him to fetch a towel that was hanging on a peg; he approached the peg but the towel was invisible to him. So she went to the peg and gave the towel in his hand and said, "See here is the towel." Sharananand learnt a valuable lesson from this. He states, "I realised service to the Guru is impossible without His grace."

A few days later he went to the outskirts of Shirdi and sat near the canal. There was a hut there and he could hear devotional songs emitting from that hut, but the singers were not visible. Then he sat down and meditated. While meditating he saw a bullock approaching him. And on that cart he saw Baba sitting looking like Lord Shiva. Baba looked fierce and angry, and his mustache was very long and it quivered. Then Baba threw a huge stone at him but it landed near his feet, this was followed by Baba pelting smaller stones at him but they failed to injure him. Then he returned to his room.

One night after everyone was fast asleep Sharananand went out and started walking towards Rahata. As he walked along he decided that he would take the vow of an ascetic; it was around midnight at that time. It was in the month of November and it was extremely dark and he couldn't clearly see ahead of him. He looked up at the sky and saw a huge golden orange sun shining; it resembled a rising or setting sun. He thought that the sun god *Surya Naryan* was pleased with his decision and hence it had appeared at midnight. He had read in the *Shastras* (book of mythology) that the sun did appear at night and now he had proof of it.

He went to the bank of the river in Rahata and sat under a tree. A short while later a *Brahma Rakshas* appeared from the river. A Brahma Rakshas is a demon who in his previous life was a very learned person but who wouldn't share his knowledge with deserving people. Such people are often condemned to live the life of a demon. Their head is illuminated and emits light and they walk with their feet up and head down. The demon returned to the river and disappeared.

Just prior to dawn Sharananand returned to Shirdi. The devotees were concerned about him and inquired where he had gone. They told him that Baba was also worried about his whereabouts and had sent a man in search of him. They entreated him not to give Baba trouble and asked him to stay at Dixit Wada and he agreed.

Ref: *Shri Sai Leela* Magazine; Vol. 65, No. 8, October 1986

***

January 17

SHARANANAND SEES MAI IN THE DWARKA MAI

In 1914 Radhakrishna Mai asked Sharananand to abstain from eating cooked rice; this was very difficult for him. Then Baba appeared in his dream and said, "Eat plenty of onions that have red skins." Swami Sharananand started doing so but after following this for some time he felt that his speech had become harsh and rude. He thought his body was unable to digest the onions and so he stopped eating them.

On one of the *Ramnavami's* Radhakrishna Mai said, "You and your wife can easily live on 20 rupees a month. Why do you need more money?" Later she asked him to get a silver lamp that cost 125 rupees, and Narvekar paid the interest of 25 rupees. Swami Sharananand thus brought a beautiful silver lamp to Shirdi. On that Ramnavami

Radhakrishna Mai lit it with wicks drenched in clarified butter and asked Sharananand to take the lamp to the Dwarka Mai. Then she said, "I will climb the steps of the Dwarka Mai and go up with you." While Sharananand was climbing the steps he felt someone tap his shoulder, so he turned around and saw Radhakrishna Mai who said, "Go up." She was in the Dwarka Mai in her *sukshma* (invisible) form, as nobody but he had seen her. She had taken a vow not to appear before Baba and the Dwarka Mai in her natural form but often visited him in her sukshma form.

When Sharananand was working at Navsari, he received a letter from Radhakrishna Mai that read, "Baba is not at all well these days. He doesn't eat anything except *kheer* (rice pudding) but the milk here is not of a good quality. So if you could send a good *Khathawari* (from the Kutch peninsula) cow that could produce 8–9 liters of milk, it would be a great service to Baba. I will make arrangements and pay the cost of the cow." Sharananand's younger sister liked the idea so much that she sold her gold chain and bought two cows that she then sent to Shirdi. Later when the price of gold fell steeply, this act saved Sharananand's sister from incurring any financial loss.

Ref: *Shri Sai Leela* Magazine; Vol. 65, No. 8, October 1986

***

January 18

SHARANANAND TAUGHT WHAT SHOULD BE EATEN

In 1916 Swami Sharananand was burning the midnight oil as he had to appear in an examination to graduate as a Solicitor. While he was studying he was plagued with worry and anxiety, thus he lost his appetite. As a result he became extremely weak. One day he heard that Dixit was going to Shirdi so he decided to send some fruits, a garland and dakshina for Baba through him. When he went to the station to hand it over, he thought he should go himself to Shirdi and return the next day, so he accompanied Dixit and arrived at Shirdi. After prostrating before Baba he went to Mai's home and told her that he had decided to stay on at Shirdi and continue studying there.

19

A short while later Mai said, "Baba has taken his seat and the devotees have offered water melon, and sweet musk melon and delectable savories. If you go and stand next to the Dhuni Mai, Baba will put my share of the offerings in your jholi. Go and bring it for me." She swiftly made a jholi out of a cloth and slung it on his shoulder and Sharananand obeyed her. When he returned from the Dwarka Mai she was having lunch; she beckoned to Sharananand and seated him beside her and gave him a portion of her lunch. He ate the food and found it extremely spicy and pungent.

The next day at lunch time, Mai fed him putting each morsel into his mouth, while doing so she mentioned each ingredient that was in it. And further broke it down recounting its calories, quantity of protein, carbohydrate and minerals in it. She also told him what effect it produced in the body upon ingestion. She said, "One must have the knowledge of the ingredients in the food that you ingest." Sharananand states, "Mai put 42 morsels in my mouth and following that my loss of appetite vanished."

One day Mai placed a banana next to his plate at lunch. Sharananand felt it was rotten in several places. When he was eating lunch he found a pellet of goat's excreta in the very first morsel of food. He took it and placed it aside. As the rest of the food was good he ate it. He then realised that Yogis teach their disciples in a similar manner as to what should and shouldn't be eaten, and what food is beneficial for them.

The next day Baba had prepared some chutney out of peanuts, desiccated coconut and some spices. He had sent some for Mai, who upon receiving it said, "Have some chutney as Baba has prepared it and you will not get this opportunity again." Sharananand ate some as Mai had requested him to but he found it very spicy. The chillies in the chutney caused him diarrhea. When Sharananand went to meet Baba, and Baba said, "When you eat what is not your share it falls out of the body thus," Sharananand understood the valuable lesson of the importance of eating food mindfully.

Ref: *Shri Sai Leela* Magazine; Vol. 65, No. 8, October 1986

***

SHARANANAND LEARNS ABOUT BIRTH, DEATH AND THE SOUL

One evening Sharananand walked out of Shirdi and wandered about; finally he found a comfortable spot on the way to Kopergaon and sat down. Then a man came to him and asked for alms; he took off some silver buttons and gave it to him. At that moment he heard Baba say, "Whenever a person comes and asks you for something tell him this, 'I am naked, so whatever you desire you may have'. For a long time he pondered over what Baba had said. If that person was a spiritually developed man or a seeker of salvation he would understand its meaning. And it is this: 'I am without any companion, I am alone; without any form, bright as fire; I am *Brahma*, so whatever you want you may have."

On another occasion Baba gave him the experience of death and dying. Sharananand states, "Once I was sleeping in Dixit Wada. That night I laid my bedding in the room on the top floor of his wada. I lay down with my head towards Baba's picture and while I was still awake I felt my soul or *atma* leave my body and settle on the wall in front of me. So with keen interest I looked there and indeed a little later I saw my atma there.

From this unique phenomenon I understood that I, Vamanrao, is now dead. And now Vamanrao has acquired a new body and is now someone else. The next morning I continued having the same experience that I had now acquired a new body and that when someone asked me whether I had a job and earned a living I replied, "Vamanrao is dead. He died a long time ago."

Then I wondered why Baba had released my atma from my body and showed it to me? What did he want me to gain from this experience? I thought hard about it. Then it dawned on me that the life force goes and returns, that is, the cycle of birth and death is a continuous process. But the atma or 'I' is immortal and it's a witness of this cycle unaffected. It watches the transactions and activities of life. This atma is full of bliss, (*Sat Chit Anand*); it is pure, everlasting, omniscient, and it is the almighty God, unaffected by maya."

The next day Sharananand woke up early in the morning and went to Lendi Baugh. The Lendi River was flooded and overflowing its banks. He crossed the river and stood on the southern side; there he noticed a strong, fair man standing there. The man wore a loin cloth with a jholi slung from his shoulder; he had a moustache and long matted hair with a small sickle stuck on top of his head. Sharananand recognised him to be Lord Shiva and prostrated before him.

P.S.: The Lendi River flowed from what is now the old Prasadalaya and traversed along the Nagar–Manmad Highway and entered Lendi Baugh and flowed between Baba's well and the Nanda Deep towards the Parayan Hall where it went underground.

Ref: *Shri Sai Leela* Magazine; Vol. 65, No. 8, October 1986

***

| January 20 |

GOPINATH MEETS BABA IN 1914

Gopinath's father worked in the Public Works Department (PWD) at Kopergaon, in the year 1914. One day his father decided to take him to Shirdi to pay homage to Baba. Gopinath was about 11 years at that time and he remembers that visit clearly. They went by bullock cart and Gopinath enjoyed the ride. Upon reaching Shirdi they alighted in the area next to the Chavadi, and went to the Dwarka Mai. Baba had gone to Lendi Baugh at that time, so they waited outside the Sabha Mandap for him.

Gopinath was thrilled to see the procession approaching the Dwarka Mai. They followed Baba; his father had brought a garland, a coconut and other offerings with him. That day there were only a few devotees, so they got a chance to enter the Sanctum Sanctorum rather quickly. His father prostrated in front of Baba and then Gopinath prostrated. Simultaneously Baba started shouting and began using foul language. The coconut that they had offered, Baba flung it away. His father cringed while Gopinath was extremely frightened and hid behind his father. Just as they were about to return home, Dixit and many of the devotees seated there came and spoke to them. Dixit said, "Baba never ever loses his temper, nor does he break his silence; it's only when he wants to shower his grace and blessings does he use abusive language. You and your son are extremely fortunate for this is his blessing in disguise. Do not for a moment consider it a bad omen."

True to his word, Gopinath Talvalkar is famous in Pune, for his brilliant academic carreer. He teaches at Pune University and has PhDs in many subjects and helps in guiding his students. He is the editor of *Anand* a children's magazine. He is also an anchor of a children's radio program at *Akashvani* Pune. He attributes his success in life to that wonderful day when he went to Shirdi and Baba blessed him in his 'strange' way.

Ref: *Shri Sai Leela* Magazine; Vol. 67, No. 10, January 1989

***

| January 21 |

LAKSHMANRAO POTDAR

Baba said, "*Arre* Lakshmanrao, give me my first salary." The experience given below occurred in the life of Lakshmanrao Potdar, a brief sketch of his life is narrated by his son Vasantrao, who was born on 4 December 1903 in a village called Edwan. Lakshmanrao was devoted to Baba and worked as a supervisor in an Engineering Company. Once he had a discussion with his boss about a business proposal that he opposed as he felt it would not be beneficial for the company. However his boss was in favour of the proposal and severely chided him, and so he went ahead with it. Lakshmanrao felt humiliated and resigned. Now he was in a fix as he had resigned from a well-paying job and had a wife and three small kids to feed.

He went home and stood in front of Baba's photograph and said, "Baba, please give me some job. I promise I will come to Shirdi and lay my first salary at your feet." Two days later a worker from that very company was at his door step with the message that the boss had re-instated him as he had realised his mistake. Lakshmanrao rejoined the Company on his previous post. When he got his first pay he decided to fulfil his vow. Taking his young son Vasantrao and his entire pay he travelled to Shirdi.

The year was 1911; he reached Kopergaon and in a rickety bullock cart arrived in Shirdi. Upon reaching Shirdi they went to the Dwarka Mai, where Baba was seated. Just then a pony came inside the Sanctum Sanctorum; it proceeded to circumambulate Baba; then lay on his stomach and prostrated before him and left. The crowd seated below was astonished to see this.

Then Baba glanced at the crowd and said, "Arre, Lakshmana give me my salary." Astonished Lakshmanrao looked around to see his namesake but nobody responded. Baba looked in his direction and said, "Arre, Lakshmanrao I am calling you. Come and give me my first salary." When Baba said, "First salary" he realised Baba was talking to him, so he and Vasantrao went and prostrated before Baba and he placed his salary in Baba's hand. Baba then turned to an elderly lady and asked her to serve them a meal.

Ref: *Shri Sai Leela* Magazine; No. 11, Vol. 63, February 1985

***

January 22

BABA APPEARS AS LAKSHMANRAO'S FRIEND

Lakshmanrao and his son Vasantrao had a hearty meal and went to the Dwarka Mai to seek permission from Baba to return to Mumbai. As they prostrated, Baba blessed them and granted permission. The train was scheduled to leave Kopergaon in the evening, so they hired a bullock cart and managed to reach Kopergaon on time. When Lakshmanrao was paying the driver he realised that he was short of money. He wondered how he would buy the tickets to Mumbai. Neither could he borrow the money as he knew no one in Kopergaon. Now he was at his wits' end, worried and helpless.

Suddenly he heard someone calling him, surprised he looked up and a dear friend of his was before him. After greeting Lakshmanrao his friend said, "I have to buy my ticket, so I will purchase tickets for all of us."

Before long his friend returned with the tickets and handed them to Lakshmanrao. They then walked into the station and his friend disappeared in the crowd. Lakshman searched for him but in vain. Finally it struck him that Baba had appeared as his friend. With tears in his eyes he thanked Baba for his help. And his faith in Baba increased hundred fold.

Ref: *Shri Sai Leela* Magazine; No. 11, Vol. 63, February 1985

***

January 23

BABA SAT AT THE DOOR AND DROVE DEATH AWAY

Vasantrao states, "Once my father was seriously ill and hovering at death's door. The doctor taking care of him finally gave up hope." He said, "If there are any close relatives you want to call please do so." My uncle Yashvantrao was summoned. That night my father's condition deteriorated further and he was running a high fever. My mother, uncle and I sat at his bedside the whole night. At midnight Lakshmanrao's father awoke and looked towards the front door and reverentially folded his hands. Then he slept peacefully through the night.

At about 5 a.m. my father got up and asked my mother for something to eat. My mother gave him some rice gruel that he ate. Then he said, "Why are you sitting at my bedside? I feel fine." While he said this he kept looking towards the door. I turned and looked in the same direction and I saw an old man seated in the doorway. He had a silver *satka* (a baton about 2 feet long) in his hand. Waving it about he said, "Let me see who dares to enter this room when I am here." I immediately prostrated with folded hands. That old man looked exactly like Sai Baba whom I had seen when I was younger. Baba was seated at the door to drive away the agents of death.

My father soon recovered and never fell ill again. My family rejoiced and thanked Baba for his compassionate caring for my father. This incident further strengthened my faith and devotion towards him.

Ref: *Shri Sai Leela* Magazine; No. 11, Vol. 63, February 1985

***

HARIBHAU VISHVANATH CHAUBAL

In 1911 Haribhau Vishvanath Chaubal visited Shirdi for the first time. His father opposed his pilgrimage vehemently. He said, "He's a Muslim fakir who stays in a mosque and survives by begging food in the village. Why do you want to meet him? There are numerous charlatans in this world who dupe innocent people. Don't waste your time going there." Nonetheless Haribhau did go; Baba welcomed him by repeating the exact words that his father had said. Haribhau realised that Baba was omnipresent as he knew what had transpired miles away. Haribhau stayed in Shirdi for 4 days; he was so impressed by Baba's divinity that he frequently visited Shirdi thereafter.

He yearned to see Baba and to pay homage to him every day; so he decided he would stay in Shirdi for long periods. In 1914 he came along with his family and stayed for 4 months; at that time he stayed with Appa Shimpi. Again in 1917 he and his family stayed in a large house that was situated behind Abdul Baba's cottage; this stay also was 4 months long.

One afternoon Haribhau's son Shankar climbed upon a railing in the Sabha Mandap just prior to the commencement of the noon Arati. Baba saw him perched there and said, "Arre your child will fall down and hurt himself. Go and get him and then start the Arati." After the child was brought down the Arati commenced.

Shankar states, "I vividly remember that one day someone brought a phonogram and kept it in the Sabha Mandap. It was turned on and everyone was enjoying themselves. That day the circus had come to Shirdi and the owner had brought an elephant to have darshan of Baba. All the children had gathered there to watch the elephant bow before Baba.

"Baba used to call me *bhau* (brother) and he was very kind to me. As I grew up and went through the ups and downs in life, first while I was a student and then when I was employed, Baba was always at my side helping me to overcome every hurdle of life. In fact, he stood by me through thick and thin. And I am eternally grateful to him."

Ref: *Shri Sai Leela* Magazine; Vol. 65, No. 2, May 1986

***

SHANKAR HARIBHAU CHAUBAL

Shankar Haribhau Chaubal was born on 13 August 1910 in Dhanu (Thane district). He was the son of Haribhau V. Chaubal and he met Baba when his father would stay in Shirdi for long periods of time. He was too young to remember his first stay there but he vividly remembers his second stay in 1917 when he was 7 years old. After *Kakad* Arati his mother would go home and prepare *zunka bhakri* (dry curry made with gram flour and onions) for Baba every day as he would come to take bhiksha daily from their home. The children would fight amongst themselves as to who would give bhiksha to Baba. His mother solved the issue by making each child take turns in offering bhiksha to Baba. Shankar would run to Dwarka Mai before Baba arrived there from his bhiksha rounds, and waited there for him. Baba would pick him up and seat him on his lap for some time, cuddle him and oftentimes wipe his nose. Baba would give him delicious food that he had received, and then tell him to go and play.

Once Shama called Shankar and said in a stern voice, "Boy you are very dirty so from tomorrow don't stand next to the railing because Baba picks you up and has to wipe your nose. The next day Shankar did go to the Dwarka Mai but quietly sat in the Sabha Mandap; Baba sent a devotee to fetch him but Shankar refused to go as Shama was standing next to Baba. The devotee was sent by Baba again, and when Shankar refused, the devotee picked him up and forcefully brought him to Baba. Baba sat Shankar on his lap and in a gentle voice asked, "Bhau are you angry with me today? Why are sitting so far away." Then Shankar told him what Shama had said. "Arre Shymia just as you are my child so is Bhau. If I don't take care of my children who will? So don't be angry with him," and saying this Baba pacified Shama. Since then Shama never objected to Shankar going to Baba.

Only the Guru will pick us up, seat us on his lap unperturbed of our shortcomings.

Ref: *Shri Sai Leela* Magazine; Vol. 65, No. 2, May 1986

***

DAMODAR NARAYAN SABNIS

Another devotee who had a close connection with Baba was Damodar Narayan Sabnis. In 1913 he was a *Mamatldar* (revenue officer) in Ahmednagar and frequently visited Sangamnere, Kopergaon and Shirdi. He was very spiritual and loved to visit saints, hence he often brought his family with him to Shirdi. His family stayed in Shirdi while he travelled to Sakori and other neighbouring villages. His daughter Santabai who was very young at that time often played with Baba.

On one occasion Shantabai's uncle was very sick and her mother took permission from Baba to go and meet him. Baba said, "What's the point of going now as it's too late." Later Shantabai's mother learned that her brother had passed away at the time when Baba asked her not to go.

Once Damodar had some urgent work in Rahuri and sought permission to leave. Baba lifted his hand up and shook it from side to side meaning, no do not go. But he couldn't miss the appointment so he drove away not heeding Baba's advice. The horses ran fast but a short while later the cart overturned and Damodar fell in front of the advancing wheels and injured himself. Here in the Dwarka Mai, Baba was shouting and abusing for no apparent reason. But by Baba's grace Damodar wasn't crushed to death.

Ref: *Sai Prasad* Magazine; 1984 (*Deepavali* Issue)

***

SHANTABAI JOSHI

Since 1913, Shantabai often accompanied her father on his visits to Shirdi. Here she gives some valuable insight about Shirdi and

Baba. "I saw Baba when I was a child, but I vividly remember how he sat under his neem tree. At that time the cemented island was not there but there was a sort of parapet built under the tree. The children from the village and I would play there in the afternoon. The tree was luscious and had plenty of yellow fruit that we would gather. In our attempt to gather large amounts of fruit, we would climb all over Baba, but not for a moment did he ever waver from his meditative trance nor did he ever scold or hit us. When we troubled him beyond measure he would take a dried branch of the neem tree and hit it on the parapet to drive us away.

Oftentimes he sang songs to amuse us; one particular song that I liked described how the moon was hiding amongst the branches of the neem tree and Baba asks it to come out and show us its face. Finally he asks the moon to give us plenty of *chapattis* (flat unleavened bread) drenched in clarified butter and sugar. The children who played with me were very poor; their parents were farmers, migrant workers and labourers who laid roads. It was very convenient for them to leave their children with Baba. They knew that their children were safe and wouldn't be harmed, as they would be looked after by Baba. Indeed we were fortunate that the Lord of the universe took care of us and wiped our 'snotty noses'. We often played in Lendi Baugh; at that time many goats and sheep grazed there. We collected the droppings of goats and all the children played a game of marbles with then. There was also a huge tamarind tree in Lendi Baugh and all the kids would throw stones in order to get a few pods of ripe tamarind that could be eaten. I would stand under the tree hoping to get a pod of tamarind and Baba would often help us.

Baba lived a life of utter simplicity, and his needs were meager. I have never seen him wear any footwear, nor did he don a new kafni although many kafnis were stacked in the Dwarka Mai. Baba never yearned for expensive clothes or jewelry. Now, I am mystified to see his *Samadhi Mandir* decked in gold, with utensils of gold all around. All this pomp and show is quite contrary to the life he lived. He, the almighty deity who has the keys to the kingdom of heaven and the supreme power to bestow salvation to his devotees, lived the life of a fakir.

Ref: *Sai Prasad* Magazine; 1998 (*Deepavali* Issue)

***

SHANTABAI'S INSIGHTFUL
REMEMBRANCES OF BABA

Shantabai states, "I have the utmost faith in chanting Lord Sainath's name. Sainath is what I still call him, as he is the saviour of the destitute. He never attracted people towards himself by performing miracles nor did he do any sort of *Tantra* (a system of mystical techniques). Even the wicked and ruthless were changed for life after meeting him, as he had equality of vision. Everyone who came to him was welcome in his Dwarka Mai.

He lived a simple life, but he had an old quilt that was made of silk and had *zari* (golden embroidery work) sewn on it. Years ago it had seen better days, but he never threw it away. There was an interesting feature about the quilt that it would change itself according to Baba's needs. I have seen this happen over and over again with my own eyes. The Dwarka Mai was a place of refuge for the stray animals of Shirdi. Often he would place a kid (young goat) on his lap and caress it. If it bleated he would give it a drink of water with his own hands. Dogs and cats sought refuge at his feet, and Baba had a special fondness for dogs. Then there was a black cow with white stripes; she and her calf had literally made the Dwarka Mai their home, and Baba would feed the cow and pat her on her back.

Another divine phenomenon that I saw was that Baba would sometimes take his unlit *chillum* (clay pipe) and puff at it, and suddenly the unlit chillum would ignite on its own accord and the smoke would rise up to the sky.

Now years later when I go to Shirdi, I can still remember Lord Sainath as I first saw him. And I thank him from the bottom of my heart for being with me my entire life and taking care of my every need."

Children take the prarabdha of people, and here animals do too.

Ref: *Sai Prasad* Magazine; 1994 (*Deepavali* Issue)

***

ANANTHRAO DANDEKAR MEETS BABA

Ananthrao Dandekar resided in Mumbai and had the good fortune of meeting Baba. He often told his grandchildren about Shirdi — "Baba called me *bhondu* (simple-minded) hence the other devotees would call me *bhonduji*. The journey in those days was tedious and I went by train to Kopergaon and from there it was either by bullock cart or horse carriage to Shirdi. I felt very blessed when I stayed in Shirdi, because I was able to stay in the proximity of my God for a week and sometimes longer. Baba had an aura of divinity around him, and as far as I was concerned, there was no other god but Baba.

During my stay at Shirdi I often pressed the feet of my Lord; they were as soft as silk and had a fragrance of sandalwood. Once while I was pressing Baba's feet he pulled them away and holding my hand said, "Bhondu stop! Get up at once and go home." I rebelliously said, "But Baba I arrived yesterday and you are asking me to leave." Baba replied, "Bhondu go home immediately as someone is anxiously awaiting your arrival." Then he gave me a handful of Udi and blessed me saying *"Allaha bhalla karega"* (Allaha will bless you). I followed Baba's orders and returned home. My wife had suddenly become very ill and she had earnestly prayed to Baba to send me home. As Baba was omniscient he had heard my wife's prayer and sent his Udi for her. My first line of treatment was to apply Udi on her forehead and have her consume some, and she recovered the very next day.

Here Baba gives us a glimpse of his omniscience.

Ref: *Sai Prasad* Magazine; New Vol. Edition, 2002

***

VAMAN NAAMDEV ASTEKER

Vaman Naamdev Asteker was born on 1 March 1906 in Akolner, a village in Ahmednagar. In 1917 when he was 11 years old he came to Shirdi along with a large group of devotees. They reached Shirdi in the evening, and Baba was sitting in front of the Dhuni Mai. It was the auspicious day of *Makar Shankranti* (14 January solstice) and Baba made Vaman sit near him and blessed him. Then he ordered him to perform *kirtans* (singing praises of god). Asteker said, "Baba I don't know how to perform kirtans." Baba told him not to worry as he would take care of it. Soon Asteker had a turban tied on his head and he started singing. He did kirtans on Tukaram's abhang on *Vithal Bhakti* and *dhyan*. A huge crowd had gathered there and they listened to his kirtan with devotion.

Asteker had gone to Akolner in October 1918, because plague was spreading rapidly in the cities. On *Dussera*, as was the custom, many villagers visited the Khandoba temple as symbolic *semolanghan* (crossing the border). Then they went to worship all the deities in the village. Asteker didn't enter the temple and sat on the steps leading to it. Then he decided to return home and started walking along the foot path when Baba suddenly stood before him. He stretched his hands out to the side as if to stop him and shouted 'Sai Baba' but Baba disappeared. The next day he heard that Baba had taken Maha Samadhi at that same time when he had seen him.

In 1924 Vaman got a job as a teacher in Korhale. In 1925 the post of the principal of the school in Shirdi was vacant and thus he got the job. He was the principal of that school till 1929. Asteker says, "Baba reassured me and guided me by appearing before me numerous times, and I am eternally grateful to him."

Ref: *Sai Prasad* Magazine; 1987 (*Deepavali* Issue)

***

SONABAI BRAHAMANDKAR

Sonabai Brahamandkar got married in 1913, and she and her husband visited Shirdi. She was the niece of Sunder Rao Navalkar who had been visiting Shirdi since 1910. Upon reaching Shirdi they went to the Dwarka Mai and prostrated at Baba's feet. Then Baba asked her husband for dakshina and he replied, "Baba you give everything to everyone, then who am I to give you anything." Hearing this Baba laughed and blessed them saying, "Allaha will bless you."

In 1914 Sonabai's husband developed diabetes and became seriously ill. He was treated for it but his health deteriorated and everyone gave up hope of his survival. She earnestly prayed to Baba and wanted to go to Shirdi to meet him. But under these circumstances she couldn't leave her husband behind nor was he in a condition to make the long journey to Shirdi. She would sit by his bed the whole night praying, and would read Das Ganu's *Arvichan Bhakti Leelamrut*.

On the third night Baba came to her door and said, "Don't be afraid. I will give him 16 more years of life. Keep giving him the medicines." From that time he started improving. Four years later a healthy baby girl was born to them. Then in 1930, exactly 16 years later he passed away peacefully.

Baba increases longevity in a variety of ways. Sometimes he reduces some life span of the next birth and increases the life span of the present birth. He can transfer the fruits of action from one being to another. The life span of a person can be increased by transferring some life span from a well wisher. In an extraordinary way he can command death to leave and grant life to an individual.

Ref: *Sai Prasad* Magazine; 1987 (*Deepavali* Issue)

***

33

NANHE BABUJI MEETS BABA

The famous musician Nanhe Babuji was born on 5 January 1911, in Rajasthan, Jaipur in the small village of Gadshimthsingh. He was born into a musically talented family, and his father was Thakur Prayelal. His father passed away when Nanhe Babuji was two and a half years old. He was brought up by his uncle Amritlal Ganghrav, also a musician in Mumbai. When Nanhe was 12 years old his uncle became his Guru.

Nanhe Babuji was 7 years old, when he accompanied his mentor, that is, his uncle on a pilgrimage to Shirdi. The young lad saw a puppy outside the Dwarka Mai and started playing with it. His uncle was sitting in the Sabha Mandap as it was time for Baba's noon Arati. When he saw Nanhe playing with the puppy, he got angry and in his anger beat the boy with a stick. Nanhe Babuji entered the Dwarka Mai sobbing and crying loudly; the devotees tried to console him but to no avail. Baba asked the devotees to bring the lad to him and made Nanhe sit beside him. Then he summoned his uncle and said in a stern voice, "Why are you after me with that cane in your hand? Don't ever beat this child again. This Nanhe Babuji will become a famous musician and vocalist one day." With Baba's blessings Nanhe became a vocalist and *harmonium* (Indian piano) maestro.

Nanhe and his uncle stayed in Shirdi for 3 months. Every day when they went for Baba's darshan, Baba gave the lad 3 *paise*. Nanhe spent 1 *paisa* on peanuts and 1 paisa on jaggery, which he relished. Baba would make Nanhe sit near him and give him *pedas* and fruits that the devotees offered to him. Nanhe did his matriculation in the Hindi medium, but studied advanced music and was a brilliant student. The king of Kashmir, Mansingh and the king of Ramgarh often invited him for concerts. Numerous concerts were held all over India and he received many accolades. He established the music school

Shri Guru Sangeet Vidyalaya in Bider and dedicated his life to music. Nanhe Babuji often said, "It was because of Baba's blessings that I was able to achieve all this and the credit goes to Baba and not to me."

The 3 months' stay at Shirdi indicates *Tri Karana Shudhi* or the cleansing of the body, speech and mind, along with the cleansing of the three bodies so that he was ready to receive Baba's grace.

Ref: *Sai Prasad* Magazine; 1996 (*Deepavali* Issue)

***

February 2

BADE MEYIAN VISITS BABA

(The next two leelas were experienced by Bade Meyian)
In 1942 Shantaram D. Thetthe met a Muslim devotee named Bade Meyian, who had met Baba in 1917. Shantaram asked him about his experience and most importantly wanted to tell him about Baba's divinity. He said, "Baba was a great *Vaili* (Muslim saint). He was like a huge ocean. How can a householder like me tell you the depth of that ocean? I was concerned about the marriage of my daughter as I didn't have any money. I had heard about Baba's greatness and philanthropy so I came to Shirdi from a small village in Marathwada. I went to the Dwarka Mai and Baba was seated on the platform with a few devotees around him. I prostrated before him and sat quietly in front of him.

Just then a Patil from the village came and placed 3 rupees in front of Baba and sat down. Baba looked at him and asked him, "Is everything fine with you and your family." He replied, "My daughter is going to get married soon and I don't have the money for it. I am up to my neck in debt. If I borrow money for the wedding I won't be able to repay it. On the other hand if I don't celebrate the wedding on a grand scale I will be the laughing stock of the village." I desperately need 3000 rupees." To this Baba replied, "Why do you worry so much? God will do your work for you. Just cast all your burdens and worries on the almighty God. Then sit quietly without worrying and see what his wish is. If he wishes he will fulfil your desire and

35

if not the work will not be done. Either way you should be content the way he keeps you." The Patil then said, "Baba what you say is true, but I am living in this materialistic world as a householder and the Patil of this village. How can I accept what you say?" Baba said, "Why do you worry needlessly; I will give you that amount. Then you can quit worrying."

Bade Meyian heard the entire conversation and he wondered how Baba was going to arrange and give the Patil the huge sum of money. He looked at Baba who was wearing a torn kafni with a dirty white cloth tied around his head. There was no box or cupboard in which he could have kept such a large amount. What could this fakir possibly give the Patil? Doubtfully Bade Meyian looked at him. At that very moment Baba put his hand into the pocket of his torn kafni and took out a bundle of rupee bills and handed them to the Patil. And said, "Count them here right now." The Patil did that and there were exactly 3000 rupees. Then Baba said, "Now go and make arrangements for your daughter's wedding."

Bade Meyian watched all this in wonder and amazement. Then he prostrated before Baba and returned home.

Ref: *Sai Sagar* Magazine; 2009 (*Deepavali Viseshak* Issue)
***

February 3

BADE MEYIAN'S DAUGHTER GETS MARRIED

Bade Meyian could not sleep a wink that night. His mind kept playing the scene over and over again that took place in the Dwarka Mai. His daughter too was of marriageable age and would soon be getting married. He needed about a thousand rupees to celebrate the wedding. He was a poor man and he wondered if Baba could help him as he did the Patil. He decided to go to Shirdi the very next day.

Early in the morning he went to the Dwarka Mai and prostrated before Baba and placed one rupee at his feet. Then he told him that he wanted to get his daughter married and needed 1000 rupees to cover the expenses. Then Baba said, "Is that right?" Then he put his hand into the pocket of his kafni and took out a fistful of coins that he asked Bade Meyian to receive in the fold of his dhoti while he heard them fall. Then Baba said, "Now go home and count them." As soon as Bade Meyian reached home, he put all the coins on the floor. There were 68 copper paise coins; at first he thought that it was a joke.

Immediately Bade Meyian returned to Shirdi and went to the Dwarka Mai. Bade confronted Baba saying, "The Patil was a rich man and so he gave you three rupees, and in return you gave him 3000 rupees. But I am a poor man who came all the way from Marathwada and I needed only a thousand rupees for my daughter's wedding, but I got 68 paise after giving you one rupee. You made fun of my poverty." Baba laughed and said, "As soon as you kept a rupee I knew that you expected to get a thousand rupees." Then Bade Meyian told him that his daughter was really going to be married soon. Then Baba reassured him saying, "Arre, your daughter is going to be married next year. Why are you worrying already? When the marriage is fixed I will see that you get the money."

Bade Meyian went home and because of Baba's blessings the harvest that he collected that year was four to five times the usual yield. Bade Meyian celebrated his daughter's wedding on a grand scale from his increased earnings, without having to borrow or beg from anyone.

Ref: *Sai Sagar* Magazine; 2009 (*Deepavali Viseshak* Issue)

***

February 4

G. J. CHITHABAR

G. J. Chithabar was born in Shirdi in the year 1915. He states, "I was extremely fortunate to be with Baba till the age of four. I would often sit on his lap and had a wonderful time. The relationship was like a doting grandfather and a spoilt grandson.

Baba never sat and indulged in idle gossip as it usually happens in small villages. He spoke very little and that too if there was a reason to do so. The other interesting fact is that though he was old, his voice was very powerful and his diction was clear up to his Maha Samadhi.

One morning he asked me to get dakshina from my father, who taught in the school nearby. I ran and told my father that Baba wanted dakshina and he immediately gave me a coin. I came and handed it over to Baba. Baba said, "I don't want the dakshina, I wanted to see what you would do. Now go and return it." I ran back and related what Baba had just said. My father immediately said, "Once you give dakshina you don't take it back. Tell Baba this and give it to him." I did as asked by my father and Baba kept the coin. I learnt a valuable lesson from this that one must give in charity whatever one can afford, and it should be done without any expectations."

Ref: *Sai Chintan*; 29 September 1990

***

February 5

BALAJI GURAV

Balaji Gurav lived with his extended family in Korhale, a small village about 8 miles away from Shirdi. His father and grandfather were *Kirtankars* (people who sing kirtan or the praise of god) and thus earned a living. Balaji went from village to village singing kirtans. Once he visited Shirdi and sang before Baba, and Baba liked his kirtans very much. He asked Balaji to sing for him. One day Dabolkar, Butti and Dixit asked him to sing a kirtan that they had composed, wherein Baba is referred to as God whose bountiful blessings are forever on his devotees. After Baba would complete his bhiksha round, he would stand in a certain place against a wall; at that time many devotees sang before him. They asked Gurav to sing the song they had composed and Gurav obliged. But Baba was filled with rage and asked, "Who has made me into a God? Who composed this song?" Gurav was terrified, and Gurav told him who had composed it. Baba calmed down but said, "Henceforth don't sing this song before me."

The next day they asked Gurav to sing the song again, but he refused as he feared Baba's wrath. They assured him that they would pacify Baba and told him not to be afraid. Gurav sang for a living and as these devotees were affluent he didn't want to anger them either. Gurav started singing the song and Baba flew into a rage; he picked up a huge stone and ran towards Gurav who fled for his life. Baba ran after him shouting, I will bury you right here. Gurav ran and hid in Dixit wada and Baba followed. Dixit very humbly asked Baba to be seated on the platform in front of the wada. Baba told Dixit to search for Gurav and bring him in front of him.

Dixit didn't know whether to laugh or cry at the turn of events. Nonetheless he brought Gurav and his partner and stood them in front of Baba. Gurav fell at Baba's feet begging him not bury him in Shirdi and that he would never sing that song again. Baba's heart melted and he hugged Gurav and told him that when he said he would bury him it meant that he wanted Gurav to stay in Shirdi permanently. Thus Gurav came to stay in Shirdi and sang before Baba three times a day.

By throwing stones Baba drove away Gurav's bad karmas, thus enabling him to stay in Shirdi permanently.

Ref: *Sai Sagar* Magazine; 1993 (*Deepavali Viseshak* Issue)

***

February 6

DAMODAR NARYAN CHANDNENE

In 1917, Damodar Naryan Chandnene along with his children Pandurang and Sitabai, and his sister Mangubai, visited Shirdi. Damodar was a staunch devotee of Maruti. By chanting mantras he could expel the venom in people bitten by snakes and scorpions. This service he did free, to help people. It was a token of his gratitude towards Maruti for his grace on him and his family. Then he became afflicted by a strange malady; if his head was pressed putrid pus flowed out of his nose. The malady became so terrifying that even if he lay down, the pressure of the pillow on his head would bring forth the putrid pus from his nose and all treatment failed to give him relief. He believed that some *tantric* had cast a spell on him and so he sought refuge at Baba's feet.

He along with his family set out from Kalyan by train, where they resided, and alighted at Kopergaon. As Damodar was in a precarious condition, his sister wanted to rest there for a day before proceeding to Shirdi, but Damodar was eager to meet Baba. They travelled to Shirdi by bullock cart; there the villagers immediately took him to the Dwarka Mai. Baba was sitting near the railing and as soon as he saw Damodar started shouting, "Why have you come here?" He used a lot of foul language, and Damodar was frightened out of his wits. Mangubai, however, asked all of them to be calm and said, "Baba is our *Sadguru* and we are his disciples and so we should be calm and quiet and listen to what he says, and everything will be fine."

A short while later Baba calmed down and asked Damodar where he had come from and why he had come. Damodar told Baba his problem and he gave all of them his Udi. He called Damodar near him and applied Udi to his entire body and asked him not to leave Shirdi without his permission. Instantaneously Damodar felt a little better.

The foul language that Baba used was directed towards the evil spirit and thus Baba drove the negativity away.

Ref: *Sai Prasad* Magazine; 1988 (*Deepavali* Issue)

***

February 7

"I WILL LOOK AFTER YOUR ENTIRE LINE OF DESCENDANTS"

Damodar and his family stayed in Shirdi for 8 days; they lived in a mud hut and the floor was covered with slurry of cow dung that had dried. The children then aged 8 and 10 had a wonderful time. Pandurung states regarding food, "We all received food that Baba had collected as bhiksha. Baba ate very little of what was left after we, the cats and dogs had eaten. Lakshmibai would bring *Bhakri* and some vegetable curries for Baba daily; she would also look after the numerous devotees who visited Shirdi. Various devotees offered confectionaries, coconuts and fruits that Baba distributed. We often played with him and climbed on his back and sat on his shoulders. Every morning we massaged his feet that were as soft as butter, with fragrance of sandalwood. Never ever did I feel a bone in his feet? Baba listened to the grievances of the devotees sitting under the neem tree or sometimes in the Dwarka Mai where the Dhuni Mai now stands; at other times in Lendi Baugh.

One day when we sat there a wonderful leela occurred. A barren couple came there to beg Baba for a child, but during the journey the wife lost her nose ring. Mentally she prayed, "I don't care if I don't conceive but I would rather get my nose ring back." They then went to the the Dwarka Mai and sat silently before Baba. Baba did not ask them why they had come. Baba as a blessing gave them a coconut and asked them to eat it. Finally the couple left, and returned to their hut and broke the coconut and lo! The nose ring was inside the coconut. Excitedly they took the ring to Baba leaving the coconut behind. Baba saw them and shouted, "Both of you came here and sat silently. I knew that you had no progeny, and had also lost your nose ring. So I blessed you with a coconut for both things, but you found the nose ring and left the coconut behind and came here. Now both of you return to your hut and eat the coconut so that you will be able to overcome the problem that lies in your path."

Damodar had by now recovered completely, and on the eighth day Baba gave him permission to leave. Again Baba shouted, "Now return home and don't come to Shirdi again." Damodar with a heavy heart wondered why Baba had asked him not to return. Damodar replied, "all right I will not return, but before I leave give us your bountiful blessings." Then Baba said, "Arre! I will look after you and your entire line of descendants. You and I have been connected with each other for numerous past lives." Then Baba gave his entire family a handful of Udi and they returned home. A year later Damodar heard that Baba had taken Maha Samadhi.

Ref: *Sai Prasad* Magazine; 1988 (*Deepavali* Issue)

***

AND HE WAS NAMED "SAINATH"

Right from the first day of school my classmates asked me how I was named Sainath. Sometimes my teachers were curious about my name as in those days Baba was not well known as he is today. I used to ask my father about it and he would say, "Your birth is due to Sainath's blessings." The years rolled by and around 1922 I pestered my father to tell me about my name. He said, "My elder brother was a Revenue Officer in a place called Mokdia, which was a small village. As there weren't any good schools in Mokdia, I was sent to Mumbai for my studies. At Mumbai I stayed with the Chaubal's and got my education. Unfortunately I didn't pass the Matriculation Exam. And as I didn't have the money to pay the fees, I didn't reappear for the exams. I started looking for employment and I got a job in the Railways. But the working hours were very long and there were too many shifts, so my wife asked me to resign. My wife was Chaubal's daughter.

At that time I first visited Shirdi, and from Kopergaon hired a *tonga* (horse-drawn carriage) that took us to Shirdi. At Shirdi I was getting some change from my wife to pay the driver when he and the tonga disappeared. As soon as I entered the Dwarka Mai, Baba shouted at me saying, "Who has asked you to come here? Go back at once." I returned home and there I received a letter asking me to join duty immediately at Port Trust Mumbai. And I have been working there since.

After a year or so I went to Shirdi again, and when my wife prostrated before Baba he blessed her saying, "Your work is done." Nine months later you were born, by Baba's blessings hence we named you Sainath. When you were about 2 years old we took you to Shirdi and Baba cuddled you while you sat in his lap." Unfortunately his surname is not mentioned.

Ref: *Sai Prasad* Magazine; 1993 (*Deepavali* Issue)
(article by Malhar S. Hrungharpure of Mumbai)

***

BABA WAITS FOR THE *BHARITH*

Sheela Chaubal states, "During the days in which my grandparents visited Shirdi the devotees prepared the meal at home and then offered it to Baba prior to the noon Arati. Many devotees had already brought their plates of food to the Dwarka Mai. My grandmother had prepared *brinjal bharith* (roasted eggplant with fried onions) with great love and devotion. Somehow she was late in bringing it and the devotees asked Baba if they could start the Arati. Baba said, "Wait a while brinjal bharith is being prepared for me." A short while later my grandmother brought the bharith. Baba saw her and said, "She brought the bharith for me." Baba ate the bharith heartely as he knew that it had been prepared with love and devotion.

When it was time to leave Shirdi, my grandparents went to seek Baba's permission. Baba gave my grandfather a picture of himself and said, "Take this picture home with you. Know that I am in this picture in your home and henceforth don't come to Shirdi." In those days my grandfather's salary was small and he had to look after a large family. It was extremely difficult to travel to Shirdi time and again, so he worshiped Baba's picture wholeheartedly. My grandparents didn't go to Shirdi after that. We are indeed fortunate that Baba gave the picture to my grandfather as we and our descendants can now worship the picture that Baba had given him.

Ref: *Sai Prasad* Magazine; 1987 (*Deepavali* Issue)

***

BABA ORDERS FASLE TO GO TO KASHI

Madhu Fasle did Baba's chores, such as sweeping the Dwarka Mai, washing his kafni and taking care of his horse. Baba fondly called him *ghodewala* (one who tends the horses). One day Baba ordered him to go on a pilgrimage to Kashi. Madhu hesitated and said, "Baba I don't know how to get there." Baba said, "Go from Shirdi to Paithan, Jalna, Balaji, Devalgaon, Omkar, Ajmer, Neemuch and then Kashi." Madhu then set out and Baba in the form of his blessings gave him an old kafni and 10 rupees that he would use as expenses on the way. Madhu had the utmost faith in Baba, and he knew that Baba would take care of him every step of the way.

The journey covered over 1,400 miles through the states of Maharastra, Madhya Pradesh and Utter Pradesh. Madhu walked to Paithan without any trouble; there he met Nandu Patil who asked where he was bound. Madhu told him that Baba had asked him to go to Kashi and he was on his way. Nandu invited him home and looked after him for 4 days. Madhu told Nandu about Baba's divinity and his experiences. Nandu took him to Jalna by his horse carriage.

From Jalna he walked up to Balaji and then to Devalgaon; there he met Ranganath Maharaj. Seeing Madhu the omniscient Ranganath said that Madhu was fortunate to live in a spiritually elevated place like Shirdi. Then Madhu continued his journey and every time he broke his journey somebody helped him. He then proceeded to Omkarareshwar by foot, and stayed in a temple for 2 days. The priest of the temple provided food and a place for him to rest. His next destination was Ajmer. On the way he got plenty of dates to eat. At some place he stopped to rest and sat by a stream and remembered Baba. Suddenly a fakir in a green kafni appeared before him and inquired as to where he was going. The fakir then warned him that there was fighting and unrest in that area. The fakir gave Madhu a large quantity of dried fruits and together they smoked a chillum. When Madhu decided to proceed, the fakir bought him a railway ticket to Bhopal. Upon parting he said, "If anyone gives you chapattis to eat on the way eat it unhesitatingly, if not eat Margosa leaves." Madhu had by now crossed into Madhya Pradesh. The rest of his wonderful journey will be continued in the next leela.

Ref: Ramalingaswami; *Ambrosia in Shirdi*

∗∗∗

AGAIN AND AGAIN THE FAKIR
HELPS MADHU

From Bhopal Madhu walked all the way to Agra. On that day it happened to be *Ekadashi*; he went to a Railway station and slept on a bench as he was tired and hungry. A *bhil* (tribal) came up to him and gave him some *chattu* (flour mixed in water to make a delicious gruel). Madhu suspected that he was a low caste person and refused to accept it. The bhil assured him that as it was uncooked flour it was suitable to eat while fasting. So Madhu ate it and continued his journey.

When Madhu reached Agra he met the same fakir who had met him on his way to Ajmer. He welcomed him saying, "Child now go to Mathura and Brindavan, but do not make friends with anyone on the way." Then he bought him a train ticket to Mathura. Madhu reached Mathura comfortably and there he met a man who was enrolling labourers to work in his tea estate. Madhu also joined as a labourer, but told him that he would not have his meals with him. The man gave him money and allowed him to eat from any restaurant. He continued giving him money for 8 days; then Madhu remembered the fakir's words and escaped from there. He then walked to Kanpur and along the way he got chapattis to eat; he then met the same fakir again. The fakir gave him chattu to eat and advised him to go to Ayodhya from Lucknow. He gave him all the information for a comfortable journey and told him where to stay and eat food. Finally Madhu went to Kashi from Lucknow, where he met Mohan Pandya, who took him home and looked after him for 5 days. At Kashi he visited the famous Vishvanath Temple and numerous temples along the Ganges.

After a dip in the Ganges he went to Prayag by train and took a bath in the *Triveni* (confluence of three rivers).

Again Madhu met the same fakir who fed him and gave him a train ticket to travel to Manmad and asked him to return home. From Manmad he walked to Shirdi where Baba welcomed him saying, "I was with you throughout your journey. I saved you on numerous occasions, during those 3 months." Madhu knew that he could not have done the pilgrimage without Baba's help. As a token of his gratitude Madhu would mix a little of the sacred water of the Ganga in Baba's drinking water as well as bathing water every day.

Do not be proud of pilgrimages, as it is Baba who sends us there and enables us to successfully complete it.

Ref: Ramalingaswami; Ambrosia in Shirdi

***

February 12

SHRIMATHI LONDE

Shrimati Londe was 11 years old in 1912 when she first visited Shirdi. Unfortunately her first name and maiden name are not given. Baba used to sit near the railing but she was afraid to go near him. The devotees brought large quantities of sweets such as pedas and fruits and offered them to Baba. Then Baba would distribute fistful of sweets to all the children. She would receive the sweets and run and stand at the end of the Sabha Mandap and eat it.

There was a huge drum kept in the Dwarka Mai and a single beat produced such a loud sound that it could be heard all over Shirdi. When she would hear it she knew that Baba would be going in procession somewhere. He often visited Neemgaon; there her brother-in-law lived. He was an officer in Neemgaon. So she would accompany Baba. At Neemgaon she would run off to her sister's home, and after eating something Baba would bring her back to Shirdi.

When my sister's mother-in-law passed away, Shama was very sad. He came to the Dwarka Mai and sat there silently. Baba asked him to go home. He replied "Why should I go?" Finally he obeyed Baba and returned home. At home he yelled loudly thrice and fell to the ground losing consciousness. After a long time he came became conscious chanting Baba's name even in that state.

Shrimathi Londe says, "Baba let us have darshan of either his left or right foot. Many a time I have seen Baba distribute shirts and caps to the poor people. If any person took of his cap in front of Baba he didn't like it too much. He said, "The cap is taken off when one makes the final journey."

Her elder sister was married to Shama's nephew. Before the girl was chosen by the family to be the bride, Shama asked Baba to choose the girl for them. Baba then jokingly said, "Shyamia are you choosing a girl for yourself?" Then Baba chose her elder sister and said, "Take only 70 rupees, 7 *sarees* and 7 *pailis* of rice (1 paili is equal to 7 kilos) from the family, and don't demand a huge dowry." However, Shama's nephew was not pleased with this and refused to get married to the girl. Then Baba said, "They have three daughters." After their marriage the couple went to take Baba's blessings. At that time, Baba took the bride and made her sit in his lap and blessed her. He then gave her a silver coin and Udi.

She says, "Because I was fortunate to see Baba and receive his blessings I led a happy and contented life"

Ref: *Sai Prasad* Magazine; 1987 (*Deepavali* Issue)

***

February 13

GANESH KESHEV REGE

Ganesh Keshev Rege worked as an Executive Magistrate in a small town called Amin and earned Rs 50 per month. In 1913 he was tormented with worry as to how he would take care of his extended family and his sons. That evening when he was returning home from work he experienced excruciating pain in his leg. The shooting pain was so severe that he had to hire a horse-drawn carriage to take him home. The doctor diagnosed him with sciatica and prescribed Aspirin. He also told him that it would take him a long time to get relief.

His eldest son, who at that time had to appear for his Matriculation exam, took good care of him. As he could not attend to official duties his officer granted him early retirement and advised him to go to Indore and recuperate. He took his wife and younger son and somehow reached Indore, but they found that life at Indore was worse.

Finally he decided to go to his in law's home at Jeergaon. After a long, tiring and tedious journey they reached there. At the station he met Naryan Dada who was the maternal uncle of his wife. Naryan Dada was shocked to see how emaciated he was. So he took him home and made him comfortable. Then he took some Udi from a box kept in his prayer room and applied it on his forehead and earnestly prayed saying, "Baba now his health is in your hands. Please don't forsake us." Then he sat at his bedside and started reading the *Tulsidas Ramayan* (epic of Lord Ram written by Tulsidas).

About an hour later Rege had a vivid vision of an ascetic who stood before him and said, "Child do not be afraid. On the third day from today you will recover your health," and vanished. As predicted by the ascetic, Rege regained his health with the Udi that Naryan Dada regularly applied on his forehead and also made him take internally with water.

Ref: *Shri Sai Leela* Magazine; Vol. 4, No. 13, *Falgun shake* 1849

***

February 14

UDI REVIVES REGE'S DEAD CHILD

In 1921 Ganesh K. Rege's daughter got seriously ill with malaria; he gave her medicines prescribed by the doctor at his place of work. But there was no improvement in her condition. So he consulted a doctor with a Diploma in medicine, but her condition went from bad to worse. Soon she became emaciated and was only skin and bones. At that time she lost her power of speech and writhed in pain, unable to tell her mother what was hurting. In agony her father told the doctor that his efforts had been futile in treating his daughter and the doctor left feeling insulted. They then tried Ayurvedic treatment. Her mother sat by her bed crying incessantly and praying to Baba to save her child.

One night she heard Baba say, "Don't be worried your child will be all right on the third day." But on that day the child's condition deteriorated; she closed her eyes and became cold, her pulse weakened and then she stopped breathing. Her mother in utter sorrow asked her husband how Baba's words could be untrue as her daughter had died. Her husband comforted her saying that it was their destiny. Rege then took his child on his lap, and told his wife to mix some Udi in some Ganga water to give to their daughter. His wife asked how he would give it to her as she had passed away. He said he would rub it on her body. She brought the mixture and drop by drop he put it in her clenched mouth, thus he gave her about five spoons of it, while his wife rubbed the Udi on their daughter's body. Suddenly she moved her eyelids and then slowly opened her eyes and looked at them. Gradually after an hour her vital signs returned to normal and finally she regained her health.

Ref: *Shri Sai Leela* Magazine; November 1930

***

February 15

APPA BALAJI SUTAR

Appa resided in Shirdi; his family was extremely poor. His father (Balaji) had a large family to feed, and was the sole earning member. Appa was the eldest of the eight children. Balaji was devoted to Baba, and would go to the Dwaraka Mai daily for Baba's *darshan*. Baba would see him approach and say, "Arre Bala, go and look after the children. Don't wander about hither and thither. The children will die of hunger. *Allah Malik,* will take care, and look after them. Do not worry. Now go; here take this Udi." Thus, Balaji never got a chance to climb the steps of the Dwarka Mai. Nor did Baba ever give him any money.

Five years after Baba's Maha Samadhi, Balaji died in 1923. With Appa being the eldest son, all the responsibilities fell on his shoulders. He looked after the family by tending to Ratnaparkhe's sheep and cattle. Appa followed a strict routine; every day after all his chores were complete, he went to the Samadhi Mandir and participated in singing the devotional songs. Then he attended to the daily reading of *Eknath's Bhagvad* (the text describing the 'Absolute' Krishna written by Eknath) by Dixit.

Prior to his father's death Appa was saddened by the thought that he was illiterate. He would prostrate before Baba and cry, "Baba why didn't you give me the gift of literacy? I too would have read the *pothi* (religious text) in your *durbar* (court). Lord it is you who has left me in this dark, ignorant and foolish state. Now what am I to do?" With these heart-wrenching words he left.

49

That night Baba appeared in Balaji's dream and said, "Arre Bala, send Appa to school. I am with you." So Balaji sold of some of his sheep and sent Appa to school. Appa often said, "It's because of Baba's grace and kindness that I can read. This knowledge is taught to me by Baba." However Appa discontinued his education after completing the fifth standard.

Appa had a burning desire to read the pothi in the Samadhi Mandir. Without wasting time he asked Kaka if he would teach him to read the pothi. Kaka replied, "Appa who am I to teach you to read the pothi. Baba himself will teach you. The only prerequisite is that you attend the reading sessions daily." Appa took Dixit's advice and, no matter what, he did not miss a single session.

Ref: *Shri Sai Leela* Magazine; Vol. 17, No. 1, 2, 3, 1940
Chaitra–vaishak shake 1862

***

February 16

BABA FULFILS APPA'S DESIRE

One night Appa dreamt that he was seated in the Samadhi Mandir surrounded by many devotees. They were listening attentively, as he read the pothi. The following week Dixit had to go to Mumbai so he asked Appa to carry on the reading sessions. Eagerly from that day Appa started reading the pothi in the Samadhi Mandir. Unfortunately he could not understand the deeper meaning. So every day he would read the required portion, then tie the pothi and put it away.

This went on for a few days. Appa soon became embarrassed, and worried as he could now read but could not comprehend its meaning. Meanwhile the devotees who attended the sessions requested him to explain the portion being read. Appa replied, "When Baba gives me a dream vision and tells me to explain the meaning, from that very moment I will do so. The reason being, that it is he who taught me to read and gave me this opportunity to read. Now the compassionate mother (Baba) has to explain and tell us the deeper meaning of the pothi." The devotees agreed with him and said, "You have complete faith in Baba, so do what you like. It will be the best for all of us."

That day was *Vaikunt chaturti* (the auspicious day when Lord Vishnu awakens from his *Yog Nidra* or slumber; it occurs in September) and early in the morning at 4 a.m. Baba appeared in Appa's dream and asked him to explain the portion being read. That very evening in his sweet melodious voice he started explaining the Jnaneshvari and the *Bhagavad Gita*, to everyone's delight.

Ref: Shri Sai Leela Magazine; Vol. 17, No. 1, 2, 3, April, May, June 1940,
Chaitra–vaishak shake 1862

***

February 17

DIVISION OF PROPERTY INVITES TROUBLE

Appa was living with his brother when he got married. Soon there were some misunderstandings and ill will between the two. It was decided that they go their separate ways. When the separation took place the assets were divided, amongst them. There is no factual evidence of the cause of the troubles Appa had to face. However, it's known that he had to pay an unknown person the sum of three hundred and fifty rupees, Appa was unaware of this, and was greatly troubled by the turn of events.

He was aware that though the villagers liked and respected him as a kirtankar, he was not affluent as he was a cowherd. So they would not lend him the money. To make matters worse, a government official came to his home to recover the money. They warned him that if the amount was not paid by a certain date he would be put into jail. Now Appa was at his wits' end. He was terribly frightened, so he left Shirdi and went to a village called Bhagwati Kohlarkarachi Wadi.

There he couldn't find any work and was penniless. He then went to Pimpalwadi gaon, which is close to Shirdi; here his condition was worse than before. Disheartened, hungry and homeless he was extremely anxious. Day and night his only thought was of repaying his debt and taking care of his family. Hopelessly he thought, "I can't

51

repay my ever-increasing debts, nor can I take care of my family, nor can I find spiritual solace." To make matters worse the local police threatened to put him into jail for some minor offence. Stealthily at night he fled to another village.

Frightened and desolate he prayed to Baba for help. He said, "Baba I am at my wits' end and I have no one to turn to. Why have you put me in so much trouble? It would have been better if I had died. Who will listen to my problems? I have but one request — either you take care of my debts or else let me die." With this prayer he fell asleep.

The compassionate Baba heard his cry for help. That night Appa had a dream; Baba appeared and consoled him saying, "Arre Appa, why are you crying like a baby? Don't be afraid and don't worry. Allaha is the saviour of everyone. He will take care of everybody. Now get up and go home." Heeding Baba's words, Appa returned to Shirdi. He went straight to the Samadhi Mandir and standing in front of it said, "Baba, you have let this disgrace of being a debtor hang like a millstone around my neck while you watch everything with utmost calm." Then he prostrated before the Samadhi and went home.

A few days later he had an irresistible desire to learn the Bhagavad Gita. At that time a *lingaite* (followers of Shiva) named Malibua was staying in the Samadhi Mandir. Appa asked him to teach him the eleventh chapter and the bua obliged.

That night he had a dream; in it Shama, Venkat Swami, Das Ganu, Kondaji Sutar and Appa were present and Baba asked each one of them to recite a *shloka* from the Bhagvad Gita. Baba then turned to Appa and said, "Appa, your recitation was the best. Ask for a boon and I will grant it" Appa lost no time and asked Baba to clear his debt and Baba obliged.

The moral of this leela is to be humble so that you can make progress in your worldly and spiritual life.

Ref: *Shri Sai Leela* Magazine; Vol. 17, No. 1, 2, 3, April, May, June 1940,
Chaitra–vaishak shake 1862

***

APPA'S LEG HAS NON-HEALING BOILS

In 1936 Appa's left leg had multiple non-healing boils. These lesions extended from his ankle to his knee and discharged fluid. He first underwent Ayurvedic treatment, then took allopathic medicines and saw several doctors but his condition did not improve.

Disgusted, by the lack of improvement he went to Nasik Hospital and slept here.

That night Baba appeared in his dream and said, "Arre Appa why are you terrified and frightened of your illness? The boils will heal. Go to Shirdi and read the pothi, as there is no one to read it. Vitthal Rao had to go to Shirvala to perform kirtans. Now go to your home at Shirdi and the boils will heal." Reassured by Baba's words, Appa left the hospital and went to Shirdi. On his way he stopped at Sangamnere and then reached Shirdi at 10 a.m. He alighted from the bus and to his utter surprise saw Vitthal Rao at the bus stand waiting for the bus to Shirvala. Vitthal Rao greeted him saying, "I am so glad you have come. Appa do read the pothi. I am going to Shirvala and there is no one to read the pothi." Hearing his words Appa said, "Baba is responsible for all the 'happenings' in this world. I am but an instrument in his hands." Appa then started applying Baba's *tirth* (sacred water) and Udi to his boils. After a few days the lesions healed completely and there was not a scar or blemish on his leg.

Ref: *Shri Sai Leela* Magazine; Vol. 17, No. 1, 2, 3, April, May, June 1940, *Chaitra–vaishak shake* 1862

***

MADHAVRAO VAMANRAO ADKAR

Madhavrao's ancestors originated from Dhanora, which is near Ahmednagar. They were affluent and owned two wada's and vast farm lands. His ancestor was well known as Swami Yogiraj and his Samadhi is in one of the wada's. Vamanrao was devoted to Lord Vitthal and frequently visited Pandarpur. Madhavrao was born on 5 September 1877. His grandfather was sleeping in the Salee Vithal Mandir when he had a dream wherein he heard a voice saying, "Get up and go home; a grandson has been born to you." He rushed home and indeed his daughter had given birth to a boy. The new born looked like Lord Vitthal to him so he named him Madhav, which is another name for Lord Vitthal.

When Madhav was about 6 months old, his mother tossed him in the air and was unable to catch him, and he fell on the sand. But Madhav was unhurt and was smiling at her. Then she realised that her child was unique. Unfortunately his mother Godavaribai died when he was only 8 years old and the responsibility of looking after his younger siblings rested on his shoulders. His father's job involved a lot of travelling so the children were looked after by their grandparents. Madhavrao was introspective and quiet by nature, and the loss of his mother had a tremendous effect on him. From a young age he accompanied his grandfather to kirtan's and the atmosphere at home was deeply religious so he developed a 'non-attachment' to material things from a young age. He would often give away his belongings to the needy.

Then his grandparents died within a span of 4 months and he now had to live with his father. He passed the Matriculation examination with honors; he knew Farsi, Urdu and English, and he also possessed a melodious voice so he studied music. Madhavrao is most famous for the Arati that he wrote and it was one of Baba's favourite Arati. Baba asked Shama to send it through Ram Giri Bua to Maina Tai as mentioned in chapter 33 of the Charita. This Arati must have been written between 1903 and 1904. Ram Janadhan wrote his famous Arati for Dnyaneshwar and the tune of Adkar's Arati is similar to it. Maina Tai told Narshma Swami that it was sent to her by Baba in 1904. It's sung at the noon and evening Arati's in Shirdi, and if there is one Arati that is sung all over the world it is this Arati.

Ref: *Sai Prasad* Magazine; 1994 (*Deepavali* Issue)

***

DEV BABA DOES *PARAYAN* OF *SHRI SAI SATCHARITA*

The *rinanubandhic* ties between Baba and Dev Baba were deep and unfathomable. Rinanubandh literally means *karmic* debt, a bond that existed for many generations. Dev Baba often went to the Bhivpuri Road temple to do *parayan* of the *Shri Sai Satcharita*. On one such occasion he completed the reading just before the Arati. And after the Arati a grand feast was arranged. The villagers knew that it was the last day of the reading, so they had gathered at the temple to partake of the feast.

Soon it was 12 noon and the noon Arati was performed. The villagers had come to attend the Arati. Although completely immersed in the Arati, Dev Baba felt a very powerful spiritual presence beside him. He opened his eyes and looked around. A tall man was standing next to him; he was dressed like a shepherd, but looked quite different from the rest of the villagers. His divine personality was overwhelming. At that time the *Mantra Pushpa Anjali* (Vedic hymn followed by the offering of flowers to the deity) had just been recited. Everyone went forward to offer flowers to the idol. The shepherd, however, stood right where he was and quietly let the flowers fall on to his own feet. Dev Baba saw this and realised that Baba had blessed him by appearing for the Arati on the day that the parayan was completed. With utter devotion he prostrated before him.

Baba is our shepherd and we are his sheep, and he looks after us as he leads us through the green pastures of life.

Ref: As related by Dr. Sainath Gavankar

***

BABA CALLS DHIGHE HIS SON

Shridharrao Janardan Dhighe resided in Mumbai. Once he visited his Uncle's home and saw a photograph of Baba. Shridharrao was fascinated by it and asked him who the fakir was. His uncle told him about Baba's divinity and it had a profound effect on Shridhar. Later he went to his village called Mahsale; there he sat under a huge *Audumbar* (holy fig) tree and wrote a letter to Baba. In the letter he wrote that he yearned to visit Shirdi and prostrate before him. He then buried the letter under the tree. Every day he mediated under that tree and hoped that his wish would be fulfilled.

Some days later his uncle visited the village and of his own accord asked Shridhar to accompany him to Shirdi. Both of them then left for Shirdi. As soon as they entered the Dwarka Mai, Baba looked directly at Shridharrao's uncle and said, "Have you brought my son along with you?" Shridhar realised that Baba knew about the letter and his eyes filled with tears as he prostrated at Baba's feet.

Dhighe with purity and sincerity of heart yearned to meet his Guru and the Guru created the opportunity for it.

Ref: *Sai Prasad* Magazine; 1988 (*Deepavali* Issue)

***

"IF YOU GIVE 4, YOU RECEIVE 8"

In 1904 Shri Krishna Purshotam Patil decided to repair his ancestral home. At that time his brothers started fighting with each other which made him lose his peace of mind. He then decided to go to Akkalkot; just before he left his friend advised him to visit Shirdi and then proceed for Akkalkot. Patil reached Kopergaon in the morning and after a difficult journey reached Shirdi at 10 a.m. As it was Gurupurnima, he witnessed *puja* being performed to Baba by Dixit, Chandorkar and others.

He had darshan and performed puja and sat before Baba. Looking at him Baba said, "Arre. When a severe blow knocks his teeth into his throat, then we will see how that wicked snake jumps about." This is a Marathi saying that when roughly translated means, "Arre .Why do you worry? You have done no harm to others, so God will do no harm to you. God will bless you with abundance. I will watch how long the wicked folk strut about." Then Baba took some sandalwood paste, rice and some petals and applied them to Patil's forehead and temples and said, "This is *Brahma, Vishnu* and *Mahesh* (Trinity)." Shama who was standing close by asked Baba as to what leela he would show them that day. Baba replied that it was the leela of the normal world. After this Patil was sent to the wada; although he didn't know anyone there, Nana graciously took care of him.

That morning Patil went to take permission to leave Shirdi, and gave Baba two rupees as dakshina; Baba asked him for two more rupees saying, "If you give four you receive eight. What you sow, so shall you reap. If you don't sow generously, how can you expect to reap a rich harvest?"

While returning from Akkalkot Patil was short of money and so bought a ticket to Poona. One of his fellow passengers advised him not to go to Poona as plague was rampant there and most of the city was deserted. The passenger then got down and bought him a ticket for Mumbai and handed it to him saying, "You can send me the amount by money order." The passenger also bought him some tea; as the train approached the station and they proceeded to board it, the passenger disappeared into the crowd. Later when Patil searched for the passenger but couldn't find him, his eyes filled with tears when he realised that it had been Baba himself who had been taking care of him.

Ref: *Shri Sai Leela* Magazine; Vol. 4, No. 2, 1926, *Vaishak shake*, 1848

***

KRISHNA PURSHOTAM PATIL

In 1905 Shri Krishna Purshotam Patil had gone for Baba's darshan. That day a villager had brought a basketful of guavas and offered them to Baba. Baba gave all the devotees one guava each but gave Patil five guavas. Then Baba asked him to stay for another day. When he was granted permission to leave, Baba blessed him. On the way back Patil was in turmoil because he had gone to Shirdi without taking permission from his superior at work and had overstayed for a day. He was frightened to rejoin as his superior would be angry with him or worse he might lose his job.

He was surprised when his boss smiled and told him, "In the Drawing Department everyone received a pay hike but you have received five rupees more from the Promotion Agent." Hearing this he realised why Baba had given him five guavas. He was overwhelmed with gratitude for Baba's kind gesture.

Ref: *Shri Sai Leela* Magazine; Vol. 4, No. 2, 1926, *Vaishak shake* 1848

***

RAMCHANDRA NARYANRAO KARNIK

Ramchandra was born in 1901; he resided with his parents in Dadar, Mumbai. When he was 14 years old, he was fortunate to have seen Baba in 1915. He along with his parents was once travelling from Mumbai to Shirdi by train; at Dondh station an affluent lady boarded their bogie and soon started conversing with his mother. The lady asked her where she was going. And when his mother told her that they were on their way to Shirdi, the lady started talking ill of Baba. She said, "Why are you going there? Baba extracts huge amounts of money as dakshina, and is it right for a sadhu to have large amounts of money with him? His mother, however, was silent during the entire conversation.

They got off at Kopergaon and travelled to Shirdi in a bullock cart. They went to the Dwarka Mai for Baba's darshan, when Baba turned towards his mother and repeated the entire conversation that had taken place in the train. Ramchandra was very impressed by Baba's omnipresence.

When they entered Shirdi they went to Dixit Wada and stayed in the wada for a week. Ramchandra states, "Baba was tall and his complexion was fair. He was wearing a kafni and a *lungi*, with a white cloth tied around his head. He never wore any footwear even when he went to Lendi Baugh. His Dhuni Mai was continually burning even then. Baba had a white horse that he liked very much. The horse would go to the Dwarka Mai early in the morning and sit there waiting for the Kakad Arati, and then it would prostrate before Baba and would leave only after Baba had applied Udi on his forehead."

Ref: *Shri Sai Prasad* Magazine; 1993 (*Deepavali* Issue)

***

February 25

"I HAVE NOT EATEN FOR A YEAR"

Till 1940 Moreshwar Joshi hadn't heard Baba's name, but his neighbour Ramchandra Sitharam Dev told him about Baba's divinity. Dev worked as a teacher in a Marathi-medium school. Every night Dev dreamt of a fakir who would say, "Come and meet me at least once." As he repeatedly dreamt the same dream, Dev was curious to know who the fakir was. He asked many people and gave a detailed description of the fakir but no one was able to tell him anything about the fakir.

One day a fakir came to his door begging for alms. The fakir was wearing a white kafni with a cloth tied around his head. He stood outside his door and shouted, "Son give me some food to eat as I have not eaten for a year." Immediately Dev said, "Then how on earth are you alive?" The fakir replied, "Come to my village Shirdi and you will know the secret of my life." Dev invited him inside his home

59

and asked him to sit. Then a long conversation took place and Dev asked the fakir many questions that he answered. Unfortunately the question–answer session isn't mentioned. Then the fakir disappeared quite suddenly. That was the first time Dev had heard about Shirdi. Dev asked numerous people about Shirdi and found out how to get there.

Then one day he decided he had to visit Shirdi. As his salary was a mere 5 rupees a month, he borrowed money from a few of his friends. He collected 20 rupees and set out for Shirdi. As soon as he entered the Dwarka Mai, Baba asked him if he had got his message. Dev was stunned as the fakir who had come to his house was actually Baba. Baba kept Dev at Shirdi for 10 days. Then Baba gave him permission to leave, but took all his money by way of dakshina. He told Dev, "Don't buy a ticket as no one will ask you for it," and Dev reached home without any problem.

Dev was very disappointed with Baba as he had gone there with great expectations but Baba had sent him home penniless. Then one day Baba appeared in his dream and said, "Arre for how long are you going to live on a 5-rupee salary. Now I will take care of you." After that Dev started earning money from everywhere and became affluent. He now owns property worth millions. Needless to say Dev became Baba's ardent devotee.

Ref: *Shri Sai Prasad* Magazine; 1994 (*Deepavali* Issue)

***

February 26

BABA MADE HIM RECITE THE DATTA *MANTRA*

Mandekar resided in Pune and was well known for his devotion to Lord *Dattatreya*. He owned a small business enterprise and thus had to visit Kopergaon frequently. On every visit to Kopergaon, he never failed to go to Shirdi and meet Baba. In 1914 on one of his business trips, he took his 15-year-old son with him. On that trip he took 1500 rupees along with him as he had to make the payment of a business transaction to someone in Shirdi. At Shirdi, Mandekar and his son went to the Dwarka Mai. Mandekar knew that Baba demanded huge amounts of money as dakshina so he decided to give the money to his son for safe keeping before he entered the Dwarka Mai. He asked his son to wait outside the Dwarka Mai while he took Baba's darshan. Mandekar went inside the Dwarka Mai and prostrated at Baba's feet and came out after receiving Baba's blessings and Udi. Then he took the money from his son and asked him to go and meet Baba.

His son then went inside and prostrated at Baba's feet; then Baba gave him Udi and shouted, "Give me the 1500 rupees at once." The lad was extremely frightened and he searched for the money. Then he replied, "I don't have the money." But Baba continued shouting for a while and the boy started crying inconsolably. Then the compassionate Baba sat him next to him and made him recite the *Datta Mantra* for about half an hour or so and later gave him permission to leave. The lad had the good fortune of reciting his chosen mantra before Baba.

The boy came outside and warned his father saying, "Whatever you do don't ever try to hide anything from Baba. He is God almighty and knows everything. Promise me that henceforth you won't do such a thing." His father became aware of Baba's divinity and humbly promised his son. Then both father and son went back to Baba and begged him to for forgiveness.

Ref: *Shri Sai Prasad* Magazine; 1990 (*Deepavali* Issue)

***

February 27

"I HAD TO TEAR THIS ABDOMEN TO GIVE YOU A SON"

Chottu Bhayia and Narayana Govind Shinde were childhood friends. In 1903, they made a pilgrimage to Gangapur. They took a dip in the *Sangam* (confluence of the two rivers). Chottu Bhayia suggested that Shinde should vow before the *padukas* (holy feet of the Lord) of Lord Datta that if he had a son within a year, he would bring him to Gangapur and lay the child at the Lord's feet. He said so because Shinde had seven daughters and no male child. Shinde agreed, and took the vow.

That very year he was blessed with a healthy son, but he did not fulfil his vow. Chottu Bhayia repeatedly reminded him about the fulfilment of the vow, but Shinde made various excuses. One day Chottu Bhayia wrung his hand and said, "*Arre* Shinde, God has a way of extracting the vow sooner or later. It is wise to fulfil it before that happens; so you better take your son and go at once to Gangapur."

In 1911, Chottu Bhayia decided to go to Shirdi along with his family. He told his friend to accompany him, but Shinde declined. He was extremely restless the entire day. So he finally decided to accompany them just as they were about to leave.

Both friends reached Shirdi the next day in the evening and had Baba's darshan. The following day they attended the noon Arati. Baba looked directly at Shinde, his eyes blazing and said, "*Arre*! You think you are very clever and smart. I had to tear this abdomen to give you a son. Just as I gave you a son, I am capable of taking him back, if you continue behaving like this." At that moment Shinde repented and mentally begged Baba to forgive him. Then Baba turned to Chottu Bhayia and said, "Is everything all right with you?" By this Baba acknowledged that Chottu Bhayia was instrumental in bringing Shinde to his feet. This incident gives a glimpse of Baba's immense love for a wavering devotee.

A few days later Shinde took his entire family to Gangapur and laid his son on the padukas. Then instead of returning home he visited Shirdi and laid his son at Baba's feet. Following this incident Shinde became utterly devoted to Baba and often visited Shirdi.

From the two leelas given above it is clear that Baba is an *Avatar* (incarnation) of Lord Datta.

Ref: *Shri Sai Leela* Magazine; Vol. 2, No. 9, 1924, *Margashirsh shake* 1846

***

February 28

BABA ASKS HIM TO BUILD A LAKSHMINARYANAN TEMPLE

In 1916, Gummadalli Lakshminarayan visited Shirdi along with a friend of his. At Shirdi they went as often as they could to sit in Baba's presence. On one occasion Baba looked directly at Lakshminarayan and said, "You have to build a Lakshminarayan temple soon." Gummadalli was an ordinary merchant and he was not affluent, so he asked Baba what the approximate cost of the temple could be. Baba replied, "6 lakhs." Gummadalli was aghast to hear this as he did not have even a tiny fraction of the money quoted; he thought that Baba was joking.

Within 2 years, Gummadalli's business flourished and he became the owner of many lakhs and could now easily spare 6 lakhs. At that time Baba had attained Maha Samadhi, but Gummadalli carried out Baba's command and constructed the Lakshminarayan temple in Secundrabad. To his surprise it cost him exactly 6 lakhs, inclusive of the permanent funds. The beautiful temple still stands there and is maintained and managed by his descendents.

Ref: *Sai Sudha* Magazine; Vol. 4, part 10, March 1943

***

February 29

"COME TO SHIRDI, YOUR RAM IS HERE"

Lakshmi Bai Tuse was devoted to Shri Ram and Hanuman. And her daily routine was her elaborate ritualistic worship. At that time she had not heard about Baba. One night she dreamt of a fakir who said, "Come to Shirdi your Ram is here. So come as often as you want." She had never heard of Shirdi. Her Guru, however, told her everything about Shirdi. In 1913, she got a chance to visit Shirdi. When she saw Baba, she recognised him as the saint she had seen in her dream.

In 1917 she again visited Shirdi as she was concerned about her property. She confided in Shama and told him that she had been gifted a vast farmland by her father-in-law. But her father had impounded the land and would not hand it over to her. Then she asked Shama to speak to Baba on her behalf. Shama, however, asked her to speak for herself. At that time Baba was standing against the wall of the Dwarka Mai. He was shouting abuses. After a few minutes he went and sat in the Dwarka Mai, near the railing. Anna Chinchnikar was massaging his feet. Laxmi Bai went up and sat down but said nothing. Baba said to Jog, "Anna has swindled Kaki and completely wiped her of all her possessions. He gives me a lot of trouble." Anna replied that he had done no such thing. Then turning to Laxmi Bai he said, "Kaki let him eat; after all it's Anna who is eating it. Do not register a complaint against him. Allah will give you enough, and there will be no dearth of food in your home. You, me and Anna will go and live in Nasik."

Laxmi Bai was surprised to hear this. Her father's name was Anna. He had swindled her of her farmland. Many of her well-wishers had suggested that she lodge a complaint against her father. However, she followed Baba's advice and refrained from lodging the complaint. A few years later she completed a course in nursing and midwifery, and lived comfortably on her earnings in Nasik.

Baba bestows peace and harmony in her mind. He teaches her Saburi because if she were to go to court daily it would cause her a great deal of anxiety and ill will. And then he assures her that he is with her looking after her welfare.

Ref: *Shri Sai Leela* Magazine; Vol. 3, No. 4, 1926

***

March 1

KESHEVDATH MEETS BABA

Saint Gurugovind was Baba's contemporary and he resided in Songiri near Dhule, Maharastra. He was a divine *Avadooth* (one who has shaken off all the worldly bonds), and with his divine omniscience loved and respected Baba immensely. He realised that Baba had finished his work on Earth and would take Maha Samadhi soon, so he wanted his favourite disciple Keshevdath to obtain Baba's blessings. Once when Keshevdath was in Mumbai he developed high fever. He was in perfect health at that time but suddenly he was drenched in sweat and his heart started pounding. Instinctively he knew that something had happened to his Guru so he immediately went to Songori along with a few devotees. There he found his Guru running a high fever; Keshevdath was naturally concerned about his Guru's health. Gurugovind, however, told him that he would be all right in a few days. Then he asked him to go to Shirdi immediately and meet Baba.

Keshevdath obeying his Guru's orders immediately set out to Shirdi. Gurugovind asked a devotee named Madan Patil to write a letter to Baba on his behalf and to hand it to Keshevdath to give to Baba. Keshevdath thus went to Shirdi and met Baba in the Chavadi. He handed the letter to Butti to be given to Baba. Baba took the letter and touched it to his forehead with respect. Then he looked at Keshevdath with love and again touched his eyes with the letter. Unfortunately we don't know what was written in that letter.

Then Baba looked intently at Keshevdath and Baba's eyes became wet with tears. Then a luminous speck of light emitted from each of his eyes and settled in Keshevdath's eyes. Keshevdath's entire being was filled with divine vibrations and he went into a blissful trance. Baba gave him *Drishti Path* for *bhakthi* or devotion.

Then Keshevdath returned to Songiri and told his Guru everything that had taken place at Shirdi. That Vijay Dassami Baba took Maha Samadhi and a day prior to it, Gurugovind lamented saying, "Alas! The light from this earth has entwined with the moonlight."

Ref: *Shri Sai Sagar* Magazine; 1994

***

March 2

"WHY ARE YOU PROSTRATING REPEATEDLY?"

R. C. Kapadi resided in Sholapur. He states, "When I was a young lad I had an extreme fondness for saints, and I was blessed by Sidharood Swami of Hubli. In 1917 my elder brother Sakharam along with his friend Rambhau Deshpande visited Shirdi. Upon returning they spoke about Baba's glorious divinity and all the leelas they had experienced there. Unfortunately shortly after visiting Shirdi my brother succumbed to influenza. But he was indeed fortunate to have met Baba and stayed in his divine presence for three days.

At that time I was a student in school and it left an indelible mark on me. I was very eager to visit Shirdi, and a few months later I got my chance. My cousin brother wanted to meet Baba so he asked me to accompany him, and I gladly accepted. In those days we had to travel by train to Kopergaon and from there by bullock cart to Shirdi. Upon reaching Shirdi we immediately went and prostrated before Baba. At that time he didn't ask us for dakshina; for the next two days of our stay in Shirdi he kept asking us for dakshina and prior to our departure our pockets were empty. We were glad to give him what he asked for as we were sure he would take care of us on our return journey.

The next day at about 8 a.m. Baba went to Lendi Baugh where a huge crowd of devotees had gathered near Sathe Wada and both of us went repeatedly and prostrated at his feet. Finally Baba said, "Arre! Why are you repeatedly prostrating at my feet? You have prostrated seventeen times already. What difference is there in prostrating once with devotion and prostrating seventeen times?" By asking these questions Baba imparts to Kapadi a spiritual pearl. It's a well known fact that one plus seven equals eight; the number 8 represents maya or illusion. (Ref: *Shripada Sreevallabha Charita*.) Thus Baba indicates 'from maya I give you freedom and take you to *"Eka mevea dwithiya"*, that is, "There is only one and none is second to it." The one prostration or number one is *Parabrahma* (supreme divine energy). Thus Baba assures him guidance from the unreal to the real.

That evening we attended Baba's radiant Chavadi procession and saw the Arati being performed to Baba there. Then Baba was given the chillum filled with tobacco to smoke, and he took a puff and passed it to the devotees seated there. When they took a puff they went into spiritual ecstasy.

On the last day of our stay we went and prostrated before Baba but didn't specifically ask for permission to leave. However, we mentally told Baba that we would be leaving. As we didn't have any money left, we walked to Kopergaon and as we had our return ticket we boarded the train. At Nasik we got off and again walked to the various holy sites and by nightfall we returned to the station for our onward journey; by then we were extremely hungry. Both of us searched our pockets, and my cousin found four 2 anna coins and bought some puffed rice, which we ate and somehow reached home. Thus we learned our lesson about 'taking permission' first and then leaving Shirdi. The three days that I spent in Shirdi is etched in my memory, and they are the most memorable days of my life."

Ref: *Sai Prasad* Magazine; 1994 (*Deepavali* Issue)

***

March 3

VINAYAKRAO GAGANAN TAKLE

He was born in 1898 in Mumbai and had the good fortune of meeting Baba, who blessed him. He was an ardent devotee and continuously chanted Baba's name. Takle grew up as a fearless young man because he was sure that Baba was there to take care of all his needs. Takle worked in a Japanese Company and held a very high position in it. He was soft spoken and polite, and was liked by his co-workers and officers. Because of his gentle nature many Gujarati merchants came to his office and bought abundant bales of cotton. He made sure that the best quality of cotton was supplied to the merchants even if the order was a small one. He didn't cheat anyone and followed Baba's teachings. Thus his company flourished and expanded, and he never forgot to thank Baba for his success. He often said, "It's because of Baba's blessings that I am successful and the company is flourishing."

Once a hooligan saw him and was envious of his affluence and style of living. He asked the caretaker of the company about him and noted his name and address with the intent to harm him. Takle heard the conversation and immediately sent the watchman home and asked him to return the next day. As Takle knew the Police Inspector he immediately informed him of the threat. The Police Officer took action and Tackle was saved from bodily harm. After living a fruitful life he passed away peacefully in 1965.

Ref: *Sai Prasad* Magazine; 2003 (*Deepavali* Issue)

*****

March 4

GADGE MAHARAJ VISITS BABA

In *Sreepada Srevallabh Charitaamrutam* (the life of Sreepada Srevallabh) it's stated that Sreepada blessed one of his devotees named Tirumala Das saying, "You will be born in Maharastra as *Gagde Maharaj* in the washer man's caste. You will be pious and render valuable service to the distressed, oppressed and miserable people. In Shiladhi village my incarnation as '*Samarth Sadguru Sai Baba*' will take place, when I will don a Muslim garb. Then you will certainly obtain my grace. You have a fondness for the image of *Baal Krishna*, so you can chant the name of "*Gopala! Gopala! Deveki Nandan Gopala!*" I will always grant you my darshan in your mental eye. And you will work for the welfare of the world as Gadge Maharaj. This is my boon and assurance to you."

Gadge Maharaj believed that "cleanliness was godliness" and was famous for sweeping and keeping the roads and alleys clean wherever he went. And he carried a broom with him at all times. He had the habit of continuously singing "Gopala, Gopala Deviki Nandan Gopala." In his early days he was a poor saint who owned only a mud pot, but had a keen desire to build a grand building for charitable work. He was quite successful in building a *dharamshala* at Pandarpur.

When he started building a dharamshala at Nasik, his funds suddenly froze. He had only a few rooms built and the work had to be stopped. He was quite disgusted by the turn of events, so he decided to go and meet Baba.

Just as he was climbing the steps of the Dwarka Mai, Baba looked at him and shouted a lot of foul abuses. Gadge Maharaj laughed heartily and so did Baba. Gadge Maharaj knew that hereafter his work would proceed smoothly. Many of Gadge Maharaj's disciples were with him at that time and were upset at what took place; their Guru was insulted and treated badly by Baba or so they thought. Gadge Maharaj hadn't told Baba the reason for his visit and neither had Baba asked him anything, yet Gadge Maharaj was extremely happy. And they returned to Nasik. As Baba had abused and driven his bad fortune away the funds soon rolled in and Gadge Maharaj successfully completed his mission.

Ref: *Shirdi Diary* by G. S. Khaparde

***

March 5

"EVEN THOUGH I LIED, BABA CAME TO MY AID"

Nivruthi Patil was born and raised in Shirdi; he had contact with Baba also as a child. Then Baba took Maha Samadhi. Nivurthi died in 1983; a few years prior to his death he was in urgent need of a threshing machine. He went to the Kopergaon dealer's showroom to purchase the machine. The agent informed him that the customer had to register his name and address first and would have to await his turn. He gave him details of the machine and told him it would cost 1100 rupees.

As Nivruthi needed the machine urgently he went directly to Kirloskarvadi. He and two of his friends met Shri Shankarrao Kirloskar. He told him his story and intent to purchase the machine. Kirloskar regretted about the unavailability of the stock at that time and asked him to return later. In the meantime Kulkarni from the Stock and Supply department turned up. He recognised Patil as he had visited Shirdi. Patil told Kulkarni a lie saying, "I was sure to get the machine as I had put a chit before Baba and the answer was that I would get it." Kulkarni told his boss that "considering everything, we should supply him with the machine." Kirloskar told him to go ahead as he was in charge of the supply department.

During this conversation a telegram came from Hyderabad, which stated that they required 61 machines against their order of 63 machines. Thus Patil was able to purchase two of the machines. He also received a hefty discount of 500 rupees on each machine. Pleased with himself he returned to Shirdi with the machines. In Shirdi he told everyone, "Even though I lied, Baba came to my aid."

Baba emphatically decried speaking lies. He told Bapu Chandorkar, "Harken to the words of your parents, and speak the truth and truth alone." Once Dixit asked Baba about this; as he was a lawyer he often had to distort the truth to save his clients. Again and again Baba told him to speak the truth. Dixit realised that he wouldn't survive as a lawyer so he left his practice. Baba always took 2 rupees dakshina from Purandhare and that dakshina was truth and honesty.

Baba granted Nivruthi the threshing machines even though he lied, because he worked as a farmer and thus had to feed people. If he was unable to get the machine, the harvest wouldn't be threshed on time and many people would go hungry. So in view of the benefit of a large group of people Baba granted this wish.

Ref: Ramalingaswami; *Ambrosia in Shirdi*

***

CHANDRABAI FAILS TO RECOGNISE BABA

Referring to Chandrabai Borkar, Baba said, "She has been my sister for her past seven births and follows me where ever I go." Once Chandrabai had gone to Pandarpur there she was inspired to perform the *Kokila Vrat* (Kokila is the Indian cuckoo. Vrat is a fast with numerous rituals). To accomplish her vow she came and resided in Kopergaon during *Shravan*. Shravan by the Hindu calendar falls in July and August and is considered very auspicious; numerous devotees perform various rituals and fasts. Every morning and evening Chandrabai would circumambulate the Dattaghat and have a dip in the Godavari. Once while performing her rituals she had an intense desire to have darshan of Baba; she hoped that somehow he would appear on the last day of her vow. On Thursday a young fakir came to her and begged for bhakri with jaggery and garlic chutney. She said, "In this auspicious month we abstain from using garlic and onions then how can I offer you garlic chutney. Besides I have come here to perform my vrat." But she had a nagging doubt that she had not done the right thing by refusing him alms, so she travelled to Shirdi.

Along with Mrs. Jog she went to the Dwarka Mai. As soon as Baba saw her he said, "She refused to give me bhakri with jaggery and garlic chutney and has now come here." Hearing this she was convinced that Baba had come on the conclusion of her vrat. She softly said that she had come to give him alms. Mrs. Jog didn't hear her and said, "She has come to have your darshan." It was then when Baba said that Chandrabai was his sister for 7 reincarnations.

Sadguru's grace is necessary to be able to recognise him when he appears before you.

Ref: Swami Sharananand (translated by B. V. Kher); *Shri Sai Baba*

***

"HENCEFORTH DON'T LOSE YOUR WAY LIKE THIS"

Unfortunately his full name and the year in which he went to meet Baba is not mentioned. His name is given as Bhai, and it is said he resided in Kholapur. Once he went to Mumbai to visit his relatives when his niece asked him to tell her about the huge scar on his forehead. Bhai said, "Oh! This scar is a gift to me from Sai Baba. When I was a young man I along with some friends went to Shirdi. I had heard that Baba tied bells on his feet and danced; and he often took huge amounts of money from devotees and shouted at people. My intent was to ridicule him and find if he had any divinity or was a charlatan. After a long tedious journey we reached Shirdi and went to the Dwarka Mai.

At that time quite a few devotees were singing devotional songs, while others were playing musical instruments. Baba was merrily dancing and also keeping beat with a pair of cymbals in his hands. As soon as we sat down Baba said, "These people have come here to ridicule me" and he flung the cymbals at me. The cymbals hit me on my forehead and I started bleeding profusely. But Baba paid no heed towards me and continued dancing. A short while later the devotees called me and filled the gaping wound with Udi and applied pressure to stop the bleeding. The bleeding stopped immediately; then Baba asked us to empty our pockets before him. After he had taken all our money and purses he said, "Now if you have seen everything that you came here to see, you can leave now"

By then it was night and quite dark; we were hungry, tired and penniless. But as he had asked us to leave we had no other choice. So we started walking towards Kopergaon; it became intensely dark and there were no street lights either. As we trudged along we realised we had lost our way. So casting our burden on Baba with faith we continued. Then we saw someone sitting on a stone smoking a chillum; I ran to him and said, "Baba we are lost. Could you kindly show us the way to the station? We will be very grateful." Baba then held my hand and it was freezing cold and I shivered. Then he walked about five steps with us and right before us was the station. Baba said, "Now I will return. Henceforth don't lose your way like this," and he disappeared. At that moment my ignorance and pride seemed to vanish. I fully realised my folly and the deeper meaning of what he had just said.

Now the question of a return ticket and food loomed before me. Just then one of my friends said, "Somehow my pocket seems to bulge, let me see what's in it?" And lo! All our purses and money was there intact; then after a satisfying meal we returned home. For the rest of my life Baba had given me a scar so that I wouldn't ever lose my way spiritually.

When we lose our way in the "unreal world" it is the Guru who holds our hands and leads us towards reality.

Ref: *Sai Prasad* Magazine; 1995 (*Deepavali* Issue)

***

March 8

BHAURAI JAYVANT MAHARAJ

Bhaurai Jayvant Maharaj was popularly known as the *Tukaram of Bhivandi*. Once he set out with three Muslim devotees of his to meet Baba. They entered the Dwarka Mai and saw Baba sitting there. There was a brilliant aura around Baba and it lit up the entire sanctum sanctorum. Baba dressed in his kafni was seated in front of the Dhuni Mai; the Muslim devotees went forward and had darshan, and then Bhaurai came to Baba. Seeing him Baba shouted with delight "Arre Shyamia, lock him up in a room." Shama understood what Baba meant by this but Bhaurai was a little perturbed.

Shama took him to Sathe Wada and gave him a room and locked him up. Then they took immense care of all his needs. They provided him with warm water to have a bath, then provided him with piping hot tea. After he had his bath and changed his clothes they took him for Baba's darshan. Bhaurai was, however, worried as he never stayed anywhere for a long period of time and he was eager to get back.

Shama then took him to the Dwarka Mai. Baba with immense love and affection seated Bhaurai next to him. Then Baba took some

73

Udi from his Dhuni Mai and applied it on Bhaurai's forehead. The rest of the Udi Baba took and rubbed it on Bhaurai's entire body and said, "Allaha will bless you." Then Baba looked into his eyes intently for a few minutes and transferred his divine energy into Bhaurai's entire being.

The transference of this spiritual energy was so intense that Bhaurai shed tears of joy and gratitude, and placed his head on Baba's feet. With utmost compassion Baba patted his back and requested him to stay in Shirdi a little longer. Bahurai, however, wanted to return along with the Muslim devotees and Baba reluctantly allowed him to leave. Bhaurai did return to Shirdi some years later but by then Baba had taken Maha Samadhi.

Never over rule the Guru's word for if the chance is missed it will not return.

Ref: *Sai Prasad* Magazine; 1994 (*Deepavali* Issue)

***

March 9

RAJARAM APPASETH VARDHAM

Rajaram was born in 1899 in a small town called Kudal in the Konkan Coast and had the good fortune of meeting Baba. He first visited Shirdi in 1914, when he was 15 years old. His elder brother and his wife wanted to visit Shirdi and they took Rajaram along with them. He states that Baba was about 6 feet tall and wore a white kafni with a white cloth tied around his head and he wandered about here and there. There was a *Pathan* residing in Shirdi at that time, and he was constantly at Baba's side and sometimes Baba got angry with him.

He states, "If a person was really poor and came to ask for bhiksha from Baba he would take out a few coins from his pocket and give it to him. And the reason for his coming to Baba would be fulfilled. Once a group of devotees came to meet Baba and stayed in Sathe Wada. That day was *Ekadashi* (day 11 of the Lunar fortnight) and one of them had observed it, so he was hesitant to go to the Dwarka Mai. The rest of the group cajoled him and finally he agreed to go. It was in the afternoon and at that time Baba usually drank lemon juice; a huge glass of it was given to Baba. Baba took two sips from the glass and he placed it before the devotee to accept; and then Baba said, "Arre, today is Ekadashi for you so you don't need this," and took the glass and drank it himself. The devotee was astounded that Baba knew that he strictly observed Ekadashi. When we were about to return home Baba asked us to go the next day. So we stayed on and all the money that we had, was all spent. The next day Baba gave us permission to leave. While we were going to Kopergaon a black dog accompanied us all the way right up to the train and then disappeared. As soon as we sat in the train, an unknown person came and handed over our tickets to us."

Ref: Sai Chintan; 29 September 1990 (Vijayadashami Issue)

✳✳✳

March 10

SAGUNMERU OFFERS BABA SWEETENED BUTTER

About 5 years after Baba's Maha Samadhi, Sagunmeru Naik had a vivid dream, wherein Baba was seated in the Dwarka Mai and Bapu Sahib Jog was performing his Arati. Sagunmeru was standing beside Baba and numerous devotees were standing next to him. All the devotees were participating in the Arati and singing the Arati with devotion. Upon completion of the Arati, Jog went forward and placed a ball of butter in Baba's hand, and to Naik's utter dismay the butter fell down from Baba's hand. Naik woke up immediately and at that time Baba's Kakad Arati was being performed in the Samadhi Mandir.

Sagunmeru realised something was amiss and Baba was notifying him about it. He thought about it seriously as he walked towards the Samadhi Mandir. He felt sure that Baba was not being offered butter mixed with sugar as *prasad* (food offering) after the Kakad Arati. Sagun knew that Baba loved the sweetened butter and he was determined to see that Baba received it.

After the Arati he asked the priest Nanu Mama whether Baba was receiving the sweetened butter daily as prasad. Nanu Mama informed him that for some reason Baba was being given sweetened cream. Sagun said, "From today I want you to come to me every day before the Arati and take sweetened butter from me for Baba." Thus for 27 years the sweetened butter was given by Sagunmeru. From 1950 the Sansthan again started providing the sweetened butter, nonetheless Sagun never failed to give a little sweetened butter till the end of his life. Sagunmeru was very close to Baba, and he could easily understand what Baba needed or wanted him to do through his actions.

Ref: *Shri Sai Leela* Magazine; Vol. 29, No. 4, October, November, December 1952

***

March 11

TARABAI H. SOMANE

Tarabai and her family resided in Girgaon, Mumbai. Her uncle was devoted to Baba and often went to pay homage to him. Her uncle Mahadev Krishnaji Chavte, took her along with him on one of his visits to Shirdi in 1914. Tarabai states, "I remember that Baba lived in the Dwarka Mai, and sat under the neem tree and smoked his chillum. I would often go and play with him, as I was sure he would give me pedas to eat. I knew that he was God, and he would surely give me whatever I wanted to eat. Baba would call out to me saying, '*Beta*, (child) come here,' and then he would give me pedas and in return I would give him marigold flowers. I knew he liked flowers especially marigold flowers as he tended to the huge garden full of marigold flowers that grew close to his neem tree."

"I have also seen Baba's Guru's Samadhi. One day I had gone stealthily to pluck some marigold flowers that were growing abundantly near the Samadhi. Baba called out saying, "Beta, do not go near the Guru's Samadhi." At that time I didn't know the reason for his refraining me from going there. Later I realised that in those days I used to wear a dress and there was a lamp lit near the Samadhi so he cautioned me not to play there lest my dress caught fire. Near the Samadhi there was a mound of mud, which one usually sees in villages as a demarcation from the next field; Baba usually sat on that mound and smoked his chillum.

I revisited Shirdi again after I got married along with my husband and his family.

***

┌─────────────┐
│ March 12 │
└─────────────┘

NULKAR WADA BUILT ON KULKARNI'S LAND

Keshev Narayan Kulkarni resided in Shirdi. He and his family were devoted to Baba. His grandfather Appa Kulkarni devoted his entire life in service to Baba, and his name is mentioned in the *Satcharita*. Keshev owned ancestral property and the land was in front of the *Gurusthan*. The Sansthan repeatedly requested him to sell that land to them, but he refused to do so time and again stating that he did not wish to sell off his ancestral property. Many devotees also requested him to sell the land but he was adamant not do so. Then Butti met with him and said, "The Sansthan needs the land to build a Wada on it, where Baba's devotees can stay when they are at Shirdi. There is an acute shortage of *dharamshalas* (pilgrims' inn) for them and I am willing to pay you any amount that you desire." But his offer fell on deaf ears.

In 1941 his father Narayan died and Keshev inherited that land and the Sansthan tried again to persuade him to sell the land to them but to no avail. The irony of this transaction was that for many generations the Kulkarni family was devoted to Baba and yet they were not willing to part with their land. Finally in August 1945, on a Thursday Baba appeared in his dream and said, "Arre! Kesheva give the land to the Sansthan and in return I will give you land that is 4 to 5 times larger." Following the dream Keshev readily agreed to sell his land and within 2 months the sale took place and on that land the Sansthan built a multi-storied building called Nulkar Wada.

77

In 1949 a cousin of his wanted to sell off his land and Keshev asked him to sell it to him as he wanted to keep the ancestral property within the family, but the cousin refused. Keshev prayed to Baba about it and Baba kept his promise by changing his cousin's mind and he finally sold it to Keshev. When the land was measured for registration purposes it was exactly 5 times larger than the land Keshev had sold to the Sansthan.

Ref: *Shri Sai Leela* Magazine; Vol. 29, No. 4, October, November, December 1952

***

| March 13 |

LEELAVATI BORKAR

Leelavathi Borkar now resides in Panvel. When she was about 2 years old her mother took her to pay homage to Baba. That visit was in 1916; of course she doesn't remember anything about it. However, her mother often spoke about Baba and Shirdi. Since then Leelavathi has visited Shirdi numerous times. She states, "I am truly blessed by Baba; he appeared before me numerous times. One night I dreamt of him as Lord *Jaganath* and he said, "Child you have come from so far off to Shirdi to have my darshan." That was in 1991 and then again in June 1992, when I was visiting my native place in Raigad. There we had gone to a famous *mutt* (an *ashram*) of Swami Samarth and there Baba appeared in ochre-coloured clothes. There he also came to our home as a beggar for bhiksha twice. A few years later he came as a serpent in my home; when I folded my hands with reverence he disappeared.

I had become an ardent devotee of Baba since 1957; I also started reading the *Sai Sthroth* every day. I never failed to light a lamp for him every evening as well as incense sticks before him. I have a great deal of faith in his Udi and I apply it all over my body after lighting the lamp in the evening. And I can certainly say Udi cures both mental and physical illnesses. I am a good example as I am now 78 years old and I am physically quite fit. I hope in the end my journey on earth ends like this — not bedridden or having to depend on anyone.

My mother had vowed that my son would cover Baba's Samadhi with a beautiful shawl. She took this vow for the welfare of my son who is physically handicapped. I was eager to fulfil my vow but I was unable to visit Shirdi. Every day I prayed to Baba saying, "Baba I have to fulfil the vow but I am unable to bring my son along with me. Please arrange for me to visit Shirdi soon," and Baba heard my prayer because a direct bus to Shirdi was soon plying from Panvel to Shirdi. Then I took my son along and fulfilled the vow. Baba has been kind and compassionate towards my entire family and we all are totally devoted to Baba."

To set right the physical handicaps of his devotees he has a straight route to Shirdi.

Ref: *Shri Sadguru Sai Kripa*; October 1993 (*Dussera* Issue)

***

March 14

DATTATREYA NAGNATH NIMONKAR

In 1917 Baba had given Somnath Nimonkar some Udi with the instruction to apply it on the child and thus save his life. Somnath thought Baba had given it for his 2-year-old son. However, when he reached Nimongaon, Dattatreya was at death's door. The 12-day-old child was gasping for air and was cold, clammy and pulseless. Somnath realised that Baba had sent the Udi for him, so he applied it on his body and the child survived. When they later went to Shirdi, Baba took the child in his lap and told Nana Sahib to call him Dattatreya, that is, God's gift. Thus, Dattatreya got a second chance at life.

About 15 days before his passing away, Dattatreya (Dada) insisted on visiting Shirdi as he said that it would be his last visit. His family admonished him for having such gloomy thoughts. They reassured him that he was fine and had no major illnesses.

About two to four days prior to his passing away Dada was continuously singing the famous abhang by Tukaram, that is, *"Ame jatho amcha gavana amcha Ram Ram ghaveya"* (roughly translated as, "I am going to my village; accept my farewell)." This was the abhang that Tukaram sang before he left for his heavenly abode.

On 10 January 2012 in the afternoon he got anxious and had severe palpitations. His daughter-in-law Sunita who was sitting by his side asked him what the matter was. He said that he was anxious and then laid his head on her shoulder. Sunita immediately took him to a local doctor, who took one look at him and said, "Dada is an aged man; instead of taking him here and there take him to a big hospital." Thus Dada was admitted to the I.C.U. of Pathak Hospital Sangamnere. The doctor started a saline drip immediately, checked him and told his son that he would not survive for more than 48 hours. Dada started improving and told his son "I know you want me to live forever but I want to go. Don't give me all these medications; just give me Udi mixed in warm water," and it was given to him.

On the opposite wall there was a photograph of Baba in his room and looking at it he said, "Baba you always stall my death, now let me go. How long will you prevent death from occurring? Now just let me go."

That evening when the doctor made his rounds he told the family that Dada would not survive for more than 24 hours, so the family had better inform the relatives and start making funeral arrangements. When his relatives came to visit him he said, "Today is Tuesday; I will go to my abode on Wednesday, *Pandurang's* auspicious day." On 11 January 2012 he passed away peacefully as he intently looked at Baba's picture.

To exit from the Intensive Care Unit of this world, the treatment of choice is Udi mixed with water.

Ref: As narrated by Sunita Nimonkar

***

March 15

SHRI JOGLEKAR

Shri Joglekar a resident of Indore was devoted to Tembe Swami alias Vasudevanand Saraswati of Garudeshwar. He was fortunate to have his thread ceremony in Garudeshwar with his blessings. After

Tembe Swami passed away, Joglekar felt desolate and alone. He felt there was no one to look after his spiritual needs and to guide him on his spiritual path. This thought haunted him day and night. One night he dreamt of Tembe Swami who said, "Go to Kopergaon"; then without telling his family or informing his office Joglekar set out early next morning. He got a room in Kopergaon and every morning for the next 6 months he walked to Shirdi. He went to the Dwarka Mai and sat in front of Baba. Baba neither spoke a single word to him nor did Joglekar tell him anything. All he did was to lovingly look at Baba with a heart overflowing with 'Guru Bhakti' (devotion to a Guru).

After 6 months he realised he had spent all the cash he had brought with him and had only 6 annas left. That day when he went to the Dwarka Mai, Baba said, "Your work is done. Now return home and do not stay here any longer." So Joglekar decided to return home. He walked to Kopergaon and had nearly reached the station when someone pulled him by his shirt from behind. The gentleman handed him his ticket and some money. Joglekar refused to take it but the man persisted and finally Joglekar accepted the ticket and cash. Then he turned around to look for the gentleman but he had disappeared. At home Joglekar's family was concerned about his whereabouts and welfare.

Just then a man came from his office and told him his boss was looking for him. He felt certain that he would be laid off, but when he reached the office they welcomed him. That afternoon he was given a packet by his boss. When he opened it he found a huge sum of money in it so he returned it as he rightfully didn't earn it. Then his boss persuaded him saying, "You have a family to take care of; accept the money as it's the pay for the past 6 months. Now go home and rest and report to work tomorrow in the morning."

Unfortunately his first name isn't mentioned nor is the year mentioned when he went to Shirdi.

Ref: *Sai Prasad* Magazine; 2003 (*Ram Navami* Issue)

***

BAALKRISHNA V. VAID

Baalkrishna V. Vaid lived in Bandra, Mumbai. He had heard about Sai Baba and his divinity. He lived near Dabolkar's home and as everyone called him *Kaka*, Vaid also called him Kaka. Once Dabolkar had invited Das Ganu Maharaj to his home to perform kirtans and Vaid and his family was also invited. Vaid heard the kirtans with rapt attention. Das Ganu gave a dissertation on Baba's divinity and leelas and provided a great deal of information on Baba. Vaid was overwhelmed with love and devotion for Baba.

Vaid suffered from hemorrhoids and was in a great deal of pain because of it. He had sought all sorts of remedies and treatments from numerous physicians and *vaids* (a person who heals by reading the pulse) without any improvement. One day he confided his problems to Dabolkar and asked for his advice. Dabolkar said, "The only remedy for all illnesses in life is Shri Sai Baba of Shirdi. Go and take his darshan and he will definitely heal you." Although Vaid's financial condition was not sound, he decided to go to Shirdi. He worked for the Railways and availed of the free pass and thus went to Shirdi.

As soon as he reached Shirdi he immediately went to meet Baba, who looked directly at him and said, "Come Bhau, (all his children addressed Vaid as 'Bhau'), I am glad that you have come. Why are you afraid when I am here? Don't worry; your hemorrhoids will get cured." Vaid was thunderstruck by Baba's omnipresence, as he hadn't stated to Baba why he had come to visit him. He bowed to Baba and went and sat in the Sabha Mandap chatting with the other devotees. Some devotee then stepped on his hand and caused him intense pain and he yelled, "Baba save me" to which Baba replied, "I had already told you to wait a while and you will be cured." From that moment on Vaid's hemorrhoids were cured and they never bothered him again throughout his life. Vaid often told devotees, "When doctors and vaids had given up hope of curing me, Baba with his divine grace cured me of this painful problem."

Ref: *Shri Sai Prasad* Magazine; 1988 (*Deepavali* Issue)

***

SHE GIVES BABA THREE RUPEES

Until the day she got married and went to her husband's home, Neeta Yadhav had never heard of Baba. The moment she entered the house, her mother-in-law asked the newlyweds to prostrate before Baba. That was the first time she had seen a picture of Baba and her heart was filled with love. Neeta then read every possible book on him, learnt the Arati's and became totally devoted to him.

During the Christmas vacation they visited Shirdi and it was overflowing with devotees. They couldn't get a room so they kept their baggage in a locker and went to visit the holy sites. Finally they visited the Dwarka Mai, which was extremely crowded. Neeta was determined to light some lamps there, so they first went to the sanctum sanctorum and worshiped Baba there. Her husband went to get the lamps while Neeta searched for a place to light them. Finally she found a spot near the *Tulsi Vrindhavan*, (container holding the holy Basil plant) and then she sat on the floor and drenched the wicks in oil. Suddenly her attention was drawn towards the entrance and she couldn't believe her eyes; she saw Baba standing there looking at her with compassion.

Then he slowly walked towards her and sat next to the Tulsi Vrindhavan and extending his hand said, "Child, give me some dakshina today." As her hands were greasy with oil, she looked around to find a cloth to wipe them. He then took out a small piece of cloth from his jholi and held it before her. Neeta was utterly confused and she thought, "I am not worthy of wiping my hands on this sacred cloth. Here the king of kings, the Kuber of the universe is asking dakshina from me and I don't know what to offer him." Finally she wiped her hands on her saree and opened her purse, but could find only three coins in it. She placed them in Baba's hand thinking, "Baba I am giving you my devotion, faith and patience." He accepted them and got up to leave and said, "Child control your temper. Never ever get angry," and slowly walked away. Neeta then saw the entire Dwarka Mai light up like myriad suns.

Ref: *Shri Sai Sagar* Magazine; 2004 (*Deepavali* Issue)

***

BABA STOPS THE BULL FROM CHASING HER

Champubai of Mumbai suffered from convulsive disorder for the past 14 years. She had gone to her in law's home in Jabalpur because she was pregnant with her daughter Shakuntala. She felt restless and weak and yearned for her mother to visit her. Her mother was at Kopergaon when Champubai wrote to her to come visit her. After posting the letter, Champubai kept worrying that the letter might alarm her mother and she might board the next train and come. Besides being far away, it would cause a lot of inconvenience to her. So Champubai wrote back again saying it was not necessary to come immediately.

As Kopergaon was close to Shirdi her mother along with her parents had visited Shirdi and had darshan of Baba's Samadhi and got Udi in which she had utmost faith. Her mother upon receiving the letter was very disturbed, and wanted to leave right away. But the more she thought about it she felt she should wait a little. With that thought on her mind she went to sleep. Early in the morning she had a terrifying dream. She dreamt that a huge ferocious bull was chasing her daughter who was fleeing from it. The faster her daughter ran the bull also kept up. She was also present there and both of them were running. Both of them knew not what to do nor could they find a solution. Just then Baba appeared and they felt relieved. He said, "Do not worry that bull will not harm you. He will leave in a short while." Then he gave her mother some Udi, who applied it on her daughter's forehead. By then Baba had disappeared. The moment the Udi was applied Champubai felt relieved of her illness and a serene peace settled on her. While this happened in the dream, physically too Champubai felt better the moment her mother had the dream.

The Udi stopped death in its tracks in the form of the bull pursuing her and it disappeared. The wonder was if Udi that was applied in the dream could have such a healing effect, imagine what it could do when applied in the waking state.

Ref: *Shri Sai Leela* Magazine; Vol. 5, No. 11–12, March 1929

***

UDI — THE PANACEA FOR ALL ILLNESSES

A devotee, whose name is not mentioned, worked as a Counselor in Thane jail. One day in December 1924 as he was about to leave for work, his sepoy came running to him. He was very distressed as his co-worker Vithu Laad had suddenly become ill. The sepoy said, "Vithu is writhing with pain, and there is a burning sensation right from his toe nail to his head. The pain is severe, as if a thousand scorpions have stung him. He has taken medications given by numerous vaids and physicians but to no avail. He is old and may not survive for long. Vithu says, "The suffering is unbearable, I don't think I will survive for long. I bid you farewell, but before leaving I have a request if by any chance you know or have of any medicines for this please send it to me."

The Counselor was now in a dilemma. He had not seen Vithu since he fell ill. Even if he had he was not a doctor, nor did he know what he was suffering from. Indeed he knew Vithu, but as the Counselor was not a medical professional he did not know how to help him. Suddenly he remembered that he had a packet of Udi in his pocket and he gave it to his sepoy. And said, "Give this packet of Udi to Vithu and ask him to pay obeisance to it with folded hands; then apply some of it to his whole body. Also mix a little in water and make him drink it."

The sepoy did this and returned and both of them went to the jail. As the Counselor was engrossed in work the entire day he didn't think of Vithu, nor did he hear from him at the end of the day when he returned home. Before relieving his sepoy he asked him to check on Vithu. The sepoy did and returned with his face beaming. He said, "Vithu followed your instructions and in no time the pain disappeared, and he got a new lease on life. He sends his heartfelt gratitude to you for sending him this panacea and saving his life."

The Counselor was overwhelmed by Baba's compassion and the power of the Udi.

Ref: *Shri Sai Leela* Magazine; Vol. 5, No. 11–12, March 1929

***

UDI POSTPONES THE BIRTH OF THE BABY

Bayotai Lele lived in Mumbai with her husband and his family. During her first pregnancy she was in Thane with her mother Venutai. She had incessant vomiting that soon became bloody. At that time she could neither eat nor drink; she lost weight rapidly and her condition became critical.

Venutai was devoted to Baba and she had heard about the greatness of Udi, but hadn't experienced it. So she went to her neighbour, Dev Mamlatdar and got some and applied it on her daughter's forehead. The effect was instantaneous. Bayotai asked her mother to give her a piece of bhakri to eat. Happily her mother brought it for her; after eating it her vomiting stopped. A short time later she returned home.

When Bayotai had completed her eighth month of pregnancy she became gravely ill. One night she had a panic attack and was semiconscious. Her husband sent a telegram to her mother to come immediately. Suddenly Bayotai remembered the Udi that her mother had given her. She asked her husband to get it and apply some on her forehead; as soon as this was done she felt all right. In Thane her mother was upset and nervous, in the meantime she received a message that her daughter was all right, due to the power of the Udi.

Bayotai had gone to her mother's home for the birth of the baby. When the time drew near she went into labour but there was a difficulty; the baby would be born under the *Mool Nakshatra* (astral influence). This was considered very inauspicious as it's supposed to be the cause of the mother's death. Now they were in a fix, and it was not possible to stall the birth. Then Venutai struck upon a plan. She applied Baba's Udi and prayed for the longevity of her daughter and said, "Baba you have protected us thus far; I have applied your Udi, now it is in your hands. Do as you wish and whatever the outcome I will happily accept it." The pains stopped and Bayotai delivered a healthy son the next day.

The respect and faith in Udi can move mountains.

Ref: Shri Sai Leela Magazine; Vol. 5, No. 11–12, 1929 (shake not visible)

***

BABA GIVES HER TWENTY TIMES MORE MONEY

Venkatrao Pendarkar the owner of the famous *Lalitkaladarsha Play Company*, decided to stage the play *Rahshi Mehtvakansh* and donate all the proceeds to charity. The play was to be staged on 25 November 1925 at the Bombay Theater. He decided to donate the proceeds to *Baba's Kayam Fund*; this fund was established by B. V. Dev and other devotees who were with Baba before his Maha Samadhi.

Venutai heard about it and decided to buy a ticket for 9 annas, but when she reached there on impulse she bought a whole pack for 6 rupees and 3 annas. She happily paid for them and returned home. At home she realised her folly as she had only 2 rupees and 13 annas left to feed her family, and there were 15 days still to go. Her mind was in turmoil, "Why would I do such a stupid thing, without consulting my son, or considering how much I had left for expenses? I bought the whole pack. But the money is to go for my favourite deity so why worry." Her son would receive his pay on the third of the next month and till then she had to manage all the expenditures with the meager amount of 2 rupees and 13 annas.

As soon as her son Gondu arrived she told him what she had done. Gondu comforted her saying, "Don't worry about it; after all it's to be used for Baba. On the other hand if we will not go for the play, the tickets could be resold and we could retrieve the money or even secure more money for them. Anyways don't bother about it as the tickets are already paid for." That month was a lean month for Venutai as it wasn't the wedding season, nor were there any festivals where she could find some work.

When Baba showers his grace, the impossible is possible. That very day a well-wisher gave her an unexpected contract for work. At the end of it she received 113 rupees out of which she paid her debts and put food on the table for her family. With tears of joy she thanked Baba for multiplying the 6 rupees 3 annas manifold and saving her family from starvation.

Ref: *Shri Sai Leela* Magazine; Vol. 5, No. 11–12, 1929 (*shake* not visible)

***

BABA'S IDOL NODS ITS HEAD

Sarojini Muley was Kaka Mahajani's daughter, and she lived in Indore with her family. She was fortunate to have played with Baba and to have sat in his lap.

A day before she started for Shirdi to attend the conference of authors of the *Sai Leela Magazine*, she and her family had darshan of Baba. It was in the morning when a vibrant voice called out saying, "Come take darshan of Sai Baba." She and her family rushed to the door to see who it was. There stood a lad about 20 or 25 years old. He was handsome and had a brilliant aura around him. He wore a top that was saffron-coloured and on it the words *Sai Ram* were printed in red ink.

Sarojini requested the lad to grace her home by coming in. He did come in but declined to sit; he carried a photograph of Baba along with Shri Dabolkar's *Shri Sai Satcharita*. They bowed to him and offered 5 rupees as dakshina. However, he declined to accept it and said, "I have come only for darshan. I do not want any money." Sarojini kept insisting that he take the dakshina and finally he accepted the money of which he retained 2 rupees and returned 3 rupees. Sarojini happily took the 3 rupees as prasad from Baba.

While leaving the gentleman said, "We will meet in Shirdi on Thursday." He walked a short distance and disappeared. Sarojini was amazed as she was indeed going to Shirdi and would be there on Thursday. She wondered how he knew this fact when she had not told him anything about her visit. Nonetheless she kept looking for him in the crowd during the morning and noon Arati. She could not see him; instead she saw the marble idol of Shri Sai Baba. The idol nodded his head. She looked again; he nodded his head and smiled as if to say, "Yes that was me and here we meet again."

Ref: *Shri Sai Leela* Magazine; Vol. 62, No. 4, July 1983 (*Guru Purnima* Issue)

***

INDIRABAI IS ASSURED OF BABA'S PROTECTION

Indirabai resided in Pendari, Ratnagiri; she was the niece of B. V. Deo and she frequently visited his home. She knew that Deo often visited Shirdi and prior to every visit he requested her to accompany him. In 1917, he and his family literally forced her to sit in the car that was waiting to take him to Shirdi. Unfortunately she refused time and again for some reason or the other. In 1930, her aunt Athyabai coerced her to accompany them and she did. At Shirdi she was filled with a peace and serenity she had never experienced before. She bitterly regretted not having come before and thought "What's the use as Baba has taken Maha Samadhi now, and is not here anymore."

Upon returning home she had a vivid dream wherein she saw she was in Athyabai's home. On a rafter she saw Baba sleeping; he had bent his arm at his elbow and cushioned his head on it, while both his legs were stretched out one on top of the other. But his eyes were open and he looked at her with intense compassion. Then he descended and walked down the stairs and went outside. There he took a bath and then washed his clothes. He then returned to the room and again lay on the rafter. At that moment Athyabai and her son Vasantrao entered the room. Vasantrao said, "Don't for a moment think that Baba's not alive; he's very much alive. And there is no reason to be afraid, as he's always here to protect us."

The thought that tormented Indirabai that Baba had taken Maha Samadhi and so it was futile going to Shirdi, vanished. She realised that Baba was alive and was always taking care of them. The thought that he was there to protect them every moment of the day and night and that he was with them every single moment, made her feel peaceful and happy.

This Leela is the confirmation of Baba's assurance that even after his Maha Samadhi he will protect his devotees.

Ref: *Shri Sai Leela* Magazine; Vol. 12, No. 1–2, 1935, *Chaitra–Vaishak Shake*

***

INDIRABAI FULFILS HER VOW

In 1930, once Indirabai had severe earache. It was so intense that she felt like throwing up. At that time she cried before Baba's picture saying, "Baba I have no one but you, please give me relief from this pain." Then she lay down and fell asleep. She had a vivid dream wherein she was in some strange place beneath a tent. It was very crowded and she was lost. At that moment an old man with a white cloth tied around his head, wearing a short white coat on top of a dhotar appeared before her. He held her by her hand and gently led her out of that crowd. Then she reached the Dwarka Mai and was standing in front of the room where the *rath* (palanquin) is kept. Suddenly she was overcome by sleep, so she slept in that room and the old man slept behind her. Then she got up and walked a short distance away and saw a Muslim lady sitting on a mattress. There were two mattresses next to her; Indirabai inquired if she could sleep on it. The lady replied, "You can sleep on it with pleasure, it's for pilgrims like you." She then said, "Why are you so miserly? Go and buy 4 annas worth of the fruit of the neem tree and everything will be all right and you will recover from your illness." Indirabai awoke startled. At that very moment there was a knock on her door. A friend had come with some medicines for her. She took the medicine and was instantly relieved of the earache. Also, it never bothered her again. She realised, "If you pray to Baba from the bottom your heart he relieves you of your troubles and gives you immense peace and happiness."

About a year later, that is, in 1931 Indirabai was bitten on her knees by some poisonous insect. The pain was intense and unbearable. It felt as if she was being pricked by a huge sharp knife. She looked to see what had happened to her knees and noticed two bite marks on her left knee, but there was no such mark on her right knee. She felt she should leave Pendari and go somewhere for some treatment and relief of the pain.

The pain was so bad that she was unable to get out of bed. She thought if she told someone about it they wouldn't believe her, and she had no way of getting herself treated. Her thoughts turned to

Baba — her only refuge. At once she vowed to send two and a half rupees to Baba's Sansthan as soon as she got some relief.

Two days later, an old Brahmin from a neighbouring village called Kingewada suddenly came to her house. Desperately she related what had happened to her. Without wasting a single moment he went into the forest and brought some medicinal plants. He ground them into a paste and applied it on both her knees. He then said, "What do I know about these medicinal plants? The almighty deity of Kinewada, Lord *Shiva* will definitely make you all right." After 2 days she felt fine and was able to do her chores without any pain. Immediately she sent two and a half rupees to Shirdi as per her vow. She was pain-free even a year later, so she decided to keep her vow and follow it every year thereafter.

In this leela the meaning of two and a half rupees could be that 'without the "Absolute" we are half; so when we offer ourselves with *shradha* (implicit faith) and *saburi* (patience), by Baba's grace we would be relieved of the pain caused by the sting of worldly affairs.

Ref: *Shri Sai Leela* Magazine; Vol. 12, No. 1–2, 1935, *Chaitra–Vaishak shake*

***

March 25

INDIRABAI WAS TAUGHT BY BABA
HOW TO COUNT THE ROSARY

About a month later Indirabai dreamt that she was asleep in bed. A huge black Bhil wearing a white dhotar was standing near her bed. His arms akimbo he looked at her menacingly. She thought he was going to kill her, so she shouted "Baba please save me." At once Baba appeared before her and Indirabai immediately clasped his feet and begged for help. Angrily Baba rolled his eyes at the Bhil and drove him away. Indirabai knew that whatever trouble was to befall her had been driven away.

Towards the end of 1931 she again dreamt of Baba; she was in Pendari at that time. In the dream she saw Baba acting the role of a kirtankar. Athyabai, Deo and she were seated in the front row listening intently to the kirtans. Baba then took two or three steps forward and stood in front of her. He had a rosary in his hand and he showed her the correct method of counting the beads. He did this by counting a few beads in front of her. Then he showed her how to recount the rosary. Then he told her to chant his name. He looked at her compassionately and said, "Child chant Sai, Sai, continuously while you do your chores."

The very next day she bought a rosary and faithfully chanted his name and circumambulated his picture 108 times. Indirabai was very grateful that Baba had given her guidance and a mantra to live by.

Baba teaches us the importance of *Naam Japa*, that is, continuous chanting of Baba's name; for when we chant his name we have direct contact with him. Baba often stressed that we should chant his name and he would do the rest, that is, he would take care of our materialistic and spiritual well-being. A few words about Naam Japa are given below.

In Kali Yuga or this Era, the only *Sadhana* that we need to do is to chant the Sadguru's name. It is easy as it does not involve any complicated Yogic practice, or ritual, and it can be done by any and everyone at any time. The chanting can be carried out by men, women and children. It can be performed simultaneously while doing other chores or household work. In Kali Yuga even if you don't see the *Avatar* yet you can chant his name. If you keep sugar you don't have to invite ants; in the same way if you continuously chant the Sadguru's name he will be drawn to you on his own accord. Also it's easy to do Naam Japa but difficult to continue it consistently. If you chant his name and put it in the bank as insurance, the interest will come of use whenever you need it. As you continue to chant his name your ego and arrogance will diminish, and your love for him will be enhanced.

Finally, in this Kali Yuga there is no greater cure to remove sins of speech than remembering your Sadguru's name.

Ref: *Shri Sai Leela* Magazine; Vol. 12, No. 1–2 *Chaitra*

***

BABA AND RAMANA MAHARISHI
ARE THE SAME

The family Guru of Susheladevi Bhaktal was Ramana Maharishi. She and her family often went for his darshan. They devoutly worshipped his padukas. When Ramana Maharishi took Samadhi, unfortunately she was in Switzerland so could not attend the last rites ceremony. The body was laid in his *durbar* for three days so all his devotees could pay their last respects. However, Susheladevi could not pay her last homage, so she was very disappointed and dejected. She returned to India 15 days later. She landed in Chenai and was very eager to visit his Samadhi.

When she was in Chenai some people approached her and spoke about the divinity of Baba. They also asked her for some donation as they wanted to construct a temple of Baba. While talking to her they invited her to visit Shirdi and have darshan of Baba's Samadhi. She told them about her Guru and said, "It's of utmost importance that I visit my Guru's Samadhi first then go for other pilgrimages." They replied that Baba and Ramana Maharishi were one and the same.

Two days later she visited Shirdi. When she went to the Gurusthan and prayed, Baba gave her darshan as Ramana Maharashi. Not only did she behold this miracle another lady named Mrs. Dongre saw it. So she stayed for 7 days and did parayan of the Shri Sai Satcharita.

Salutations to your guru ultimately reach Lord Datta.

Ref: Ramalingaswami; *Ambrosia in Shirdi*

***

BABA SAVES HER FROM DROWNING

Ramchandra Amtithram Deshmukh was a resident of Shirdi, but wasn't devoted to Baba. Then his aged mother came to live with him. His mother, however, had visited Shirdi in 1918, and had met Baba and was totally devoted to him. Despite her age, she attended all the Arati's and used Udi every day. She never failed to go to the Dwarka Mai and worship Baba's photograph there.

There was a well on the land near their home and everyone was aware of it. Early one morning at about 4 a.m. when Ramchandra's mother was going to the latrine she fell into the well. No one was aware of the accident. At about 5 a.m. a village woman came to draw water and found the old lady floating in it. Somehow they managed to pull her out.

Immediately they got a doctor to examine her. The doctor shook his head and said, "It's due to Baba's grace that she is alive. The depth of this well is about 48 feet deep, and the water is very cold. She is aged, frail and weak; the cold that she was exposed to for such a long period of time can cause hypothermia. And as a consequence of the hypothermia it could be fatal. Just keep her warm and give her plenty of hot fluids and apply Baba's Udi on her entire body." Then the doctor left.

Ramchandra's mother was drenched from head to toe; her daughter-in-law removed her wet clothes. While doing so she was surprised to find that the old lady had not been hurt or bruised or cut anywhere. She got her into dry clothes and then gave her a cup of hot tea; then she asked her how she had survived when she didn't know how to swim. Ramchandra's mother said, "When I fell into the well I called out to my saviour. Sainath only you can save me from drowning. Immediately my Sainath came running and held me with his thousand hands. So I was afloat till the lady came to draw the water from the well." Then she chuckled and said, "I am sure that it is Baba who sent the lady to draw water from the well so early in the morning."

94

A short time later after having the tea, Ramchandra's mother felt better and went about her normal routine. She often said that she survived because of Baba's grace.

Sadguru protects us with his thousand hands from drowning in the well of life.

Ref: Ramalingaswami; *Ambrosia in Shirdi*

***

March 28

THE FROG HEARS THE PARAYAN

Once Ramchandra Deshmukh's daughter fell ill. She had high temperature and was admitted to Dr. Gondkar's hospital. The child was given treatment, and her blood and urine reports confirmed the diagnosis of typhoid fever. She was started on antibiotics, but the fever was relentless. She was getting weaker by the day. The mother was ardently devoted to Baba, so she would administer Udi mixed in water twice a day to her daughter. The child remained hospitalised for 45 days.

The father was vexed as the child had not recovered fully, though she showed improvement. The mother, however, continued giving her Udi tirth and no other medicines. Her husband taunted her saying, "When the medicines did not help, do you think Udi tirth will cure her." The mother kept silent and continued administering the tirth. Three days later the child recovered completely and started eating and even playing. The mother thanked Baba and told her husband to behold the greatness of Udi and Baba's grace. In fact, she forced him to believe in Baba.

Deshmukh then purchased a Marathi Satcharita and started doing parayan. He did the reading aloud; one day a big frog came and sat next to him and listened to him read. This occurred every day for 7 days and after the completion the frog disappeared. The frog symbolizes spiritual evolution or transition from a lower level to a higher one. It also symbolizes purity, rebirth, fertility and luck.

That year Deshmukh decided to get his eldest daughter married, but was unable to so due to ill health. Then he cried before Baba's photograph. "Baba you were relieving me and my family from all kinds of problems although I had no faith in you in the beginning. Now I pray to you from the bottom of my heart to fulfil my eldest daughter's wedding and give me good health."

In January the next year Deshmukh's elder brother and the parents of the prospective groom came to visit him. After the marriage was agreed upon, Deshmukh decided to conduct the marriage in a simple but befitting way. They prepared the marriage feast for 500 people. But unexpectedly 800 people turned up. Deshmukh was desperate to save his family's honor. He ran to the Dwarka Mai and beseeched Baba to come to his rescue. Then he took some Udi and put a little in all the vessels containing food and boldly served it. All the guests were served satisfactorily and there was surplus food enough for 200 more guests.

Ref: Ramalingaswami; *Ambrosia in Shirdi*

***

March 29

"HOW DID YOU FORGET ME?"

P. N. Chettiar and his wife resided in Chennai. They were devoted to Sai Baba and Saint Harnath. They went to Nellore for a month where they sang devotional songs of both the Sadgurus. Then they returned to Chennai. There they continued singing devotional songs of Haranath but omitted singing devotional songs of Baba. However, they performed Arati of both the saints.

In 1939, Chettiar's wife fell seriously ill, and had seizures and a paralytic stroke. This resulted in her inability to move both her lower limbs, thus she could neither stand nor walk even a few steps. She very strongly felt that this illness was a result of slighting Baba, by omitting singing his devotional songs. However much her husband tried to reassure her, she could not be consoled.

Then she dreamt that she was in a garden in Nellore; it was the same place that they had conducted devotional songs of Baba and Harnath. In the dream she was running as she was being chased by two Muslim boys. She them remembered Harnath and begged him to help her. Immediately one of the boys chasing her disappeared as soon as she prayed to Harnath.

Now only one boy was chasing her; the boy began to chuckle and laugh and said, "Am I not Sai? How did you forget me? Now give me 40 rupees and your illness will be cured." She woke up and told her husband about the dream. At once they vowed to fulfil the dream by sending 40 rupees to the Shirdi Sansthan. About half an hour following the dream she noticed that she could move her leg slightly. She was extremely happy and started chanting Baba's name with enthusiasm. By next morning she could walk a few steps, at first with support and later in the day she walked without support. Since then the couple regularly began to worship and sing devotional songs of Baba in their home.

Ref: Ramalingaswami; *Ambrosia in Shirdi*

***

March 30

HE SAW BABA WATERING THE PLANTS

(The next three leelas are about Bhagwanji Desai and his experiences with Baba.)

Navin Bhagwanji Desai resided in Jalalpur, Gujarat with his family. He became devoted to Baba and considered him his guide, saviour and God. Baba gave him some wonderful experiences. One night Navin had a vivid dream, wherein Baba asked him to come to pay homage to his Samadhi in Shirdi. Immediately Navin found himself in front of the Samadhi. To his utter amazement he saw Baba himself atop the Samadhi. Baba beckoned him to climb on the Samadhi. Then Baba came towards him and put *tilak* (vermilion mark) on his forehead. Then he spread a towel and placed 300 silver coins on it. Each coin was a huge silver coin of one rupee denomination. He then tied them in a bundle, gave them to him, and asked him to leave. So Navin got down from the Samadhi and was about to leave, when Baba called him back. This time Baba took a small piece of jaggery (unrefined brown lumps of sugar) from a small silver bowl and put it in his mouth and then gave him permission to leave. After this he found himself in his home. Navin thought this was an auspicious sign.

Some time later he visited Shirdi; he was provided accommodation in Nulkar Wada. It was the multi-storied building in front of the Gurusthan. He sent a heartfelt prayer to Baba begging him to give him a divine appearance, if Baba had accepted him as his devotee. During this visit he stayed in Shirdi for 3 days. On the last day of his stay he had a wonderful vision; he saw Baba watering the plants behind the Samadhi Mandir. He then returned home with his heart bursting with joy and gratitude. Needless to say his faith grew by leaps and bounds.

A Sadguru's will always prevails.

Ref: Ramalingaswami; Ambrosia in Shirdi

***

March 31

A DOG TAKES HIM AROUND SHIRDI

On one of his visits to Shirdi, Navin was guided and helped by Baba in a strange manner. Navin was allotted a room in the Sathe Wada on the ground floor. After he had darshan of the Samadhi Mandir and all the other places, he returned to his room. There he found a stout black dog seated in front of the door. The dog wagged its tail and greeted him as if he was waiting for him. When he opened the door, the dog entered and went straight to his bedding and sat on it. After resting for a short while Navin decided to do some shopping because he had a long list of articles that he had to buy as gifts for his friends and family.

The dog reading Navin's thought got up and led him to the shopping area. Then he preceded him and stood before a certain shop. Navin made some of his purchases from there. The dog then led him to various shops and he easily found what he wanted. As soon as his shopping was complete Navin returned to his room, all the time being led by the dog. Again the dog went and sat on his bedding. In the meantime, Navin's mother got a meal ready for him and the family.

When the meal was served, the dog got up, walked to the plate and took a bite of all that was served and then returned to his seat. The dog symbolizes the *Vedas*; they absolve all impurities. The dog is also the symbol of a guide. Here the dog guides Navin around Shirdi.

After the family had eaten they wanted to vacate the room. Navin mentally prayed, "Baba thank you for your guidance and help. I now need to vacate this room; please enable me to vacate the room and return home safely." As soon as the prayer was complete, the dog got up and walked out of the room and was not found anywhere.

Ref: Ramalingaswami; *Ambrosia in Shirdi*

***

THE FAKIR WHO WAS FED AT THE WEDDING

Navin's brother was illiterate; he was a kind and gentle person. Because of his illiteracy, no parent was forthcoming with a proposal of marriage for their daughter with him. This was a big problem for him and he was saddened by it. One of Navin's neighbour's friend from his village was getting married, so the neighbour asked Navin if he would host the bride-to-be and a few relatives in his home, to which Navin readily agreed. After the marriage the bride, the groom and a few relatives came to Navin's home to thank him for his generosity; at that time he threw a small party and they left.

After their departure he stood in front of Baba's photograph and wept. He breeched Baba to perform his brother's marriage soon. A week later an old man who had attended the marriage arrived with a proposal for Navin's brother. He had seen Navin and his brother, their home, their demeanour and was determined to betroth his daughter with his brother.

Thus, Baba settled his brother's marriage. Navin went to Shirdi and placed the invitations in all the sacred places, and requested Baba to attend the marriage and bless the couple. The marriage took place with great pomp and show. At about 12 noon a fakir walked up to Navin and asked to be fed. Navin fed the fakir in a befitting manner as he would an esteemed guest. Then he emptied his pocket that contained 21 rupees as dakshina, with tears of joy in his eyes. Sadguru fulfils even the smallest trivial wish. Here taking dakshina of 21 rupees signifies that one has to surrender 10 *indriyas*, 7 *saptha dathu* (body) and 4 *antakarna chatatrusya* (ego complex).

Ref: Ramalingaswami; *Ambrosia in Shirdi*

***

BABA TAKES 6 DEGREES OF HIS FEVER

Way back in 1943, D. K. Rao had first heard of Sai Baba, but had not paid much attention to him. Subsequently his parents became devoted to Baba and frequently visited a Baba temple.

In 1947 he had high fever and pain in his chest. The doctor diagnosed him as suffering from pneumonia and treated him for it. There was some relief but it was short lived; he had a relapse and his condition worsened. His brother got him hospitalised at Stanley Hospital. The doctor examined him and aspirated 36 ounces of fluid from his left lung and placed him on antibiotics. That afternoon he was injected with calcium gluconite, and he reacted to it. His temperature shot up to 106.8 degrees and he had rigors. They sponged him with cold water to bring down the temperature.

His parents immediately went to the Baba temple and prayed for his recovery and brought Udi and applied it on his forehead. Rao, however, was unaware of this as he was asleep. At the dead of night he woke up because he felt as if there was someone sleeping next to him. He saw the brother of the patient in the bed next to him get up and say to him, "Don't be afraid. I am taking away 6 degrees of your temperature." Then he blessed him with his right hand and walked across the ward and disappeared. Rao asked his servant who was lying on the floor if he had seen anybody walk across the ward. Sleepily the servant answered that he had not. Rao then called the nurse and questioned her; neither had she seen anyone.

The next morning Rao's parents arrived with milk and breakfast for him, hoping that he would eat something. He narrated his experience to his parents; at that very moment the brother of the patient in the next bed also arrived. Rao asked him whether he had visited his brother at night. Surprised at the question, he said no. From that day his temperature came down and Rao soon became normal, after about 3 weeks of the fever wreaking havoc. He was discharged from hospital in good condition. Even now he gets a thrill and ecstasy when he remembers how Baba cured him and took his temperature upon himself.

Baba never ever leaves his devotees in the lurch.

Ref: *Shri Sai Leela* Magazine; Vol. 66, No. 5, August 1987

***

BABA THE ARAB IN SAUDI ARABIA

In Saudi Arabia the enforcement of the law is very strict and harsh, and no mercy is shown. Nandu Haldankar along with his friend was living there. They had a Muslim cook who would prepare meals for them. One day the cook started acting up; he poured salt into their meal. When the two friends came home for lunch, they could not eat even a morsel. Nandu lost his temper and jumped from his chair and lunged towards the cook, who escaped and hid in the mosque nearby. Nandu followed him to the mosque and slapped him. The irate cook lodged a complaint against him stating that "Nandu had assaulted him while he was carrying out his *Namaz* (daily prayers)."

The police took immediate action and locked Nandu in a cell for 22 days till the trial began. The punishment would be the loss of one upper and one lower limb. Nandu's friend wrote to his parents and informed them of the grim consequence. Nandu also wrote to them and asked them to forget him, but he requested them to go to the Baba temple and pray for him, although there was no hope of his acquittal. Nandu said that Baba was his last resort and nothing else could prevent the outcome.

His parents didn't know what to do; they took his horoscope to an astrologer, who hearing about the crises politely returned the horoscope and asked them to pray fervently to Baba. Nandu was sentenced by the authorities and was taken by the police who would execute the orders. The order was to chop the hand that Nandu had used to slap the cook as well as the loss of a leg. At that very moment an Arab arrived on the spot and spoke to the *kazi* (priest) in a very soothing voice. Finally the Kazi agreed to set Nandu free, provided he pay the damages, which was indeed a huge amount. The unknown Arab paid the hefty damages and Nandu was released.

One fine morning Nandu stood in front of his parents with all four limbs intact, and a heart full of gratitude for Baba.
Baba's grace is unfathomable; the only prerequisite is to have shradha and saburi.

Ref: *Shri Sai Leela* Magazine; Vol. 64, No. 5, August 1985

***

"COME TO SHIRDI; I WILL CURE YOU"

Jesus aged 5 resided in Spain; he had leukaemia and was treated with chemotherapy and radiation. Although in remission, he had the debilitating side effects. Then he stopped responding no matter what drugs they gave him.

Finally the doctors gave up hope and asked the parents to take him home as they could provide him with only supportive therapy. In short, the doctors said that he was dying. They took him home and contacted the, *Make A Wish Foundation* that grants the wishes of terminally ill children.

That night Jesus dreamt of an old man with a white beard and kafni who said, "Jesus come to Shirdi and I will cure you with my ash (Udi)." The next day Jesus told his parents about the dream and emphatically said that he wanted to meet him. His parents knew nothing about the old man or about his whereabouts. The next day his father needed some spices, so he went to an Indian store to buy them. There he saw Baba's photograph hanging on the wall; he inquired about him. The shopkeeper said that his shrine was at Shirdi, India, and he gave him the picture.

Everyone was against this idea, of Jesus going to India but as it was his last wish it was agreed to take him to Bombay and then to decide what to do. With all his medical papers Jesus and his parents disembarked at Bombay. In the airport they saw many photographs of Baba and enquired about Shirdi. A devotee settled them in a cab and directed them to Shirdi. The first person they met there was Sivanesan Swami, who got them a room at Gorodia's and asked them to return after taking a shower and a meal.

Now Jesus started pestering his parents saying, "I want to meet Baba as he will cure me with his ash." The parents were taken to the Samadhi Mandir but there was no human being there. Swamiji told them that Baba had taken Samadhi in 1918. Now who would give them ash? Swamiji reassured them that Jesus would get cured as promised by Baba. Then Swamiji got a wheelchair and took Jesus for darshan;

he also put some Udi on his forehead and some on his tongue. He then asked them to return for the Arati; by then Jesus asked for some milk and something to eat. They gave him milk and two slices of bread, which he ate and managed to retain. Swamiji had given them quite a lot of Udi and asked them to put it in all the beverages and the food that Jesus ate. This was done and by the next Arati, for the first time since he had been ill, Jesus sat up on his own. To make a very long story short, he started improving with every passing hour. They stayed at Shirdi for 2 days and then returned home.

There they met their oncologist who was sure Jesus had by now died in India. Surprised to see Jesus walk into his office, he at once drew his blood and sent it for various tests. But what astonished him most was there was not a single blast cell. In disbelief he sent the blood thrice to different laboratories and every specimen came back negative — not a single cancer cell. Since then, Jesus and his family visit Shirdi on every anniversary of his cure.

Baba draws his devotees from the remotest corners of the world.

Ref: As narrated by Swamiji

***

April 5

THE BHOPAL GAS LEAK

L. S. Narayan was a resident of Piplani, Bhopal. On 2 December 1984 he celebrated the wedding of his daughter. Late that evening he went to the railway station to see off the bridegroom's party, because they were leaving by the Indore–Bilaspur Express that departs at 11 p.m. However, the train was late by an hour, so Narayan was there past midnight. After they left he thought he would spend the night in the waiting room, as the *auto-rickshaw* (a form of transportation in India) would demand exorbitant amounts due to the late hour. With this thought on his mind he exited the station.

Just then an auto-rickshaw drove up to him and the driver said, "*Sahib* I am going to Piplani, I will drive you there for 4 rupees." The driver had asked him for the regular fare. Surprised he looked at the driver whose face looked very familiar. But Narayan just couldn't remember who he resembled. He racked his brain trying to remember, but by then he had reached Piplani.

The next day he heard of the lethal Union Carbide gas leak. It took the lives of so many people near the railway station, and maimed many more, whereas he had returned home safely. Then he remembered who the driver resembled, the driver was Baba. With tears of gratitude he ran to his shrine where Baba's photograph was kept and thanked Baba for saving his life. It also struck him that the driver (Baba) had taken only 4 rupees as dakshina and in return had given him the gift of life.

Baba takes any and every form to save his devotees.

Ref: *Shri Sai Leela* Magazine; Vol. 64, No 5, August 1985

***

┌─────────────┐
│ *April 6* │
└─────────────┘

HE WALKED OUT OF THE POLIO WARD

S. M. Banerjee was an employee of the Central Railways when his son got polio. There was an epidemic of polio in 1949 and his son was admitted in J J Hospital. It was a heart wrenching disease and was known as "ascending polio". It started with paralysis of the lower limbs and ascended, paralysing the muscles along its path. If the chest was involved, the child would start frothing and could not breathe. Some of the children were placed on *iron lungs* and given ventilation. But, if it spread further to the neck it was fatal. Then the treatment was to carry out a spinal tap, extract the fluid and give the spinal cord hot fomentations that were excruciatingly painful.

As Banerjee was posted to Manmad, he got his son admitted and left. The mother used to be with the child, sitting on a stool the whole day and night. She could sleep on the floor if she desired. The child's condition was stable, in that the paralysis did not ascend.

Just after his arrival at Manmad, one of his trolley men asked him about his problem and gave him a wonderful solution. He told him about Shirdi that was nearby and recounted the leelas of Baba. He asked him to go there and pray to his Samadhi, and his child would be cured. So Banerjee proceeded to pay homage to the Samadhi.

At Mumbai his wife was exhausted, and for the first time she gave up her vigil. Seeing her son fast asleep, she curled up on the floor and fell asleep. At midnight her son woke up and not finding his mother there, sat up in bed all by himself. Slowly he climbed down and stood steadily on his feet and started waking towards his mother. The nurses ran to hold and support him. This happened when his father was fervently praying for his recovery at Shirdi.

He was the first child to have "walked" out of the polio ward after 6 weeks of hospitalisation. He then went on to become the captain of the cricket team. This miracle was witnessed by all the doctors and staff of J. J. Hospital. Needless to say Banerjee and his wife were eternally grateful to Baba and became staunch devotees.

We are attacked by "ascending poliomyelitis" of the unreal world. With Baba's blessings we too can walk out of this polio ward, freely.

Ref: *Shri Sai Leela* Magazine; Vol. 64, No. 5, August 1985

***

April 7

THE IDOL ASSUMED HIS PHYSICAL FORM

In June of 1994, Neha Bhatji had an extraordinary dream. In the dream her parents, her husband and she were about to visit Shirdi when it suddenly became very dark and some problem occurred so her husband cancelled the trip. She was extremely saddened by the turn of events, so she went into a room to be alone. There she saw a beautiful idol of Baba and she started shedding tears. Neha stood before the idol and said, "I am like a famished person who is suddenly led to a table which has a feast laid on it. Then as I am about to put the first morsel into my mouth it's snatched out of my hand. Don't you want me to visit you?

Then the lips of the idol started moving so she looked intently at it. Then her tears of sorrow turned to tears of joy as the idol turned into his physical form. Then Baba said, "Why are you so sad. My blessings are with you. Now offer that coconut to me." Neha took the coconut and placed it before him. He then said, "Don't give me that coconut as it has already been offered. Offer me another coconut." Neha went and bought another coconut and kept it in front of him. Baba said, "Now tell me three of your earnest desires and I will fulfil them." Neha said, "What I desire the most is that you bless me and be with me at all times." As she was about to state her second desire she woke up. And this is what she prays for every day, that Baba should bless her and her entire family eternally.

Offering of coconut indicates total surrender by breaking the hard shell of *chitta vikaras*.

Ref: *Sai Prasad* Magazine; 1994 (*Deepavali* Issue)

***

April 8

BABA SAVES HIM FROM THE *RAZAKARAS*

Seth Ratilal Chimanlal was a resident of Sholapur and he witnessed the power and protection of prayer in a very tense situation. On 25 May 1945 he was travelling in a first class compartment of the Madras Mail in which his co-passengers were Jagdish Munshi, a solicitor; his wife, Naidu an agent of the Central Bank; and Gopalrao, a well-known cotton merchant of the Cotton Marketing Company. Nothing to note happened and they passed their time playing cards, joking and chatting.

The train was then passing the Nizam's territory and Ratilal became uneasy in his mind, as that area was the centre of militant activity and a seat of racial riots. Ratilal followed his intuition and started praying to Baba. The train neared Gangapur and an army of *Razakaras* forced the train to stop. They were shouting, "All Muslims get down; kill all the Hindus." Ratilal ordered his companions to pull down the shutters and lock all the doors of the compartment that they promptly obeyed. They could hear the wailing and shrieks of the passengers from the other compartments as they were robbed and beaten violently. Now his companions joined Ratilal in his prayers as Baba was their only refuge.

Baba came to their rescue in the form of a burly Pathan and created an optical illusion of a well-guarded compartment and protected Ratilal. The Razakaras seeing that the compartment was well guarded turned their attention to the other compartments. Thus, Ratilal and his companions were saved from their brutal attack. After the savage rampage the train slowly arrived at Sholapur and to safety.

At Sholapur statements were obtained from all the passengers by officials from the Collectors Office. They had come to survey the damage caused by the Razakaras; then it was noted that only Ratilal's compartment was the one that had been saved. Ratilal and his companions were then questioned and they all answered in unison, "All this is the grace of Sai Baba."

Prayers from the bottom of the heart never go unheard.

Ref: Swami Sharananand (translated by B. V. Kher); *Shri Sai Baba*

***

April 9

BABA SPOKE FROM HIS PORTRAIT

G. S. Jaiswal a resident of Punjab was gifted a portrait of Baba by Dr Babaji. He was affluent and owned a house and vast acres of land. Then terrorists started harassing him and asked him to leave Punjab. Two of them entered his home in his absence and crippled his dog by binding his limbs and stuffing his mouth with cloth. Then they viciously attacked his son in the same manner. They bound him and tried to suffocate him with cloth.

There in the bedroom hung the portrait of Baba watching over his son. The terrorists happened to glance at it and they left. Had their departure been delayed Jaiswal's son would have suffered irreparable damage from asphyxiation or lost his life. Just then their neighbour came to his home and witnessed the terrible scene. Immediately she set the boy free and took him to her physician. The physician told her it was a miracle that the child hadn't died; on examining the child he found him to be all right. Nevertheless he asked her to watch for any seizures or loss of consciousness. Casually she told the doctor that Baba had been there to guard him and watch over him.

A few days later there was a letter from the terrorists. Jaiswal wondered what they would threaten him with next. He was astounded when he read it so he re-read it. The letter stated that Sainath had spoken to the terrorists from the portrait and advised them to give up this heinous and criminal way of living. They also assured Jaiswal that he would not be harassed henceforth as they had turned over a new leaf.

Thus it was evident that Baba not only saved his son's life but also brought about a radical change in the lives of the terrorists.
Only Baba can make the impossible, possible. His presence in any form will emit rays of protection.

Ref: *Shri Sai Leela* Magazine; Vol. 66, No. 4, July 1987

***

April 10

BABA GIVES HIS SON BACK

On 6 June 1984, Mr. T. T. Vijay Kumar lost his son, Vikram who succumbed to burns. This left the couple in a state of shock and depression. In July the couple made a pilgrimage of the temples of south India, and their only prayer to all the deities was to, "give them back their son." The distraught father did not go to work for 3 months. Then one night he dreamt of Baba. In the dream he was waiting to have Baba's darshan along with other devotees. Suddenly Baba stood before him; Vijay prostrated at his feet and held them tightly. Then he asked Baba about his son. Baba replied in English, "You will get your son back." Then Vijay inquired about his job and Baba reassured him saying, "You will get a job soon." He immediately told his wife about the dream. At that time she was pregnant.

On 10 March 1985 the couple was blessed with a son. They named the child Sai Karthik. His second son resembled Vikram both physically and temperamentally. His son Sai was born in the month of March, exactly 9 months after they had lost Vikram. Many of Vijay's friends and relatives remarked about the striking resemblance between the two children. In January 1986 they took Sai to Shirdi to show their gratitude and receive blessings from their Sadguru.

Baba always releases his devotees from the clutches of distress.

Ref: *Shri Sai Leela* Magazine; Vol. 66, No. 9, December 1987

***

April 11

HE CAST HIS BURDEN ON BABA

In December 1984 S. Sreenath made a pilgrimage to Shirdi. After attending the Arati he went for darshan and stood in the queue. As the queue was moving slowly, he casually started talking to the devotee in front of him. The devotee was from Nagpur, so Sreenath requested him to tell him how he became devoted to Baba.

The devotee on hearing his request turned and looked at him; his eyes were filled with love, devotion and implicit faith. He said, "Once I had a severe attack of pain in my abdomen. I got treated by an allopathic doctor, and instead of getting cured, the pain aggravated severely. This treatment went on for some time, and when I could endure the pain no longer I stopped taking the medicines. On the advice of friends and family I started a regimen of ayurvedic medicines and that resulted in the swelling of my entire body. Two days later the swelling subsided but my body started to shrink and wither.

Due to the untoward reactions of all these treatments, the soles of both my feet peeled off. The reaction was so severe that the nerves became exposed. With the result of which I could not place my foot on the floor and so became bedridden. My wife was desperate and asked me to try some other medicine or get admitted into a hospital. I had had enough of these treatments, so I refused to take any more treatments or see any doctor.

I lost all hope of recovery or even being able to walk again. At that desperate moment I remembered Baba's assurance of, "Cast all your burdens on my shoulders and I will bear them." I started taking Udi mixed in water regularly three times a day after chanting Baba's name. However, I did apply butter to the soles of my feet and bandaged them with cotton gauze. I did this with implicit faith, and it took 6 long months before I recovered my health completely. Along the way I learnt a valuable lesson of shradha and saburi. And

110

now I am here to pay homage to him and express my gratitude to my Lord Sainath."

Baba's assurances are "Universal Laws."

Ref: *Shri Sai Leela* Magazine; Vol. 66, No. 9, 1987

***

April 12

SHRI MOTA BABA

Chunilal Atmaram Bhavsar was born on 4 September 1898 at Savali in the old Baroda state and later he became famous as Shri Mota Baba. A short account of his life is written here because he was blessed by Sai Baba 20 years after Baba's Maha Samadhi. Mota Baba hailed from a community that dyed cloth. He passed his Matriculation examination in 1919. He had a few mentors along his spiritual path, but he considers Dhuniwale Dada and Sai Baba his Sadgurus.

In 1938 (20 years after Baba's Maha Samadhi), Mota Baba was at Karachi and had gone to the seashore. Suddenly Sai Baba appeared before him and asked him to walk into the sea. Without hesitation he started walking and soon the water was above his head. Then he lost consciousness; when he did regain it he found he was on the other shore and his clothes were dry.

Once on *Eid* he had an irresistible desire to attend the Namaz. His relatives advised him not to do such a foolish act, because he would stand out in the crowd by the way he was dressed, in a dhoti and turban, and might also get beaten up. Not heeding their advice he attended the Namaz. As soon as it was over, he came out and Baba appeared before him and said, "Well done. Now remove all your clothes and go home naked." Hearing this strange command he was quite perplexed. To move through the streets of Karachi naked was inviting trouble. Not to obey the command of his Guru meant failing the test and losing the spiritual benefits forever. So he asked his friend to keep his clothes outside his home. As soon as he removed his clothes he was full of bliss and did not remember how he ran home. He only remembers a British Sergeant shouting, "Sai Baba, *Eid Mubarak*" (greetings for Eid).

111

Thereafter Baba taught him certain Yogic practices and gave him supernatural visions. On Ram Navami day in March 1939, Baba gave him the experience of non-duality and made him a self-realised soul forever. In the short period of 15 years Mota Baba had achieved all this. About Baba he said, "He gave me the final touches in my spiritual progress." To express his gratitude he wrote and published a hymn in praise of Baba the *'Sai Stavan'* of 17 stanzas in Gujarati.

During his *sadhana* (penance) days Mota had gone and stayed at Shirdi for a month. Abdul Baba on seeing him remarked "Oh, he's one of us."

Ref: Lt. Col. M. B Nimbalkar; *Shri Sai Leela* Magazine; Vol. 65, No. 2, May 1986

***

April 13

BABA CLAIMS THE *ANNADAN* AS *SAMEDHA*

Mr. Sarma was a librarian in a Government college. On 20 December 1982, he went to work as usual. At about 11 a.m. two Brahmins came to his house and asked for some *samedha* (uncooked grains and pulses). At that time his wife attended to them, as his grandmother was sick and was in the next room. One Brahmin inquired about Mr. Sarma and told his wife that he knew her husband very well. He told her that he used to give him dakshina regularly whenever they met. The landlord's daughter was present there at that time and she said that she had never seen these Brahmins. His wife went inside and related everything to his grandmother who asked her to go ahead and give them samedha, so his wife gave the Brahmins some rice and they left.

When Sarma returned home after work that day, his wife related all that had happened that morning. At first Sarma was surprised as he had never offered any dakshina to any Brahmins. Then he remembered that he had forgotten to send money to the Shirdi Sansthan that month for *Annadan*. Then he realised that Baba had claimed the Annadan through the samedha.

Ref: *Shri Sai Leela* Magazine; Vol. 62, No. 2, 1983

***

MUNSHI'S EXPERIENCE OF SAI BABA

Jadesh K. Munshi and his wife were devoted to Baba, but a heart wrenching incident occurred in October 1959. Their one-month-old daughter got severely dehydrated and was admitted to Beach Candy Hospital. She was administered oxygen and even blood transfusions over a period of three weeks, but continued to run a high temperature. All the eminent doctors were treating her, but they gave up hope of her survival as the fever was relentless. On 14 November early in the morning the parents were told that the child was having difficulty in breathing despite the oxygen inhalation, and her chances of survival were remote.

The parents went home for a short while to change and rush back to the hospital. As soon as they reached home Munshi took an agonizing decision. He said, "We have been praying to Baba for several years now. It has been said that if we looked up to him and sought refuge in him, he would look after us. The survival of our only daughter means a lot to us. My decision is that if the child survives, our conviction that Baba looks after us in times of distress would become conclusive. If the child does not survive we will end our worship as Baba has failed us." This decision was made from utter desperation, dejection and helplessness.

When they returned to the hospital another senior doctor was consulted and he to came to the same conclusion. Suddenly a young doctor who had accompanied him said, "Doctor I have been observing this child for some time; though she has been running a very high temperature, she has not lost consciousness. Could it be that she has malaria instead of septicaemia?" The senior doctor was aghast at the thought of malaria prevailing in a top-notch hospital. Nonetheless he said, "You can give her a shot of Quinine as there is not much left in the child."

After the shot was given the temperature gradually and steadily came down. And by evening it was normal and remained normal. Needless to say all the doctors were baffled. The child did not run a temperature ever since and was hale and hearty. Consistent with their promise, they took their daughter to Shirdi by car. As they neared Shirdi, the child put out her hands and said her first words "Baba, Baba." After this miracle Munshi's family, friends and even the servants became devoted to Baba.

Ref: *Shri Sai Leela* Magazine; Vol. 65, No. 11, February 1987

***

April 15

BABA BREAKS HIS ADDICTION TO LIQUOR

In 1982 S. S. Raj got a job in the Gulf, but his dream of a good life was shattered and he was unhappy and depressed. So he turned to alcohol for comfort and soon he had used up most of his savings. Then he decided to return to India; in Mumbai his life was worse as he was broke, jobless and had nowhere to turn. One day his friend R. Naryan asked him whether he had ever been to Shirdi. He replied, "If I had money wouldn't I have bought a few more drinks." His friend not heeding his remarks persuaded him to go to Shirdi with him.

That was in October 1984; upon his return from Shirdi Raj got a small job. As soon as he had saved some money, he visited Shirdi again. But this time he surrendered himself at Baba's feet and prayed for a better life. Upon his return he secured a well-paying job and now was devoted to Baba. However, he could not give up his addiction to liquor. His health was deteriorating and he was miserable; in desperation he prayed to Baba to save him from the clutches of liquor.

One day a friend of his offered him a job in Doha. He knew that alcohol was strictly prohibited in Doha. Raj thought that this was Baba's unique way of detoxifying him, so he accepted the job. He stayed in Doha for 2 years and by then he was completely rid of his addiction.

He returned to Mumbai and then visited Shirdi to thank Baba for saving him from destruction and death. With his savings he started a small business and soon his business started flourishing. He was eternally grateful to Baba for saving him from rack and ruin, and giving new meaning to his life, which was full of happiness.

Ref: *Shri Sai Leela* Magazine; Vol. 67, No. 10, January 1989

***

"BABA SAVE ME," AND BABA DOES

Sada S. Ghode, a resident of Shirdi wished to pay homage to *Shani Dev*. On *Shani Amavasya*, that is, the dark night prior to the new moon in April and September. He and his cousin named Janeshwar set out early in the morning in the month of September. Sada drove a rickety Honda CD 100 and his cousin rode pinion. As it is, the Honda was not as sturdy as a motorbike, and this one was not very travel worthy. As soon as they were on the highway, Sada accelerated to full speed; he had no protective helmet on. Probably he thought he was immortal and accidents happen only to others.

They were about a mile from the Asthagaon Bridge and in the opposite direction an Ambassador was travelling at full speed going towards Shirdi. Suddenly a bicyclist appeared from nowhere and tried to cross the road. To save the bicyclist, Sada moved to the oncoming traffic lane and the Ambassador hit him head on. All he remembers of the accident was that he cried out *"Baba baccho"* (Baba save me).

The next thing he realised was that he was lying in a field about 20 feet away from the highway; his cousin had been thrown on the edge of the opposite side of the highway. The bike was blown to smithereens. At first both of them thought they were dead. Sada, however, did get a bruise on one elbow while his cousin got a bruised ankle.

The devotees who were going to Shirdi were sure they were dead and immediately called the police. In the field Sada lay dazed for some time thinking he was dead. Then he moved his legs; they seemed all right so he checked the rest of his body and found everything was all right. Then it dawned on him that Baba had saved his life after he had cried out for help.

Ref: As narrated by Sada S. Ghode

***

"BABA SAVES HIM AGAIN AND AGAIN"

Sada S. Ghode and the trustees of Kohrale Mandir decided to build a huge hall for the pilgrims who walked to Shirdi. Most halted at Korhale before covering the last leg of their walk. The village was infested by cobras and vipers, so for the safety of the pilgrims who slept out in the open, the hall was being constructed.

The hall, a huge stone building looked more like an old fortress. The height of the walls was about 15 feet high and the stone masons were working on the top. As there was no crane for the workers to stand on, they had built a scaffolding of bamboo. Some of the masons were working below chiselling the stone while others were atop the platform. The masons asked Sada to check on the alignment of the stones, so he climbed on the scaffolding to check but then slipped and fell. Below there were stone boulders strewn about. For a second he "blacked out" and landed between two boulders. Had he not missed the boulders by half an inch, his skull would have shattered. He got up, wiped off the dirt and found that he had sustained no injury, except for a few bruises.

All the workers rushed to help him and inquired if he was hurt. "No," he replied "Baba takes care of them who render service to his devotees."

In 1996 Sada had gone to Amravati to meet the descendents of Dada Sahib Khaparde, to photograph and collect material for my forthcoming books. He was eager to see the *hookah* (Indian pipe) that Dada Sahib and Baba smoked together on many an afternoon. He reached Amravati and booked into a hotel on Raj Kamal Chowk, and made an appointment with the family to visit them the next morning.

The next morning he visited them, heard their experiences and had a pleasant chat with them. While returning to the hotel he came to Raj Kamal Chowk, when he heard Baba say loudly, "Sada cross the road at once." This was repeated thrice. In a daze he obeyed and walked right into an auto rickshaw that was coming in from the opposite direction. The driver was furious with him and got out of the vehicle shouting at him. Just then there was a loud noise like a canon going off? Then it rained balls of fire as the electrical wires overhead broke and came crashing down. By then Sada had crossed the road and the driver had followed him shouting abuses at him. The auto rickshaw was on fire, but Sada and the driver had safely crossed the road. Thus, Baba saved Sada's life and that of the driver too.

Ref: As narrated by Sada S. Ghode

***

April 18

FINALLY HE VISITS SHIRDI

Although he lived and worked in Kolhar District, Ahmednagar, it never occurred to Murlidhar Rajhans to visit Shirdi. Kolhar is just 35 miles away. Then in 1960 his uncle gifted him Baba's photograph that he hung on a wall at his home. Rajhans neither venerated, nor garlanded it. Ever since Baba entered his home in the form of the photograph he gradually started changing. He started doing parayan of *Navnath's Pothi*, in succession till *Datta Jayanthi* and completed reading the book 60 times. On Datta Jayanthi he sat under the *Audumbar* tree and did parayan of the *Guru Charita*. During this period he easily passed his examinations and became an Electrical Supervisor, and got promoted. He was able to look after his family's needs well. This was due to Baba's grace but he didn't realise it then.

On *Gokul Astami* (the day that lord Krishna manifested as a new born baby in Devki and Nand baba's home), he prepared everything for the puja and around 10 p.m. he fell asleep on the floor. Then he had a vivid dream wherein he was seated on the floor chanting his Guru Mantra and Baba appeared and began walking slowly towards him. There were two disciples on either side holding Baba by his arms, just like in his photograph 'going to Lendi Baugh'. As Baba approached Rajhans, he lifted up his hand and blessed him. It didn't occur to Rajhans to prostrate at his feet; he just said, *"Shri Sadguru Sainath ki jai."* He woke up startled with his heart thumping wildly. He was overwhelmed by the thought that Baba was in his home and

117

he didn't even realise it. The next day the *Gopal Kala* festival was at Shirdi, so he went and attended it and thereafter he frequently visited Shirdi.

There he earnestly prayed that after retirement he would like to spend his life in doing some service for Baba. Whenever he did parayan of the Pothi, he prayed to Baba to enable him to do some service for him. Years rolled by and his date for retirement drew near. One day his boss told him that he had gone to Shirdi and there they were recruiting people for various jobs. He knew Mr. Bane the recruiting officer so he submitted his name. Rajhans sent in his application and he was selected. At first his pay was 100 rupees but by the end of the year due to Baba's grace it was raised to 1000 rupees. Rajhans states, "My time spent at Shirdi was the happiest period of my life."

Ref: *Sai Prasad* Magazine; 1992 (*Deepavali* Issue)

***

April 19

"AT LONG LAST MY BABA HAS COME"

Dr. P. S. R. Swami couldn't mentally accept the fact that his eldest son who was 10 years old had passed away. He poured medicine into his mouth but it remained there. He shook him and shouted, "Swallow it," but his mouth remained open. No matter how much he tried to close it, it would not close as rigidity had set in.

In utter despair he asked his wife to throw the photograph of Baba in some dung hill. By then he had reached the end of his tether, spiritually. Then with brutal impudence he asked his wife if she had prepared his meal, saying, "He is dead anyway, I don't want to die too." She replied that she had already cooked for the younger children so if he desired he may serve himself.

Then he served himself a full meal. He sat for a long time with the plate in front of him. At that moment his mind said, "What are you trying to do? Your first born is dead and you are going to gorge yourself in this despicable way." Shocked at his horrible act he looked

118

in the direction of the bed on which his son lay. It was then that his eyes beheld the wonderful form of Baba. He stood at the gate, exactly like the photograph of his bhiksha pose. He wore a torn kafni, a cloth draped on his head, the *tumrel* in his right hand with his left hand on his shoulder.

He shouted to his wife, "Look outside and see who has come." Hearing the urgency and emotion in his voice she ran out and lovingly said, "At long last my Baba has come." Dr. Swami was now sure it was Baba himself and that Baba had not forsaken them. His heart was full of gratitude for Baba for coming at the nick of time and saving him, for he might have polluted the food in front of him. He then took the plate full of food with reverence and put it in his tumrel. He received it and went away.

As Dr Swami entered the house, his son opened his eyes and said, "Father I am thirsty, give me some water." This occurred in March 1944 — 26 years after Baba's Maha Samadhi.

Ref: *Shri Sai Leela* Magazine; Vol. 65, No. 6, September 1986

***

April 20

"A SINCERE PRAYER CAN WORK MIRACLES"

Mr. Kalyanpur had the scare of his life on 12 May 1973. He awoke in the middle of the night feeling quite sick. And to make matters worse he just could not move his right arm. In anguish he remembered his mother and three of her sisters who had had a paralytic stroke before the age of sixty. He could ill afford to inherit this gene from his maternal side. As he was a bachelor, his housekeeper would have to bear the brunt of his stroke. "Baba" he called out plaintively, and turned his head towards the small shrine where Baba's idol was housed. In the darkness he could not see it but he felt Baba's presence in the room. A feeling of calm reassurance settled on him and he fell asleep.

His housekeeper came in and prepared his breakfast. She did not notice that he had performed Baba's Arati with his left hand, and also had his breakfast awkwardly with the same hand. Finally he asked her to call the doctor who lived next door to check him. The doctor came at once and checked him, and asked him to get hospitalised.

His housekeeper then understood the gravity of his illness. "How long will it take you to recover? When will you be back?" she asked. Without realising it he said, "In exactly 5 days." From the experiences of his mother and aunts he knew that it was a slow and tedious journey to recovery. He felt Baba had prompted the reply.

In hospital he was looked after by a gentle Parsee doctor who was spiritual and believed in the power of prayer and divine grace. He was treated and given intensive physiotherapy. The fifth day was a Thursday. When he woke up he felt the power returning to his paralysed arm, but he was too excited to move it. His doctor came to see him and was pleased to see his swift recovery. Kalyanpur told him that he had prayed to Baba for speedy recovery. "Yes," said the doctor, "A sincere prayer can work miracles, as in your case. Continue to have faith and everything will go well for the rest of your life."

Ref: *Shri Sai Leela* Magazine; Vol. 64, No. 1, April 1985

***

April 21

MAYAGONDA BEGETS A SON

Mr. G. S. Kalyanpur a resident of Hyderabad, was gifted a photograph of Baba in the *ashirwad* (blessing) pose. Many of his friends and neighbours would stand before it and petition Baba with their requests. And uniquely they all were granted.

His friend Mr. Mayagonda had two daughters and no son. He was a Jain, and had for many years had prayed to the *Jain Trithankaras*, (24 enlightened spiritual guides) but his desire for a male child remained unfulfilled. One afternoon he, his wife and two daughters came to Kalyanpur's home. "I need your Baba's help," he said in a desperate voice. "My wife is expecting our third baby. She's afraid it will be a girl again, because a reputed specialist has tested her foetal chromosomes and declared it to be a girl again."

Mr. Kalyanpur took the family to the photograph and conducted puja for them. He prayed to Baba to bless them with a male child and vowed that the son would be taken to Shirdi and placed on his Samadhi. A wonderful incident occurred just as he finished praying. There was a knock on the door and the postman handed him an envelope from the *Shirdi Sansthan* containing Udi and prasad.

Full of wonder and delight, he called his friend saying, "Mayagonda, Baba has answered your prayers so promptly by sending his blessings through this Udi and prasad. You will most certainly get a son, no matter what the chromosomes predict. Take the Udi and prasad; apply the Udi on her forehead and give your wife some internally mixed in water so that she and your son will be fine."

On 3 January 1982 Mayagonda was blessed with a healthy son, Siddhartha. When he was 3 months old the parents fulfilled the vow and took Siddhartha to Shirdi and thanked Baba for blessing them.

Ref: *Shri Sai Leela* Magazine; Vol. 64, No. 1, April 1985

***

April 22

BABA RECEIVED THE DAKSHINA AT THE WEDDING

The parents of Yatin Dandekar were staunch devotees of Baba. His father, Vinod Dandakar, would get up early in the morning and perform puja of Baba's idol. Then he would read a chapter of the Shri Sai Satcharita without fail. In the evening he would light a lamp and incense before Baba.

The marriage ceremony of Yatin's elder brother, Ashish was to be celebrated on 4 June 1994. One evening his father told Yatin that Baba would attend the wedding. Yatin states, "I remember that evening very clearly; it was the 27 of April. At 6 p.m. my father said this with such certainty that I nearly burst out laughing. He further added that Baba would come after the *Mangal Astaka* (Shloka recited at the wedding invoking the blessings of the deities) was recited by the priest. He would be in the hall and I should give him some dakshina."

It was very hard for Yatin to believe this, but he had a lot of respect for his father so he kept quiet. However, he thought long and hard about what his father had said. At that time he had just attended a course on parapsychology and had learned that the mind was very powerful and sometimes an individual who intensely believes in something can feel and see that thing.

The wedding took place and at noon after the Mangal Astaka had been recited Yatin immediately went and stood at the entrance of the hall to see if Baba would appear. He waited for some time but couldn't see Baba. Then he said, *Aum Shri Lord Mahadeva* you incarnated as Lord *Khandoba* and you are my family deity. Lord Shiva if you truly came on this Earth in the form of Sai Baba then you will appear before me." Then as he started moving away from the entrance he saw a tall man with bright shining eyes standing before him. He had a white jholi slung on his shoulder. He wore a long white shirt, but what struck Yatin most was that he wore huge *Kholapuri* slippers. They were so large that he had never seen such a large pair in his life before. He took the slippers off at the door. Yatin immediately went to him and gave him the dakshina that he had kept for Baba. Then he sat in the very same pose of Baba sitting on the stone, and Yatin was now certain that he was indeed Baba. So he immediately fell at his feet. And when he got up he had disappeared.

Yatin was quite confused and he searched for him everywhere but alas! He had disappeared and was nowhere to be found.

Ref: *Sai Prasad* Magazine; 1994 (*Deepavali* Issue)

***

April 23

BABA RESIDES IN THE KORHALE TEMPLE

Dayaneshwar Salunki Patil was a resident of Counti Mahaankal of District Sangli. He had studied up to the seventh class, but even as a young lad he was very spiritual and loved the company of saints. As soon as he was old enough to read and understand, he undertook reading the Gita and soon he could recite it from memory.

Once Gadge Maharaj visited his village and Dayaneshwar wasted no time in meeting him. The meeting was the turning point of his life. Gadge Maharaj was sitting near a gutter, plucking grass. On seeing the young boy he asked him to bring a sickle. Dayaneshwar ran home and brought it. Gadge Maharaj took it and handed him a broom and asked him to sweep his surroundings. Since then he has swept all the places that he visited. Besides reading the various scriptures and religious books, he also made numerous pilgrimages.

One day he happened to stop at the Korhale Temple and asked Rahul for a broom. Since then he has been staying there, and he is looked after by the temple trust. One night he was sleeping in front of the Dwarka Mai photograph in the temple. At midnight he had a wonderful vision of Baba. Baba emerged from the padukas in the temple in front of him and walked towards him and said, "Don't leave this place for I reside here," and saying this disappeared. A short while later Baba appeared again and bent his knees as if to sit but there was no chair or platform for him to sit on. Then he extended his bowl for taking alms towards Dayaneshwar and disappeared. By this Dayaneshwar understood that he should also sustain himself on alms. No matter what delectable food is cooked at the temple, every morning Dayaneshwar goes for bhiksha. He goes and stands in front of five houses for a short period and whatever food he collects he mixes it all up and then eats it.

Ref: As narrated by Dynaneshwar

***

April 24

BABA AND SWAMI SAMARTH ARE THE SAME

Shailla Sarodhaya a resident of Mumbai states, "Shri Sai Samarth and Shri Swami Samarth are one and the same." Her mother was utterly devoted to Swami Samarth and visited his mutt in Dadar daily. Shailla was born on a Thursday; after her mother had attended the Arati at the mutt she returned home and went into labour. During her childhood, Shailla had numerous dreams that convinced her that both the saints were the same.

Shailla had a series of dreams regarding the two saints. In the first dream she was praying to the picture of Swami Samarth when it changed into Baba's picture. This interchange took place thrice. In the next dream she was walking towards the picture of Swami Samarth in the mutt and as she came close to it, it transformed into the photograph of Baba sitting on the stone.

Once, she completed the reading of Swami Samarth's *Charita* (*Guru Leelamrut*) in 7 days. So she sent some money for the *Abhishek* Puja of his Samadhi and padukas to the Sansthan at Akkalkot, along with a letter. The postage stamp was defective and the image on it was upside down, but as she had bought it from the post office she stuck it on the letter and posted it. It was to reach the Sansthan on Thursday; early that morning she had a wonderful dream. In the dream she was seated in a huge hall along with a group of friends and was chatting. When a huge tall man came there and asked, "Whose surname is Sarodhaya." She got up said, "That's me." The man then led her into a large room and said, "You have passed your matriculation examination and yet you don't know how to stick a postage stamp?" Then he showed her the defective stamp stuck on a huge long box. Opening that box he said, "Now have darshan of Sai Baba." Like a child she placed her palms together and humbly looked into the box. There she found Baba lying in it smiling, his eyes moved to take a good look at her. "I had sent the money to Akkalkot for the puja of Swami Samarth's Samadhi instead I got a chance to pay homage to Baba lying inside his Samadhi. However I consider myself blessed and fortunate to have seen the interior of Baba's Samadhi. All the above dreams convinced me that both the saints were one and the same."

Ref: *Shri Sai Sagar* Magazine; July and August 2005

***

UDI HEALS PHYSICAL AND MENTAL ILLNESSES

For the past 6 months the wife of Mahadalkar, a resident of Bandra Mumbai was extremely ill. Various remedies, treatments and hospitalisations later, her health continued to deteriorate. The doctors were of the opinion that she had tuberculosis and would not survive much longer. On Thursday, 11 December 1941 her condition became worse and she hovered at death's door.

The family thought her end was drawing near so they started chanting the name of Lord Ram. She became extremely angry and agitated and yelled, "Stop this nonsense." The family was terrified at the sudden change in this pious lady, and the vehement outburst. The family thought that she was possessed by an evil spirit, so the husband got his friend Abha Sahib Pendarkar to check her. He came to their home at once and started reciting the *Ram Raksha* (a hymn beseeching Ram for protection). Hearing this she turned her fury on him and yelled at him to leave her alone. He asked her husband to go immediately to Galvankar's home and fetch some Udi. Galvankar was Dabolkar's son-in-law and had Udi given to him by Baba.

Her husband got the Udi and stealthy entered her room, but she rolled her eyes in anger and ordered him to throw away the packet that he had brought. Everyone was convinced that she was possessed so they restrained her and applied a little on her forehead, and forced some down her throat. She calmed down immediately and slept peacefully.

After this she started improving and allowed them to tie a talisman filled with Udi around her neck. A few years before this Mahadalkar's first wife had passed away, but her last rites had not been performed properly, nor was the *shrada* (the yearly ceremony of appeasing the manes) performed. The spirit of his first wife had possessed his second wife, but the Udi healed her both mentally and physically.

Ref: *Shri Sai Leela* Magazine; Vol. 18, No. 8–11, October, November, December and January 1943, *Ashvin, Karthik, Margashish, Paaush shake* 1863

***

SHE SERVES BABA THE MEAL AND IS CURED

Sriramulu was in deep trouble; his wife was seriously ill, besides he had to look after his young children and then go to work. Every morning he fervently prayed to Baba to heal his wife. One morning Baba appeared at his doorstep. Not believing his eyes he asked him who he was. Baba replied "What a fool you are. You will know who I am, only if you know who you are." Here Baba in one sentence imparts the greatest spiritual truth. The spiritual truth being *Aham Brahmsa me* stated in the Yajur Veda. It is to experience the state that I am not the body or mind but the *sakshi* or witness that is Brahma.

Sriramulu invited Baba in and requested him to have a meal with them. "I have come just for that. Tell your wife to serve me the meal now." He fetched his wife and she served the meal with great difficulty. Sriramulu dashed off to the market to get some bananas to offer Baba. When he returned Baba had already left, but his wife had recovered.

One day Sriramulu's wife was upset that she had lost a beautiful picture of Baba. That night Baba appeared in her dream and threw a large number of pictures of his on her and asked her to pick the picture of her choice and she did. The next day a devotee friend of theirs visited them. He had gone to Shirdi and had brought a picture for her. He then gifted her the same picture that she had chosen in her dream the previous night.

Ref: Acharya E. Bharadwaja; *Shri Sai Baba the Master*

***

"NO ONE CAN ESCAPE THE EFFECTS OF *KARMA*"

Her sight was failing and this was a cause of constant worry for Sushilamma. She felt that the deterioration of her sight would cause her to be dependent on others and they might resent it and not take care of her. So she fervently prayed to Baba. On day she dreamt of Baba wherein Baba told her about the law of karma. He said, "Why do you grieve about your sight. If you wish I will grant you your sight, but remember you will have to experience the same fate in your next life. No one, not even me can escape the effects of Karma. Think about it seriously and decide if you want to finish this balance of karma in this life or the next." She woke up before she could tell him what she desired. Yet she continued to pester him for better eyesight. The doctor operated on her and sent her home with a patch on her eye.

One night while she slept on the terrace, a bat struck her on her eye and the patch fell down. She woke up with profuse bleeding from that eye. The doctor on examining the eye said it was damaged beyond repair. She persuaded the doctor to do his best. He bandaged it and kept her in hospital for a few days. That night she dreamt that Baba himself removed the bandage and she could see clearly. The doctor examined her the next day and was astounded to see her miraculous recovery, as she could see quite clearly.

Then she became worried about her next life and prayed for it. Baba was angry with her and said, "You come up with some problem or the other. Now feed 11 blind people and offer 11 coconuts to God, and you will be freed from this evil karma forever." Sushilamma carried out Baba's orders and was content and at peace.

Her only son was betrothed to be married; eagerly she invited her whole family. But her brothers refused to attend the marriage due to some misunderstanding. Sushilamma cried in front of Baba's picture. That night Baba appeared in her dream and said, "Why do you worry about everything, big and small? Just go on chanting this, "*Shri Rama Rama Rameti. Rame Rame manorame. Sahasra nama tattulyam.*

Rama Rama varanane. Then you will have no more difficulties." The meaning of the verse is "By uttering the name of Lord Shri Rama three times the mind gets purified and it is equivalent to chanting the *Vishnu Sahasra Naama."* She related the dream to her husband who told her that it was a powerful mantra and she should keep chanting it.

The Vishnu Sahasranama or the thousand holy names of Lord Vishnu is a powerful *sothra* (chant in praise of the Lord). As the chanting of it is difficult and takes time, one can reap its benefits by just chanting the four lines that were given by Baba to Sushilamma. Thus, Baba had bestowed on her health, spiritual instruction and warded off many difficulties

Ref: Acharya E. Bharadwaja; *Shri Sai Baba the Master*

***

April 28

THE MUSLIM SAINT WAS INDEED BABA

Shivshankar Dixit was full of despair when he was diagnosed to have tuberculosis. One night he had a dream wherein he saw a picture of a Muslim saint and bowed to him. At that moment, mysteriously the Muslim saint appeared before him and applied *vibhuti* (sacred ash) on his forehead and assured him that he would soon recover and be well. Following this his condition improved without treatment and he realised that it was a visitation. One of his friends told him that the 'Muslim' saint that he had seen might have been Sai Baba.

Four days later, some children were playing in his yard and they left a picture of Baba seated on a stone, which was kept on top of the Samadhi. Dixit picked it up and recognised the Muslim saint who had appeared in his dream; he looked exactly like Baba in the photograph. Later Dixit visited Shirdi and found a marble idol of Baba on the Samadhi and not the photograph. He made enquires about it, and was informed that Baba's photograph was placed on the Samadhi till 1954. Then the marble idol had been installed there. The picture

128

of the Muslim saint that he had seen in his dream was indeed the photograph of Baba which was earlier kept on the Samadhi.

Then he started praying to Baba as Lord Dattatreya, who was his chosen deity.

Ref: Acharya E. Bharadwaja; *Shri Sai Baba the Master*

***

April 29

THE EXPERIENCE OF A CHRISTIAN DEVOTEE

Mr. B. Adrishtarao was a resident of Hyderabad; in September 1978 he was in a very troubled state of mind. One of his well-wishers gave him a picture of Baba, and assured him that he would get relief by merely keeping the picture with him. Thus, he kept it in his pocket, even though he was a Christian by faith. His wife also agreed to burn incense and bow to Baba every morning.

Three months later his wife became seriously ill, followed by loss of consciousness and was admitted to the Government Hospital. Despite treatment, there was a slim chance of her survival. It was difficult for him as he had four children and the youngest was just 5 months old. In desperation he prayed to Baba to save him from the impending calamity and look after his welfare. His wife regained consciousness and recounted her experience. "I had a terrifying dream; my uncle who had died recently was dragging me by my hair through the window. Baba leapt up and dragged the dark form of my uncle and threw him into a blazing fire. I appealed to Baba not to be so ruthless. Baba said, "He is solely responsible for all the hardships that you and your family are going through. And he must definitely be punished." Then I requested Baba to be seated. He replied, "My child your husband is at the end of his tether looking after the children. So I will go there. Do not be apprehensive, for you will recover in a few days."

Indeed she recovered after a few days but was extremely weak. This life-changing experience turned her into an ardent devotee. Later she had another dream in which two fakirs entered her home and made a sign of a cross on her chest and went away. That was when her doctor had advised her to get her chest radiographed. Casting her burden on Baba's shoulders she did not abide by their advice, nor did she take any of the prescribed medications. However, she took Udi twice a day and thereafter she steadily improved.

Ref: Acharya E. Bharadwaja; *Shri Sai Baba the Master*

***

April 30

BABA SPEAKS FROM THE CALENDAR

Once a Parsee gentleman named F. M. Bhangara was gifted a calendar with Baba's picture on it. He, however, did not know who he was. One morning he had an irresistible urge to bow to him and he did. But he didn't say anything to his wife least there be an argument, as his wife was very orthodox. Mr. Bhangara, however, had a great regard for saints and would go and meet them whenever the opportunity arose. The next day he was surprised to see a garland on the calendar. He inquired about it to his wife. She replied, "Yesterday while I was dusting the pictures in that room a mysterious voice emitted from that picture and said, "Child garland me daily and it will do you a lot of good." This occurred twice, so I placed a garland on it." A friend of theirs heard about it and asked him to get it framed and place it on their altar. Following this his wife garlanded it regularly.
Some time later the voice from the picture asked his wife what she desired. She replied, "Look after my husband's welfare and bless us with a child." A week later Mr. Bhangara's superior, on his own accord, gave him a pay raise for no apparent reason. And a year later they were blessed with a baby boy. Solutions to their problems flashed through their minds when they prayed to Baba's picture, and even trivial wishes were fulfilled. Not only this, they asked about their friends and relatives and received valuable solutions.

Once Bhangara had to go to an official camp; his wife insisted that he return that very night. Just before leaving he bowed to Baba and he heard him say, "Son you will not return home today." To

130

confirm if the message was true he set out early in the morning. While travelling on the Ghats, they took a turn and the brakes failed and the car came hurtling down the slope. There was a ravine on one side and a hill on the other side, and it was a dangerous situation.

The driver told him not to panic as he could crash the car into a tree as safely as possible. But whenever he tried to do so there was a vehicle coming in the opposite direction and they narrowly missed a collision. This happened everytime he tried to stop the car. Bhangara then remembered Baba's message and that it signified imminent death. A palmist had read his palm a few years ago and had foretold him of his accidental death. Then he prayed to Baba, "Baba I know I have to die one day. Save my life this time for the sake of my family, I beseech you. Henceforth, I will never doubt your words and messages."

The next moment the car stopped as it hit a stone on the road, and the tire was damaged. The driver changed the tire and they reached their destination 7 hours later. Thus there was no chance of his returning home by that evening.

Ref: Acharya E. Bharadwaja; *Shri Sai Baba the Master*

***

EVIL SPIRIT DEFEATED BY THE *UDI-TIRTH*

Unfortunately no details are given about this couple, such as their names, dates or place of residence.

Her spouse was a doctor and she was well educated. Suddenly she developed a strange incurable disease. She would suddenly lose consciousness that often lasted for hours. The best doctors were consulted and numerous remedies tried, but there was no improvement in her symptoms. The doctor's father advised him to take his wife to Shirdi, on the suggestion of a friend who told him that many rare and incurable diseases were cured there.

The doctor along with his friend took his wife to Shirdi. There they asked her to accompany them to the Samadhi Mandir, but she refused. They tried several times but she was adamant. Finally they dragged her and made her prostrate before Baba and his Samadhi. Baba's Udi mixed in water was put into her mouth. Next evening after praying to the Samadhi she fell on the ground and started speaking, "I am a female Bhil spirit. And I entered this woman's body one day while she was standing below a tamarind tree on her way home. The tirth and Udi have made me powerless and I am defeated, hence I will leave her body forever and never trouble her again." Baba's Udi-tirth has the unique power to burn the wrong and evil doings and convert it into *ananda* (bliss). Time and again Udi has shown its powerful effect, then and even now, decades after Baba's Maha Samadhi that it's just as powerful. Thus the lady's malady was cured and the couple returned home happily.

Ref: *Shri Sai Leela* Magazine; Vol. 4, No. 2, March–April 2004

***

BABA CURED HIM WITH HIS MEDICATIONS

Once, Nityanand Paul of Miraj and his friend were travelling to Pune. From there they wanted to proceed to Vanuri. Enroute the bus broke down and the repairs delayed them by two hours, hence they could not board the connecting bus. As the next bus was due the next morning, his friend decided that they stay overnight in another Christian friend's home. That night the conversation turned to Baba and to his wonderful leelas that many devotees had experienced.

Paul had been suffering from tuberculosis for the past 15 years. Upon hearing about the miraculous cures that people had experienced, he told his friend that he would like to accompany him on his next visit to Shirdi. His friend readily accepted, and they set out the very next day. At Shirdi Paul caught a cold and his symptoms became aggravated, and he incessantly coughed up blood. He was treated by Dr. Gujarati, and got some relief. He went to the Samadhi Mandir and piteously begged Baba to either cure him or give him death at his feet.

Then he returned home. Later an old man came to his residence and enquired about his disease. He assured him that his treatment would cure him permanently, but he would have nausea and vomiting while taking the medications. Paul accepted and started taking the treatment, he suffered terribly for the first week, and gradually the side effects began to subside by the third week. His condition improved rapidly. Paul was so glad that his sufferings had finally ended. He regretted that the old man had not taken a fee from him, nor had he given his name or address; hence he could not trace his whereabouts. Then he realised that the old man was Baba who had cured him as promised.

Ref: Ramalingaswami; *Ambrosia in Shirdi*

***

HOW MEHTA GOT RID OF THE EVIL SPIRITS

A devotee of Baba named Dayabhai Damodardas Mehta worked as a hardware merchant in Mumbai. He resided in a multi-storied building near Madhavbagh. Once he developed high fever and was diagnosed as having typhoid. The people in his building were convinced that the spirit of a carpenter was harassing the occupants residing in that building. His neighbours brought a talisman and tied it around his neck to ward off the evil spirit. The moment the talisman was tried around his neck his fever shot up. Neither his medications nor the cold compress had any effect on it. The doctor was summoned; he changed the medications but to no avail. Mehta was restless the whole day; at night he screamed in his sleep, "Baba save me." At that moment he felt that the evil spirit was sitting on his chest. There was a picture of Baba in that room. And he distinctly heard a voice emit from the picture saying, "Why are you afraid? I have been protecting you since morning. But you need to get rid of that talisman." The spirit dissuaded him from doing so, but Mehta obeyed Baba's orders and threw the talisman away.

The next morning he found the talisman lying in the corner and his temperature had steadily returned to normal. Some time later he had a relapse because of not following the prescribed diet. He vowed to go to Shirdi and offer a dakshina of 101 rupees if he recovered. From that moment on his health improved rapidly and he later fulfilled his vow.

Ref: Swami Sharananand (translated by B. V. Kher); *Shri Sai Baba*

***

"MY BANK IS IN SHIRDI," SAID THE ASCETIC

Gangadhar Lakshman Jakhadi resided in Dadar. In 1949 he worked as a cable operator at the Kalyan Railway station. One afternoon on his way to lunch he saw an ascetic seated on a bench. He beckoned to Jakhadi to sit beside him, and he narrated the life story of his father. He had worked for Gopalrao Butti of Nagpur, a close devotee of Baba. In the course of the conversation the ascetic said he was devoted to Lord Dattatreya, and he had just returned from Mahur, a famous pilgrimage place of Lord Datta. Then he asked Jakhadi to buy a ticket for him to Badrinath where he would be going next. He told Jakhadi to put his hand in his jholi and take the money for the fare.

Jakhardi put his hand in the jholi and found it was full of coins; he was not greedy so he took out only the amount of money that he needed. The fare was 35 rupees and 12 annas and he returned the change. Again the ascetic asked him to put it inside his jholi. When he put his hand in it, it was empty. Seeing the look of astonishment on his face the ascetic said, "My bank is at Mahur, Gangapur and Shirdi. When I need the money it comes and when the need is over it goes back. Sai Baba is an incarnation of Lord Datta; visit Shirdi as often as you can and you will be blessed." In this leela the ascetic aptly says, that his bank is in Shirdi. Our lives revolve around this bank Shirdi, which is the centre of the Universe. The fixed deposit in our life is our *Sanchit Karma*, that is, the stock acquired through the good and evil works of the present and all the past births. The interest accumulated is our prarabdha karma, that is, it is that part of the stock that is to be worked out in this life. This we can withdraw or sometimes end up as an "over draft" or negative balance. Any new deposits we make is *Kriyaman Karma*, that is, the actions of our present life with merits and demerits to be experienced in births yet to come. The 35 rupees are spent to reach him, with the 12 annas to be utilised for *Kayena Vacha*. The verse means, "My body, my speech, my mind and all my senses, my intellect, my innate being — all these I offer to you."

135

From that time Jakhadi started worshiping Baba as Dattatreya and he never failed to visit Shirdi especially on Datta Jayanthi.

Ref: *Shri Sai Sagar;* January–March 1980

***

May 5

BABA SENDS HER THE POSTER OF HIS FACE

Inscrutable are the ways of Baba for with him nothing is impossible. A few years ago Sandhya and Ajay Gupta had brought a group of devotees with them from Agra to Shirdi. Namrata yearned to accompany them but she had fractured her arm a few days ago so was unable to go. Her husband Saroj Avasthi, however, accompanied the Gupta's. Prior to their departure Namrata said, "Sandhya I would love to have a poster of the face of Baba's idol in the Samadhi Mandir." Sandhya immediately gave it to her as she had a couple of posters with her.

They reached Shirdi and everyone went for Kakad Arati. Saroj left the hotel early as he wanted to have a cup of tea. Before returning to the hotel he bought another two cups of tea for the Gupta's. He proceeded to the hotel when he heard someone say, "*Arre Agra wale bhai rukko,*" (Oh! brother from Agra, wait); he wondered who could know him at Shirdi. He turned around and saw a fakir smoking a *bidi* (tobacco rolled in a dried leaf) and walking towards him. He had a jholi slung on his shoulder. The fakir asked him his name and then he took out a small book from his jholi and placed it in his shirt pocket. He said, "Read this book. So you are coming for the Arati; we will talk during the Arati," and he disappeared. Avasthi upon reaching the hotel narrated everything in detail to Ajay.

The next day they returned home. His wife immediately opened his suitcase to look at the things that he had bought. Avasthi was telling her in detail about the fakir; it was then that she noticed a photograph that was rolled up and tied. She opened it at once and saw that it was a poster of Baba's face — exactly what she had wanted. Full of excitement she asked him if he had bought it for her. He glanced at it and said with astonishment, "Where did that poster come from? I totally forgot to buy one for you." He took it from her hand and scrutinised it; then he saw a small hole in the corner and that hole was caused by a lighted bidi.

Ref: As narrated by Saroj Avasthi

***

May 6

SHE HAD BEEN PRAYING TO BABA ALL ALONG

Her mother was devoted to Baba since her childhood, while her daughter Manjula was devoted to Lord Krishna. She prayed to Baba but did not know too much about him or what he looked like. Her mother worshipped a picture of Baba that was only the bust. Nor had she seen a full length picture of him. At that time life was fine and she did not have any major problems or worries.

One night she had a vivid dream, wherein there were two rows of devotees standing, and Lord Krishna was walking between the rows inquiring of each devotee about his welfare. He was moving rather slowly and she was standing at the very end of the queue, and it seemed that he would never reach her. In despair she cried, "O! Lord will you ever reach me?" At that very moment Baba came from behind Krishna, overtook him and stood in front of her. He looked directly at her and spoke in Kannada and said, "He is me and I am him. Why are you anxious and worried? I am there to worry about you and look after your welfare," and saying this disappeared.

Manjula describes the scene thus, "Baba took long strides; he was holding his kafni in his characteristic manner and he came up to me. At that moment I felt serene and at peace. For the first time I saw Baba from head to toe, dressed in a torn kafni with the cloth tied around his head and I realised that I had been praying to him all this time."

Ref: As narrated by Manjula S. of Bangalore

***

BABA TAKES THE FORM OF HER FATHER AND WALKS HER HOME

This touching leela happened to Kandalgonkar's daughter. Once Dattatreya Kandalgonkar decided to do a *saptha* or read the Shri Sai Satcharita in 7 days. During those 7 days he did not go out of the house as he felt he would be unable to complete the number of chapters required to be read for that day. His daughter who lived in Bandra visited him every evening, when she brought his dinner and other necessities with her. Her routine was to go every evening from Bandra to Dadar where he lived, deliver the meal and then return home. She was a great help to him and he looked forward to her visits, although the visits were short. In fact, she delivered the meal and left as she had a long way to travel. On the seventh day she arrived at his home and found it was locked; Dattatreya had gone grocery shopping as he was going to prepare a sumptuous meal for the conclusion of the saptha and had invited his family and friends for it. She waited a long time and because it was getting late, she left. By the time she reached Bandra station it was dark and the road to her residence was desolate; she was terrified.

Suddenly she saw her father at the station, who was waiting to accompany her home. Little did she know that Baba had assumed the form of her father as he was concerned for her safety. Then both of them walked home; when they reached home she asked him to stay for some time, but he refused and left. The next day when her father visited her she rebuked him and said, "You never came in yesterday even after I entreated you." Her father was surprised at what she said, for he hadn't met her the previous day as he was busy shopping. It was then that they realised that it was Baba who had walked her home whereas her father had not even met her the previous day.

Ref: Swami Sharananand (translated by B. V. Kher); *Shri Sai Baba*

***

"ALLAHA BHALLA KAREGA"

Sandhya grew up in Hyderabad; when she married Ajay Gupta she moved to Agra after her marriage to Ajay Gupta. Ajay had just completed his apprenticeship as a lawyer. As his law practice was not yet established, the young couple had to struggle to make both ends meet. Sandhya decided to go to Hyderabad and purchase some pearls so she could start a small business selling pearls and pearl jewellery. The Gupta's were travelling by train to Hyderabad, and at Balsara station Sandhya got down to buy a magazine; she was engrossed in reading it while her husband laid next to her. Suddenly she heard a compassionate voice say, "Raju, don't worry your venture will be successful and will flourish. *Allah bhalla karega.*" She looked up to see who had called them because both of them had the same nickname, Raju.

Outside her window there stood this fakir with a *biksha patra* (begging bowl) in his hand. He was dressed like Baba in a kafni and had a cloth tied around his head. She was mesmerised by his eyes that glinted like emeralds in the darkness. She woke her husband and both of them saw and heard Baba say, "Allaha bhalla karega." Then Sandhya and Ajay both gave him a rupee and he blessed them and vanished. At that time there was a downpour of rain, but Baba wasn't wet nor had the other passengers seen or heard him. Ajay immediately got up and looked out of the window. But there was no platform for the fakir to stand on; instead the train was speeding through a forest.

After Baba had showered his bountiful blessings on them, they never looked back. Needless to say Sandhya is a successful diamond merchant with a huge jewellery shop named *Sai Kripa* and Ajay has a successful law practice. Both their sons own businesses.

But the best part of this leela is that Ajay who was a skeptic became devoted to Baba and visits Shirdi once a month and sometimes even 2–3 times a month.

Ref: As narrated by Ajay and Sandhya Gupta

***

SMOKE EMITS FROM THE UNLIT CHILLUM

He had the good fortune to stay in Shirdi for 3 months, and the stay was job related. In 1953, Vasudev Gangadhar Lele a resident of Dombivili came to Shirdi along with chief engineer, D. P. Nagarkar. The Shri Sai Baba Sansthan Shirdi had called an Engineering Company based in Pune to carry out some extensive work at Shirdi.

At that time Lele was not an ardent devotee, but as he had the time so he attended the Arati in the morning and evening. In 1953, the idol of Baba was not there and in its place there was a photograph. One Thursday there were about 60 to 70 devotees from Chennai who were very enthusiastically performing worship of Baba. Lele went for the evening Arati and the main priest performed the Arati; then the priest took a chillum that was unlit and held it to Baba's lips. The devotees shouted loudly, *Sainath Maharaj ki jai.*

What Lele saw left him dumfounded; he didn't know if he was awake or dreaming. He pinched his hand and realised he was quite awake. Lele saw smoke emit from the unlit chillum. The priest offered the chillum to Baba three times and each and every time there was smoke. It was then that Lele became an ardent devotee.

Prabhune, a devotee from Pune narrates an interesting anecdote about Baba's magical chillum. "Years ago there were very few devotees visiting Shirdi. In those days there wasn't any tiled flooring in the Dwarka Mai and the floor was rather uneven. A slurry of cow dung used to be applied to the floor daily. I went into the sanctum sanctorum and worshiped Baba. Then I noticed that a chillum was embedded in the wall where Baba's *Kolamba* (earthen pot in which Baba kept the food collected from bhiksha) is now kept. I asked the caretaker why Baba's chillum was embedded in the wall. He replied "Oftentimes smoke emits from this chillum, as Baba must be smoking it." Prabhune was intrigued and he eagerly asked, "And when did this happen?" The caretaker said, "That I can't say as there is no fixed time." Then Prabhune went and laid his head on the chillum.

Ref: *Shri Sai Leela* Magazine; Vol. 48, No. 12, March 1970

***

THE WOODCUTTERS DONATE THEIR LAND

V. P. Chetty was a resident of Chennai; he dreamt of Baba on Thursday early in the morning. In the dream Baba ordered him to build his temple, and then took him by his hand to the site where the temple was to be erected. Baba even pointed to the spot where his photograph was to be placed. So Chetty went to check the land and appraise it. He was disturbed to find that the land was being used as a dumping ground for garbage, and was filthy and foul smelling. That land belonged to the community of woodcutters. But as Baba had specifically asked for that place so Chetty requested them to sell it to him for a good prize. He also told them that Baba's temple would be erected here.

The woodcutters told him that the land was not for sale nor did they know who Baba was. Chetty tried his level best to convince them but as they were adamant he left. He returned a few days later hoping that they would have changed their minds and indeed they had. So he inquired as to what brought about this change. They told him that while they were returning from the forest the next day they met a fakir. The fakir had a powerful magnetic personality and he asked then to give him the land to live on. As the whole community was impressed by the fakir they decided to donate the land for the temple.

Chetty took out a small photograph of Baba that he carried with him at all times and showed it to the woodcutters and asked them, "Is this the fakir who met you in the forest?" Of course it was Baba. A small temple was constructed and on 15 June 1940 a portrait of Baba was installed in the temple by B. V. Narsimha Swamiji.

Ref: *Shri Sai Leela* Magazine; Vol. 17, No. 1, 2, 3, 1940,
Chaitra, Vaishak, Jesth shake 1862

***

HE TESTED BABA'S POWER

Although he had some formal education but he did not have the qualifications of an Engineer. Yet Vithoba M. Fand applied for the post of an Engineer in the Department of Railways. His application was rejected, but Fand had set his heart on getting it. His uncle Kashinath Dube saw his morose, dejected condition and advised him to seek refuge in Baba. Dube also gave Fand a picture of Baba and asked him to worship it with faith and devotion. Fand agreed to do so on the condition that he would experience the powers of Baba within 2 months.

A month later a vacancy for the post of an Engineer rose again and Fand re-applied. In the meantime another officer had taken charge of the applications and appointments. Fand was recommended by a friend who was a devotee of Baba, and knew the officer well. Finally three applicants were shortlisted; one was an ex-employee with 10 years of experience; the second was the son of the head clerk working in that office and the third was Fand. The ex-employee was rejected and the other two were to now appear in an examination. Naturally Fand was apprehensive as he was less qualified. His uncle encouraged him and told him to have faith in Baba and apply Udi and appear for the examination.

During the examination the son of the clerk got terribly confused and could not answer the questions; Fand, however, answered the questions correctly and got the job. Thus with Baba's grace he got the job that he wanted and became an ardent devotee. He often said, "With a great deal of pride and a bloated ego I set out to test Baba's power although I didn't have the qualifications, and yet in the end with Baba's grace I got the job that I didn't deserve. And in the end I humbly became devoted to him."

Ref: Swami Sharananand (translated by B. V. Kher); *Shri Sai Baba*

***

MANTRA RECEIVED IN HER DREAM

Surajbai Kasiwal resided in Khamgaon, Bihar; once she dreamt of Baba. In that wonderful dream Baba clearly instructed her to chant *Sai Nath, Sai Baba* continuously. She was extremely happy and immediately started doing the Japa. In her zeal to do the chanting, she stopped performing her daily routine of performing ritualistic worship of the deities in her home.

On the fourth day she had another dream wherein she saw a magnificent court. In that court four thrones were placed. All the thrones were on the same level and were identical in shape and size. On the first throne Baba was seated on the next throne Shantinath was seated, then Padmaprabhu and Mahavir. These were all the deities that she worshiped. She turned and asked Baba a question. Baba smiled at her and said, "Look. Shantinath, Padmaprabhu and Mahavirprabhu are here, so ask them whatever you want to know." There ended the dream. When she woke up the next morning she pondered over the dream. She concluded that Baba wanted her to continue her daily worship with devotion of her chosen deities and continue chanting the mantra that they had given to her.

Surajbai was fortunate to receive the mantra in her dream, but Baba did not want her to forsake her chosen deities, so he reappears in another dream on the fourth day to remind her of her daily duty. Surajbai followed Jainism, and the three 'enlightened sages' that she worshiped were seated next to Baba. Each sage has a symbol attached to him; Padmaprabhu has the lotus symbol, which represents purity; the lotus grows in a murky pond yet it is unaffected by the murky water. Shantinath has the symbol of a deer, which represents the mind that leaps from one thought to another and is rarely still. Mahavir has the symbol of a lion who is the king of the forest and represents control. These are *Trigunas* or qualities that originate from the Parabrahma thus their very source is Baba. The four deities are seated on identical thrones and at the same level signifying that all of them are equal. Hence, Baba asks her to place her question before her chosen deity.

143

Here Baba wants her to continue her ritualistic worship of her chosen deity while chanting her mantra after that. Chanting Baba's name does not require any ritual, yoga or Sadhana. It can be chanted while walking, sitting or doing household chores. The only prerequisite is love, devotion and faith.

Ref: Swami Sharananand (translated by B. V. Kher); Shri Sai Baba

***

May 13

THEIR PROBLEMS WERE SOLVED THROUGH DREAMS

Dinkar Vasudev Joshi was an atheist, but deep in his heart he yearned for Baba's grace. "If only Baba would give me *sakshatkar* (appear in person) or give me some unforgettable experience, I promise that I will be devoted to him for life."

At that time he worked as an art teacher in Billmoria and Tata High school. Time rolled by and he met an enlightened man named B. N. Phadkar and got many delightful experiences. Often Phadkar would appear in his dream and warn him of some crisis that would take place and give him valuable advice. Soon a very close relationship developed between them.

One summer it was unbearably hot and humid; Joshi's eldest daughter Narmadabai was very sick at that time. And day after day her condition worsened, and finally she was at death's door. At that time Phadkar had sent a portrait of Baba to Joshi to be enlarged and thus this beautiful portrait of Baba came to reside in Joshi's home.

Early one morning at about 5 a.m. his wife had a dream. In the dream Phadkar's daughter was with Baba who said, "Baby, because of you I have come to stay in Joshi's house. His daughter is very sick, and this is what I want you to do. Take this coconut and go to Joshi's home and give it to him, and assure him not to be frightened as there is no reason for fear." And 2 days after this dream Narmadabai started improving and soon became hale and hearty and is still healthy. Joshi got proof of Baba's divinity and he and his family became ardent devotees.

144

Joshi then composed hymns on Baba. On every Thursday and Ekadashi he would perform Arati to Baba and sing the hymns that he had composed.

His neighbour was Chimanlal Nirmal; he worked as a clerk in the Postal Department. He and his wife would attend the Arati. Once he told Joshi, "If Baba performs a miracle and removes my troubles I will be totally devoted to him." At that time there was some theft in his department and Nirmal was held responsible for the loss; so a huge sum of money was being deducted from his pay.

On that Sunday, that is, three days after he told Joshi of his resolve to be devoted to Baba, his wife had a dream. In the dream Baba came to his home and said, "I am Sainath, and I have come to your home, so give me bhiksha." His wife replied, "But you do not look like Baba in the photograph." To which Baba replied, "Just go and see the photograph." The wife ran and looked at the photograph and indeed the features were identical and there ended the dream.

From that day their troubles disappeared; her husband's salary was paid in full, as the thief was found. Needless to say they both became ardent devotees of Baba.

Ref: *Shri Sai Leela* Magazine; No. 2, 1926, *Vaishak, shake* 1848

***

| May 14 |

BABA ASSURES EXONERATION

A senior official once imposed a fine on G. G. Shriyan for a very flimsy reason. He was extremely hurt and humiliated. Being an ardent devotee of Baba, his first thought was to take refuge in Baba. That evening he rushed home and stood before Baba's photograph and poured his heart out. "Baba it isn't the fine that upsets me so much. Although that is a needless waste of money but it's the reason for this unjust fine that makes me cry. Now it's up to you to set this matter right."

That night he had a vivid dream in which Baba consoled him and assured him that he would be exonerated. The next morning he found that the concerned official had withdrawn the fine imposed on him without an appeal. He was mortified to learn that the official had now placed the blame on a junior officer.

The junior officer followed Shiryan's advice and prayed to Baba. That night he saw Baba in his dream and Baba promised him relief in 73 days. Thereafter the junior officer decided not to appeal or apply for redressal. He was pleasantly surprised when his immediate senior took it upon himself to represent his case on the seventeenth day. The case continued and on the seventy-third day the outcome was ruled as "Null and void," and the fine was cancelled.

Years ago, Shiriyan and his friend had cordially agreed that their children would get married when they became of marriageable age. This took place in 1924. But when his daughter came of age to be married, his friend refused to fulfil his promise. His friend went back on his word because his son had passed the matriculation exam and was studding in college. He got greedy and asked Shiriyan for a huge dowry, and as it was not forthcoming the engagement was broken. He was looking to get a better prospective bride who would bring a lot of dowry along with her. Naturally Shiriyan was hurt by the turn of events, so he prayed to Baba for help and advice. Baba appeared in his dream and assured him that he would get the same groom within 2 years. Then Shiriyan heard that his friend was offered a huge dowry by another family; he prayed to Baba fervently. Again Baba appeared in his dream and assured him, that all would be well and his daughter would marry the same boy.

His friend left no stone unturned to secure an affluent bride for his son. But no such thing happened and his son began getting restless and disgusted by the turn of events. Finally the son lost sleep as his conscience pricked him every time he had to meet a girl. Eventually the old pact between the two families was restored. And the marriage of the young couple came to be celebrated within 2 years. Thus Baba's words came true.

Ref: Dr. A. G. Munsif; *Sai Baba the Perfect Master*

***

"CELEBRATE RAM NAVAMI HERE ITSELF"

It was Madhukar's routine to celebrate Ram Navami in Shirdi every year. He states, "On that day I would cover myself with the blanket that I had asked and received from Baba. Then I participated in all the festivities and returned home on the third day after the festival ended." In 1937 Madhukar had made all preparations to go to Shirdi along with a few of his friends, but Baba had other plans for him. That night he had a dream and Baba said, "Why are you coming to Shirdi? I am here, so celebrate Ram Navami here itself."

He bowed to Baba's wish and made preparations for the celebrations. The program was to be conducted exactly as it was done at Shirdi. S. N. Chafaker of Pune came to his residence and requested him to allow him to narrate the *Tulsidass Ramayana*. Mudhukar was delighted and asked him to do so on Ram Navami day. Strangely Chafaker didn't know that Ram Navami was but a few days later.

Another surprise was that in that building Susheela Mansion a Police Prosecutor was also residing who on his own accord wished to read the *Gurucharitra* on Ram Navami day. The Gurucharitra was Baba's favoured book to be read aloud to the assembled devotees. So the parayan started at 4 a.m. and completed at 5 p.m.

Then 11 Brahmin married couples were served their meals, and given gifts and dakshina. After this was over, trouble started. The guests were to be served their meals on the terrace, but a fierce gale blew away the banana leaves. The futile attempt to bring everything under contraol went on from 7 p.m. till 9 p.m.; by this time around 300 guests had gathered, who were tired and hungry. Madhukar's friend, Ramrao Kothare, seeing all the chaos placed a coconut before the photograph of Baba and sincerely prayed to Baba to forgive them for any mistake they may have unknowingly committed. He begged Baba to bless the function and enable them to complete it. About 15 minutes later, the wind ceased and everyone had the meal.

The possible meaning of this leela is that, the blanket given to Madhukar by Baba acts as a mantle of protection; nonetheless the fruits of his karmas have to be borne or eaten. Baba asks him to perform the festival in his home, yet the fierce gale prevents them from eating the meal for 2 hours. Baba has removed the karma's that are ready to be eaten in the form of the gale. Then his friend begs Baba to forgive them for any mistake they may have committed unknowingly. Thus, realisation sets in and the devotees are able to have the meal."

Madukar was convinced that Baba resided in his home and his very life was taken care of by Baba.

Ref: *Shri Sai Leela* Magazine; Vol. 17, No. 1, 2, 3; 1940,
Chaitra, Vaishak, Jesth shake 1862

***

May 16

HE WITNESSED THE HEAD-ON COLLISION OF HIS CAR

V. S. Aiyer was a resident of Calcutta, and devoted to Baba since 1940. His brother once had a serious head on car collision in Ranchi. Aiyer was not aware that his brother had gone to Ranchi at that time. The occupants in the front seat of the other car died after 24 hours of hospitalisation, while the other passengers sustained serious injuries. Members in his brother's car were badly shaken but no one was seriously injured. His brother, who was at the steering wheel, was miraculously standing outside and witnessing the collision. He was not hurt except for a small scratch while trying to get out. How exactly this happened his brother was unable to recount. The only conclusion was that Baba's grace saved him.

The police took the case and the proceedings began at the Ranchi court. The defense meant considerable expenditure, personal inconvenience and a doubtful verdict. Aiyer consulted Baba by placing numerous chits; he was directed to pay his contribution to his brother's employer for the legal expenses. He paid 100 rupees and explained to him his inability to contribute more. The employer was, however, determined to proceed with the case, whatever the cost may be. Extraordinary things started happening; certain officials were transferred during the court proceedings. Meanwhile Baba appeared in his brother's dream and reassured him. After long drawn court proceedings his brother was acquitted.

A few years later Aiyer's wife suffered from excruciating pain in her abdomen. All kinds of remedies and treatments proved futile. Over a year passed and she gradually became emaciated and he despaired for her life. Her husband applied Udi daily along with the prescribed medicines. When he could no longer bear to see the torture she was going through, he cried in front of Baba's photograph. "Baba, is it right that thou the embodiment of mercy should look on while my wife is writhing in pain? Possibly she is suffering due to her previous karmas. But having come to thee would thou still permit the results of karma to operate. Hence forth I will not give her any medicines, but only your Udi. Her recovery or passing away is in your hands." After his prayer the pain slowly but surely started decreasing and completely disappeared after a few months.

Ref: *Sai Sudha* Magazine; Vol. 2, No. 9 & 10, February–March 1942

*****

May 17

THE OPEN *DHUNI* BLAZES IN TORRENTIAL RAIN

D. Shankrayya resides in Hyderabad and has been devoted to Baba since a long time. Being a devotee it was but natural for him to visit Shirdi. In Shirdi he had the privilege of being under the guidance of Sivenesan Swamiji. Swamiji advised him to perform congregational *Naam Jap*. Naam Jap is singing Baba's name continuously for a certain period of time be it for 24 hours or a week. When it's sung continuously for a week it's called *Naam Saptha*. The mantra that's sung by his group is *Aum Sai Shri Sai Jaya Jaya Sai* and was given to them by Swamiji.

From 25 May 1988 to 6 June 1988 Naam Saptha was conducted by him and his entourage in Penuconda. It was their custom that whenever a saptha was conducted they would have a dhuni (sacred fire) and this one was an open dhuni. It was lit with all rituals. The dhuni contained dried neem leaves from the *Gurusthan*, half-burnt incense sticks from the Dwarka Mai, and Udi, besides the usual sandalwood chips, clarified butter, cow dung cakes and wood.

On the second night Shankrayya went to sleep at 2 a.m. Then it started raining; at first it was but a drizzle but soon it poured in torrents. As there was no covering over the dhuni, it soon stood in a puddle. His companions woke him and told him what had just taken place. Nonchalantly he replied, "Baba is there to look after his Dhuni Mai," and went back to sleep. The next morning he went to make his offerings to the dhuni and was extremely glad to see that the fire was blazing as if someone was continuously pouring clarified butter into it.

Naam Jap is the 'life boat' that ferries us across the stormy ocean of our lives.

Ref: As narrated by D. Shankrayya

***

May 18

SHE ESCAPES FROM WAR-TORN BURMA SAFELY

In the year 1942, Krishnamurthy Iyer was very concerned about the welfare of his cousin sister. She was in Rangoon, Burma; it was being heavily bombed due to the war. Her mother was an ardent devotee of Baba so she sought refuge in him and prayed that her daughter return home safely. One night Baba appeared in her dream and reassured her. He said, "Do not worry your daughter is pregnant and is on her way back to this country; she will arrive in a few days." A few days later her daughter knocked on her door and surprised her; this confirmed Baba's statement.

Her pregnant daughter had suffered seriously as she had walked all the way from Burma to Calcutta. Her mother at once got her admitted to the Vellore A.M.M. Hospital. But the doctors there declared that her body had been ravished by malaria and malnutrition, and her chances of recovery were slim. Her mother was shocked to hear

150

this and she immediately brought some Udi and applied it all over her daughter's body. Steadily her condition began to improve and soon she was discharged. Later, she had a safe delivery and both the mother and child were all right.

During her pregnancy the daughter yearned to eat *burfi* — an Indian confectionary — but her mother could not afford to buy it. That Thursday the mother and daughter went to a Sai Baba temple to offer their prayers; the offering that day was burfi! The person distributing the prasad gave her a handful of the burfi that she ate to her heart's content.

Ref: Sai Sudha Magazine; Vol. 3, Part 6, December 1942

***

May 19

BABA'S NAME A MANTLE OF PROTECTION

The next two experiences are of a Judicial Officer whose name is not mentioned. He states, "I have a great deal of reverence for sages and saints. One summer I was fortunate to meet Bala Swami at Vridachalam. He looked like a boy, though he was much older. He was a linguist, but he had taken the vow of silence. When we prostrated before him, he was writing something on a paper with his left hand as his right hand was held up above his head for many years as a form of penance. We sat in his presence for about 10 minutes and then wanted to take leave of him. At first he nodded his assent, then as we were leaving he signed to us to stay. Then he turned to me and gave me the scroll of paper, on which was written Sai Baba's name a 108 times. He instructed me to keep the paper with me at all times, and to write Baba's name a 108 times daily.

At parting he distributed Udi to all of us and then we proceeded for worship at the Vridachalam temple.

I was not inclined to follow any of his instructions, and I gave the scroll of paper to my son. After worshiping the deity in the temple, we were circumambulating Shiva in the big temple. By then it was dusk, but it soon got quite dark when I was stung by some noxious

151

creature on my big toe. I used my flashlight to see what it was, but couldn't see anything. Rapidly the excruciating pain ascended to my hip joint. As the pain was unbearable, my relative wanted to fetch a carriage for me as our room was about 2 miles away. It was then that I realised that I had made a mistake by not keeping the scroll of paper with me. I took the paper from my son and kept it in my waist cloth. Within a few moments of doing this, the pain rapidly decreased from elsewhere in my body, except on the toe where I had been stung. Thus, I was able to walk back and slept well that night. The lesson was learned, and I kept the paper with me as Baba's mantle of protection. Needless to say I became devoted to Baba."

Ref: Sai Sudha Magazine; Vol. 3; Part 1, 2, 3; October 1942

***

May 20

HE REALISES THE POWER OF CHANTING BABA'S NAME

The Judicial Officer did not follow any of the instructions given by Bala Swami except to keep the scroll with him. The power of Baba's name struck home a month later. The Officer was in a train going to Tirupati. He states, "At a station a peon of the Department of Railways got into my compartment howling with pain. He was stung by a scorpion on his right forefinger; it was swollen and the pain was traversing up to his shoulder. He pleaded to all and sundry to do something to relieve his intolerable pain; he begged us to pronounce some mantra for relief. Not being a *mantravadi* (a person who thought the recitation of mantras can rid the body of poison), I kept quiet for some time. But the heart-wrenching cries of the peon touched my heart, as I remembered my own experience a month ago. I resolved to try the effect of my charm, that is, the scroll with my Sai Mantra.

I bade the peon to come near and I took out the folded scroll and touched him with it. I started with his neck and made passes downwards to his right forefinger, all the while mentally repeating Baba's name a 108 times. As soon as this was done, the man's pain

152

started subsiding and it became localised to his wrist. I repeated the procedure a second time and the pain became localised to the area that was stung. I told him that the localised pain would remain for 24 hours and I put my scroll safely away. I now have sufficient proof and sufficient faith in Baba's name that I write his name a 108 times daily in a book. I have also realised the power of Naam Jap."

Ref: *Sai Sudha* Magazine; Vol. 3, Part 1, 2, 3; October 1942

***

May 21

A KAFNI-CLAD HAND TOUCHES HER FOREHEAD

Ambujam a resident of Chennai was an ardent devotee. She actively participated in the numerous programs of singing devotional songs and selflessly did strenuous service. She was always willing to lend a helping hand in each and every activity of the temple. On the night of 25 May 1942 she felt the onset of labour pains. The midwife was away, so she went to the local doctor but he was not available at that time to render aid. Ambujam was devoted to Baba so she started chanting his name. That night Baba appeared in the mother's dream and said that he would take care of her delivery, which would take place the next day.

The next day Ambujam had unbearable pains, nonetheless she continued chanting Baba's name. As the time of her delivery drew near, she saw "this wonderful kafni-clad hand appeared from nowhere and touched her forehead" and within moments she had a safe and easy delivery. Thus, her son was born normally. The only problem was that he cried incessantly and no amount of cuddling could calm him. Ambujam was not worried as Baba had taken care of the delivery. She told her mother not to worry as the boy was "Baba's child". She then got a little Udi and smeared it on his forehead and the baby stopped crying. The baby slept peacefully and allowed his mother also to get some rest. Thereafter he gave her no trouble at all.

Ref: *Sai Sudha* Magazine; Vol. 3, Part 1, 2, 3; October 1942

***

THIS "GLORIOUS LIGHT" IS SAI BABA

In 1965 her little daughter brought a photograph of Baba and placed it near the photographs of her ancestors. Unfortunately the names of the mother and daughter are not mentioned. Before going to bed she looked at the picture and felt overwhelmed with love and devotion. That day was her daughter's birthday, that is, *meher roz* (in Parsee). She hoped that with Baba in her home he would bestow his *meher*, that is, beatific grace on them.

As her husband was out at sea she could not inform him, but she had a nagging doubt that he would be displeased. Unlike her, her husband did not believe in saints and fakirs. She feared that he in a fit of temper would throw the photograph out. When his ship reached Calcutta port he wrote and said he would arrive home shortly. When he returned home and saw the picture he was shocked and asked her why she had put the picture there. She begged him not to remove it as she had been praying to it all this while. And hoped he would not get rid of it.

Then he told her that while he was at Calcutta he had a vision. Wherein he heard someone say, "Look who has come" without opening his eyes he inquired as to who it was? He was told that it was Sai Baba and he replied that he did not believe in him. The voice persisted again and again. The third time he opened his eyes and saw a "Glorious light" the voice then slowly said, "This is Sai Baba."

Ref: *Sai Sudha* Magazine; Vol. 36, part 11, November 1976

***

"DON'T YOU HAVE FAITH IN MY UDI?"

On 4 June 2007, Anil Sahebrao Shilke felt extremely unwell while returning home from work. Suddenly he started sweating, his throat became parched, and his abdomen was painful and bloated. The symptoms increased in severity by the minute so he went to a shop so that he could make a call home. He dialed the number but he could not speak and fell on the floor unconscious.

When he became conscious he found himself in the I.C.U. of Chinchvad Hospital. The doctor informed him that the blood tests and scans revealed that both his kidney's had "shutdown" so he would be on dialyses starting that day. The dialyses would continue after he was discharged every Tuesday and Friday for the rest of his life. The diagnosis and prognosis sent a chill down his spine and he felt helpless. In desperation he prayed to Baba and said, "Baba don't give me this life of dependency on dialysis, instead give me death."

On the 17 June he went home and exactly a month later the *palkhi* (palanquin) procession would start walking from Pune to Shirdi. Anil was distraught as he had participated in the procession for the past 8 years and he intended to walk this year also. Again he earnestly prayed to Baba saying, "Due to ill health, I can't walk this year. Baba, please restore my health so that I can walk with the palkhi next year. Baba if I can run in front of your palkhi like a horse next year, I promise to offer a silver horse to you with gratitude." Then he applied a little Udi to his forehead and fell asleep.

That night he was awoken by a loud voice that said, "Do you have no faith in my Udi?" Anil woke his wife and asked her if she had heard the voice; she thought that he was delirious and got worried. Then he fell asleep, and this time he woke up at 5 a.m. and he was sure he distinctly heard the Kakad Arati. Again he woke his wife and the whole family got up but none of them heard the Arati except him.

This was the turning point; about 2 hours later he passed some urine. This was good news as he had not passed a drop of urine for the past 15 days. His condition also improved considerably, and when he visited the hospital a few days later his blood tests had improved dramatically. He did not require dialyses sessions any longer. Anil's improvement was rapid and sustained. He did walk to Shirdi along with his wife and friend, and he also offered a silver horse to Baba as promised.

Ref: *Sai Anantha*, Vol. 5, No. 17, July 2010

***

SAMUEL SAVED FROM ACID BURNS

Ramakrishna N. Samuel of Mumbai was a skeptic and did not believe in God or saints. But in 1946, he started carrying a small photograph of Baba with him everywhere and at all times. His office was situated at Byculla Bridge, in a predominantly Muslim locality. The officials had arranged for a lorry to carry all the workers to and from work. Every day about 60 people were crammed into the lorry and transported out of the Muslim neighbourhood.

On 7 November a catastrophic event took place. At 5 p.m. everyone got into the lorry and as they passed through that neighbourhood they were stopped by a group of people who threw bulbs of nitric acid on then. There were shrieks as many of them were burned by the acid. A few of the workers lost their eyesight; others had burns on their faces; while some had splashes of acid all over them. Their clothes were burnt, and they were writhing with pain. Ramakrishna was standing next to a person who had been splashed with acid, but strangely Ramakrishna was not burnt. The only damage that occurred to him was that the back of his coat got burnt, and there were a few splinters of glass in his pocket.

They then proceeded to the nearest police station and filed a complaint, and took the injured people to J. J. Hospital. Ramakrishna attributes his not sustaining any burns to Baba's grace, and the photograph that he kept with him acted as a protective armour.

Ref: *Sai Sudha* Magazine; Vol. 9, part 6, November 1946

***

BABA'S TEMPLE IN MATUNGA

Especially in Maharashtra, there are numerous temples of Sai Baba. In Matunga, Mumbai adjacent to the Kabutar Khana there is a temple that's filled with spiritual vibrations and Baba's presence is perceived by numerous devotees. One Thursday, early in the morning, Yasvant Karpadey and his mother went there to pay homage. As Yasvant had his shoes on, he waited outside the temple while his mother after buying a platter of offering joined the long queue. He knew that it would take some time for his mother to return, so he folded his hands and prayed from outside; then he went and stood under a tree beyond the temple premises. A few moments later he clearly heard a voice saying, "*Allaha tera bhala karega* (Allaha will bless you)." Astonished he looked around but there was no one around, so he folded his hands again and paid homage. He wondered where the voice had come from; he felt that the voice had emitted from the temple. Then he went inside mentally chanting Baba's name; he sat down looking at Baba's idol. After 5 minutes had passed, in the place of the idol Yasvant saw Baba sitting there physically. Baba was smiling and a short while later he nodded his head. He couldn't believe what he had just seen, so he pinched himself. He was certainly awake and full of bliss; mentally thanking Baba he exited the temple. After the above incident Yasvant frequently visited the temple and experienced numerous leelas, like Baba's aroma filling his car prior to any journey he undertook. On another occasion, the moment he entered the temple he saw Baba blowing Udi on him. Once he felt Baba standing near him, and then later he saw him actually walking about in the temple.

Once his daughter was standing outside near the entrance of the temple; she was worried about the forthcoming harvest in her fields. While standing there she distinctly heard Baba saying, "Now go my child, Allaha will fulfil your wish." A few days later her fields that had been confiscated by someone illegally were returned to her without any problem, and the harvest was plentiful.

Kashinath Laad a devotee once visited the temple and was astounded to see Baba's idol put his foot forward so that Kashinath could place his head on it. Then his body became weightless and Kashinath felt he was flying in the sky. Numerous other devotees have experienced such varied experiences in this temple.

Yasvant says, "Any devotee who is unable to visit Shirdi due to lack of money or has any other problem, should definitely visit this temple."

Ref: *Sai Prasad* Magazine; 1998 (*Deepavali* Issue)

***

BABA SAVES RAGHUNATH'S WIFE AND CHILDREN FROM THE FLOOD

He was at work in his office at Khirkie when he heard that the Panchet and Khadakvasala dams of the Mula River had broken. The water flowed furiously and flooded Pune. Raghunath S. Gondeswala resided in Pune with his wife and three small children between the ages of 3 and 9 years. As he was devoted to Baba since childhood and prayed to him in matters big and small he sought refuge in him. "Baba you have taken care of me since I was 10 years old and have never forsaken me. I don't know how my wife will cope with three small children; please save them."

When Raghunath reached Pune he realised the gravity of the situation; he had to wade in waist-deep water to reach home. All modes of transportation had stopped plying the roads. Somehow he managed to reach home by about 7:30 p.m. He found his house locked. When he opened it, he saw that everything was damaged, except for a picture of Baba that was hanging on the wall. The flood waters had reached up to the frame, but the picture had been spared. He was extremely glad to see that Baba's picture was safe. His worried thoughts then turned to his wife and children. But in his heart he knew that Baba had saved and protected them.

Raghunath asked his neighbours about his wife and children, and was relieved to learn that they were safe. They had shifted to his sister's home who lived in the suburbs of Pune. At the time that he had been praying to Baba for the welfare of his family, his sister had come to their home when she heard of the disaster. Being concerned about their safety, she had taken his family along with her, as she feared their home would get flooded and they would be in trouble.

Ref: Ramalingaswami; *Ambrosia in Shirdi*

***

"BABA WILL DEFINITELY SAVE MY SON"

The 10-year-old son of K. Arundati Amma was very mischievous. One day he was playing with a small iron nail, and subsequently swallowed it. But as luck would have it, instead of passing into his stomach it got lodged in his trachea. His mother saw him gasping and realised what had happened, and summoned a doctor.

The next day the child was taken to the hospital where he had an x-ray of his chest; the diagnosis was confirmed. The child was taken to the operation theater and under anaesthesia a tube was passed into his trachea. Through that tube in the trachea a magnetised rod was passed. However, the nail could not be extracted and the procedure was unsuccessful. Following this procedure the child then started running a fever and the doctors stated that infection had set in. Besides this the child could not ingest any food and started getting weaker by the hour. Drastic measures were taken to reduce the fever, and the doctor said, "The nail has to be taken out, but to give the child anaesthesia is very risky." While the doctor was making up his mind about performing the procedure, the mother earnestly prayed to Baba to save her son. Then she told the doctor, "Baba will save my son, so I give you my consent for the procedure; you go ahead with the operation."

The doctor after taking her consent tried the procedure again and this time it was successful. Gradually the child recovered his health. The doctor was impressed by the mother's unshakable faith; her strong conviction that Baba would save her son even under such hopeless circumstances, turned the skeptic into a believer. The doctor became devoted to Baba.

Ref: Ramalingaswami; *Ambrosia in Shirdi*

***

THE OLD MAN'S BREW CURES HIM

Since April 1939, L. Shrinivasrao was afflicted by a strange ailment and he felt exhausted all the time. Various tests were performed but they were inconclusive. Then he attended Baba's Arati held in the home of his friend Gopal Iyer, and received Udi and prasad there. He had never seen a photograph of Baba before and was instantly drawn towards Baba. And throughout the Arati he looked intently at Baba's picture.

The next day he had an appointment with his doctor. In the doctor's office he met an old man about 80 years who had a jholi slung over his shoulder. The old man came up to him and gave him some herbs and asked him to make a brew of it and drink it throughout the day. He also told him he would be cured within 2 weeks. As the man was a total stranger, Shrinivasrao was hesitant to accept it, let alone drink the concoction. But because he had been trying everything else, he accepted this too and returned home. Reluctantly, he began following the directions given by the old man, and soon began to see improvement in his health.

He started thinking of the mysterious old man, and was astonished when he realised that he was Baba. The old man resembled Baba; he was only dressed differently. He had worn a torn white shirt over a white dhoti. Shrinivasrao felt that Baba had blessed him; his faith in Baba increased by leaps and bounds.

Ref: Ramalingaswami; *Ambrosia in Shirdi*

***

SHRI SAI BABA RAKSHAK

Avayambal resided in Kiranur with her husband. Once there was a disagreement between them, and Avayambal left home and began to stay with her parents. After a month or so she realised the stupidity of her actions and repented. She was anxious that her husband would come and take her back but there was no sign of him. She confided her problem to a friend who was an ardent devotee of Baba.

He listened to her sympathetically and asked her to buy a small round sheet of gold and bring it to him. She spent 6 rupees and bought the sheet. He took the sheet and etched the mantra, "*Shri Sai Baba rakshak*" (Sai Baba, the saviour) on it. He placed it on the altar and started intense ritualistic worship of it.

A week later her husband came and took her home. Avayambal asked him whether he had forgiven her as she was curious that he had come to fetch her just after the intense worship of Baba was conducted. He told her that an old fakir with a long white beard, wearing a kafni with a cloth tied around his head had appeared before him. The fakir sternly ordered him to bring his wife back home. She realised that Baba had appeared before her husband as her saviour; this increased her faith in Baba.

Ref: Ramalingaswami; *Ambrosia in Shirdi*

***

May 30

VIOLENCE TURNED INTO COMPASSION BY THE SADGURU

L. Rajan Iyer resided in Mumbai. He was a violent, abusive person and he hesitated at nothing and spared no one. His family and even his parents suffered his torture. His mother was a saintly person but that did not deter him from hitting her. On one occasion he had an argument with his elder brother and he flung a pair of scissors at him; the wound required three stitches in his waist. The police were a constant feature in his life.

The turning point came in 1976, when a Parsi gentleman advised him to go to Shirdi. He gave him a ticket for the movie *Shirdi Ke Sai Baba*. Thankfully Rajan did watch the movie and felt an incredible urge to visit Shirdi. Impulsively he boarded a bus to Shirdi. During the journey he was befriended by a family who looked after his needs and at Shirdi they introduced him to Sivanesan Swamiji.

Swamiji looked after all of Rajan's needs and advised him to sleep in the Dwarka Mai. That night Rajan received the pain and violence that he had given to others all along. He hoped to sleep soundly that night but instead he felt as if someone was drawing out, with both his hands, all the flesh from his heart and lungs; he could not ward him off as he was immobilised. The pain was unbearably excruciating. The next morning he told Swamiji about his awful experience. Swamiji said, "Baba has removed all your bad thoughts and violent behaviour, and burnt them in the dhuni." From that day Rajan changed for the better, and he became devoted to Swamiji and Baba.

Rajan's thoughts kept turning to Baba's devotee Bhagoji Shinde, and he started working with *Lok Seva Sangam*, a Leprosy Eradication Centre at Sion Mumbai and learnt about leprosy. One day he received a letter from Sister Rosmina of St Rapheal Convent, asking him to join her in a project for leprosy in Jambodhi near Indore. He didn't hesitate to join her; there he spent all his time and energy washing and cleaning the patients' non-healing wounds with tender loving care. His days were filled in alleviating their pain and suffering, instead of causing it.

Each patient became a human being with worries and aspirations. Their children needed to be looked after and this was of utmost importance to Rajan. He got them admitted into a school in Pune that cared for such children, and undertook the task of rehabilitating them. Some of the patients were cured but had deformities, so Rajan taught them to grow vegetables and flowers that could be sold in the market for a price. This way they didn't have to resort to begging.

Thus 20 years passed after he first visited Shirdi and he was at peace with himself; his violence had now transformed into love, caring and compassion. This is a life that Baba would have liked and applauded. What a transformation — to turn from utter violence to utter compassion.

Ref: L. Rajan Iyer; *God's Rainbow*

***

BABA VISITS THE CHOLKAR'S HOME

This unbelievable leela occurred in the home of Rangu — a Cholkar resident of Dahisar. His daughter had completed two readings of the *Shri Sai Satcharita* on a Thursday. Then she prepared delicious savories and confectionery as offerings, and eagerly awaited Baba's arrival. She had read the Charita with love and devotion, and was sure that Baba would appear to her in some form or the other, as stated in the Charita.

A short while later Baba came and sat in the veranda of her home. She saw him and held his hand and brought him inside the house. She was dismayed as his hand felt as hard as stone. No sooner had this thought crossed her mind, his hand became as soft as a child's hand. He spoke to her in Hindi and asked whether she would give him either dakshina or a blanket. Happily she said, "Baba you can have everything that I possess because everything is yours." She seated him comfortably in a chair and performed Arati and gave him the prasad. He ate everything that she offered and then took out 8 annas from his pocket and gave it to her.

After he had finished eating she took him to her "worship room". There he pointed to a picture and asked, "Whose picture is that?" She replied that it was his picture. Then he said, "Badrinath, Haridwar, Rameshwar, Shirdi are all one and the same." Then he gave her a beautiful picture of himself and left. The wonderful miracle was that he left the imprint of his foot in her "worship room" and another in the place where he ate the prasad.

Then Baba went to a temple nearby and asked the priest there to give him the 2 annas that he had in his pocket. The priest immediately gave it to him. About an hour later he returned to the Cholkar home. Cholkar's daughter had just finished cooking lunch. As soon as she saw Baba she ran to him and said, "Baba you did not stay for lunch; please come inside and have some lunch." He obliged her by coming in; she then served the lunch that she had just prepared and sat at his feet. Baba started eating the food. When she asked him to give her some of the consecrated food, he gave her some of the food from his plate. At that very moment her sister-in-law entered the room and sat down. Baba turned to her and asked her to give him a bedspread and 1 rupee as dakshina. She immediately gave it to him and asked him to bless them. He gave his blessings saying that they would do well in life. Then Baba went away. Cholkar's daughter followed him, but after taking a few steps he disappeared.

Ref: Ramalingaswami; *Ambrosia in Shirdi*

***

PANDEY'S WONDERFUL VISION

Shri Pandey worked as a Business Contractor in Vithran, Kalyan. On 13 August 1952 he visited Shirdi; he hoped that Baba would bless him with some unusual experience. He decided to stay on at Shirdi till he got some experience. On the twenty-first during the noon Arati he went into deep meditation. In his meditation he saw Baba lift his right hand bending it at his elbow. Then he saw a powerful light emit from the palm of Baba's hand. The light soon became a huge circle and in it he saw Lord Rama, Hanuman, Krishna and Datta. When he came to his normal state he was curious as to what it could mean.

He wondered who would be able to explain to him the meaning of the vision; he did not know anybody in Shirdi, nor could he find a *sadhu* who could enlighten him. When he went to Dixit Wada for lunch, he met a devotee named Dongre. They sat next to each other during the meal and started conversing with each other. Then he related the beautiful vision that he had in the Samadhi Mandir and asked Dongre what it could possibly mean? Dongre said, "The light emitted from Baba's palm and in it you saw those deities? It means that Baba is one and the same as all those deities." Pandey was satisfied by the explanation as well as with his stay in Shirdi, and he returned happily home.

Ref: Ramalingaswami; *Ambrosia in Shirdi*

***

THE FAKIR CURES HIS STOMACH ACHE

Nemichand Jain owned a jewellery shop in Secundrabad; on one Tuesday in 1960 a strange incident took place. A tall, well-built fakir stood outside his shop and waited patiently. Nemichand was rather busy that day so he didn't notice the fakir. An hour later when he was free, he asked the fakir what he wanted. The fakir immediately replied, "Five Annas." Nemichand searched in his cash register but could find only 4 Annas; the fakir, however, would not accept either more or less money. Suddenly the fakir said, "Are you suffering from severe stomachache?" On hearing this Nemichand was surprised as to how the fakir could know this. In fact, he had tried all kinds of treatments and visited numerous specialists for his stomach ache, all in vain.

The fakir said, "I will give you a medicine that will cure it but you will have to follow my instructions carefully. First, you have to stop your present medicines. Second, you have to start worshiping Sai Baba from Thursday as you will get relief by that day. You have to offer him some confectionery on Thursday if this is not feasible you should light two incense sticks and prostrate before his photograph. Will you be able to do this?" Nemichand readily agreed to this. Then the fakir asked him to cup his palms together and he put some Udi in it. The Udi he took out of his jholi. He then instructed him to take some orally and apply some on his forehead for the next 2 days. Nemichand did this and 2 days later he was pain-free. The fakir came again on Thursday and stood outside Nemichand's shop. Nemichand was delighted to see him and asked him how much dakshina he should offer him. The fakir replied. "One rupee and four Annas" Nemichand was able to find a rupee coin but not the four Anna coin that was there a short while ago. He made a hectic search for it but by then the fakir had disappeared. Nemichand searched for him everywhere but could not find him.

Ref: *Shri Sai Leela* Magazine; Vol. 64, No.12, March 1986

***

June 3

BABA APPEARS AS A COBRA

On 10 September 1983 Dinanath Gupta a resident of Jabalpur had high fever accompanied with weakness. He rested for 2 days and did not step out of his house. A doctor was summoned and he took the medicines as advised, but to no avail. The fever would come down when he took the medicine, but it would soon rise again. On the twelfth he went to work and he was all right during the day, but as soon as he came home the fever rose again.

Thursday was a very important day for him as he had been fasting on that day since 1948 and worshiping Baba with all due rituals. He went to work as usual and at 4:30 p.m. experienced the upper part of his body shake violently; it was as if someone was inside his body churning and shaking it. His colleague Murthy also saw this strange phenomenon. The shaking abated about 2 hours later and Dinanath immediately went home and lay down; then the fever started and reached 105 degrees.

The next day his entire body was shivering; his wife saw this and started crying. There was a photograph of Baba above his bed; she went and prayed to it and then gave Dinanath a glass of water mixed with Udi, which he was able to drink. His wife summoned a doctor who gave Dinanath some medicines but told her that he was gripped by an evil spirit. His wife contacted a tantric who came the next day and through the recitation of mantras was able to capture the evil spirit. The evil spirit was taken away and at midnight its last rites and cremation were performed. While the cremation was being done a cobra appeared suddenly; the tantric folded his hands before the cobra and said that the spirit had been expelled successfully; hearing this, the cobra left. The tantric acknowledged the cobra as his Guru who is Lord Datta, and was satisfied that the cobra which is symbolic of 'removal of Karma' had appeared there during the cremation. Hence, he was assured that Dinanath would recover completely. Dinanath recovered after that, but by then he had lost a lot of weight and was pale as a sheet.

It was then that he realised that Baba had appeared in the form of the cobra and taken care of him. He recollected the numerous times that Baba had appeared before his devotees in the form of a cobra.

Ref: *Shri Sai Leela* Magazine; Vol. 64, No. 3, June 1985

***

June 4

BABA APPEARS AND AVERTS DEATH

The doctors had given up hope, and they informed G. B. Tamahane that his brother would not survive past midnight. Tamahane resided in Chendani and his brother was hospitalised because he was in coma. He and his brother-in-law were at the bedside waiting anxiously, and hoping that things would take a turn for the better.

Tamahane's brother-in-law was devoted to Lord Ganpathi and was reciting his mantras. Tamhane, however, sat quietly and looked lovingly at his brother. Soon the clock struck 12, and to his astonishment he saw the smiling face of Baba bending over and looking intently at his brother. He states, "It took place within a few moments, but I could clearly see Baba's face his white beard, and eye brows, the usual piece of cloth tied around his head. I cried out loudly to my brother-in-law, "Oh! Look at Sai Baba standing there." His brother-in-law looked up but in vain, as Baba had disappeared. But since that very moment Tamahane's ailing brother started recovering and with Baba's grace recovered completely, and is doing well.

Tamahane further states, "Before this incident occurred I hardly believed in Sai Baba, but this touching incident aroused me from my ignorance and I became a staunch devotee of Sai Baba."

Ref: *Sai Sudha* Magazine; Vol. 15, part 9, February 1955

***

BABA HELPS HIM BUY A HOUSE

In 1949 G. B. Tamahane intended to purchase a house. Fortunately he contacted a person who was devoted to Baba. While they were making the deal, the owner of the house said, "Everything will go as per your plan, because Baba informed me in a dream that my house will be sold to a person whose name starts with the initial "T" and the amount you are willing to pay is exactly the amount that Baba specified."

Tamahane made a contract to purchase the house, but at that time he did not have the full amount, so he paid half the amount immediately. He requested the seller to wait for 2 months while he got a loan for the rest of the money. He tried his level best to procure a loan from an insurance company and his bank but all in vain. As a last resort he thought of getting the loan from his office, but he knew that his office would not sanction such a large amount.

The next day the seller contacted him and told him that he had received a message from Baba that he should try for the loan from his own office and it would be sanctioned. Tamahane accordingly applied for the loan from his office. To his astonishment the usual office rule was overruled and the full amount was sanctioned on the very date the seller had told him. Further, his office did not ask him for any security nor was his house mortgaged. Thus Baba helped both of them — Tamahane got the house and the owner successfully sold his property.

Ref: *Sai Sudha* Magazine; Vol. 15, part 9, February 1955

***

"WHY FEAR WHEN I AM HERE"

It was with anxiety and sadness that 19–year-old Ganesh went to R. Radhakrishna's home in Hubli. With tears he narrated that his elder brother Ramani had met with an accident and there was no hope of his recovery. Ramani worked as a mechanic in the Railway Workshop at Hubli and on the night of 5 April 1985 left for Tiruvarur along with his friends to attend the marriage of a friend and co-worker. After attending the wedding he left Tiruvarur all alone for Hubli. He reached Mayavaram station at 3:30 p.m. where he had to board another train. While boarding the train he slipped and fell on the platform dashing his head on a stone.

This resulted in a serious head injury and he bled profusely from his mouth and head. The staff at the station identified him as a Railway personnel from his Railway pass. He was given first aid and then rushed to Tanjore General Hospital. They informed his parents about the accident. His mother and uncle immediately left Hubli and reached the hospital at about 10 p.m. the same night. It was heart wrenching to see him lying in a comatose state.

On the tenth his uncle sent an express telegram to Srinivas, Ramani's father to come immediately and bid farewell to his son. Srinivas was unable to do so as he was suffering from severe asthma. He went to his prayer room and prayed, "Baba, please save my son," and prostrated before him. The next day was a Thursday and Ganesh went to Radhakrishnan's home. They performed the evening Arati and prayed for Ramani's recovery. Then they proceeded to Gopinath's home where there was to be the Congregational singing of hymns. At the end of the program everyone observed silence for 5 minutes and prayed for Ramani's recovery. When Radhakrishnan opened his eyes and looked at Baba, he saw Baba smiling and making a reassuring gesture. Then he clearly heard Baba say, "Why fear when I am here. Just cast all your burdens on me and I will surely bear them." Then he asked Ganesh to go home and reassure his father that his son would be saved.

On the twelfth Ramani had regained consciousness at 8:30 p.m. exactly at the time Baba had made the reassuring gesture, and a week later he was discharged from hospital.

Ref: *Shri Sai Leela* Magazine; Vol. 65, No. 3, June 1986

***

BABA LOOKED AT HIM THROUGH THE CAR WINDOW

Pravin V. Dhairvan resided in Vile Parle, Mumbai. His friend Dasai lived opposite to them. One day Dasai came over to their home and told them that he had seen Baba standing on the steps leading to their home. Pravin and his family were utterly devoted to Baba whom they considered their family deity and Sadguru.

When Pravin started working he moved to Dadar; later when he got married his wife was the granddaughter of the famous Shyamrao Jaykar. Pravin states, "By Baba's grace my wife was very devoted to Baba. I called my father-in-law, Surinder Jaykar, 'Baba'. On 29 January 1998 my father-in-law passed away. Thenceforth every year on his death anniversary both of us took a platter of his favourite food to his wada in Vile Parle and offered it to his departed soul. A few years ago on the anniversary we set out with the food; on the way my wife wanted to do some shopping so I dropped her off and proceeded to the wada. Just as I was about to open the gate, I met Dhanjaya a friend of mine and we chatted for some time and he left. Then I entered the compound and was about to park the car when I clearly saw Baba standing close to the car and looking intently at me. I was astounded and started shouting, "Baba! Baba" I halted the car and got out as quickly as I could but by then he had disappeared. I searched for him everywhere and asked every possible person near the wada whether they had seen Baba, but nobody had seen him. Then I called Dhanjaya and inquired if he had seen Baba while he was leaving the wada. But no one had seen him. I eagerly awaited my wife to return and I told her that I had seen Baba, but was unable to prostrate at his feet as he had disappeared."

My wife said that we should go to Shirdi as soon as possible and we did just that. In the Samadhi Mandir I begged for forgiveness for my inability to clasp his feet. Pravin states, "I am sure Baba has forgiven me, because since then through all the difficult times in my life Baba has come to my aid. At every turn and through all the ups

and downs of my life I have felt Baba's presence with me, guiding
me and taking care of me."

Ref: *Shri Sai Sagar;* January–March 2011

***

June 8

BABA CHIDES HIS STRICT *SOVALAE*

Narayan Chiplunkar and his family resided in Dadar, Mumbai. On
the auspicious day of *Navami* (ninth) *Phalgun* (according to the
Hindu calendar the month of February and March), Baba appeared
in his home. "It was the most memorable day of my life. Early that
morning I was performing ritualistic worship to Baba. Every day I
get up early and after my bath wear the *sovalae* (silk *Dhothi* prepared
with rituals to attain a state of purity; thereafter that person does not
touch anybody or any object as it's considered impure) and conduct
my ritualistic worship. I was totally engrossed in my worship when my
wife and son exclaimed excitedly, "Nana look there and see who has
come to our home." I looked across the room and saw Baba standing
there. Baba had on an ochre kafni, and a golden aura surrounded
him. His eyes glinted like emeralds and golden rays seemed to emit
from every pore in his body. I got up and went and stood before
him with folded hands and head bowed with respect. Then Baba
said, "How is everything with you? Is everything all right?" And
have you recognised me?" I replied, "Yes I have recognised you your
divinity, and I bow before you to receive your blessings and follow
your orders." Then Baba said, "When are you coming to Shirdi?"
With a great deal of delight I replied, "Whenever you order me to
come I will surely be there."

Then I extended my hand to give him dakshina. And Baba said,
"Whatever you want to give me you can give it to me in Shirdi."
Eagerly I replied, *Maharaj* I have some dakshina to give you and I
cannot take it back." Then Baba said something strange; "Is it because
you are sovalae (by rituals a state of 'purity' is attained) that you refrain
from touching me?" Without saying another word I took his hand
in mine and placed the dakshina in it. Then Baba said, "Do come on

172

Ramnavami to Shirdi," and then he raised his hand and blessed all of us. Then just as suddenly as he had appeared, he disappeared. But for the next few days the spot where he stood shone with a brilliant light. Then all of us said together, "That was Baba who came to our home and blessed us." From that moment our lives became as sweet as nectar and we tasted the ambrosia that Baba had poured in our lives."

Ref: *Sai Prasad* Magazine; 1994 (*Deepavali* Issue)

***

June 9

"BABA'S CALLING ME. HE HAS A NEW BED FOR ME."

Over the years numerous devotees requested me to narrate my experiences, as I have been praying to Baba for over 65 years. My entire family is devoted to him, and our day starts and ends with his name. Baba in his kind compassionate way has been showering his grace on us. Up until now I have written the experiences of other devotees, but the next few leelas occurred with me and my family.

"My grandmother passed away in 1953; she had not been well for a few days prior to her death. She had, had cataract surgery when something went wrong and she couldn't see very well. My mother who was devoted to her asked me to sit by her bedside, lest she fell down while going to the bathroom, etc. I loved that chore as my grandmother would tell me many mythological stories. One evening while I was sitting by her bedside, she looked up at the corner and started clapping her hands in ecstasy. I ran to my mother and said, "Come quickly granny is behaving in a strange manner." My mother came at once and saw her sitting up in bed; and then she beckoned to my mother to come near her. My grandmother then pointed to the corner and said, "Look they are performing Arati in *Vainkunt* (abode of Lord Vishnu). Can you see Lord Vishnu decked with gold and diamond jewellery?" Then she went on to describe the huge Kohinoor diamond on Lord Vishnu's chest. Of course neither of us could see all this.

173

The next day at midnight she got up and was trying to open the front door and go out. My mother rushed to her side and asked her where she was going. She replied, "Don't try to stop me, can't you see Sai Baba is calling me. He has a lovely new bed for me and I have to go." The next day she told my father that she would pass away that night. She asked him to sit by her side and see that she does not die between a certain period of time. My father sat by her side and she passed away peacefully at dawn. All of us put a little Ganga water in her mouth and then my father placed a tulsi leaf in her mouth and she closed her eyes forever.

My grandmother who vehemently opposed Baba's photograph being kept in the house later had become an ardent devotee. And during the time of her passing away, Baba himself came and took her to her final abode.

Ref: As witnessed by Vinny

***

June 10

BABA GUARDS OUR PLOT

My father retired from the Ordnance Factory in 1963 and moved to Pune. He chose Pune because the climate here was pleasant, but most importantly Pune was close to Shirdi. In those days there were no private buses plying that route. Hence, he would board the State Transport bus at 6 a.m. and reach Shirdi just before the noon Arati.

My grandmother wanted to own a home but unfortunately she passed away before her dream came to fruition. My father was determined to fulfil her desire and so wanted to build a house. He managed to buy a plot of land in a desolate area in Aundh. At that time Aundh was a village and there was only one bus leaving Aundh in the morning and returning in the evening. Nonetheless my father went to the city and searched the markets for the best, but cheapest building materials, and got them delivered to our plot. There was only one street light on the road in front of the plot and a family lived on the opposite side of our plot.

That family, the Mayyia's, hailed from Karnataka and as my mother had been born and bred in Mangalore, she and the family quickly became friends. One day my mother casually asked Mrs. Mayyia to keep an eye on the plot as there were a lot of robberies taking place and vast quantities of building materials were being stolen. Mrs. Mayyia however said, "Why are you worried Mrs. Prabhu, your Muslim watchman is so good. He walks around the premises the whole night saying "Allaha Malik." My mother was aghast because we could not afford to hire a watchman nor did we have one. My mother said, "What watchman?" Mrs. Mayyia went on to say, "The old man with a beard and a cloth tied around his head," and she proceeded to describe Baba. My mother's throat was chocked and with tears in her eyes she said, "O! He watches over us every moment of our lives." My mother was astounded that Mrs. Mayyia was fortunate to see Baba while she unfortunately couldn't see him.

In *Sreepada Sreevallabha Charitraamrutam* the meaning of "Allaha Malik" is described beautifully in chapter 45. Sreepada Sreevallabha states, "In Arabic, *Aal* means *Shakti* and *Aha* means *Shaakta* or one who possesses this energy, that is, Shakti. Therefore, 'Allaha' means the form of Shiva and Shakti, thus the word Allaha is acceptable to the Muslims also. Malik means the master."

Ref: As narrated by Varija Prabhu

***

June 11

"MY JOURNEY BACK HOME ENDED ABRUPTLY"

In 1963 I was studying in the third year of medical college, when I became very sick. I began suffering from a relentless high temperature and was admitted to hospital; however, every investigation done was negative. Every possible antibiotic was given to me but to no avail. With every passing day the fever raged on, and I became emaciated and critically ill.

One day I stopped breathing and the doctors rushed to resuscitate me. And I had an out-of-body experience. I was flying or moving through a strange tunnel that was tapering towards the end. As I floated towards the apex clouds, a glowing fluorescent light floated toward me from either side. I moved on and at the end of the tunnel there was a blue light beckoning me; it was a deeply silent peaceful place.

At that moment I was revived and my own breath sounded like thunder. Baba had pushed me back to earth with all its ups and downs. Silently I shed tears, when I told my mother this; she summoned the doctor who thought I was hallucinating and gave me a sedative injection. I never spoke about it again, as I thought I was crazy. But when I went to the U.S.A., I read about the 'near-death experiences' of children who had fallen into Lake Michigan and were revived 10 to 15 minutes later, all of them had had a similar out of body experience that was slightly different from mine.

But this made me wonder why I came back? What was the purpose of my life? Have I made a difference in even a single person's life? I don't know if I have, but every morning I get up and thank Baba for protecting me through the night. Also when I have to walk alone in some unknown place especially at night I ask Baba to cover me in his blue light and I know I will be safe."

Ref: As narrated by Vinny

***

June 12

BABA GIVES ME THE DIAGNOSIS

It was a Thursday of 1984; as usual I went to my clinic an hour before we started seeing patients. I had a photograph on my table of Baba sitting in front of the Dhuni Mai; it was my habit to spend this time praying. I would beseech him to help me with every patient that I saw on that day. Suddenly there was a knock on my door and the nurse entered my office. She said, "I know I am not to disturb you at this time but I want you to see a 3-month-old child that is quite sick and the child has laboured respiration." As we walked to the examining room I asked her the usual questions, about diarrhea, vomiting fever and drug ingestion to which she said, "Negative'.

I examined the child and I could not find anything wrong except dehydration and rapid breathing, I had no clue of the diagnosis; desperately I prayed to Baba. Then I heard him say loudly, "Diabetic Ketoacidosis." I was shocked; I turned around and said, "What Baba

176

the child is only 3 months old." Baba repeated the diagnosis three times. I got the blood and urine tested. Within a few minutes I got the results — "blood glucose 350 and urine was positive with ketones." The lab technician came to see the child as he could not believe the age of the child as he thought the child was 3 years.

While all this was happening, the child's condition was fast deteriorating. I asked the nurse to bring an I.V., but the veins of the child had disappeared, and the child was in shock. Again I pleaded, "Baba please put the I.V. in and administer the fluids, and immediately I got the vein on the very first attempt. Then again I heard Baba say, "Now ship the child to Children's Hospital." I had to laugh in that tense moment, "Wow, Baba talks the medical jargon too."

As this leela is very big it will be continued as the next leela.

***

June 13

BABA APPEARS AS CAPTAIN RODRIGUEZ

I asked the nurse to call 911, that is, the Emergency Service and send the child to Children's Hospital. The ambulance arrived a short while later; it is customary to take the patient to the nearest hospital and from there the child may be transferred. But the nearest hospital did not have a Pediatric Department. However, the fire fighter who came was Captain Rodriguez. The team went and saw the child; I asked them if they could please take the child to Children's Hospital, as the baby had diabetes. To my relief the Captain readily agreed, which was unusual. As the child was in such a critical condition it was 'air lifted' to Children's Hospital.

I then went to my office closed the door and cried my heart out; I thanked Baba for his mercy. Finally I laughed and said, "Baba I always knew that you know everything about everything, but I did not know that you spoke 'American English;' you said ship the child?" I called the Hospital an hour later and was informed that after performing a CAT scan and other tests the child was stable. Then the doctor said, "Doc how did you suspect and diagnose the child to have diabetes?" I replied "O! That was divine intervention." She thought I was crazy and put the receiver down. The senior doctors also asked me the same question and every time I said it was divine intervention, they hung up. But I know Baba is the one who gave me the diagnosis.

Finally I called the Fire Department who took the child to the hospital and asked to speak to Captain Rodriguez as I wanted to thank him. They said, "Yes we did take the baby to Children's Hospital but there is no one called Captain Rodriguez.

I saw his name tag and wrote his name on the chart, so I asked the nurse and she confirmed that it was Captain Rodriguez. Then I realised that my Baba had come as Captain Rodriguez and saved me and the child's life. That child did well and was discharged and many papers were published on it, but all the accolades go to Baba.

Ref: As witnessed by Vinny

***

June 14

BABA SAVES US FROM THE RIOTS IN MUMBAI

In 1991 my sister Asha and I had come to India. We landed at Santa Cruz airport so we could take either a cab or a flight to Pune. We went to the cab stand but all the cab drivers were huddled together saying they should go home as soon as possible. I wondered why they would want to go home so early in the morning. We asked them to take us to Pune but they did not pay any heed to us; they kept saying that things may turn violent at any time. Asha said, "Let us take the flight to Pune for which we already have tickets."

By then all the seats were booked. Not knowing this or what was happening we went to the ticket counter and handed our passports and tickets. As a formality the lady took my passport and a card-sized photograph of Baba fell out. She reverentially picked it up and said something very strange, "There are no seats available and it might get dangerous. Just stay beside me and I will seat you on this flight." Not knowing what was happening we stood close by.

178

Then the aircraft arrived, and she started calling the names of the passengers. The names of the passengers that were a family of 4 or 5 she called loudly. But the name of a couple she called softly she did call the names thrice but so softly that they did not hear it. Then turning to us she said "Now just go," and literally pushed us into the boarding aircraft.

The flight took off and it was the last for many days as riots had broken out between the Hindus and Muslims as a result of the Babri Masjid. As the aircraft flew over Mahim we looked out of the windows and saw Mumbai burning. Thanks to Baba and the kind lady we reached Pune safely and were not stranded in Mumbai Santa Cruz airport.

Ref: As witnessed by Vinny

***

June 15

BABA ORDERS ME TO CROSS THE ROAD

My clinic was situated in a ghetto and often there were muggings and violence, so most of the staff left the clinic in a group. On day a mother brought her son just as I was about to leave the clinic. The nurse advised the mother to take the child to the Emergency Room, but the mother was determined to have the child checked by me. I obliged her and examined the child, got the medicines and gave the child a dose; after reassuring the mother I asked her to bring the child again the next day.

By then it was quite late and I left the clinic alone. When I punched out I noticed the time. In the evening I usually walked home. I exited the clinic and walked around the corner when I noticed a group of teenage boys huddled together. It struck me they were talking loudly and belligerently. I was not afraid for I thought they know me so they won't harm me. Just then Baba said loudly, "Cross the road."

Instinctively I crossed the road and kept walking and reached home. Every evening I watched a Channel called Eye Witness News; this channel gave all the hoary news of the events around the city. There was a 'Gang War" between two rival gangs and one gang shot

179

at the other from the roof of a high rise building. Many teenagers were killed, hurt and maimed. Many innocent children and bystanders were also hurt some crippled for life. And all this happened just after Baba asked me to cross the road and walk to safety.

Ref: As witnessed by Vinny

***

June 16

FOR MY CHARITA I RISKED MY LIFE

Once in 1985 I had gone to visit a friend of mine on the south side of Chicago. The south side is mainly a black neighbourhood and is riddled with gangs, muggings and violence. We sat and talked for a long time and it soon became dark. Unfortunately she had to go elsewhere and could not drive me home. I told her not to worry as I would take the bus back home; she remarked, "You are very confident to go alone on the south side." I replied, "Why should I be afraid, I have my Bible, that is, my *Shri Sai Satcharita* with me." She laughed at me and I left.

It was a dark, cold night in December, and I was glad when the bus arrived. I got in and sat in the third row not directly behind but in the opposite side, so the driver could see me from his rear view mirror. At the next stop a group of hefty boys sat behind me. My hand bag was by my side and the zip was open. At the next stop the group of boys jumped on me and snatched my bag and exited the bus. I jumped up and followed them; my only thought was my Shri Sai Satcharita is stolen. The gang swiftly took whatever cash they could find and threw my bag and fled.

Strangely the driver waited a while there. I collected my bag ascertained that the book was there and re-entered the bus. The driver said, "Lady you ought not to have gone after them they could have shot you. What was so precious in that bag that you risked your life?" Through tears of joy I screamed, "My Sat Charita. My Bible! How can I live without it?" He gave me a strange look and drove on.

I had always known the power of that book, but now I became even more aware of it. It was indeed Baba physically protecting me through it. I knew that it was not a mere book, and when it was

180

preserved in my place of worship its auspicious vibrations drove away misfortunes and spirits of darkness. I recollected the many times that I had carried it to interviews, meetings and presentations and by its grace had been successful. During lonely and hard times I have held it to my chest and it has given me solace. I can write volumes about its glory, but I will end by saying if there is one book that you wish to possess it is this book.

Ref: As narrated by Vinny

***

June 17

HOW I LUCKILY MISSED THE TRAIN THAT WAS BOMBED

On one of my vacations to India I visited Shirdi; there I met an aged man who was very knowledgeable and answered many of my questions, so I called him Guruji. Guruji lived in Ambarnath and often he would write to me and give me news about Shirdi. Sometimes he would write about a book he had read on Baba, often with an explanation of some passage in it. I felt very happy receiving his letters in Chicago. A few years later, while visiting Pune, I decided to visit him at his home in Ambarnath. Guruji's home was right in front of the railway station and I could see the trains approaching the station from the balcony of his home.

At that time there was a lot of unrest, and incidents of bomb blasts in various trains had been occurring. After a comfortable stay for a few days, I decided to return to Pune. We stood on the balcony and when the train was approaching Guruji said, "If you walk at a fast pace you will catch that train." So I touched his feet and left. But as I approached the road I saw some delectable custard apples and bought some as my father liked them. For some reason I dillydallied and bought my ticket. I entered the station and saw the last bogie leaving the platform; I knew I would not be able to board that train. I thought I would catch the next train which was due in an hour.

Then I saw some emergency trains go in that direction and there was a lot of flurry amongst the railway staff. I finally asked them when

181

the next train to Pune would arrive; they said they did not know. I went to the official on duty and asked him what had happened as no train had arrived and it was midnight; they told me that there had been a bomb blast about 15 minutes after that train had left the station and many people were seriously injured. When I heard that, I knelt down and thanked Baba for making me miss that train and for protecting me. Finally I caught a train going to Kanyakumari and reached Pune at 6 a.m.

Ref: As narrated by Vinny

***

June 18

BABA HELPED ME DURING MY *PADA YATRA* TO SHIRDI

After my father retired from his job he settled in Aundh; I would visit them during my vacations. Often times during the month of June I would go to Shivaji Nagar and watch the *Varkari's* walk to Pandarpur. The Varkari's are a sect of devotees who carry palkhi's and walk to Pandarpur. I was thrilled to see the devotees singing and dancing in ecstasy. I thought if only there was a palkhi to Shirdi I would surely participate in the procession.

Years rolled by and in 1996, I got my chance to join a palkhi that was going to Shirdi for *Gurupurnima*. I went and registered my name and paid my dues. When I informed my mother about my decision to walk to Shirdi she advised me against it, because of all the hardships I would have to face. I assured her that if it was too hard for me I would return home. I made all the arrangements and set out, but at the very first halt someone stole my medicines, walking shoes and sleeping bag. I bought some sandals and continued walking. On the third day we reached Shirur and there was a steep climb and I was reeling like a drunkard.

Just as I was about to fall a devotee named Rohi Dass came and helped me. But the hill loomed in front of me and it seemed insurmountable. So I asked him to hold me by my arm, 'like Butti held Baba while going to Lendi Baugh,' and we started talking. At that time I had worn a loose white shirt, loose pajamas and had tied a thin wet white towel around my head. Rohi Dass asked me what I did for a living, when I told him I was a physician he jerked his hand away. Little did I know that he had had a dream a few days ago wherein he was helping a physician dressed like me. At the next halt he asked the palkhi in charge if there were any physicians in the group, and as I was the only one he considered it Baba's order and helped me all the way to Shirdi. When he finally told me about the dream I was overwhelmed. I thanked Baba for sending a perfect stranger to take care of a stubborn devotee who wanted to walk to Shirdi.

Ref: As narrated by Vinny

***

June 19

TWA 800 BLEW UP IN THE SKY

In June 1995 my sister Asha and her husband decided to visit Paris. At that time a number of airlines were offering packages to Paris and London. They booked a flight on TWA for Paris. A few days later her husband said, "Since we are so close to London let's add London to our travel package and travel one way by the Chunnel." Asha was thrilled at the idea of travelling by the Chunnel and readily agreed. So they called the airline and a price was fixed; 3 days before the date of travel her husband called for the tickets and they were told that they would have to pay 200 dollars on each ticket, which was more than the set price that was quoted. This enraged her husband and he cancelled the tickets. Her husband then booked their tickets on Air France without any problems and they reached Paris. Air France had also provided them a beautiful room near the Louvre.

They settled in and Asha was eager to go sightseeing, but her husband lay on the bed and said he wanted to watch TV; she chided him and said, "It's not even 12 hours since we left New York and what news can CNN give you about New York." Nonetheless he switched on the TV and started screaming. Asha was having a quick shower and did not understand what had happened. She came running out of the bathroom; her husband was pointing to the television screen.

183

There was the vivid scene of TWA 800 burning away. It had burst into flames 8 miles out of New York Airport.

Asha states, "Sai Baba the omniscient God knew what was going to happen and made us change our tickets from TWA 800 to Air France just for a mere 200 dollars and saved our lives."

Ref: As narrated by Asha

***

June 20

A KAFNI-CLAD HAND PULLED HER TO THE TOP

On 20 June 1978, it was a sad day for Rajani Sharma, a resident of New Delhi, for on that day her father passed away. She was dejected and worried as her mother was frail and ailing, and her youngest brother was only a year old. Although she worked, she wondered how she would look after her family. On the third day of her father's cremation it was a ritual to visit a temple and Rajani did just that. Rajani visited the Hanuman temple at Connaught Place; there she found a relief brass metal image of Baba. She was drawn to the image as it was Baba in the *ashirwad* pose (Baba with his hand lifted to bless). Little did she know at that time that Baba would play such a significant role in her life. Nonetheless she brought him home and placed him in her payer room. She said, "I have lost my father and henceforth you are my father." At that time she knew nothing about Baba.

A few days later a friend at work asked her to accompany her to a temple at Lodhi road. When she entered the temple she was astonished to see Baba's idol when she realised that she had brought him home a few days ago. One night she had a vivid dream; in the dream she had gone to the Lodhi road temple and after exiting it she found a huge granite wall blocking her from getting her sandals. So she started climbing the wall; like a lizard she scaled the wall. Just as she was about to reach the top she started sliding down. And lo! A kafni clad hand reached out and pulled her up and there the dream ended.

184

That was the turning point and she became an ardent devotee of Baba, and thereafter Baba held her hand through thick and thin. Her brother then started an export business and slowly their financial condition stated improving. Then she bought an apartment in Shirdi, and visits Shirdi frequently and stays for long periods of time.

Ref: As narrated by Rajani

***

June 21

A FAKIR INSTRUCTS THEM ABOUT THE TEMPLE

In December 1984, J. Meerebai and a few devotees formed the *Shri Sai Seva Mandali*; they sang hymns and worshiped Baba. In 1983 a group of about 50 devotees visited Shirdi. There they met Nana Sahib Rasne who said, "Baba bade me to meet you and guide you on the important work you are about to do. You are going to construct a temple at Vijaywada shortly." The group was surprised to hear this as they had not planned to do so.

In 1985 Nana's prediction started coming true. A plot of 750 sq yards on the banks of the river Krishna at Guntur was donated by Gopal Singh. The foundation stone was laid in June and about 500 people were fed. After most of the devotees had left, Baba appeared there as a fakir. He blessed the temple saying that it would flourish. Then he asked them to give him a little prasad. After a thorough search they found a little prasad stuck to one of the vessels and it was served to him. He said, "I am from Maharashtra. I came here 20 years ago and now I have come for this purpose." He then circumambulated the temple area three times and vanished.

While they were counting the collection an unknown person on a motorbike stopped there and gave them some money. Surprisingly the amount was 9 rupees; he took the money and gave it to Giridhar Singh and asked him to spend it on service to Baba. Then he wrote a mantra *Aum Guru, Aum Namo Sai Ram, Guru Sai Ram* and asked them to inscribe it in bold letters next to the idol. He also ordered them to plant a neem and a *karol* tree (a Christmas tree and is believed

185

to shower its blessings on everyone around it) on either side of the temple. Then he vanished and was not found anywhere.

A week later two members of the Mandali had a dream in which Baba assured them that he indeed had come that day to the site and had blessed them.

Ref: *Shri Sai Leela* Magazine; Vol. 64, No. 10, January 1985

***

$$\boxed{\text{June 22}}$$

HER DEAD SISTER WAS SEATED BESIDE BABA

B. R. Jyothi was a 19-year-old student studying in the Pre University course at Bangalore when she passed away on 28 March 1986. She was devoted to Baba, recited the *Vishnu Sahasra Naam* daily and read literature on Baba.

On the twenty-seventh she complained of her inability to pass urine and at 4 p.m. she collapsed near the door of the bathroom. Dr. Vinod came and checked her immediately and rushed her to a nursing home close by. Jyothi was constantly chanting Baba's name. She was given the best possible treatment. Her grandfather had a terrible dream early in the morning and was awakened hearing his own screams saying, "Go away. Go away." In his dream he saw a huge dog rushing towards him to attack him. Simultaneously Jyothi was murmuring, "Some one is dragging me to the cremation ground."

Her grandfather was summoned and was told there was no hope of her survival. He went to her bedside and held a photograph of Baba before her. She gazed at it reverentially and a little Udi was given to her. A few minutes later she breathed her last. Her younger sister was devastated by the loss and could not be consoled. On the thirtieth she had a dream in which she saw Jyothi seated beside Sai Baba, following this she was consoled and became calm. Her grandfather told her what Baba had said to Dixit when the latter requested him to revive a boy. Baba had said, "Do not get entangled in this. He has entered a new body. In that body he will do good work that cannot be accomplished in this body. If I draw him back then the new body

186

will die and this body will come to life. I will do it for you. Have you any idea of the responsibility of this act, and are you prepared to take it up?"

Ref: *Shri Sai Leela* Magazine; Vol. 66, No. 6, September 1987

***

June 23

BABA STOOD BESIDE WITH A LANTERN IN HIS HAND

She was a Tamilian and Tamil was the only language she spoke. Her name was Kamal Ammala and she resided in Matunga, Mumbai. Kamal was devoted to Baba; in 1944 her only son was recruited in the army. She was agonised by the thought of what might happen to him in the Army, so she decided to seek refuge in Baba. She went to the railway station and asked for a ticket to Shirdi; she did not know that the train did not go up to Shirdi. The booking clerk was devoted to Baba, so he gave her a ticket to Kopergaon. Somehow she managed to come to Shirdi along with some pilgrims. She also managed to get a room near the Samadhi Mandir.

At 8 p.m. she went out in the darkness not knowing that the steps behind the Samadhi had no railings at that time. She fell down on the paved floor near the well and was badly bruised. The knees and forehead of this 60-year-old lady were bleeding badly. She met Mr. Balvalli and told him in Tamil that she had fallen down the steps and bruised herself. He offered to take her to the doctor but she refused. Then she told him this incredible leela. She said, "When I fell down I saw a man standing next to me. I looked up and saw it was Shri Sai Baba himself. He was standing with a lantern in his hand. Then he gently passed his hands over my body especially the parts that hurt. He also assured me that I would be all right the next day, so I don't need any treatment." Then she retired to her room and slept well as if she did not have any pain. At midnight she dreamt of Baba who assured that he would take care of her son, so she need not worry or fear for his safety.

Ref: *Sai Sudha* Magazine; Vol. 5, No. 8, June 1945

***

NEVER HAS A DEVOTEE BEEN THROWN INTO DESPONDENCY

From his nineteenth year V. N. Murtirao of Bangalore was tormented by a convulsive disorder. He was treated with anti-convulsants without any improvement. Various alternative remedies and even charms were tried, but nothing worked. Many people took advantage of his situation by suggesting various quacks who promised a fast cure for his disease. They swindled him of a lot of money, and this continued for about 17 years.

Then one day a friend gave him a little Udi and asked him to stop all these useless treatments. He also advised him to caste the entire burden of anxieties and worries on Baba and pray to him. Murtirao started praying at once, not with any faith but merely to get relief from the disease. From that day on the fits did occur but when he was at home or in the office, and not on the street. The attacks became milder and there were no aftereffects. Sometimes when he became aware of a fit's onset, he put a little Udi in his mouth and managed to stave off the attack.

Murtirao was quite content with this but his mother and brother were anxious about the slow recovery. On two occasions without his knowledge they consulted some *mantricks* who claimed to possess powers to cure his disease. A mantrick is one who through the recitation of Mantras and rituals can cast or remove spells. After each consultation Murtirao became worse; the convulsions came on fast and furious. And finally he started behaving like an 'imbecile'.

While he was in this state Baba told his mother in a dream, "Am I not here to look after him? Why did you go elsewhere? Never has a devotee of mine been thrown by the wayside. He is not having as many attacks as before. Within 3 or 4 months he will be completely all right. Do not do anything now that will make him worse. Be content at having his convulsions cured slowly." Thus it came to pass; Murtirao got completely cured and developed immense faith in Baba.

Ref: *Sai Sudha* Magazine; Vol. 5, No. 8, June 1945

***

UDI RESTORES THE CAT'S SIGHT

A little girl named Surya of Bangalore was an ardent devotee of Baba. She was very fond of a little kitten. One day a cat found its way into her home, and her parents allowed Surya to keep it. A few days later her mother took Surya and her sister to Malleswaram temple to attend the *Sai Bhajans* (hymns). When they returned home they found that the cat had viciously attacked the kitten. The cat had brutally mauled the kitten with the result that both his eyes bulged out of their sockets. The eyeballs were torn and bleeding. The kitten lay moaning and mewing piteously in a corner.

Surya was distraught and heartbroken to see this as the kitten would lose his eyesight. She picked up her pet and ran with him to Baba's photograph and cried, "Sai why can't you restore the sight of this poor kitten?" Then she took some Udi and smeared it all over the wound saying, "Baba save my pet from blindness." Strange as it may sound, after a few minutes the bleeding stopped and the eyeballs were restored to their normal position. Needless to say the kitten recovered and could see as clearly as before.

A few years later, a series of calamities befell the family, and they were poverty stricken. In disgust the family ceased their worship of Baba and remained estranged from him for some years. Then they moved to Chennai but still forsook Baba. Two months later the mother heard a command, "Do *bhajans*." The family started singing hymns at home and sometimes in the temple. Soon their faith started increasing so also their financial condition. The mother was a linguist so she started holding discourses on Baba in various languages, as a gesture of gratitude.

Ref: *Sai Sudha* Magazine; Vol. 13, Part 9, February 1953

***

THE *HAKIM* CURES HIS RASH

J. Ram Murthy was a military officer; he hailed from Madurai and was devoted to Baba. In 1943 he was transferred to Ambala Cantonment for an advanced military training. He was delighted as his residence was surrounded by a forest of beautiful trees. Some time later he developed a rash over both his arms that itched intensely. The doctor diagnosed it to be a severe case of *tinea corporis* or ringworms. The treatment lasted for many days which Ram Murthy followed strictly, but to his dismay the rash spread all over his body. He suffered a great deal every morning when he attended the physical training. There was intense itching and bleeding as a consequence.

He was hospitalised by his officer who witnessed his suffering; the treatment given to him was intensive but to no avail. Ram Murthy was reduced to tears because of the futility of it. That evening a young lad entered his hospital room and told him that he would take him to a hakim who could cure him. Ram Murthy wondered how the boy had managed to enter the room, let alone enter the premise because of the tight security all around. However, the boy was insistent and something about him convinced Ram Murthy to follow his advice. He got permission from his officer and accompanied the boy. The boy took him deep into the forest where there was a thatched hut and the hakim was seated there. The hakim took a look at his rash and gave him a small jar of ointment with instructions for its application Sceptically Ram Murthy followed his instructions very carefully.

That night he slept peacefully as the intense itching had abated. The next morning after he showered he checked his skin and was delighted to see that the rash had disappeared completely. It was then that the whole scenario of the events that took place made him realise that this was Baba's leela. As soon as the doctor arrived he asked for his discharge from the hospital, which was granted. Immediately he set out to find the young lad and the hakim. Upon reaching the spot he was amazed to note that the hut, along with the young lad and the hakim had disappeared.

Ref: *Sai Sudha* Magazine; Vol. 5, No. 12, May 1945

***

"UDI CAN CURE ANYTHING AND EVERYTHING DOCTOR"

In 2003 Rahul was a young lad of about 18 years and resided in Korhale; he looked after the Sai Baba temple there. His duty was to take care of the pilgrims who came to the temple at night. That summer at about 8 p.m., he was walking back to the temple when he was bitten by something. As the village is infested by scorpions he thought it was a scorpion bite. There was intense pain and burning in his foot. Just then Prasant his friend walked by and saw him groaning with pain. Presuming it was a scorpion bite he took him to an Indian shaman, who could heal him by his spells and incantations.

Thus two hours passed but the pain became excruciating and the foot became blue. Prasant who worked in the Primary Health Centre realised that he may lose his foot so he brought him to Shirdi. Immediately he called Sada and both of them got Rahul admitted into Sainath Hospital Intensive Care Unit. The blood test was positive for viper venom; where did such a rare and dangerous snake come from?

To make a long story short, Rahul was given the anti-venom shots, but Rahul's condition worsened by the hour. The doctor finally shook his head and said, "He won't make it as paralysis has set in, he is incoherent and is losing consciousness. Only a miracle can help him. Inform his parents of his condition." Sada replied, "Doctor, Baba's Udi can cure anything and everything, and Baba will save him." Meanwhile Rahul had become cold, clammy with a very feeble pulse. Sada got a handful of Udi from home and vigorously rubbed it on his entire body. The whole night he sat at his bedside and prayed. At about 5 a.m. when he fell asleep, he felt someone patting him and asking him to get up; it was Rahul. He was sitting in bed, asking to be taken home.

A strange change occurred in Rahul; before the bite he was irresponsible and did not care for the temple. Since his recovery he turned into a responsible, kind and caring person. He says, "What can Baba's Udi not do, it brought me back from death, and changed me so much that I often wonder if I am the same Rahul."

Ref: As witnessed by Sada and Prasant

***

191

BABA POURED AMBROSIA IN HER MOUTH

During the summer vacation of 1942 Draupatibai V. Parab came to Mumbai to stay with V S P (his full name is not mentioned) for a month. When she arrived she ran a slight fever, which soon developed into pneumonia. Her fever shot up to 104 degrees and she had a hacking cough with blood-tinged phlegm. The doctor was summoned who said, "Considering her advanced age, frailty and the high temperature she needs to be hospitalisd as her condition is critical." But Draupati was terrified of hospitals and refused to be admitted. The doctor also told her relatives that Draupati's chances for survival were very slim. But Draupati was content to die at home than in a strange hospital. So V S P and Draupati sought refuge in Baba, along with the treatment prescribed.

On Saturday the tenth at 1 p.m. Baba appeared; he had his jholi slung over his shoulder, wore a kafni and had a cloth tied on his head. He first washed his hands and feet at the tap in front of their home and entered Draupati's room. He stood at her bedside and said, "Don't be afraid. The old lady had recovered fully from her illness in this house. Have you come here again to get sick?" The whole family witnessed this memorable event and was struck by the compassion in his voice. Then Baba poured some ambrosia into her mouth, and asked the family to bring some cooked rice and *dal* (cooked pulses). Then with tender loving care he fed some of it to Draupati. He then gave the following instructions, "Do eat any food for the next four days. There is a temple of *Jari Mari* on the outskirts of this town; offer a *pan Vida* (rolled beetle leaf with areca nut and other ingredients) there, one beetle nut and raw rice; place these offerings on the right hand side. Before doing this take a bath and think of me. Before leaving the house prostrate to my photograph and then leave." The old lady followed Baba's instructions with a great deal of faith and determination.

Needless to say the lady recovered fully and was very grateful to Baba.

Ref: *Shri Sai Leela* Magazine; Vol. 18, No. 8–10, October–December 1943

***

BABA'S WORSHIP NEGATES THE SPELLS OF BLACK MAGIC

Venkatraman lived with his family in Mylapore, Chennai. His father was employed in the Railways and lived in Hyderabad. There was a lot of ill will between them and some of their relatives. And the relatives resorted to witchcraft, to take revenge. One day an old man appeared before Venkatraman and gave him the following advice. "Make a thorough search of your home, and you will find some chits of paper. On these chits the words, *"Pilli Suynam"* (spell of black magic) will be written in Tamil, along with some ashes from the crematorium. Immediately burn those chits of paper and thoroughly wash your home on every Saturday. Also offer *Pongal* (sweet rice) offering to god." Venkatraman went home and found numerous chits of paper with ash on them; he burnt them immediately. He followed the advice given by the old man.

About 10 days later a relative came to his home and gave him 20 mangoes. No sooner had his relative left, the old man turned up riding a motorbike. He warned them not to eat the mangoes, as it would bring great misfortune on the family. He then asked Venkatraman to fetch a knife and cut one of the mangoes. Inside the mango was a small quantity of ash and a jasmine flower. The old man then trampled upon the mangoes and threw them away. He then said he was hungry and would like to have some food. Venkatraman gave him a meal of rice, *sambar* (pulses cooked with vegetables) and buttermilk.

Some days later his father returned home and Venkatraman related everything to him. His father told him the elderly gentleman was B. V. Narsimhaswamiji, who on 13 March 1946 came to their home and removed the black magic as ordered by Baba to do so. Narsimhaswamiji performed Baba's worship and gave them a picture of Baba and Udi. Ever since Baba's worship was started, they are leading a peaceful and happy life.

Ref: *Sai Sudha* Magazine; Vol. 7, Part 4, September 1946

***

BABA'S IDOL PERSPIRES INDICATING THE FIRE

Though I cast off this mortal body (take *Niryan*), I am eternally alive and immortal; know this as the truth, then behold and experience my fame and leelas — this is a promise that Baba made.

Shambaji Sawant a resident of Mumbai was a staunch devotee; he also had the good fortune to become a trustee of the Sansthan. He did some splendid work and was responsible for telecasting Shirdi and Baba's daily worship through a television show on *Doordarshan*. During his tenure as trustee he often visited Shirdi. Once he was seated in the Samadhi Mandir and meditating. Sawant often got an irresistible urge to look at Baba's face during mediation, so time and again he would open his eyes to look at Baba's idol. A few hours later when he looked at Baba's face he saw the idol perspiring. The perspiration started from the forehead and soon a drop trickled down Baba's beard and fell down. The priest who was there wiped it and looked at Baba's face with wonder. Soon Baba started perspiring profusely; at that very moment Sawant heard some people yelling, "Fire! Fire!"

There were some rooms between the Samadhi Mandir and the Dwarka Mai, and the room directly behind the Dhuni Mai was engulfed in fire. Of course the fire was deftly and quickly extinguished. Sawant said, "Baba started sweating and he was trying to tell us that the room was on fire. But we are so stupid that we could not understand him."

Ref: Shambaji Sawant; *Saianubhav*

***

194

THROUGH DREAMS BABA FORETELLS WHAT IS TO BEFALL HIM

S. Subharao was an advocate from Gooty. In 1942, his maid who also cooked for him went to her village. She was away for 5 months and he had to do all the household chores. One day a vessel containing boiling, pepper water slipped from his hand and fell on his left calf and legs causing severe scalds. He at once remembered Baba and applied Udi to the burnt area. The pain was severe, but he continued chanting Baba's name and was able to sleep that night. He got up early next morning and examined the scalded area. He was pleasantly surprised to see that the scalds had completely disappeared, leaving almost no trace. As he had no pain or discomfort he was able to go to work as usual.

On 30 September 1942, Subharao dreamt that Baba was sitting on a wooden box in grave anxiety and concern in front of a cloth shop. That was the shop that Subharao frequented often, and he wondered why? This dream was followed by another dream; here Baba was sitting happily in his home near his shrine. Two days later Subharao slipped and fell from the steps of that cloth shop. He sustained a head injury and blood flowed profusely from the wound. Besides all these injuries, he also lost consciousness for a short while. Some time later he felt better and walked home. As soon as he entered his home he went to the shrine and applied Udi profusely to the injured area. The next day he felt all right and went to work as usual. He states, "Baba's Udi did wonders in the above two incidents in my life. I assure you that the application of Udi with intense faith in Baba is a panacea for all ills."

Ref: *Sai Sudha* Magazine; Vol. 3, part 1, 2, 3; October 1942

***

VIA A DREAM BABA TELLS HIM TO EAT A LOT OF UDI

In June 1946, S. Subharao an advocate from Gooty suffered from a bout of dizzy spells. This caused his head to reel and his body was unstable that resulted in his falling down anywhere and at any time. This posed a hazard to his life as he was 66 years old and his going out could result in a fall. He bought himself a stout walking stick and relied on it for support. Even the stick did not ensure that he would be safe as he narrowly escaped falling on the road twice or thrice. He was at his wits' end and feared he would be housebound, or would have to risk falling on the road with the on-coming traffic. Things came to a headon on 3 July 1946, when his head was reeling at night as he lay in bed. Then he prayed to Baba intensely asking for help as he feared going outside the house.

In the early hours of the morning he dreamt of Baba, who appeared as a Judge sitting on a raised platform while Subharao was standing before him. Baba handed him a big packet of Udi that was to be consumed in large quantities. While returning home with the packet, Baba sent another small packet of Udi through another devotee. The devotee placed the packet of Udi in his breast pocket. The result was that with the packet of Udi on his person he was able to climb a huge mound as well as slowly descend on the other side. This brought him into the heart of a big busy city full of life. Subharao understood that if he used the Udi profusely, it would get rid of his dizziness. So he began to keep a small packet next to his body, so that it could protect him and Subharao could continue to do his work. Thus it came to pass.

Ref: *Sai Sudha* Magazine; Vol. 7, Part 4, September 1946

***

HE'S TOLD TO RECITE THE
HANUMAN CHALISA REPEATEDLY

On 17 July 1946 Advocate S. Subharao again fell ill. That morning he got up feeling hot and feverish. On the previous day he had consumed only liquids as he was unwell. That night before he went to bed he meditated on Baba and sought his help. Baba responded to his call and appeared in his dream and made him recite the *Hanuman Chalisa* (a hymn in praise of Lord Hanuman) and asked him to repeat the recitation frequently. With each recitation Subharao felt better and the dream ended. So the next day he did just that; he prayed to Lord Hanuman by reciting the hymn. By the end of the day he was all right.

On the eighteenth he again dreamt of Baba; the dream occurred early in the morning. In the dream he and Baba were invited to a large dinner party. Baba appeared as an Advocate and sat very close to him and enquired about his health. Baba also encouraged him to continue to recite the Hanuman Chalisa. Subharao was touched by Baba's concern and kindness. He states that Baba helped him overcome his major and minor ailments. He felt that the dream proved that Baba and Lord Hanuman are one and the same.

An interesting anecdote about Lord Hanuman is given in chapter 45 of *Sreepada Sreevallabha Charitra*. Sreepada meets Hanuman absorbed in chanting Lord Ram's name and the following conversation takes place between them. "You have transcended time and have become immortal. You have to incarnate in this Kali Yuga, that is, fourth or Iron Age, commencing before the Christian era and ends with the destruction of the world. You are a part of me." Then Hanuman replied, *Amsavatars* (divine descent) merge with their original nature after completing their mission on earth, and lose their value and importance. But the Amsavatar that I am going to take must be constantly connected to the *Moola Twatta*, that is, the root or the source. I should possess all the wealth of strength and power of your ancient moola twatta. Then Sreepada replied, "After I have completed my Swami Samaratha incarnation, when the time comes I will incarnate into you and reign as Sainath. I will announce unequivocally that my incarnation is within you. And you will be famous as *Samartha Sadguru*", that is, manifestation of divinity in human form.

Hanuman replied, "You are Lord Datta himself, non-duality will be accomplished when we become one. So grant me absorption into the essential nature of Lord Datta." Sreepada decided that on Datta Jayanthi, the consciousness in Hanuman would be transformed into Lord Datta. And thus it came to pass.

Ref: *Sai Sudha* Magazine; Vol. 7, Part 4, September 1946

***

July 4

BABA IS AWARE OF HER VALVE REPLACEMENT

(The next two leelas are how Baba showed his concern for Sunita during her pre- and post-operative period)

Sunita Arote resided in Mumbai with her husband and daughter. Lately she had been feeling tired and had shortness of breath. Thus she got admitted in Bombay Hospital for a 'checkup'. After she had a complete workup the doctor told her husband that Sunita's left mitral valve was not functioning properly and it would have to be replaced. He also told him that the surgery was risky in her current weakened condition. Nonetheless it would have to be performed as soon as possible.

Sunita's husband broke the news to her very gently and reassured her that Baba was there to look after her. Sunita burst into tears and cried her heart out, but they had to make a decision and fix a date for the surgery. Finally the date was set, and two days prior to the surgery she was admitted for the pre-operative workup. She had brought a small photograph of Baba that she kept on the table next to her. She also had Udi and Baba's *Astothar* (the 108 names of Baba) that she read daily.

On the day prior to surgery she had a vivid dream, wherein she was admitted in a huge ward with many patients. There were numerous people there and she lay quietly watching them. Then a small boy about 8 years old made his way through the crowd and came forward shouting, "Who is Arote from Shirdi?" Sunita lifted her hand as she had resided in Shirdi prior to her marriage and said, "I am Arote from Shirdi." Then he said, "Baba has sent me to ask you which valve of yours is to be replaced. Is it the right valve or the left valve? She replied, "The doctor told me that the left valve is to be replaced." After hearing her reply the small boy left. When her husband came to meet her she narrated the dream to him. Her husband told her not to worry as Baba was fully aware of her surgery. Sunita was now confident that Baba's grace was with her and nothing could go wrong.

On the day of the surgery she got ready early in the morning and prayed to Baba. Then she read the Astothar and the room was filled with Baba's aroma. Sunita then felt confident that Baba was indeed there to look after her. Needless to say the surgery was successful.

Ref: *Sai Prasad* Magazine; 1998 (*Deepavali* Issue)

***

July 5

BABA TOOK GOOD CARE OF HER

Sunita Arote had her mitral valve replaced in Bombay Hospital; her husband was anxiously waiting outside for the doctor. Finally the doctor met him and told him that the operation was a success. He thanked the doctor profusely then shed tears of gratitude at Baba's feet. Sunita was in the I.C.U. for a week and later shifted to her room. In the room she was sponged and her personal hygiene was taken care of. The nurse had sent a very young student nurse to comb her hair. The student nurse was about 13 years old. Sunita was surprised to see such a young nurse. She conversed with her; the student told her that her name was Joythi. Sunita then asked her where she resided. Joythi replied, "I live in Shirdi and my home is next to the Samadhi Mandir." Sunita immediately replied, "I too live in Shirdi." Then the student left. Sunita pondered over the conversation thinking, "But there is no house adjacent to the Samadhi Mandir." Joythi came every morning and evening and took very good care of her.

On the fourth day Sunita felt very well and she awaited Joythi's arrival but another nurse turned up. Immediately Sunita asked her, "Why hasn't the student nurse Joythi come today?" The nurse said, "Which student nurse? There is no nurse called Joythi." In wonder Sunita replied, "Joythi who lives in Shirdi." The nurse again said, "My dear there is no nurse called Joythi who lives in Shirdi working with us," and she left.

Then it dawned on her that Baba had appeared as the little boy and the young Joythi to take care of her. Her eyes filled with tears at Baba's kind caring compassion.

Ref: *Sai Prasad* Magazine; 1998 (*Deepavali* Issue)

***

July 6

MY CHARITA ISN'T A PILLOW; READ AND UNDERSTAND IT

A M. Narshima Prasad is now a healthy 70-year-old man, but in September 2006 the chances of his survival were slim. He was an atheist and drank alcohol from the moment he awakened till the moment he went to sleep at night. His wife was devoted to Baba, and he often drove her to the Sai Baba temple and waited outside the temple for her.

In the month of September he was rushed to the hospital as he was getting drowsy and losing consciousness. He was admitted and his blood tests were done. At that time his abdomen was bloated as it was full of fluid and his liver was totally damaged by alcoholic cirrhosis. The doctor told his family to take him home as he would not survive for more than 2 days. He further stated that the liver enzymes were so high that even a liver transplant would fail. As Prasad was slipping into a coma he was kept in the hospital and palliative treatment was started.

His friend Nagesh Reddy came to visit him and brought a *Sai Satcharita* along with him. Seeing Prasad's serious condition Nagesh kept the book on his chest and prayed for his survival. Prasad, however, took the book and kept it under his pillow as he did not plan to read it. Then he slipped into a coma. At midnight he opened his eyes and asked for food and re-lapsed into a coma. The doctor was informed and treatment was continued. 48 hours later Prasad again opened his eyes and asked for a meal, and again became comatosed. Thus 60 hours had passed; it was then that Baba appeared and touched him on his shoulder and asked him to come with him. Then he took him to the bathroom and helped him wash his feet; then he took him back to the room. Baba seated him on a chair and stood behind him and passed his hands over his body. Baba told him "My *Chaitra* is given to you not to be used as a pillow; it has to be read and understood. You have a lot of work to do, so I will cure you." Then Baba disappeared. Prasad, immediately started reading the Chaitra, and completed reading it by 6 a.m. The doctors were astounded to see him sitting up and reading. Needless to say his blood tests came back normal, and he is healthy. He now does *annadan*, distributes clothes and blankets to the needy, and follows Baba's teachings. He neither drinks nor smokes, and is an ardent devotee of Baba.

Ref: As related by Shankrayya

***

July 7

UMAPATHI FOUND AND BROUGHT HOME

On 26 January 1944, 10-year-old Umapathi, the son of S. Kasi Viswanadhan residing at Secunderabad was missing from home, at about 2 o'clock. A thorough search proved futile. The next morning the police was informed and every hospital was contacted about the missing child. The father in his anxiety feared that the child may have been run over by the military vehicles that were plying the streets. Or worse he might have been kidnapped. In desperation he consulted an astrologer and a palmist who assured him that the boy was safe.

Since December 1940, Kasi had been praying to Baba, so he sought his grace and prayed fervently. His agony was compounded by the fact that just a year ago his eldest son aged 13 had succumbed to typhoid fever. Six days passed since the boy was missing. At last Kasi stood in front of Baba's photograph and said, "If it's my lot to lose my child due to past bad karma, I will try to bear it. But how can I bear the thought of someone attributing this mishap to me solely for worshipping you." On 1 February 1944 he cried out to Baba saying, "Whether my son is found or not, whether you give me more suffering and agony, whether the worst fate may befall me, I have sought refuge at thy lotus feet and I shall not budge an inch. Let thy will be done." Kasi felt calm and fell asleep.

At 4 o'clock he had a dream which he narrated as follows: "a tall white-robed fakir was beating a boy and dragging him towards me. Then he made him sit by my side and he served us confectionary and made us eat them." The next morning just as he stepped out of the house, the post man delivered a telegram which stated "Umapathi brought home safely." He later found out that the boy had gone in search of his mother who had gone to Chennai for a short time. Luckily the boy boarded the correct train and reached Chennai, where the police took him into custody as a missing person. And he was brought back by his brother-in-law.

Surprisingly he boarded the correct train or else would have reached Delhi. Secondly throughout this period the child never went hungry as he was being fed by someone or the other throughout his journey.

"We are like Umapathi who runs away from our true home, that is, the Sadguru's feet, and needlessly search here and there. And the Guru knows that we are harming ourselves, so he resorts to either granting our wishes or gives us some sorrow and drags us back. Then he removes it and seats us beside him and gives us confectionary to eat."

Ref: *Sai Sudha* Magazine; Vol. 5, Part 4, September 1944

***

| July 8 |

MUTE GIRL'S FIRST WORD IS "SAI BABA"

Although Rajalakshmi was 9 years old, she spoke not a single word as she was dumb from birth. Her father T.R.S. Mani was extremely dejected about her future. He was devoted to Baba and found solace in him. On the night of 28 March 1942 he dreamt of Baba who ordered him to come to Shirdi and worship his Samadhi. Immediately he and his daughter went to Shirdi. He took his daughter to the Samadhi Mandir; the little girl clapped her hands with joy and cried out, "Sai Baba, Sai Baba." Rajalakshmi then started going to school and day after day her speech started improving. How apt this leela is, "We devotees have to first silence this chatter that goes on continuously, by keeping silent. Only then it's possible to silence the mind. Thus it was but natural that her first words were "Sai Baba." Baba asked Dixit to stay upstairs in his wada for 9 months in solitude. The number 9 represents the unalterable or the eternal *Parabrahma*

In 1944 he again visited Shirdi and presented a Benaras silk shawl worth 500 rupees, and a silver lamp of the height of his daughter. Now his daughter is an ardent devotee, and she sings all the hymns of Baba

Once, T. R. S. Mani, had an urgent task of depositing some money. The money was in two bags. One bag contained nickel change of 50 rupees, and another bag contained silver change of 50 rupees. He set out at 4 a.m. with the bags tied to his waist. Unfortunately it was very dark and there was no moonlight or any street lights along the desolate way. He walked along the side of the road, chanting Baba's name. Suddenly the bags got untied and the cash scattered hither and thither. He thought, "If I leave this place to get a lamp it would be unwise as some passerby may strike his foot against the coins and carry them away." So he sat down and waited.

A short while later, someone came along and remarked that the money aught to have been secured within the waist cloth more carefully. The stranger bent down to help him and strangely while he was doing this the sky lit up as if it was dawn. Mani could clearly see the coins that he gathered. The stranger asked, "Where is the bus stand?" As Mani did not reply, he left and again darkness fell. It was then that he realised that the kind man was Baba. Who else could change the darkness into dawn and back again to the original time.

Ref: *Sai Sudha* Magazine; Vol. 5, part 7, September 1944

***

BABA APPLIES UDI ON HIS FOREHEAD

Sashi Prabha resided with her husband in Pune while her family resided in Madhya Pradesh. Her great grandfather had started praying to Baba way back in the 1920s.

Her husband did believe in Baba but was opposed to the idea of saying "Baba did this and Baba did that incessantly which many Sai devotees do." Sashiprabha's nature was just the opposite; she acknowledged and thanked Baba for every deed in her life. It was her habit to apply Udi on her forehead every night before they went to sleep. But on the forehead of her husband she did apply but rather hesitantly as he might scold her.

There was a picture of Baba above their bed. Once she couldn't apply Udi because of her 'periods' she stood in front of the picture and said, "Baba today I cant apply Udi on my husband's forehead, please take care of him through the night." Then she turned on the night lamp and went into the adjacent room to sleep. A few minutes later she saw her husband sit up in bed for a short while then he drank water and went back to sleep.

The next morning he narrated what took place the previous night. He said, "I was not fully asleep when you prayed to Baba and retired for the night. At that moment I felt a huge finger of a man touch my forehead exactly in the spot that you apply Udi every night. I was terrified and sweating, so I got up looked around as there was no one, but there was Udi on my forehead so I drank water and went to sleep." Both of them realised that Baba had applied Udi on his forehead.

Ref: *Shri Sai Sagar* Magazine; 2004 (*Deepavali* Special Issue)

***

BABA SCARES DEATH AWAY

Unfortunately the name of this devotee is not mentioned. He states, "My second daughter was not keeping good health since I got transferred to Calcutta. At that time Baba advised me in a dream to send one rupee to Shirdi. I did this immediately as I have great faith in Baba. I had premonition that something terrible would happen to my daughter. On the night of 27 April 1941, the child's condition was going from bad to worse. We prayed to Baba and put Udi in the child's mouth and rubbed some on her body. I could not sleep because I was extremely anxious. At 2:30 a.m., *Yama* (the lord of death) dressed in black with bells around his waist entered through the front door of my home. Simultaneously Baba came out swiftly from my 'prayer room' and shouted "*Huth, huth*" and drove Yama out of my house. Then at that hour Yama entered the next house and carried away one child. I could hear loud wailing that their child had died. I peeped out of the window and saw a crowd of people, and everyone was lamenting the death of their child. I then woke up my wife and related everything that had happened. Then we bowed down and thanked Baba for his protection. We were thrilled at the fact that Baba was protecting us even after so many years of his taking Maha Samadhi."

Ref: *Sai Sudha* Magazine; Vol. 2, No. 3, August 1941

***

"KNOW WHO YOU ARE THEN YOU WILL KNOW ME"

In June 1947, Narsingarao of Nellore admitted his wife in Government Hospital at midnight, as she had no foetal movements. To make matters worse she was unable to deliver the still born. The doctor removed the baby but his wife developed high fever and convulsions for 12 days.

The next morning he was served a notice of dismissal from his temporary post as a clerk in the Revenue Department. He was at his wits' end as the treatment was expensive, and he was unemployed and penniless. His children were small and there was no one to look after them. As usual he placed his burden on Baba's shoulders; his friends at work paid his hospital bills, and the neighbours took the children home and looked after them.

On the thirteenth day his wife was discharged, but her leg was swollen and painful. Dr. Subbramiaha a friend of Narsingarao treated her free of cost and provided the medicines for her. Gradually she recovered and was able to walk a little. During this period Narsingarao chanted Baba's name continuously and sang hymns in praise of him.

One morning he walked out of his house and saw Baba begging for alms. He was in a state of shock for a short while. Narsingarao then walked up to him and blurted, "Sir, may I know who you are?" He said this in English and Baba also replied in English, "You are a fool; if you know who you are then you will know who I am." Baba in one sentence taught him a great spiritual truth, of *Aham Brahmsa me* (Yajur Veda). To experience the state that I am not the body or mind but *Sakshi*; that is, a witness (*Brahma*).

Then Narsingrao invited Baba to his home and have some food. Baba accepted the invitation saying, "I have come just for that." After Narsingarao had seated Baba comfortably he began to serve him. Baba stopped him from serving and said, "I want your wife to serve me." She managed to serve Baba with a great deal of difficulty. After having eaten he rested for a short while and Narsingarao went to the market to buy some fruits for him. Alas when he returned Baba had disappeared, but Narsingarao's wife was restored to perfect health after this event.

One day Narshingarao's wife was on the way to the market to get Baba's picture framed. Unfortunately she lost it; desperately she searched for it but couldn't find it. She wept bitterly as she felt Baba had left her and some disaster was sure to take place. But no such thing happened; still weeping she went to sleep. That night Baba appeared in her dream and said, "Why are you weeping thus? Here, pick any picture of your choice and worship it daily." The very next day a devotee who had just returned from Shirdi came to her house. He gifted her with the very same picture she had chosen in her dream. They have preserved the picture as a precious gift from Baba. After she received that picture her troubles ceased, both mentally and physically. Her husband secured a permanent job and financially he became well off.

Ref: Ramalingaswami; Ambrosia in Shirdi

***

July 12

HE FOLLOWS BABA TO THE DWARKA MAI

The devotee probably wishes to remain anonymous as he has given the initials of his name as P. S. He was suffering from a disease for a long time in 1950. He consulted various physicians and tried all kinds of treatment but did not get any relief. Then one day he found a photograph of Baba in an old book of medicine and began to worship it. Early in the morning he would go to a park and sit in a secluded place under a tree and meditate. Then he would pray to the photograph and chant the "Astothar."

One night he had an interesting dream wherein, an ascetic resembling Baba was leading him, while he followed. The ascetic took him across hills and streams, a path that was strewn with thorns. It was very difficult for him to follow the ascetic, nonetheless he persisted in following him. At last they reached a *Masjid* (mosque) and the ascetic disappeared. The dream ended there. Soon after this dream he started recovering from his illness and became healthy again.

In 1953 he visited Shirdi and went to the Dwarka Mai and was pleasantly surprised to see all the relics there. He had seen all these relics in the Masjid in his dream in 1950. It was then that he realised that Baba had brought him to his Dwarka Mai. In *Shri Sai Satcharita* chapter 22 Baba talks of his Dwarka Mai thus, "When you sit on her lap she gives you full protection as given to a child. And there then remains no cause for worry. She protects you from grave dangers, and you overcome all difficulties of life." These words Baba said to Baba Sahib Mirkar. In the case of P.S. he made him tread a difficult path to reach the Dwarka Mai. And upon reaching it his Karma's got destroyed and the Dwarka Mai cured his illness and gave him the gift of health.

Ref: *Sai Sudha* Magazine; Vol. 16, Part 12, May 1956

***

July 13

HE MEETS A PERSON WITH LEPROSY AGAIN

A devotee named Narsinghrao accompanied Narsimhaswamiji on one of his visits to Shirdi. On the second day they went to Sakori, at Rahatha where he saw a person afflicted with leprosy who was begging for alms. Then Narsinghrao promised to give him 4 annas when he returned, but he forgot all about it.

Since Biblical times, such unfortunate patients were considered the scum of the Earth and were banished from society. In *Sreepada Charitra* the disease is considered as the highest form of punishment as these patients are filled with lust and cannot control their sexual desires. A snake does not bite such a person as snake venom was administered to them as treatment for the disease." To call a person a leper is a derogatory and unkind term so I have used the term person with leprosy.

Upon returning to Shirdi, Narsinghrao went to the Dwarka Mai and prayed to the photograph there, but the face of leprosy patient appeared in the photograph instead of Baba's face. He ran to Narsimhaswamiji and told him what had just happened. Swamiji advised him to put the 4 annas in the donation box, which he did promptly.

Later he went to the Samadhi Mandir and again the person with leprosy appeared instead of Baba's idol. He was quite perplexed and begged Baba to forgive him, for his apathy and indifference towards the patient. When he was returning home, the bus stopped at the same place and he saw the same person with leprosy in the very same place. The patient came up to him and begged for alms which he readily gave with humility. But it surprised him that there were so many passengers yet the man asked only him for alms.

Baba demonstrated to Narsinghrao his omnipresence. Only the Sadguru has the power to remove such karma. Probably Narsinghrao was to contact the disease in this or his next life and Baba had taken this karma on himself and removed it by taking alms from him. He asked and received alms only from Narsinghrao and did not ask alms from the other passengers.

Ref: *Sai Sudha* Magazine; Vol. 2, No. 3, August 1941

***

$$\boxed{\textit{July 14}}$$

HOW BABA BLESSED MANI SAHUKAR

Mani Sahukar a resident of Mumbai, was going through a difficult period in his life, and was dejected and unhappy. That was in 1942; at that time Narshima Swamiji was in Mumbai and a neighbour brought him to her home. He knew that things were not going well for her. He took her aside and said, "Don't worry. Why don't you take refuge in Sai Baba?" At that time Mani knew nothing about saints and fakirs. She asked, "Who is Sai Baba?" Swamiji placed a packet containing the books written by him in her hand and said, "There is a beautiful picture of Baba in there for you," and blessed her and left. She was touched by his kindness, his advice and gift but was not impressed. She put the packet away and continued to be unhappy.

Her husband, however, read one of the books and was totally impressed. He said, "Sai Baba seems to be a great saint. Why don't you read these books they might help you," but she remained unmoved. After a few days she took out the picture and got it framed and placed it on the night stand next to her bed. This she did to please her husband. The next afternoon as she lay sleeping in her bed, she was blessed with a lovely visitation. Just as she was dozing off to sleep, she saw Baba's picture light up with a translucent glow. Baba in the picture suddenly started tenderly smiling at her. Then his hand emerged from the frame and he beckoned her like a mother would to her child. She dreamt that at that moment she jumped out of bed and ran towards him. Baba blessed her by laying his hand on her head.

She woke up with a start and was filled with joy and ecstasy. She was thrilled as she could feel his hand placed gently on her head for a long time. From that moment her life changed and she got a new lease on life. In one stroke her apathy, unhappiness, and dejection all vanished and the seeds of devotion were sown in her heart. After this she never looked back.

Ref: Ramalingaswami; Ambrosia in Shirdi

***

July 15

HOW BABA TREATS HER THROAT AILMENT

In 1950, Mani Sahukar was afflicted by a strange throat ailment that was accompanied with congestion and severe grittiness. Numerous doctors and specialists, both allopathic and homeopathic, could neither diagnose it nor treat it successfully. She was desperate as she sang Classical Hindustani music. She tried every form of treatment without any success. After singing for about 10 minutes her voice would become so hoarse that she would have to stop.

After 6 months of this torture she visited Shirdi and stood before Baba's Samadhi and cried for help. After she came out of the Samadhi Mandir she visited a friend who was staying in the Sansthan premises. She went to her friend's room and spent some time with her. She then returned to her room in Sathe wada at about 7:30 p.m. She opened the lock and entered the room.

As she was removing the pin that fastened her saree to her left shoulder she heard the rustling of paper and a small packet fell on the floor. It was neatly folded as if by a chemist or a doctor. The packet was about two inches long. Perplexed she picked it up and found that it contained six tiny white tablets, which resembled homeopathic medicines. Picking them up, she ran to her friend's room and related everything. Before she could finish her friend said, "You understand, don't you that this is Baba's prasad. What are you going to do with it?" Mani unhesitatingly ingested all the tablets and returned to her room.

When she returned home she found she could sing without any hindrance, pain or congestion of the throat. Her heart overflowed with gratitude, and needless to say she became devoted to Baba.

Ref: Ramalingaswami; Ambrosia in Shirdi

***

July 16

BABA HAD BLESSED HIM ABUNDANTLY

In 1957 A. H. Dharmadakari was studying in Nagpur for his final B. Sc. exam. He had a room on the first floor of Ramdas Peth building; his father was also staying with him at that time. He had some chores to do and as he was exiting the building with his bicycle he noticed an ascetic dressed in an ochre-coloured robe standing outside the building. Looking directly at Dharmadakari he said, "I have come from Shirdi and I am on my way to Kashi, so give me some money for my journey." Dharmadakari informed him that the money belonged to his father and thus could not give it to him. The ascetic said, "You have kept a 10-rupee bill in your book; give that bill to me." Astonished to hear this as no one knew that he had indeed kept a 10-rupee bill in his Chemistry book. Without thinking twice he ran upstairs and gave him the money.

The ascetic then asked him to extend the palm of his hand as he wanted to give him some holy water from Shirdi. The ascetic placed his *Rudraksh* (*Utrasum*) garland on his palm and water flowed out of it, which Dharmadakari drank.

Following this he placed a flower from Baba's Samadhi on his palm and asked him to close his fist, while concentrating on Baba. A short time later he asked him to open his fist and lo the flower was converted into consecrated rice. Then the ascetic blessed him saying, "Henceforth everything in your life will be great as Baba had

211

blessed you abundantly. The Sadguru turns the flower into *Akshada* or consecrated rice, which is symbolic of auspiciousness and prosperity. So in the future Dharmadakari will have no problems in his daily life and his progeny too will be prosperous."

Dharmadakari went upstairs to keep the rice and when he returned the ascetic had vanished and was not to be found although Dharmadakari searched for him everywhere. Indeed since that time no matter what hardships came his way, Baba always took care of him.

Ref: *Shri Sai Leela* Magazine; Vol. 44, No. 6, September 1965

***

July 17

HOW HER STOMACH AILMENT WAS CURED

Sushila Nanivadekar, a resident of Mumbai, was devoted to Baba for the past 27 years. Every morning and evening she performed ritualistic worship of Baba. After the worship was completed, she offered Udi to every member of her family to apply on the forehead and take internally. She and her family never left home without Udi.

Sushila was quite content with her life but for one problem; she had bouts of stomachache. Many doctors were consulted and many tests performed but the cause was unclear. The various treatments and diet changes proved futile, and finally she gave up and learned to live with it. Her faith in Baba was unwavering and she made numerous visits to Shirdi. In 1979 she visited Shirdi and had a vivid dream in which she was an old man with a lady by his side. The old man pointed to her and told the lady, "She is troubled with severe pain in her abdomen for a long time. You should take care of her," and there ended the dream. Many times when she visited the Samadhi Mandir she saw that very same lady there. Sushila was eager to ask her who she was but hesitated to do so.

On her next visit to Shirdi that lady happened to sit beside her in the Samadhi Mandir; seizing the opportunity she did ask her. The lady told her she was an employee of the Sansthan and worked in Sainath Hospital. It then dawned on her why Baba was asking that lady to take care of her. Needless to say, after that dream her pain gradually subsided and never bothered her again.

This is *Swapna Dristanth* or curing a person via a dream by taking her karma upon himself. This, Baba can easily accomplish as he is *Kaala Thetha* (one who has transcended time). The lady works in the hospital, but Sushila never goes there. The hospital duty is taken over by Baba on himself and Sushila got rid of her abdominal pain.

Ref: *Shri Sai Leela* Magazine; Vol. 67, No. 10, January 1989

***

$$\boxed{\textbf{\textit{July 18}}}$$

BABA LIFTED AND PLACED HIM IN A CORNER

At the onset of the monsoon, Madhukar Vkare a resident of Badlapur decided to clean the roof of his home. He was concerned that the electrical wires running to his home were all right and free of any debris. He worried about an accidental 'short circuit' and a fire resulting from it.

The front of his home had an awning about 6 feet high while the roof top was about 15 ft high. He climbed on the roof and cleaned it thoroughly, but he slipped and fell and with him the awning fell with an explosive sound. The awning was supported by huge wooden pillars and was made of metal sheets that were cemented over. Hearing the noise his neighbours ran to help him. There was a huge pile of debris, and everyone feared the worst.

Madhukar was found standing safely in a corner, unhurt. He said, "Just as I was falling, I saw a bright dazzling light before my eyes and then I felt someone lifting me and placing me in this corner. The only recollection I have is that the person whose hands lifted me was clad in a white kafni." Then he went inside and stood before Baba's photograph and thanked him for saving his life, and the lives of both his small children. His children had just returned from school a few minutes before the awning fell. They had entered the house to

213

keep their school bags; had they been under the awning they would have been crushed to death.

Ref: *Shri Sai Leela* Magazine; Vol. 67, No. 10, January 1989

***

July 19

HOW BABA'S IDOL CAME TO HIS HOME

It was under an unusual circumstance that Baba's clay idol came to be housed in his home. Eknath Dharmaji Kamble was an atheist while his wife was devoted to Baba. His neighbour Ravindra Joshi was a dear friend and an ardent devotee of Baba. Joshi had bought a small shrine and placed it in his prayer room, and then his wife went and bought the clay idol. When she brought the idol home, she found to her utter dismay that the idol was about 2 inches taller than the shrine. Now Joshi was faced with a dilemma of what should be done with that idol. His friends suggested the immersion of the idol, but Joshi was totally against it.

Joshi asked Usha Kamble if she would accept the idol, and she readily accepted. The next day while Eknath was at work, Joshi went immediately and got a carpenter to make a shelf to seat Baba. Then with all rituals Baba was housed on the shelf and *peda* (confectionary made of milk and sugar) was distributed to everyone. After all the ceremonies were completed Usha started crying as her husband would soon return home and would be upset and angry when he saw Baba's idol in the house. So the Joshi family stayed with her so they could bear the brunt of his anger and hopefully pacify him. Joshi placed a peda in Eknath's hand and told him everything. Eknath said, "You are a dear friend so I will not offend you by refusing the peda. However, do not expect me to pray or take care of the idol." Thus, Baba came to stay in his home. This event was followed by a lot of squabbles and bickering between husband and wife. Usha, however, looked after the idol and prayed to it sincerely.

Ref: *Shri Sai Leela* Magazine; Vol. 68, No. 9, April 1989

***

THE DOOR BELL RANG EVERY TIME HE FELT SLEEPY

A few weeks later, Kamble heard that the Departmental exams were to be held soon, which if he passed would enable him to get a higher post and a pay raise. A week later the date for the exam was announced. He decided to do his best and set up a time table for his study. But he could not concentrate, as there was no peace at home; the time for the exam was too short, and the course to be covered was too long. One day out of desperation he began to cry in front of Baba's idol, "Baba, to progress at work and get a better income for my family I want to pass this exam. If I do pass I will stay alive, but if I do not pass I will commit suicide and end it all. Baba if there is no peace and harmony at home then why should I keep your idol here?" Now there were 15 days left for the exam, and there was peace in the house. His routine was to go to sleep early and get up at 2 a.m. to study. Kamble was tired and anxious, so if he felt drowsy he would have a shower and resume studying. One night, he was overcome with sleep, so he took a nap. He was startled when the door bell rang; it was 3 a.m. He went and opened the door hesitantly but there was no one at his door. So he continued studying.

As the exams drew near, his wife Usha was extremely anxious and seized by doubts. She worried that he may fail, and carry out his threat. She prayed to Baba continuously. One afternoon a fakir dressed like Baba came to her door. She ran inside and found a rupee coin and gave it to him; he held it in his hand for a short while and returned it. So she got some wheat and lentils and gave it to him. The fakir did not accept it and said, "I have not come to beg alms from you, but to tell you this. Why do you worry so much? Your husband will definitely pass the exam. Be calm and peaceful. Everything will be all right." When her husband came home she narrated everything to him. Kamble did not pay attention to her and continued studying.

Every night if he yawned the bell rang, it continued to ring every time he got drowsy and nodded off to sleep. Even if he took a break or a 'cat nap' the bell rang loud and clear. It was as if someone was watching him from the outside. Indeed it was Baba watching his every move.

Ref: *Shri Sai Leela* Magazine; Vol. 68, No. 9, April 1989

***

July 21

AFTER HIS EXAMS THE DOOR BELL STOPPED RINGING

Kamble was determined to find out who was ringing the bell so persistently. He asked his neighbours if they had rung the bell. All of them looked at him strangely and said, "Who would get up at that hour and ring your bell. One night he sat outside his door, right under the bell. He nodded of to sleep and again the bell rang, but there was no one there. Finally the examinations took place and he passed the written exam. Next there was the oral exam, which was to be held a week later. So he started preparing for it with renewed vigour. Every night the bell rang and woke him so that he could study. Kamble passed the oral exam with flying colours. That night he slept soundly; the bell had stopped ringing. Then he realised that Baba had been ringing the bell, so that Kamble could study. He was overwhelmed with love, devotion and repentance so he promised to take his family to Shirdi.

Due to the responsibilities of his new post he was unable to do so. Kamble states, "I am a Buddhist by religion. This leela occurred in 1988. I did not write about it thus far, nor tell anyone because I feared they would make fun of me."

Ref: *Shri Sai Leela* Magazine; Vol. 68, No. 9, April 1989

***

216

THE MAN FORCED THE PACKET OF MONEY ON HIM

Nandani Kamble states, "During the early 1950s very few people in Mumbai were aware of Baba's divinity and the spiritual atmosphere of Shirdi. But in our family we had a picture of Baba in our prayer room, and we knew that Baba could come to our aid in difficult times." Her father had gone to Shirdi in 1915 along with his uncle and had prostrated at Baba's feet when he was about 6 years old. Unfortunately his name is not mentioned.

One evening a friend of his came home and informed him that he was going to Shirdi a few days later and asked her father and mother to accompany him. He said he would be staying in Shirdi for 3 days, and if her mother also came along her arthritic pains would disappear after she returned. "My father liked the idea very much but the question of finances weighed on him. He was the only earning member and had a large family to look after. Although at that time the room rent in the Sansthan and meals cost a minimal amount, he still had to buy two tickets for the train journey to Shirdi.

Her father worked in the Port Trust and would return home at night fall. Two days prior to his date of departure, he was returning home at night when a Parsee gentleman came hurriedly towards him from behind and said, "Sir your packet has fallen out of your pocket so pick it up." He turned around and saw a packet on the ground and replied that it wasn't his packet and walked on. The gentleman insisted that he had seen it falling from his pocket. Finally the gentleman picked it up and thrust it in his pocket and disappeared. My father returned home with the packet and handed it over to my mother. She opened it and found 60 rupees in it. That was the exact amount for the train fare of two tickets to Shirdi. Both of them looked at each other and knew that Baba had given them the fare. Thus, they went to Shirdi and had a wonderful trip.

When her mother was returning home she wanted the Arati book *Sainath Sagunopasana*. But it was out of stock at that time. It was also not available in the bookshops in Mumbai. A few days later the postman delivered a small parcel to them. They opened it and found the Arati book in it. Who could have sent it?

The address in the front was their address but the senders name was not mentioned, just the Shirdi post mark was clearly visible. My father hadn't given his address to anyone, so he decided that Baba had sent it. He treasured it as Baba's prasad, and it is still preserved in our home."

Ref: Sai Prasad Magazine; 1994 (Deepavali Issue)

***

```
July 23
```

KABIR UNDERGOES MAJOR SURGERY

Her son Kabir aged 10 was to have major surgery for thiospondilitis, and his mother Sumangala Vaid was worried about it. She worried how Kabir would bear the pain post surgery, and where would they get the money to pay the hospital bills. Suddenly she heard someone at her door; there was a fakir who asked her to give him 25 paise. She didn't have any change, so she gave him a 2-rupee bill, but he insisted that he wanted only 25 paise. She searched in vain and finally he accepted the bill and left. She was surprised that he didn't go to any other apartment, and then she realised that it was Baba. After this incident she got money easily from numerous friends for the surgery. In April 1999 the surgery was conducted successfully. The doctor told her that she would have to take utmost care of him for the next four days and then maybe he would be able to bear weight of his feet. To the surprise of the doctors Kabir started walking on the third day.

The reason for his rapid recovery was Baba's grace and Udi. A day prior to surgery a devotee named Appa Shelke dreamt of Baba. Baba said, "Are you still sleeping. Get up, the boy is sick." Appa had a grandson and he was fine, so he went back to sleep. Then he heard the same words again so he thought it was his imagination and fell asleep. The third time Baba said, "Are you going to get up or should I whack you with my satka."

Appa went to his daughter's home and found his grandson in good health. His next stop was Shivaji Nager temple; there he asked

218

Baba to solve the puzzle and let him know who was sick. Then he heard some devotees voicing their concern about Kabir's surgery. Now where was he admitted? As soon as he exited the temple a rickshaw driver said, "Come I will take you to K.E.M. Hospital and drove him there without accepting the fare. Now where was Kabir admitted in such a huge hospital? There he met a nurse who said, "You must be looking for Kabir," and took him to his bedside. Appa then gave Sumangala, Baba's Udi and wished her son a speedy recovery and left. He knew that when Baba wanted something he made the impossible possible.

Ref: Shri Sai Sagar Magazine; 2003 (Deepavali Issue)

***

July 24

BABA APPLIES UDI ON KABIR'S FOREHEAD

In April 2002 Kabir had to undergo another major surgical procedure for thiospondilitis. The surgery was successful but Kabir was in a great deal of pain and cried continuously. Sumangala tried to comfort him but he continued to cry. A gentleman wearing a white suit entered his ward and said, "Just apply some Udi on his forehead and he will stop crying." Sumangla wondered how he knew that she was devoted to Baba besides she didn't have Udi with her at that time. The gentleman then took out a packet of Udi from his pocket and applied some on Kabir's forehead. The packet was from the Shivaji Nager's temple convention that had taken place a short while ago. He then said, "I visit the Shivaji Nager temple and also walk with the palkhi to Shirdi." As Kabir had quietened down Sumangala thanked him and asked him his name. He replied, "Does it matter what my name or surname is? My daughter is admitted in room number 24 and I came to see her. While passing by I heard your child crying so I came in. Sangita Patil a devotee who visits Shivaji Nager temple had told me about your son's surgery so I came to visit him also." Then the man ran his fingers through Kabir's hair with love and left.

As Kabir was sleeping comfortably Sumangala went to visit the gentleman's daughter but the room was locked. She inquired where the patient had gone. The nurse said that no one had been admitted there for the past week. A week later she met Sangita and asked her about the gentleman who came to visit Kabir. Sangita in surprise said, "I didn't know that Kabir was undergoing surgery that day then how could I have told anyone about it?"

Sumangala had tears in her eyes; she thanked Baba for being there physically every time Kabir underwent a surgery.

Ref: *Shri Sai Sagar* Magazine; 2003 (*Deepavali* Issue)

***

July 25

"USE THIS *UPARNA* AND WIPE YOUR NOSE"

Parvati Vaid a resident of Mumbai was an ardent devotee and treated Baba like a dear friend. Whatever happened to her, big or small, during the day she told Baba about it. She never asked Baba for materialistic things and whatever happened in her life good or bad she accepted it as Baba's blessing. Every morning she knelt in front of Baba's picture and prayed, "Baba you are my saviour; please don't forsake me. Always keep you hand on my back and caress me."

One night she was fast asleep when the phone rang. It was midnight; startled she woke up. She went to receive the call when she tripped and fell. Her head hit the floor hard, and she began to also bleed profusely from her nose. She said, "O god what am I to do now? With what shall I wipe my nose and stop the bleeding?" At that very moment she felt someone pass his hand over her back. Simultaneously he gave her a snow white *uparna* (small cloth that is worn over the shoulder) and said, "Here use the uparna to wipe your nose." Instinctively she replied, "The uparna is so clean and white, why spoil it? Give me a handkerchief."

Hearing their mother fall, both her children ran to help her. Her daughter brought her a handkerchief and ice and finally the bleeding stopped. Parvati lay in bed and thought over the incident. Who could have passed his hand over my back and given me the uparna? With immense joy she realised that Baba had finally answered her prayers.

Ref: *Shri Sai Leela* Magazine; Vol. 65, No. 2, May 1986

***

July 26

LORD KRISHNA COMES OUT OF BABA'S IDOL

Around 1996 Zulekha Chadda bought an apartment in Shirdi as she was devoted to Baba. She wanted to spend time in Shirdi reading the *Charita*, and chanting Baba's name. Her dearest friend was Naseem who was an orthodox Muslim; she also came to Shirdi every month but only to collect the room rent that her hotel Sai Village earned. She knew nothing about Baba nor did she bother to visit the temple or the Dwarka Mai.

One day Zulekha asked to accompany her to the Samadhi Mandir. She told Naseem that it was Baba's *Dargha* (mausoleum) thus it was all right to go. Zulekha got passes for the evening Arati and both of them went. They entered the Samadhi Mandir and were right before Baba's idol. Naseem was enraged to see the idol and was angry with Zulekha. She gave Zulekha a piece of her mind and threatened to leave. By that time the Samadhi Mandir was full of devotees and it was impossible to leave. The Arati started and Naseem was still grumbling. Zulekha told her to be quiet for a little while as the Arati was going on.

Suddenly she felt her friend nudging her and saying something. Zulekha turned towards her to tell her to be quiet and was shocked to see her friend. Naseem had tears rolling down her cheeks; her palms were together as in prayer. She said, "Look at Lord Krishna he came out of that idol and is playing his flute. Can't you hear it? It is celestial music, and I have never ever heard such beautiful music in my entire life." Zulekha, however, heard only the evening Arati.

Ref: As narrated by Zulekha

***

SHE SURVIVES THE TERRIBLE TRAIN ACCIDENT

Shraddha (faith) and *Saburi* (patience with fortitude) was Pramodini Joshi's mantra and she lived by it. This leela is ample proof of it. Pramodini was returning home from work along with her friends by the Virarh local train on 17 April 1978. They boarded the train, which was packed to suffocation as two of the previous trains had been cancelled. The train proceeded to the next station when it collided head on with the Ahmedabad Mail. She states, "Somehow the Ahmedabad Mail was on top of their train, crushing it with its impact. Thus all the fans and light bulbs smashed into the passengers, and many were electrocuted. I could hear everyone screaming for water and begging their favourite deity to save their lives. Till the very end I was chanting Baba's name and pleading for my life. The next morning I was taken out of the wreckage and placed amongst all the dead females. I can't remember how I was taken to K.E.M Hospital but I was admitted there. I was taken care of by Dr. Bhavdekar and Dr. Dhir; I stayed in the hospital for 8 agonising months, as my body was crushed beyond recognition.

It was decided that both my feet would have to be amputated from the hip, and my right hand amputated at the shoulder. Then they took me to the O.T., but Baba had other plans. I had to undergo 10 major operations on my feet and my skull was reconstructed with plastic surgery. They also asked me not to look in the mirror. During this time my father passed away from grief as he could not tolerate this tragedy. The most disheartening event was that I lost three of the fingers of my right hand and was left with my thumb and little finger.

For the next 4 years my mother had to take care of me like a little child as I could neither feed myself nor take care of myself, nor could I walk. During this ordeal neither my mother or I lost faith in Baba, we were constantly chanting his name. A lady doctor at K.E.M Hospital rehabilitated me, she fitted me with a Caliper shoe so I could walk independently, she taught me to write with two fingers, and take

222

care of myself. After 8 months of intensive rehabilitation, I wrote the words "Sai Gajana Maharaj".

Then there was no looking back; the Bombay Telephone and the *Mahanagar Telephone* gifted me a Public Telephone Booth, in Borivili. Every day I travel by the Virarh local, to get to the booth, as I am the only earning member. I am sure that Baba and Gajanan Maharaj will take care of me."

Ref: Pramodini D. Joshi; *Saianubhav*

***

July 28

THE PARROT WAS MERRILY SINGING *SAI RAM*

Actor Giriraj Gumatker states, "Baba gave me ample proof of his divinity and supreme spiritual energy and turned a stubborn atheist into an ardent devotee." In 1981 the producer Mr. Kumarsen, of *Sai Baba* a theatrical performance in Marathi requested me to play the role of Baba, as the original actor was ill. "Thus I had a short time to learn my lines and rehearse the part because 9 January 1981 was 'opening night' that too in Mahapshala Goa, where I was born and bred. The dramatic opening was that, I as Baba would be seated with a chillum in one hand and a parrot on my right shoulder in utter darkness, and then slowly the lights would come on. Kumarsen had a pet parrot for this scene, but I had very little time to rehearse with it, and neither did the parrot know me.

Then on the opening night when I went to my seat I realised that the parrot was not there. I groped in the darkness for it but to no avail. I called out to Kumarsen but the countdown for the curtain to go up had started. Maybe it had flown away or flown to the roof top. In desperation I said, "Baba if you are really a supreme power, bring back that parrot and perch it on my right shoulder." The curtain went up and there was a thunderous applause; the audience had accepted me in the role of Sai Baba. Now where was the parrot? I slyly looked at my right shoulder and to my delight the parrot was seated right

223

there merrily singing *Sai Ram*." I thanked Baba from the bottom of
my heart, and this was the first proof of his supreme power."

Ref: Giriraj Gumatker; *Saianubhav*

***

July 29

BABA SPOKE GIRIRAJ'S LINES FOR HIM

Slowly but surely Giriraj's faith in Baba was growing. Then it was
decided that the play was to be enacted in Shirdi and that too on
Ram Navami day. Hoards and hoards of people had gathered there to
see how Giriraj played the role of Sai Baba. Mr. Kumarsen the producer
of the play had permanently assigned him to play the role Sai Baba.

In that play Giriraj had to enact the role of Baba in his youth,
then Baba in his middle age and finally as Baba in his old age, all
this when Baba's popularity was at its zenith. He spoke his lines
well. Then the play entered into Baba's old age; it is then that Giriraj
remembered that Baba had a thunderous voice, but the words failed
to come out. Suddenly his attention was drawn to the footlights, and
he saw Baba's face looking at him intently with a flicker of a smile
on it.

After the play ended he went to the producer who was seated
with his staff and apologised for being unable to speak his lines. The
producer and the staff were congratulating him. They said, "Why are
you apologizing; you did speak your lines and that too extremely
well. It sounded as if Baba himself had spoken them for him." Then
he remembered that Baba indeed had been sitting in front of him and
speaking for him. Finally he states, "If you have shradha and saburi,
Baba will definitely come running to your aid."

Ref: Giriraj Gumatker; *Saianubhav*

***

224

BABA SAID, "MAKE HIM DRESS LIKE ME"

Once my young son, Viraj aged 3 years had a 'fancy dress' competition at school. This was a short while after I had enacted the role of Sai Baba. My wife, Vidya had given his name for the competition, so she asked for my suggestion. I told her not to worry as there was plenty of time left. I really did not pay any heed to her, and went about doing my work.

One evening I was walking home when I saw a photograph of Baba hanging on a neem tree. There were a group of people there and they were performing Arati to it. I stood there for some time and wondered when this photograph had been placed there. Why had I never seen it? The fact was that I did not pay any attention to it. Nonetheless I paid homage to it and turned to walk home.

"Arre, make him dress like me," I heard Baba distinctly say this to me. Stunned, I looked around but there was no one in sight. Then I thought, why can't I dress Viraj up as Baba? My wife was at the door and was frantically telling me that the competition was on the next day. I assured her that I would personally dress Viraj like Baba for the competition, and that is what I did. Viraj returned from school happy that he had won the first prize. Since then I have happily and successfully dressed up my friends' children like Baba for competitions and plays. But that voice saying, "Arre. Make him dress like me," still rings in my ears.

Ref: Giriraj Gumatker; *Saianubhav*

***

225

THE MAN HELPED HIM REDEEM HIS MONEY

Pandit K. Rajdhan was a famous music composer of Marathi music and lived in style. In outward appearance he looked affluent as he owned two cars and a beautiful home. In reality, sometimes he was unable to get 100 rupees to spend but his wife was optimistic and would say, "Don't worry Baba will surely find a way out."

Between 1974 and 1978, Rajdhan had to face some difficult times, and he constantly worried about his income. Once he needed some money to pay his bills and he asked his wife how much money she had; he was aghast to hear that she had only 100 rupees. He was extremely dejected and wondered where the money would come from. As he was at his wits' end, he prayed, "Baba only you can save me."

At that very moment the door bell rang and a Life Insurance Agent was there asking him to buy an Insurance policy from him. What irony here he was pinching pennies and that man was asking him to buy a policy for 500 rupees. He vehemently refused, the agent asked him, "Why not." Rajdhan told him he already had some policies but was unable to redeem any money from them. The agent asked Rajdhan to show them to him as he would help him get his money back. Untrustingly Rajdhan thrust his file at him. The agent carefully went through the file and told what amount he was eligible for on each policy, but that Rajdhan would have to go to the company Head Office to collect the amount; saying this the agent left. The next day Rajdhan did exactly as he was told and finally got a sum of 15,000 rupees. He wondered who that man was who had visited them; he had not told Rajdhan his name nor did he ever call or return to sell any policy. Rajdhan says, "Of course it was Baba. I do not fear the darkness as I have lit the lamp of love for Baba in my heart."

Ref: Pandit K. Rajdhan; *Saianubhav*

***

BABA GIVES MALTI A MANTRA IN HER DREAM

So vivid was the dream that Malti S. Bhosle, residing at Pune, remembers every detail of it even today. In the dream she was in a bus bound for Shirdi; suddenly she remembered that she did not have any money with her. Her sister-in-law who was sitting beside her said, "Don't worry I have enough money with me;" at that moment they reached Shirdi and alighted from the bus. Malti didn't know which way to proceed when she saw Baba sitting on a stool. He looked directly at her and said, "If you want peace, shall I tell you what you have to do? Just keep chanting *Aum Sainath, Jai Sainath* continuously." Her sister-in-law said, "Look Baba is wearing a shawl on which Mohamed Khan is inscribed. So Muslim's also must be coming to him," to which Baba said, "For me every devotee of every caste, community and religion is equal. Every night I cover myself with every shawl that is offered to me," and the dream ended there.

Malti had this wonderful dream in the year 1981, and since then she longed and yearned to go to Shirdi. Finally she did visit Shirdi and the reason was that for a long time she was suffering from hematemesis (a disease characterised by bouts of vomiting blood). Every possible investigation was done, every possible specialist was consulted, and every possible mode of treatment given but with no result. She and her entire family were worried about her health. At Shirdi, Malti cried before Baba's idol, saying, "Baba please let the bleeding stop by the time I return home to Pune. This is my only request." She had a wonderful stay at Shirdi, and the wondrous fact was that she stopped bleeding by the time she reached Pune, and never again suffered from the disease.

Malti states, "Regarding the mantra that Baba gave in my dream, I try my level best to say it each and every day. Sometimes I am

227

unable to do so, nonetheless Baba has not let my disease return, and I am eternally grateful to him."

Ref: *Shri Sai Leela* Magazine; Vol. 65, No. 7, October 1986

***

August 2

HER X-RAYS BECAME NEGATIVE WITHOUT MEDICATIONS

This leela was also experienced by Malti S. Bhosle, a resident of Pune. In 1984 Malti was suffering with a bout of chronic cough. It was a persistent, hacking, wheezy cough and she coughed both day and night. Malti had never heard anybody cough the way she coughed in her entire life. Her concerned family took her to doctor who gave cough medicines and lozenges to suck on but it didn't work. Then the doctor got her chest X-ray taken, and she was told that she had tuberculosis of the lungs. Malti felt as if the very ground on which she stood had given way and she had fallen into an abyss.

Her family thought it was best to get a second opinion, so they consulted a pulmonary specialist who got another X-ray taken, and confirmed the diagnosis. He advised her to go to Mumbai and referred her to a hospital; he told her that she would have to take treatment for a period of 3 months without missing a single dose. Malti was very upset as she could not bear the thought of leaving her children behind. She returned home and in desperation started taking Udi orally. Then on Thursday, she placed her head at Baba's feet and cried, "Baba you are my only refuge; I need a miracle to happen; when I have my X-ray taken again next week I want it to turn out to be negative."

A week later she got the X-ray done and the doctor was shocked to see that it was negative. So he got all the films together and checked and compared each one and told her it was a miracle as this film is negative. When he said the word "miracle" Malti again saw Baba sitting on the stool for a few seconds. Malti said, "I know that each one has to bear the karmic burden of this life, but when Baba is there to lighten the burden why should I panic. Baba's Udi is the panacea for all sicknesses."

Ref: *Shri Sai Leela* Magazine; Vol. 65, No. 7, October 1986

***

August 3

AND THE WHEEL DIDN'T CRUSH HIS HEAD

They were returning from their farm when this incident took place. On 24 December 1988 Jyothsana Patil had taken her 3-year-old son, Sai to her farm in Alibaugh, Raigad. Her husband had gone at dawn to fill numerous sacks with the harvested rice. The sacks were then loaded on to a bullock cart; Sai sat on one of the sacks and they proceeded home. His parents were walking behind the cart.

They had gone a short distance when Sai slipped of the sack and fell behind one of the bulls, right in front of the wheel. The cart was moving; his mother saw this and screamed, "Baba save my son." Baba heard her plea and the bulls stopped in their tracks. The wheel, however, had passed over Sai's hand and was about to crush his head. Sai's father immediately got under the cart and lifted the wheel as much as he could. The farmers in the neighbouring fields heard Sai's mother shout and rushed to help. The farmers lifted the wheel off his hand and someone extricated his hand from beneath the cart. Sai's hand was fractured and his forehead was bruised by the wheel. Joythsana can only imagine what would have happened if the cart filled with sacks of rice had gone over her child's head. She immediately thanked Baba for saving her child from a terrible accident that would have surely caused death. Sai was treated for 8 days by the doctor and his fractured hand was placed in a plaster cast. Soon his bruises healed and he was fine. Everyone was wonder struck by this miracle.

Ref: *Shri Sai Leela* Magazine; Vol. 68, No. 8–9, November–December 1989

***

HER TUMOUR WAS BENIGN

For the past 2 years Neeta Seth's voice was slightly hoarse. And although her throat hurt a little she did not pay much heed to it. She was busy with her work and had little time to get it checked so she kept postponing going to the doctor. Then suddenly one day she became voiceless; her lips moved but not a sound came out. Then she panicked and wondered what had happened to her. She got herself checked by various doctors and faithfully took the prescribed medicines without any improvement. Two weeks passed with no results; then she tried alternative medicines and consulted an ayurvedic and homeopathic doctor and took their medicines but she could not produce a single sound. Then an otolaryngologist diagnosed her with having a small growth on her wind pipe. She was shocked to hear this and she started worrying about it day and night.

One day her sister, an ardent devotee of Baba, told her to seek refuge in Baba. She said, "Every morning put a pinch of Udi in water and drink it; also apply a little to your forehead. And light a lamp with clarified butter before Baba and earnestly pray to him." Neeta did as she was told and in a few days her voice returned and the pain in her throat also ceased. Her father was delighted but concerned; he suggested that she should have the growth checked. The doctor agreed with her father and scheduled a bronchoscopy. Under anaesthesia a bronchoscope was inserted in her wind pipe and the growth was removed and sent to pathology. Neeta had to wait for a few days for the report, and she was worried. "What if the growth is cancerous? What side effects would she undergo after chemotherapy?" She again sought refuge in Baba and prayed that her growth not be cancerous. She promised Baba that if the growth was benign she would visit Shirdi and gratefully cover his Samadhi with a beautiful shawl. Finally the report came and it was a benign growth. Neeta kept her promise and since then she has had no problems, and is Baba's ardent devotee.

Ref: *Shri Sai Leela* Magazine; Vol. 68, No. 8–9, November–December 1989

***

"TAKE CARE OF YOUR PARENTS AND YOU WILL PROSPER"

Sandhya Samant a resident of Dadar, Mumbai had this dream early one morning. "*Jai Gurudev Datta,*" (Hail Lord Datta Guru) he said in a resounding voice in her dream. She saw a tall man standing at the door; he had an ochre-coloured cloth tied around his head, and wore a white shirt and dhoti. His forehead was marked with a *Tripund* (three horizontal lines of Lord Shiva), and his face shone with a bronze aura around it. She asked him to come in and be seated as she was making a grocery list. She murmured the items that she needed; hearing this, the man said, "Are you preparing for a *Satya Narayan* puja (ceremonial worship of Lord Satya Narayan)?" He went on to bless her saying that everything would be fine with her. As soon as he blessed her she woke up. Early next morning Sandhya related her dream in detail to everyone in her family.

At about 7 a.m. she heard the same voice, saying "Jai Gurudev Datta." Her mother-in-law said, "Someone is at the door taking the Lord's name. Run and open the door." Sandhya opened the door and there stood the same man she had seen in her dream a few hours ago. There was a cot near the door and he sat on it and asked them to continue with their morning chores. They offered him a cup of tea that he drank. Her father in law had just completed his morning worship and came into the room, followed by her husband.

He asked Sanjay, Sandhya's husband, to bring a flower that was offered during the worship. Sanjay brought a rose and placed on his outstretched palm; he held it for a few minutes then asked Sanjay to put it back on the altar. He placed his hand on Sanjay's head, blessed him, and then said, "Take good care of your parents. The more care you take of your parents the more you will prosper," and left. Sanjay went in and picked up the rose and found a large shiny silver coin with the imprint of Baba's padukas on it like the one sold in the Sansthan beneath the rose.

Ref: Sandhya Savant; *Saianubhav*

***

BABA SENDS A HELICOPTER TO RESCUE THEM

In Worli, Mumbai there is a fort that was built by Shivaji Maharaj by the sea, and in the left courtyard is a beautiful temple of Baba. Adjacent to the fort is *Kohli* (fishermen) wada, that is, the place where the fishermen community live. Early one morning Andral Kohli and his son set out to sea; at about 8 a.m. they reached the middle of the sea and cast their nets. The father and son were engrossed in conversation, unaware that dark menacing clouds were gathering overhead. And before they realised it, the sea turned turbulent and they were caught in a storm. To make matters worse, it started raining in torrents. Before long their boat sank and Andral and his son were far away from the coast. They looked around for help but all the other fishermen had left.

Andral and his son prayed desperately to Baba to save their lives. When Andral realised that they would not make it to the shore, he regretfully said, "Babu I have never ever missed Baba's noon Arati; no matter what, I have always managed to attend it. Today I will miss it, as our boat has sunk and there is no way we will reach the shore. Today I will say it in my mind as this will be my last Arati." Then he embraced his son, as he knew that he would drown soon, and continued praying.

At that very moment an Air Force helicopter was hovering overhead. He wondered if the helicopter was there out of curiosity. But it had come to rescue them; the rescue was accomplished and they were taken to Sea Rock Hotel's Security Department. The officer was devoted to Baba and had a picture of him on his desk. The officer said, "When the weather was turning bad I was restless for some reason. Then I heard a voice say repeatedly, "Look at the sea." I looked through my binoculars and saw you. So I telephoned the Air Force Department to send a helicopter to rescue you. Since you have been at sea for so long, please have a drink."

Andral thanked him for saving their life and refusing the drink said, "I would be glad if the helicopter could drop us off at the Sai

232

Baba temple in the fort near Kholi Wada." The Officer obliged and just as they got down the bell started ringing for the noon Arati. Andral washed himself and dripping wet he went for the Arati. With tears rolling down his checks he stood in front of Baba and began to sing the Arati.

Ref: Andral B. Kohli Garg; *Saianubhav*

***

August 7

"I TROUBLE BABA NEEDLESSLY"

Shrikant Madhukar Pathak, a resident of Mumbai says, "We trouble Baba with our own doings and actions, and he patiently bears with us and helps us in times of need." On 17 April 1989 he was travelling from Pune to Mumbai by the Deccan Express train. On that particular train they have a bogie that gets filled at Lonavala Station. So to have a comfortable journey, Shrikant stepped out of the train at Lonavala before it had halted. While doing so he missed his step and fell in the narrow space between the platform and the train.

Shrikant had the habit of constantly chanting Baba's name and was doing so when he fell. He said, *"Jai Shri Sai Baba,"* and the first wheel of the bogie moved towards him, he repeated it three more times and was about to be crushed to death when the train came to a complete halt." A huge crowd had gathered there as they saw him fall, but Shrikant managed to crawl back on to the platform. His back had a few bruises but there were no serious injuries. The officer, Mohan had also arrived on the scene; he took Shrikant to the Railway hospital where first aid was given to him along with a cup of piping hot tea.

Astonished Mohan said, "For a person of your built it's impossible for you to be alive. Besides, seven people have fallen like you did and no one has survived. You are lucky you got a second chance." Shrikant took out a picture of Baba that he always kept in his purse and said, "Baba is my saviour; time and again I take stupid actions and time and again he saves me from disaster and even death."

Ref: *Shri Sai Leela* Magazine; Vol. 68, No. 8–9, November–December 1989

***

THE TERMITES HAD INVADED BABA'S PHOTOGRAPH

Dr. M. K. Rajgopalachari was gifted a photograph of Baba. At that time he did not know anything about Baba nor was he eager to find out. He gave the photograph to his assistant and asked him to get it framed to put it in his home amongst the other photographs. Early that morning he got a vivid dream, wherein a fakir dressed in a kafni and a cloth tied around his head, entered his bedroom. The fakir walked close to his bed and stood looking at him intently. Rajgopalachari was astonished to see that left leg below the knee had pus and blood oozing out of it, and it dripped on the floor. Concerned that his marble flooring would get stained he got up took the flash light that was close to his bed and looked around. The fakir slowly walked away and left. The floor was fine, so Rajgopalachari went out and searched for him but he was nowhere to be found. He returned to his bed and kept thinking about the incident, and finally fell asleep

The next day he went to his work as usual, but he was preoccupied with the dream. His wife repeatedly questioned him but he gave her evasive answers. But the wound in the fakir's leg obsessed him. That evening he went to his office and saw that his assistant had put up the framed photograph of Baba above his chair. He gasped when he saw that exactly at the site where the pus and blood was oozing, the photograph had been invaded by termites. Immediately he took down the photograph and cleaned it. Then he went to the framers and asked them to have it cleaned professionally and mounted and framed.

Ref: *Shri Sai Leela* Magazine; Vol. 17, No. 10, 1940, *Paush shake* 1862

***

THE PLACEBO WORKED AFTER APPLYING UDI

A few days after the incident of the termites invading the photograph of Baba Dr. Rajgopalachari experienced another leela of Baba. His neighbour's son had been sick for a long time. The parents had got the best doctors to take care of him. Everyday Rajgopalachari's wife told him about the child's condition, or rather its deterioration.

One day his wife was very upset when he returned home. She told him that her neighbour had asked him to come and check her child. He told his wife that it was futile as various experts had treated the child and the child was at death's door. Nevertheless on the insistence of his wife who was ready to go even without changing her clothes, he decided to go. He thought that his visit would pacify both his wife and the neighbour. So he decided to give the child an injection more as a placebo than as a medication.

When both of them reached the child's home, Rajgopalachari was shocked to see the child. Then he took out the injection from his bag; the mother of the child asked him if she could first apply some Udi on the child's forehead before he administered the medication. Rajgopalachari asked the mother to do so, but she insisted that he apply it, and placed a small packet of Udi in his hand. Casually he asked about the vibhuti. She told him it was Udi from Shirdi Sai Baba. He did as asked just to satisfy the child's mother and returned home.

Early next morning the mother came to his home and excitedly asked him to visit her son before leaving for work. So he and his wife went there; he couldn't believe his eyes when he saw the child sitting up in bed and playing. His faith in Baba grew by leaps and bounds. As this incident occurred right before his eyes, he was now eager to learn more about Baba and soon became an ardent devotee.

Ref: *Shri Sai Leela* Magazine; Vol. 17, No. 10, 1940, *Paush shake* 1862

***

UDI NEGATES THE EFFECTS OF A JOLT OF ELECTRICITY

Seema A. Bartakke, a devotee from Sangameshwar, Ratnagiri states, "Sai Baba is the most accessible deity. If the devotee has unconditional faith, Baba is ever ready to shower his grace on him. He comes running when the devotee is in trouble or in a difficult situation; all the devotee has to do is to earnestly call him and he's there. My entire family is devoted to Baba and he has never failed us in difficult times."

Seema's younger brother had the habit of reading every night before he went to sleep. One night at about 10 p.m. he got a book and went to switch on the table lamp which happened to be faulty. The moment he touched it he got a severe jolt of electricity; then he fell on the ground with the lamp on his chest. Seema was awake and wanted to switch off the main, but she couldn't reach it and the table and chairs in the room were all metallic. She started shouting on the top of her voice. There was no male member in her house, so she opened the front door and yelled for help. Her neighbours hearing the commotion came to help, and then one man rushed and switched off the main.

By that time her brother was in a serious condition. He was lying on the floor limp as a rag and his extremities had gone cold. He was frothing severely from his mouth and his eyes had rolled up. Seema and her family were upset to see his condition, and everyone began praying to Baba. The neighbour who had turned off the main also made arrangements to take Seema's brother to the hospital, and an ambulance arrived a short while later.

Seema earnestly prayed saying, "Baba, only you can save my brother," and she put a little Udi in her brother's mouth. When they reached the hospital her brother regained consciousness; the doctor examined him and gave him some tablets. Seema states, "Baba gave my brother a second chance at life. It was Baba's Udi that negated the ill effects of the jolt of electricity. Udi has the power to breathe life into anyone."

Ref: *Shri Sai Leela* Magazine; Vol. 68, No. 5, August 1989

***

THE POWER OF UDI AND NAAM JAP

Baba said, "Show me anyone who has sought refuge in me and has been cast aside." This is one of the 11 promises that Baba made and it came to pass in Bhagyashree Navghare's life. In 1985 her father was diagnosed as having hypertension and to make matters worse he suddenly suffered a stroke. During the stroke he lost consciousness for a short while, followed by paralysis of the left side. Immediately Bhagyashree put a little 'life-sustaining' Udi in his mouth and rubbed a little over the paralysed side too. Three times a day she gave him a dropper full of *tirth* (holy water obtained from the daily bath given to Baba's idol). Every morning she massaged the paralysed limbs with the oil obtained from the drippings of the "ever-burning lamps" in the Dwarka Mai. This 'holy' treatment worked as a life support. Once when he had a setback, both his eyelids started drooping and he had double vision; with intense faith Bhagyashree continued her father's treatment. Her father was checked by their family physician who advised them to get him admitted in Nair Hospital for a neurological workup.

Numerous X-rays were taken and they all were 'Normal'. Then a CAT scan was done and they had to wait for 4 days for the report. Bhagyashree and her family chanted Baba's name continuously day and night. A day before the results came, a doctor on his rounds asked her mother if she was given a red card. This card would enable them to receive blood if needed during any op ration. Hearing this, her mother burst into tears and cried inconsolab. Finally the results were obtained, and as the scan was normal her father was discharged from the hospital that very evening.

Ref: *Shri Sai Leela* Magazine; Vol. 68, No. 5, August 1989

***

BABA WATCHED OVER THE LITTLE GIRL THE ENTIRE NIGHT

During the summer vacations of 1987, Rachna Ambarker had taken both her daughters to Pune, where her mother lived. Her daughters asked their grandmother to make *chaklis* (a savoury that is deep fried) for them to eat. Rchana's mother prepared the dough, and fried a few and served them. Rachna's older daughter Swati was playing on the cot, while her younger daughter was seated next to Rachna, and everyone was having a wonderful time.

Then disaster struck; Swati somehow fell off the cot and literally fell into the pot of boiling oil. The oil splashed all over her face, head and body; luckily it did not ignite. Rachna and her mother did not hesitate for a minute and rushed Swati to the nearest hospital. Swati was given the necessary treatment and the doctor advised Rachna to bring her daughter early next morning, if the swelling around her eyes increased even a little. He told Rachna that if that occurred he would have to perform a small operation to save Swati's sight. Hearing him say the word operation, Rachna felt as if the very ground below her had given way. Swati was crying all the while due to the agonising pain, so the doctor gave her an analgesic and sedated her and sent her home.

Rachna and her mother were continuously chanting Baba's name and praying earnestly that Swati should recover. Swati slept peacefully while her mother sat beside her, praying the whole night. In the morning when Swati woke up, Rachna noticed that the swelling around her eyes was negligible, and Swati seemed rested. Rachna asked her how she felt and if the pain was tolerable. Swati replied, "I feel fine, as Baba was with me the whole night. He nimbly passed his hands over all the burnt parts and took away the burning pain and swelling. Even now he is passing his hands over me. Look there he is, can't you see him?" Rachna looked around but couldn't see Baba. However, she gratefully thanked Baba for healing her daughter and making her pain-free.

Ref: *Shri Sai Leela* Magazine; Vol. 68, No. 5, August 1989

***

BABA COMES TO MEET THE LITTLE GIRL

Parimalam was born in Lulur in Coimbatore district in Tamil Nadu. Her father was an atheist while the rest of her family was very devout. She was very fond of her uncle as he was devout and many *Sadhus* and saints visited him. Her uncle often asked her to serve meals to them.

When Parimalam was only 10 years, she was fortunate to see Sai Baba. Most devotees yearn their entire life to have a dream, let alone a vision. It happened in 1960; early one morning she ran out of the house and saw an ascetic sitting on a huge stone. His face was luminous as a thousand suns shining all at once. Delighted she said, "Sir please wait I will call my uncle immediately." He beckoned to her saying, "I have come to meet you. You are a good girl, and you will do well in life." She rushed to get her uncle and when they returned he and his stone had disappeared. Everyone thought that the event was a figment of her imagination.

After this incident Parimalam began to foresee the future and started predicting events before they even happened. Yet no one took her seriously. She did not know about Baba at that time. In 1967 she got married and moved to Chennai. One day by chance the couple visited a Sai Temple in Myalapore. There she saw a photograph of Baba and felt she knew him. Then the scene of her childhood meeting flashed through her mind. She gleefully told her husband all about the meeting but he paid no heed to it. Then a friend gifted her with an idol of Baba; simultaneously she got information about him easily and became devoted to Baba.

This leela and the subsequent leelas were experienced by S. S. Parimalam of Chennai.

Ref: *God's Rainbow* as narrated by S. S. Parimalam

***

239

THE PIANO PLAYED DURING THE ENTIRE BRAIN SURGERY

Some years later Parimalam started having severe abdominal pain. She went to a doctor who could not diagnose her pain; the severity too was not lessened by the medications she was given. After a while the doctor gave up, saying it was an 'un-diagnosable' pain. As the pain was severe and accompanied with nausea, it was not a psychological pain. Disgusted she gave up taking her medications; then along with her pain she experienced dimness of vision and obesity.

One day just as she was leaving for work she had an episode of losing and regaining her vision. She rushed to the hospital and was immediately scanned for a brain tumour that was present and needed surgery. She calmly went for the surgery with a request that Baba be with her. The surgeon who was devoted to Baba readily got a small statue of Baba and placed him in front of her.

When she was 'under' anaesthesia the surgery began, but she could hear the doctors talk with astonishment about the size of the tumour. Suddenly she saw an indescribable light that changed from violet to green and then to gold. Then she floated towards it in a narrow lane; on either side of the lane were computers that were recording everything. "Don't even think of anything lest it be recorded," she thought, and it was. Finally she floated to an open space and she heard the most beautiful piano music. The music played for 5½ hours and then stopped; the stopping coincided with the completion of her surgery. Then she felt the sutures being applied and later she being placed on the stretcher and taken to her postop room.

Two days later she narrated everything to her doctor; he threw up his hands in amazement and said, "Oh my god!" The operation took place on 24 August 1999.

Ref: *God's Rainbow* as narrated by S. S. Parimalam

***

BABA HEARS HER PLEA TO TAKE HER FATHER UNTO HIM

Years rolled by when Parimalam's father was diagnosed to have cancer. She spent her time looking after him, but the treatment was painful and soon infections set in. She was agonised to see her father's condition deteriorate. Then she prayed to Baba saying, "Baba! I am unable to see my father in such a condition. Will you not take him unto thee?" At 1 o'clock her mother came to relieve her to take care of her father. She slept below the cot and she dreamt of her father. In the dream her father said, "My little girl I am leaving you now. I cannot lie on this wooden cot anymore." Then he gave her a few seashells and a few dried branches, as they were the only assets he had accumulated thus far.

She clung to him but he forcibly pushed her aside and vanished. She cried out "Daddy! Daddy!" and woke up and she realised that the inevitable had occurred, that her father had passed away. The doctor was summoned and he checked his heart and he said that her father was no more.

She narrated her dream to many people seeking the meaning of it. An uncle told her that he had merged into Baba. Parimalam felt that Baba had heard her prayer and given him salvation. Now she feels Baba is her father.

Ref: *God's Rainbow* as narrated by S. S. Parimalam

***

241

THE DEAD FOETUS WAS DELIVERED NORMALLY

Around 1978, the Mahajan family was sitting together chatting and having tea. At that time Mrs. Mahajan was pregnant, when her husband suddenly said, "If this child dies in the womb, I don't want you to be disturbed or worried at all as Baba is there to take care of you and everything will be all right." Sunil S. Mahajan had a premonition that this child would not survive. He got up immediately and applied some Udi to his wife's forehead and gave her some orally. Every night before she slept, Sunil prayed to Baba to protect his wife and gave his wife some Udi.

Eight days later his wife had labour pains and she was admitted to the hospital. The doctor examined her and told Mahajan that she would deliver about 3 to 4 hours later. The doctor looked very worried but Majahan did not pay any heed to it as he was continuously chanting Baba's name. A short while later the doctor and nurses were running hither–thither and the family knew that something was wrong. Mahajan asked his sister to immediately take some Udi and apply it on his wife's forehead and give her some by mouth.

Finally a stillborn girl was delivered. The doctor told the mother about the tragic news, but Mrs. Mahajan was calm and accepted the news without crying. The doctor wondered about it. Then she called Mahajan into her office and said, "The baby died in the womb 8 days ago. As the child was shrivelled and had dark patches all over the body, it is indeed a miracle that the baby came out normally along with the sac intact. This normally does not happen; in most cases the child has to be delivered by surgery. And most importantly if the sac had ruptured in the uterus it would have caused a fulminating infection and your wife would not have survived. So she has in fact got a second chance and a new lease on life."

Ref: *Shri Sai Leela* Magazine; Vol. 65, No. 8–9, November–December 1986

***

RANE FINALLY VISITS SHIRDI

The next few leelas were experienced by Ananth P. Kane a resident of Pangi, Goa.

He yearned to go to Shirdi but couldn't for some reason or the other, so he did a *parayan*, that is, read the *Shri Sai Satcharita* and complete the reading in a week. Kane's son was residing in Mumbai and was ill for over a year, and he repeatedly asked his parents to stay with him for some time. In September of 1973, he and his wife went to Mumbai and stayed with him. His wife pleaded with Rane saying, "Mumbai is so close to Shirdi so we must make pilgrimage there during this visit. Please let us not miss this opportunity." Rane agreed; he made reservations on a bus that would depart 2 days later. While he was returning home he remembered that someone had told him, "If you do parayan of the *Charita* you should offer dakshina to Baba. And the very same coins and rupee bills should be put in the donation box at Shirdi." Now he was in a fix because unfortunately he had left the dakshina on the altar at home. He immediately called a relative and asked him to send that money by registered post.

On the day of their departure the registered post had not yet arrived, so Rane had to cancel the tickets and buy tickets by train for the next day. Rane was feeling quite unwell that day, and the doctor told him that he had high blood pressure and it was inadvisable for him to undertake such a long journey that day. The next day the registered post arrived and they left for Shirdi along with a relative who had visited Shirdi quite often. They had a wonderful pilgrimage and visited all the sacred places in Shirdi. It was indeed a thrill to see and touch all the sacred articles used by Baba, but they had to return a day later as their relative couldn't extend his leave. Although he did visit Shirdi, his trip was unsatisfactory because he yearned to stay there for a few more days, so he consoled himself thinking that his next visit would be for a longer time.

Ref: *Shri Shri Sai Leela* Magazine; Vol. 54, No. 10, January 1976

***

"I LIVE UNDER THE NEEM TREE," SAID THE FAKIR

Rane was strolling on Chowpati early one morning when he met a fakir who was about 55 years old; the fakir had a divine aura around him. The fakir wore a kafni and had a bunch of peacock feathers tied together like a wand. Rane immediately took out a coin from his pocket and gave it to him. The fakir accepted it and asked him if Rane knew Hagi Malang. As Rane said no, the fakir then asked him if he knew about Shirdi Sai Baba. Delighted Rane replied, "Yes I know him and I have just returned from Shirdi." Then the fakir said the most unexpected thing. He said, "Even after visiting Shirdi you haven't recognised me?" So Rane took a good look at him and indeed he saw the same beard and moustache, and Rane realised that the fakir resembled Baba. The fakir continued, "Now you must have recognised me. I live under the neem tree that you saw in Shirdi. It's your good fortune that you met me here on the street of Mumbai. And what brought you to Mumbai?" Rane told him about his son's ill health. The fakir asked Rane if he would give a message to his son.

The fakir continued saying, "Give me a coconut and a shawl right now." Rane was regretful of his inability to do so as the shops were closed. "Never mind, but promise to give it to me. Now give the money you have in your pocket." Rane handed him the 5 rupees that he had. The fakir then blessed him and walked away. Rane ran after him to ask him what message he was to give his son, but by then the fakir had disappeared.

Rane wondered if the fakir was really Baba. What was he to tell his son? His son had just recovered from a prolonged illness and was unable to join them on their trip to Shirdi. When Rane told his family about his meeting with Baba, no one believed a word of what he said.

Ref: *Shri Sai Leela* Magazine; Vol. 54, No. 10, January 1976

***

BABA HAD PULLED HIM TO SHIRDI

Rane returned to Goa in early December and 2 weeks later his nephew visited him and told him he would be going to Shirdi as usual on the thirty-first. Rane asked him if he would take a coconut and a shawl and offer it at Baba's feet. His nephew said, "Sure, but why don't you accompany me to Shirdi?" Rane thought that he had just recently visited Shirdi, but instead he said, "Will we be able to get the tickets?" His nephew assured him that he would arrange everything. Rane asked his son to meet them at Pune so that they would all proceed to Shirdi.

At Shirdi they were allotted a room in Sathe Wada, and they attended every Arati and worshiped Baba to their hearts content. On Thursday they went for the palanquin procession, and did not know where to stand as it was very crowded. Just then an old man in a *chopdar's* (mace bearers) uniform took them to the door of the Chavadi and said, "This door will open soon; then you can enter and participate in Baba's Arati." Rane wondered who that old man was.

On the first they offered the shawl that was draped on Baba and on the Samadhi, and the coconut was placed at Baba's feet. That evening after the Arati, Bholenath Samel had a program of devotional songs and the Sansthan gave him one rupee along with the coconut that Rane had offered. Rane felt that the fakir who had asked him for a coconut had accepted it. But the question still remained as to what message the fakir wanted to give to his son. Finally he decided that as his son was unable to accompany his parents on their previous visit, Baba had pulled him to Shirdi like a sparrow with a string tied to his feet.

After Kakad Arati they collected tirth of Baba's morning bath in a bottle. Just then a priest came up to Rane and said, "You are leaving today, so accept this prasad and gave him a huge peda. Rane wondered how that peda happened to be on the Samadhi when everything was put away. How did the priest know that they were leaving that day?

Soon it dawned on him that all this was the doing of Shri Sai Baba and Rane was filled with joy.

Ref: *Shri Sai Leela* Magazine; Vol. 54, No. 10, January 1976

***

| August 20 |

HE SET A TEST FOR BABA AND BABA OBLIGED

Virendra P. Panday ordered, "No Sadhu, fakir or beggar should be allowed inside the compound of my house or be allowed to loiter in the vicinity." Panday worked as a business contractor in the Bombay Water Supply Scheme in Vaitrana near Kalyan. At that time Vaitran was a densely forested area, and many Sadhus and fakirs duped and looted his staff members there. Besides Panday was a sceptic and a doubting Thomas, hence the strict warning. He also had a huge amount of money at his residence which was for the daily wages that he had to pay the labourers. Pandey was well educated and did not believe in saints and was a hard-core atheist.

Many years ago he happened to visit Shirdi by chance with a cousin who also gifted him with a picture of Bāba that he put away in a trunk in the attic of his home. A few years later his family residing in Bihar had to face a great deal of difficulties and Baba solved them, yet he thought it was a fortunate coincidence and good luck. In fact Baba helped him twice to overcome extremely difficult situations yet Panday was wavering in his faith.

Panday decided to test Baba's divine powers by putting impossible demands before him for Thursday 6 August 1952. He stood before Baba's picture and said, "Baba tomorrow is Thursday; I want you to come to my residence in the form of a sadhu or fakir for alms between 12:30 and 1 p.m. At that time I will put the first morsel of food in my mouth as it is my lunch time. So I want you to appear not before or after that time. And lastly I want you to bless me not in the usual way of placing your right hand on my head but by passing it from my head to foot so that every part of my body is blessed. If these

246

impossible demands are met, I will dedicate my life in your service and will never ever doubt your divinity."

Early in the morning on Thursday a friend visited Panday and gave him a box of confectionary that Panday placed in front of Baba's picture so he could give it to the fakir. Then at the stroke of 12:30 he sat down for his meal and waited for the fakir but no one appeared. Just as he was about to put the first morsel of food in his mouth, he saw and heard Baba asking for alms. He sat there in a state of shock, but his cook ran and gave Baba a coin. He wondered how this fakir had entered the compound. He invited him to have a meal; after the meal the fakir blessed him by running a bunch of peacock feathers from his head down to his feet. This incident assured Panday that Baba had blessed him, and he became ardently devoted to Baba.

Ref: *Shri Sai Leela* Magazine; Vol. 29; No. 4; October, November, December 1952

***

August 21

"IT'S WISE TO FINISH *PRARABDHA* NOW"

During *Dussera* (October) of 1949 G. Naik an ardent devotee of Baba came to Shirdi. He stayed in Shirdi for 2 months, for his own well being and mental peace. He thought that he would simultaneously perform some service for Baba. On the night of *Khojagiri Purnima* (a festival on full moon during October) he had a vivid dream, wherein he saw an idol made of marble. Then he saw Baba enter that idol from the right side. At that time Baba's face resembled the face of the Dwarka Mai portrait. Then Baba said, "Now go; I will do your work for you," following this Baba started crying uncontrollably for about 5 minutes and Naik woke up.

On August 1951, Naik completed his work and was satisfied. Then on 30 September he was in great trouble; it was unavoidable so he shed copious tears. He remembered the dream and said, "Baba had warned me that I would cry uncontrollably but I could not comprehend its meaning or its gravity."

About 4 days before the unavoidable disaster, Baba warned him again but he failed to understand it. There were three adults in his family and he felt one of them would face insurmountable problems but could not figure out who that person was. Alas! It was him, and then he realised that what is destined to happen will surely happen. But as he had sought refuge at the feet of his sadguru, he knew that Baba had taken three-fourths of his trouble on himself and lessened the gravity of the situation. He also realised it was better to face the fruits of his karma in this life itself rather than carry them forward.

Unfortunately Naik does not state what kind of troubles he had to face.

Ref: *Shri Sai Leela* Magazine; Vol. 29; No. 4; October, November, December 1952

***

August 22

HIS WORK IS ACCOMPLISHED

One night Naik again dreamt of Baba. In the dream Baba was sitting on a low stool in the Dwarka Mai pose, that is, the pose in the famous portrait painted by Shyamrao Jaykar. A man was standing next to Baba who looked like a Brahmin in appearance. Naik went and stood before Baba who said, "Why did you call out to me?" Naik said, "Baba, I didn't call you." Then the Brahmin said, "Baba he has some urgent business with the Government, for which he is willing to pay a thousand rupees." Hearing this Baba said, "Is that right? Now you can go." Following this, Baba asked the Brahmin to draw the curtain and there ended the dream and Naik woke up.

The next day was a Thursday and Naik was pondering deeply on his dream. As Naik could not understand what Baba wanted to convey to him, he decided to meet a colleague of his and take his advice. This colleague was a friend and a trusted advisor. Upon meeting his friend he on his own accord said, "Don't worry your work is done." Naik was surprised that indeed his goal was accomplished with the payment of a thousand rupees. The money that he had paid to the Government was also returned to him subsequently, thus all his troubles came to an end because of Baba's abundant grace.

Ref: *Shri Sai Leela* Magazine; Vol. 29; No. 4; October, November, December 1952

***

August 23

CHRONIC RASH WAS CURED WITH *TIRTH* BATH

Sadashiv D. Joshi now a resident of Sholapur and employed in the Chitle Agricultural Products states how he became devoted to Baba. In 1947 he resided in Lakshmivadi about 3 miles away from Shirdi, and worked as a clerk in the Godavari Sugar Mills. Nanda his son suffered from a chronic skin disease. The disease was characterised by hives and intense itching, that appeared in large groups in succession and left scars before invading another site. Nanda was treated first by the Mill physician, then by Dr. Patvardhan of Kopergaon, where he was given Penicillin shots but without improvement. Dr. Patvardhan finally asked his father to get the boy admitted in K. E. M. Hospital in Mumbai; by this time Joshi had spent a huge amount of money for his treatment. Joshi was unwilling to take his son to Mumbai, as his son's condition was deteriorating rapidly.

As a last resort he decided to seek refuge in Baba. The irony was that Joshi knew about Baba's miraculous powers and he lived so close to Shirdi yet it did not occur to him to take his son there. Finally one Thursday he came along with his son to Shirdi and earnestly prayed for a cure. The next morning he collected a bucket of tirth after the Kakad Arati and vigorously bathed Nanda with it. This he did regularly for a week and lo! the rash along with the itching, disappeared. The astonishing fact was that Nanda's skin had no scars blemishes or any trace of the disease. Joshi said, "It was Baba's grace and the wonderful power of his tirth that enabled my son to have baby soft skin. But the most wonderful fact is that this incident made me into an ardent devotee. Now I visit Shirdi as often as I can."

Ref: *Shri Sai Leela* Magazine; Vol. 29; No. 4; October, November, December 1952

***

AND THE LAMPS KEPT BURNING
BRIGHTLY

In 1943 Rajabhau M. Sirdeshmukh a resident of Sholapur, was seriously ill with malaria. For 2 years the fever raged on relentlessly. Although numerous doctors treated him, he also received nine injections of Quinine without any improvement. He spent vast amounts of money on doctors' fees and medicines and his condition steadily deteriorated.

His father was very concerned about his health, so he turned to prayer as a last resort. In April 1943 B. V. Narshima Swami visited Sholapur, and Rajabhau's father was fortunate to meet him. On the very first meeting his father told Swamiji about his son's ill health. Swamiji gave him a small photograph of Baba and said, "Pray to Baba with devotion. Keep this photograph in front of you and tell Baba all your problems and difficulties as if he was standing in front of you." His father stopped all the medicines and told Baba about his son's condition every day.

In late 1943 both father and son visited Shirdi. They got a room in Sathe Wada and the father immediately went to the Samadhi Mandir and earnestly prayed for his son. At this point his son was in a critical condition. That night his father dreamt of Baba. In the dream he saw Baba lighting a lamp and then turning to him said, "Look how brightly the lamps are burning. Why are you worried? I will pour more oil in the lamps and they will continue burning," and then Baba filled the lamps with oil. At this point Rajabhau's father woke up.

From the very next day Rajabhau's condition started improving steadily, and for the next 10 years he was free from malaria. Rajabhau was so grateful to Baba for curing him that from 1951 he began staying in Shirdi. He rendered selfless service to Baba. He helped the staff during Baba's Kakad Arati's and Baba's morning bath rituals. Rajabhau said, "It was only because of Baba's grace I recovered from this dreadful disease."

Ref: *Shri Sai Leela* Magazine; Vol. 29; No. 4; October, November, December 1952

***

"MAKE MY IDOL AND PADUKAS, AND YOU WILL PROSPER"

Since 1930, Venketesh R. Matdhar a resident of Davangiri worked for the Congress Party as a volunteer. Although he worked earnestly, his financial condition was bad, and for the past 20 years he and his family faced abject poverty. He was the eldest brother and had a large family to look after. To make matters worse he was imprisoned off and on; then in 1942 he went 'underground' and his family suffered a great deal. Although the country had gained independence, his financial condition did not improve. Along with change came the rising cost of living and Venketesh was at his wits' end.

One day a friend visited him and told him about Baba. He gave Venketesh a picture of Baba and asked him to pray to Baba with devotion and tell him about all his problems. Vanketesh was attracted to the picture and prayed to Baba with devotion. Things started to change and he soon got a job in the Neera Company and was able to look after his family, and also visited Shirdi with them.

About 5 months later he had a wonderful dream, wherein he was sitting on a huge boulder. The boulder was in the middle of a vast river. The river was crystal clear and beautiful. Suddenly he saw Baba swimming towards him, and then Baba went beneath the boulder and came out on the other side. Baba then swam around the boulder and mounted it and stood in front of Venketesh. He immediately prostrated before Baba, and when he looked up at Baba, he saw him seated on a beautiful throne. Then Baba placed a silver idol of Annapurna in Venketesh's cupped palms. Baba said, "Make an idol of mine along with padukas then everything will be all right." At that moment Venketesh woke up.

Following this dream his financial condition started improving rapidly. His younger brothers also got employed and he was free of worries. Thus Venketesh visited Shirdi to thank Baba, and take a vow in front of Baba's Samadhi that he would follow his orders. Lastly he states, "Baba takes utmost care of his devotees and worries about their welfare day and night. All that a devotee has to do is totally

251

surrender to him and cast all his burdens on him and he will surely take care of him."

Ref: *Shri Sai Leela* Magazine; Vol. 29; No. 4; October, November, December 1952

***

August 26

HOW SHE GOT BABA'S PRASAD

Sushma M. Pavar a resident of Netherlands states, "I have been praying to Baba since my childhood and he is my chosen deity. Previously I used to work for Cooperage Exchange. To reach my office I had to board a bus at V.T. station. One morning I was waiting for the bus that happened to be late.

Hence, I was looking hither and thither for it. Just then I saw a man approach his friend; he told him he had just returned from Shirdi and had brought Baba's prasad with him. He then gave him some prasad. I yearned to get some prasad too but as I didn't know that man so I didn't expect him to give me some. Then the bus arrived and I got in and went to my office.

After I had lunch, my friend Seema placed a small piece of peda that was no larger than a pea in my hand. Delighted I told her how I had yearned for Baba's prasad, this very morning. I was astonished to hear her reply, "My sister's friend gave her a small piece of peda as she had just returned from Shirdi; she gave me a small portion of it. I kept it before Baba and this morning after taking my bath I was about to put it in my mouth when I turned to Baba's picture and I saw your face in it. I felt Baba wanted me to give it to you." With tears of joy I accepted the pea-sized prasad. How kind my Baba is; like a caring mother he fulfils even the smallest wish of his children."

Ref: *Shri Sai Leela* Magazine; Vol. 29; No. 4; October, November, December 1952

***

MESSENGERS OF DEATH DRIVEN AWAY

On 28 March 1989, Baba and goddess Tulja Bhavani averted a calamity in the home of Dilip S. Laande. He and his family resided in Barshitakali Akola. His mother was devoted to Baba and Tulja Bhavani; she read the *Charita* every day and often did parayan of it. She also fasted on Tuesday for Tulja Bhavani and his home was filled with spiritual energy.

That night was *Holi Purnima* (Holi is the festival of colours and Purnima is the full moon night), and his mother went outside behind the house to use the washroom. When she did not return after quite a long time, Dilip's younger sister noticed her absence and went out to check on her. Her mother was swirling round and round; she realised that she was under the influence of some spirit. She immediately went inside and got some Udi and applied it on her mother's forehead and mentally sought Baba's help. After this her mother lost consciousness and began talking incoherently. Her condition soon became worse and she was thrashing about her hands and feet. The family then got her admitted to the hospital; she was examined by the doctor and given some medicines.

About an hour later she got up and looked around and said, "I am fine and I am going home right now," and they all returned home. Later that night she told her husband, "Two hideous demons were trying to take me away and were dragging me, when suddenly Baba and Tulja Mai appeared and beat them mercilessly and drove them away." Her husband realised that the deities had saved her from death, as the two demons were the messengers of death.

Ref: *Shri Sai Leela* Magazine; Vol. 68, No. 8–9, November–December 1989

***

"I AM WITH YOU ALWAYS"

(The next two leelas were experienced by Prasant Uhake.)

When Prasant Uhake a resident of Bathul, Madhya Pradesh dreamt of Baba he knew nothing about him. All this changed on 12 March 1980 and he became an ardent devotee. At 6:05 a.m., Baba wearing a white kurta and a dhoti with a border appeared and stood close to Prasant's bed. His alluring bearded face shone like a thousand suns and Prasant's bedroom was filled by this magnificent light. Baba said, "Don't be frightened and worried," Prasant asked, "Why should I be worried?" Then Baba said, "I am with you always. On this date next year come to Shirdi." In the dream Prasant went to touch his feet but Baba had disappeared by then. He woke up with a feeling of disappointment for being unable to touch his feet. But Prasant was full of peace and intense joy.

Later that morning he met his friend, Sachin Saxena and related his dream to him hoping Sachin would help him understand its meaning. Sachin said, "You are extremely fortunate that Baba blessed you by appearing before you. Now you should obey him and go to Shirdi." He then told him where Shirdi was and how to get there. Sachin also told him about Baba's divinity and gifted Prasant with a *Shri Sai Satcharita* to read. Prasant took the *Charita* and as soon as he reached home opened it and saw a picture of Baba in it. He immediately cut it and placed it in a frame and kept it on his table and prayed to it.

Some days later he requested Baba to enable him to get a Gas Agency. This he did by writing his request on a piece of paper that he rolled up and placed it behind the picture. On 27 August 1980 he succeeded in getting the agency along with the required license to operate it. Baba also let him know three days prior to getting the agency that he would succeed.

Ref: *Shri Sai Leela* Magazine; Vol. 62, No. 7, October 1983 (*Punytithi* Number)

***

HIS MEMORABLE VISIT TO SHIRDI

The date 12 March remains etched in his mind. On 10 March, Prasant went and bought a ticket for the Punjab mail to go to Shirdi. He had gotten all the necessary information as to how to go to Shirdi and where to stay from his friend, but as he didn't have any reservation he decided to go standing all the way to Shirdi. Just then a coolie appeared before him; he was rather old and had a short beard and wore a badge that was number 12. Prasant told him he was going to Manmad, but he didn't have any reservation. The coolie took him to a compartment and placed his luggage on seat number 12. When Prasant asked him what his charges were he smiled compassionately and said, "Son you are going to Shirdi, aren't you? When you return bring some prasad for me. Now don't forget," and saying this, the coolie disembarked the compartment and got lost in the crowd. A short while later the ticket collector entered the compartment; Prasant told him that he didn't have any reservation and if he was allotted a berth he would be grateful. The ticket collector asked him to take seat number 12 and told him that if the person whose seat it was did not turn up he could have it.

Prasant had a comfortable journey to Manmad and the train pulled into the station exactly at 6:05 a.m.; that was the time Baba appeared in his dream. From Manmad he boarded a bus to Shirdi and the seat that he got was number 12. Upon reaching Shirdi a small boy took him to a hotel where only one room was available for 50 rupees a day. While opening the room he was astonished that it was a number 12. Prasant attended all the Arati's and performed Abhishek. Before leaving the temple he laid his head on Baba's padukas when he heard Baba say, "I know that you have come to my Shirdi."

Prasant returned home on the twelfth at about 4 p.m.; on the way back he pondered about the mystery of the number 12. He felt Baba wanted to assure him that he was with him all the way from Bhopal to Shirdi. When he reached Bhopal he searched for the coolie but was unable to find him. Then he realised that the old coolie was actually Baba.

Ref: *Shri Sai Leela* Magazine; Vol. 62, No. 7, October 1983 (*Punytithi* Number)

***

SAI BABA'S SHACKLE

(The next two leelas were experienced by K. M. Bhagvati, a resident of Mumbai.)

Till he was 6 months old K. M. Bhagvati was a healthy baby; then he fell ill and his condition became critical. The best medical treatment failed and his parents were desperate. One day a fakir appeared at their door and asked his mother if her son was seriously ill; then he told her to seek refuge in Sai Baba of Shirdi. His mother went inside to inform her sister-in-law about the fakir and when both of them came to the door the fakir was not there. Later they informed his father about it and he immediately went to Shirdi. He prostrated before Baba and told him about his son's critical illness. Baba asked him to make a silver anklet and put it around his son's ankle. Then his father sought permission to leave but Baba detained him for one more day. When he finally got permission to leave, he was 3 hours late for the train, but that day the train too was late by 3 hours. He returned home and followed Baba's orders.

Bhagvati wore the anklet for 32 years and it became 'almost a part of him' as it did not cause any discomfort. He and his family lovingly called it *Sai Baba's bedi* (Sai Baba's shackle). As he grew older, it was enlarged by adding more silver and thinning it to fit him till it weighed 5 *tolas* (1 tola is equal to 11.65 grams). Thereafter no more silver was added; but it was thinned and large enough to fit him. Needles to say he became hale and hearty soon after he wore the anklet.

In 1950 Bhagvati asked his father, "For how many years should I wear the anklet? When should it be removed? And what rituals should be followed for its removal?" His father said, "Go to Shirdi and after removing it place it on Baba's Samadhi and offer floral tributes to Baba's Samadhi. While you are at Shirdi, ask the Sansthan if we can render any service to them as a token of our gratitude." Shortly after this his father who was healthy died suddenly of a massive heart attack. Bhagvati then went to Shirdi along with his family priest and placed the 'bedi' on Baba's Samadhi.

Ref: *Shri Sai Leela* Magazine; Vol. 69, No. 6, September 1990

***

THE SAMADHI MANDIR LIGHTS UP

It was in November 1950 that K. M. Bhagvati went to Shirdi for the removal of his bedi. His family priest removed the anklet and placed it on Baba's Samadhi. They had brought a beautiful *'chadder'* of flowers from Mumbai. A chadder is a long horizontal garland strung with numerous perpendicular garlands to form a veil. The chadder was placed on the Samadhi with devotion and immense gratitude.

At that time the structural work of the Samadhi had just been completed, but the electrical installation was yet to be done. Bhagvati immediately requested the Sansthan to allow him to do it and they consented. He was very glad as his family business had been of Licensed Electrical Engineers and Contractors and his firm was called Bhagvati and Company. Upon returning home his brother, an electrical engineer readily agreed to undertake the installation.

The work was completed quite satisfactorily and in time. On the day of the inauguration, a short time before the lights were to be turned on they were unable to do so. The best materials had been used, the staff was very competent, and the system had been checked and rechecked. In spite of their best efforts, the lights wouldn't light. The manager who was devoted to Baba sat in front of the Samadhi and prayed begging to be forgiven for any mistakes that they had made. And lo! the lights went on, and the entire Samadhi Mandir was lit up brightly. Bhagvati felt elated that he and his family had been able to contribute their mite of gratitude in this form. Unfortunately his full name is not given nor the name of his father who had the good fortune to meet Baba.

Ref: *Shri Sai Leela* Magazine; Vol. 69, No. 6, September 1990

***

UDI REACHES HIM IN THE NICK OF TIME

(The next two leelas were experienced by a middle-aged man who worshiped a goddess.)

Chodagem P. Vitthal a resident of Machlipatnam worked in the stationery department of the LIC. Once he bought a ticket to Shirdi from a tourist agent and paid the fare in advance. On the day of departure the tour got cancelled for some reason. After that he was travelling in a bus in Andhra Pradesh when it met with an accident. He was seriously injured and went into a semi-conscious state; he had to be admitted in a hospital in Guntur. He was promptly treated but he remained unconscious for a long time. When he gained consciousness he was in a terrible state and his pain was unbearable. When he was writhing in pain he remembered Baba and abused him for the state he was in spite of his wanting to visit Shirdi. He thought, "If you are God and as great as your devotees claim you to be, you will relieve me from this torture."

At that very moment he received a packet of Udi from Shirdi that was addressed to him. He applied it to all the injured areas and that gave him immense comfort and within a few minutes he was relieved of pain and became calm. How the Udi reached him in the nick of time is a miracle; that too when no one knew him in Shirdi nor was his name and address registered with the Sansthan.

Ref: From the book titled *Sai the Mother, Anasuya the Amma*

***

ANTAGONISTIC DEVOTION
(*VIRODH BHAKTI*)

On 16 November 1988 Vitthal went by a tourist bus to Sabarimalai in Kerala to worship Ayyappa Swami. While returning the bus made numerous unscheduled stops in places like Goa, Mumbai and Shirdi. This was done at the request of the passengers. He was surprised that he was visiting Shirdi unexpectedly and this had been his original wish. At Shirdi he ran out of money and had no money for lunch. He did, however, have a lot of prasad with him that he had brought from Sabarimalai. However, he could not eat it as it was in the bus that was locked and there was no one to open it. His stomach was growling with hunger. He couldn't purchase a coupon for meals from the Sansthan at subsidised rates as he didn't have the money.

Again he vented his anger on Baba, for mercilessly treating him and keeping him without food at Baba's own place. He thought, "Baba is renowned for extending immediate help, succor and relief to those who think of him. And in Shirdi my stomach is growling with hunger."

Just then two lady passengers told him that they had two extra meal tickets with them and asked Vitthal if he could give it to some needy person, as they were going to a hotel to eat. He told them about his situation and offered to pay for them later. Then he went to the Sansthan *Prasadalaya* and had a sumptuous and delicious meal.

The above two leelas are about *Virodh Bhakti* (antagonist devotion) and yet Baba responded immediately to Vitthal's needs.

Ref: From the book titled *Sai the Mother, Anasuya the Amma*

***

HIS *SAPTHA* WAS ACCEPTED

In December 1967 K. R. Gopinath began the worship of Baba, which was initiated by a Brahmin friend of his. At that time Gopinath was residing in Hidkal Dam near Belgaum. At first he did a *saptha* of the *Guru Charitha* and concluded it on Friday. That very night he was blessed by Baba who appeared in his dream and asked him to attend the job interview the next day. The following day a person was waiting with a letter for him to appear in the interview. Not only did he do well in the interview but got the job immediately without trouble. He was quite restless after joining it as he felt his previous post was better, but with Baba's grace he succeeded in introducing a better pattern of accounting and received many accolades for his effort.

About 3 months later he went to Kerala as his bride was residing there. Just prior to his marriage he performed a saptha of the *Shri Sai Satcharita* in his hometown. On the seventh day he had invited many of his friends and relatives for the feast. When preparations for the Arati were being made, a black cat turned up and ate the prasad that was kept before Baba's photograph. He was elated that Baba had accepted the saptha and the prasad. This miracle surprised everyone who was present. Then everyone partook of the spiritual feast and kept wondering of the glory and significance of Baba who was present in all living beings.

Ref: *Shri Sai Leela* Magazine; Vol. 53, No. 11, 1975 Feburary

***

BABA APPEARS AS A SERPENT

K. R. Gopinath states, "My faith in Baba increased with every passing day. I was reciting *Sai Mantra* the whole day on my birthday in 1968. In the evening my wife and I performed puja and

Arati to Baba. Suddenly I felt the presence of Baba in the room. I looked around but couldn't see him, but the spiritual energy persisted and became very strong. Then my attention was drawn to a shining piece of gold in front of Baba's photograph. Soon I realised that it was a serpent about 6 feet long. I was overwhelmed with love for Baba and was immensely happy.

My wife was dumfounded with this Sai leela. I instructed her to fetch some milk which we placed in front of the serpent. It drank the milk and disappeared. I thanked Baba for accepting the milk on my birthday. Soon my little puja room became a place of worship for many Sai devotees.

One day a saint came to our home and when we narrated what had happened in our puja room he said, "This is an unusual blessing that you have received, and it's a glorious act of Sai Baba."

Ref: *Shri Sai Leela* Magazine; Vol. 53, No. 11, 1975 Feburary

***

September 5

BABA INSTRUCTS HIM NOT TO FAST

Every day Anil K. Rasal a resident of Mumbai read at least one chapter of the *Shri Sai Satcharita* with very few interruptions; this was in 1983. On 31 August, which happened to be *Janmastami* (day of birth of Lord Krishna), Rasal read chapter 41 that describes how Baba blessed B. V. Dev in his effort to read the *Dnyaneshwari* (sacred Hindu book). Rasal hoped that he would one day be blessed to read this book also. He was pleasantly surprised to receive a packet of Udi from Shirdi on that very day and he considered it as a good omen.

The next day he started reading the *Dnyaneshwari* and completed reading two chapters. After a few days he met Dnyaneshwar Manebua who had mastered the book by over 30 years of regular reading and gave discourses on it. Manebua readily accepted to help him with his reading and explained the portion read. Manebua also asked him to fast on *Ekadashi* (eleventh day of lunar fortnight) but Rasal was hesitant as Baba disliked fasts. He thought, "Baba is my sadguru and until I get clear instructions from Baba I will not fast."

The next day was *Kartik* (the month of November by Hindu calendar) Ekadashi and Rasal dreamt of Baba. In the dream Baba held him by his right hand and led him to a place where Dnyaneshwar (Hindu saint) was sitting and gave him some *pithle bhakari* (Pithle: gram flour curry. Bhakri: thick bread of millet or sorghum) and asked him to give it to Rasal. Dnyaneshwar did as he was told by Baba; in this way, Rasal was instructed by Baba not to observe the fast.

Ref: *Shri Sai Leela* Magazine; Vol. 64, No. 5, August 1985

***

September 6

CHANTING BABA'S NAME ENABLES SPEEDY RECOVERY

Illness in a family usually becomes the cause of loss of income, disruption of daily routine, agitation and loss of peace of mind. And if the illness is chronic all these factors are increased exponentially, and this is what happened to K. L. Shah. Shah was a resident of Surat; he owned a small business and was not very affluent. In 1950 he had a stroke that resulted in the paralysis of his right side. He tried every available remedy, but his physical vitality as well as his financial resources were almost exhausted.

A friend of his happened to meet him and he told Shah to devotedly chant Baba's name; he also gave him a small picture of Baba. Shah was at his wits' end so he followed his friend's advice. The resultant recovery was remarkable. Within a short span of a few months Shah was able to walk and ride a bicycle for miles through the crowded streets of Surat. He then realised the power of chanting Baba's name.

Ref: *The Spiritual Symphony of Shri Sainath of Shirdi*

***

262

THE BRILLIANT LIGHT DRIVES
DEATH AWAY

He resided in Baroda and was a retired gazetted officer of the government of India. This is the wonderful leela experienced by K. F. Master. Once he suffered from obstruction of the kidney, which had affected his bladder and prostrate gland. As a result he suffered intensely and frequently passed bloody urine. His doctor admitted him in the State General Hospital for surgery. A complete workup was done prior to the surgery and a high percentage of glucose was detected in his urine. As he was a diabetic, the idea of immediate surgery was abandoned. To save his life, a catheter was inserted into the bladder through a wide opening made through the abdomen. Unfortunately his condition started deteriorating with every passing day. Finally uremia set in and he lapsed into coma. The doctor who cared for him was an eminent surgeon who practiced in England; having vast experience in his field, he realised that there wasn't the remotest possibility of his patient's survival. He told the patient's family of the grim prognosis and suggested that they could take him home if they so desired.

Harshad Mehta was a dear friend of the family. And he went to the hospital along with Dr. D. M. Shah, a renowned surgeon in Baroda. Mehta asked the doctors and nurses if there was the remotest possibility of survival but they unanimously said that he would not survive for more than 6 hours. Dr. Shah also examined him and agreed that the chances for survival were slim. Dr. Shah was devoted to Baba so he applied some Udi on his forehead as a last resort.

The family brought him home and started making preparations for the last rites. Mehta went to Master's home the next day and was surprised to see him alive. After the Udi was applied he opened his eyes and looked around; then he started speaking. He told his family that 50 huge men clad in silk robes were about to lift his cot and take him away. At that very moment a brilliant light shone and the 'cot bearers' fled in panic. That happened to be the moment the Udi was applied on his forehead. Master also recovered from his dreadful illness slowly but steadily.

Ref: *The Spiritual Symphony of Shri Sainath of Shirdi*

***

BABA SHOWS HIM THE CAUSE OF FEVER

Dr. Bansilal Shah aged 35, was the son of the renowned physician Dr. Dhirajlal of Baroda. In 1952 he was ill with pneumonia and admitted into hospital. The best available care was given to him, and all eminent physicians and surgeon took care of him. The pneumonia was treated and x-rays were normal but the temperature persisted. For 2 months the fever persisted with unfailing regularity and there was no improvement in Bansilal's condition. A course of all the antibiotics were administrated to him but to no avail. Repeatedly all the investigations were reported as normal yet the temperature remained high. The case baffled the medical staff.

One day Dr. Dhirajlal (father of Bansilal) was performing his morning worship of Baba when he had a vision. In the vision he saw a large pocket of pus in the abdomen. Its connection with his son's case was obvious, but since all the medical evidence was contrary to this he thought it was own agitated imagination. The vision, however, repeated with greater vividness two more times.

Dr. Dhirajal told a surgeon friend about it, who was also Baba's devotee. The surgeon immediately examined Bansilal's abdomen and found a very painful area in the abdomen; he got it x-rayed and a large mass was detected. On aspiration four ounces of pus was aspirated, so Bansilal was taken to surgery and exploration of his abdomen was done. Exactly in the spot that Dhirajlal had seen in his vision, was a huge pocket of pus; about 2 liters of pus was removed. Following this Bansilal's health rapidly recovered, and both father and son thanked Baba.

Ref: *The Spiritual Symphony of Shri Sainath of Shirdi*

***

HIS SOUL RECOLLECTS HIS PAST ASSOCIATION WITH BABA

H. V. Desai and his wife Ratnaprabha resided in Mumbai and were happily married for the past 10 years. They were ardently devoted to Baba but they didn't have any children; this troubled them a great deal. Ratnaprabbha was the editor of a popular Marathi daily; she was well known for her translation of the famous novel *Divya Chakshu* written by Ramlal Desai into Marathi.

The Desais left no stone unturned; the couple got themselves checked by numerous specialists in the field of infertility but all the doctors said that Ratnaprabha would never be able to conceive. One day the couple happened to see a picture of Baba and was attracted to him. Immediately they got that picture of Baba and started praying to him with devotion. They also read all the literature written on him and took refuge in him.

Two years later they were blessed with a beautiful healthy baby boy. When the child was about 2 years old they brought him to Shirdi. As soon as the child entered the Dwarka Mai he clapped his hands with joy and said, "Baba, Baba." He ran into the sanctum sanctorum and when the mother placed his head on Baba's padukas he repeatedly kissed them. He also exhibited an extraordinary familiarity with all the articles there and soon became the centre of attention. Everyone who saw this was convinced that the soul of the child was intimately associated with Shirdi from some previous birth. The Desais are living a life of peace and contentment with their ever growing faith.

Ref: *The Spiritual Symphony of Shri Sainath of Shirdi*

***

BABA'S ENTIRE BODY WAS COVERED WITH MEASLES

When Lakshmibai G. Khaparde's son Balwant suffered from bubonic plague, Baba said, "The sky is overcast. The clouds will burst and pour down rain and then the sky will be clear. Why fear?" Then Baba lifted his kafni and showed her the buboes he had taken upon himself. This is a similar leela. Dinaben Ilavia a Parsi lady and her family were devoted to Baba. Some years ago her small child contracted an extremely virulent attack of measles. Later the two younger children also were infected; now all three of her children were extremely ill. The fever was dangerously high and she was at her wits' end. One afternoon Dinaben was seated at their bedside praying fervently to Baba and begging for their recovery. Suddenly she was dazzled by a brilliant light and in that light she saw Baba. In a soothing compassionate voice he said, "Do not worry my child. Your children will be all right soon." It was then that she could see him clearly and was stunned by what she saw. Baba revealed his body to her and his whole body was covered with the malignant rash. That evening the fever subsided and soon the children recovered fully. After this miracle, Dinaben's faith increased by leaps and bounds.

Ref: *The Spiritual Symphony of Shri Sainath of Shirdi*

***

BABA ANSWERS HER CALL

Atul's parents Malti and Harshad Mehta kept a constant vigil next to his bed as his condition was precarious. In 1949 Atul was extremely sick and hovering at death's door with typhoid, and was admitted in a hospital. Dr. Thakorbhai and his wife Dr. Indumati Patel gave him the best possible care. They were also friends of the family and didn't hesitate to check on him, at any time of day or night. But Atul's fever relentlessly raged on. The doctors told them about the seriousness of his condition and the complications that could occur. They asked the parents to inform them at once if they noticed the stools were bloody or even blood tinged.

One evening the parents noticed that Atul had passed blood-stained stools, and informed the nurse. The nurse asked them to contact the doctors immediately. Malti immediately ran to the next ward to make the call. His father sat by the bedside praying to Baba. At that time Atul's abdomen was distended a lot and he appeared worse than ever.

The doctors arrived within 15 minutes of the call, when the miracle took place. As Malti ran to the next building where the telephone was, she had a vision. She saw Baba in an ochre-coloured kafni and not the white one that he usually wore walking with her. He walked along side up the winding staircase and stood beside her while she made the call, and Baba at the other end had answered her call. Just as she completed the call the bloating disappeared and gradually the temperature started coming down.

The doctors examined Atul and asked them not to panic that much. It was only after the nurse showed them the blood-stained stools did they realise the gravity of the situation and the wonderful miracle that took place. Thereafter Atul's condition started improving and gradually he became healthy again.

Ref: *The Spiritual Symphony of Shri Sainath of Shirdi*

***

September 12

BABA APPLIES UDI AND SHE DELIVERS EFFORTLESSLY

P. V. Satyanaryan of Guntur narrated how Gopichand became devoted to Baba.

Gopichand resided in Kurnool and worked as the Director of Publicity for the Government. In 1954 his wife was admitted to the

Government Hospital for a 'difficult delivery'. Three days passed and there was no relief; Gopichand was very worried. On the third day, he chanced to pass by a Baba temple. In his deep anguish he said, "People say you are God; you possess vast powers and that you come to the rescue of the distressed. If this is true, then come to my aid now and see that my wife has a safe and painless delivery. Then I will believe in your omnipotence."

By the time he reached the hospital he found that his wife had already had an easy and safe delivery. She gave birth to a male child. When he met his wife, she told him that "An old man with a beard and *angarkha* and a *satka* came and sat on her bed and said, 'My dear child, don't worry; I have come to give you relief. You will have a painless delivery here and now.' So saying he applied Udi on my forehead and made me drink water mixed with Udi. No sooner did I drink the water than I delivered this child. I have no pains now. I am now safe and all right." Gopichand asked the time when the old man came to visit her. She told him the time; Gopichand was then convinced that Sai had appeared before his wife immediately after he had challenged him. And Gopichand was convinced of his omnipotence. He mentally bowed and thanked Sai for the timely help given to his wife. The grateful father named that child Sai Baba. All those who knew him felt the shock of this tremendous transformation. Gopichand passed away a few years back; his son, Sai Baba is now a grown up young man.

Ref: *Shri Sai Leela* Magazine; May 1975

***

September 13

BABA PULLS THE BULLOCK CART TO SAFETY

In 1949 a group of devotees set out from Hyderabad to visit Shirdi. It was a very tedious journey as they travelled for about 20 hours by train before they alighted at Kopergaon. Kopergaon was a tiny station and the train hardly stopped there for more than two or three minutes. The group had lunch and set out by bullock cart to the town. It was the monsoons at that time and the unpaved pathway was slushy and muddy. With a great deal of difficulty the bullock cart arrived at the shore of the Godavari River. There were no buses in those days from Kopergaon railway station. One had to cross the river, to catch a bus to Shirdi. The present road overbridge was under construction at that time.

On reaching the shore, the party found that the low level bridge across the river Godavari was almost submerged in water. A ferry boat was plying from one shore to the other. A cartman suggested that he would take the party by his cart to the other shore over the low-ebb bridge across the river and they agreed. When the cart was half way through, it started raining. The river became furious and the level of the river began rising with every passing minute.

The cartman lost his control of the bullocks as the water current was fast and soon they were floating on the water. One of the cart's wheels got stuck on a boulder. There was no parapet wall on the low-ebb bridge and the water force was pushing the cart, endangering it to fall into the river. The members of the party were chanting Baba's name. They lost hope of survival and were prepared to meet a watery grave with the Lord's name on their lips.

Suddenly from nowhere, a middle-aged man appeared before the bullocks and took control of the bullock cart. The cartman removed the boulder and the stranger piloted the cart slowly towards the other shore. The river became calm as the stranger pulled the cart cautiously to the other shore. Then the clouds cleared and there was sunshine.

Ref: Ananthula Neeraja; *Shri Sai Leela* Magazine; June 1975

***

September 14

BABA HIMSELF CARRIED THEM ACROSS THE FLOOD

Although his parents were utterly devoted to Baba, B. R. Kakade did not worship any deity. In his childhood he thought it was a waste of time and energy. His father did not chide him for this but sought the help of his elderly friend. The friend requested the son to read some religious books aloud as he was unable to do so. And this brought a transformation in him.

In 1927 Kakade aged 16 years was staying with his father in Baroda when there was a terrible flood. The flood divided the city into parts; he and his father were on one side while his younger brother and grandmother were on the other side. They tried to cross a bridge that was quite high but the police objected as it was dangerous. Not heeding their advice they proceeded and waded in water. Soon the water was up to their neck. Now they could neither turn back nor proceed further because of the fury of the water. They were trapped in the water and were sure they would soon die. His father silently prayed to Baba to save both of them.

Suddenly a tall man, about 7 feet tall, appeared from nowhere; he had a beard and a cloth tied around his head. He shouted loudly asking them to stand where they were. Then he walked through the flood water and carried both of them to the other side where the grandmother and brother were waiting anxiously. The son asked his father who their saviour was. His father said, "Of course it was Baba; he heard my earnest prayer and immediately rescued us." Kakade looked around for their saviour but Baba had disappeared.

Some years later Kakade visited Shirdi and brought some Udi with him. At that time a dear friend of his had been blessed with a baby girl. Unfortunately she had palsy of her upper limbs. His friend was dejected as the progress was slow and didn't produce the desired results. Kakade gave him a little Udi and asked him to rub it on the affected limbs with devotion. As he was not a devotee, his friend hesitated but due to Kakade's persistence he did so. With the very first application there was tremendous improvement that surprised the friend and the physician. His friend saw the result right before his very eyes and thus became an ardent devotee.

Ref: *Shri Sai Leela* Magazine; January 1974

***

HOW BABA PULLED HIM TO SHIRDI

In 1955 N. Purnacharanrao accompanied a friend to a Baba temple in Bhimavaram; at that time he knew nothing about Baba. He was fascinated by the idol and soon became an ardent devotee and visited the temple frequently.

He longed to make a pilgrimage to Shirdi. In 1967 he was to go to Pune on an assignment; he was delighted as he would also visit Shirdi. But at the last moment the assignment was cancelled. In October 1967 he was asked to proceed to Pune immediately for a stay of 8 weeks. At that time he was hesitant as he had moved his family to another city because he was transferred there. Thus he would have to leave his family for 2 months without any adult male member to look after their needs. On one hand his family would be all alone on the other hand he would lose the opportunity of going to Pune and hence to Shirdi.

There was no time left to think and decide as he either had to leave for Pune the next day or apply for a leave for 2 months and stay on with his family. That night he tossed and turned restlessly. Finally he fell asleep at midnight and a few hours later he had a wonderful dream. He states, "Suddenly I saw Sai Baba surrounded by brilliant white light. The intensity is beyond my power of expression. I trust that this brilliance cannot be described and explained by any person with the exception of some great spiritual master. In the midst of this white, brilliant, divine and powerful light I saw the idol of Sai Baba, in pure white from head to foot. But the eyes of the idol were human and they were looking at me with compassion. I could not withstand the divine vision and I woke trembling with fear. After 5 minutes I went back to sleep. Within half an hour I had the same vision again. I woke up nervous as I couldn't withstand the brilliance of the light."

Next morning he decided to proceed to Pune and visit Shirdi. When he entered the Samadhi Mandir he was amazed to see the same idol that he had seen in his dream. Formerly he had visited temples where the idols were of different colours and he was not aware that the idol at Shirdi was white.

Ref: *Shri Sai Leela* Magazine; January 1974

***
271

BABA ACCEPTED THE ALMS AND SAVED HIS WIFE

On Thursday 19 January 1984 at 6:30 a.m., Narendranath Mungara and his colleague hailed a cab to take them to the railway station. They were returning to Aurangabad. The driver wanted to eat breakfast so they stopped at a small teashop and ordered bread and tea. Mungara saw a picture of Baba in the adjacent shop and closed his eyes in silent prayer. The bread arrived and the shopkeeper went to fetch the tea. Mungara had just unwrapped the bread when he saw a young Muslim fakir at the entrance. He had a green cloth tied on his head and had a loose white Kurta over a lungi. He had a small black bowl suggesting he came begging for alms. Surprisingly he asked nobody for money or alms. With a smile and a calm look on his face he stood there. Mungara's heart was filled with inexplicable joy. He nodded his head calling him and offered a few slices of bread with devotion. The fakir accepted them and raised his hand in blessing and swiftly walked away without asking anyone for alms. In his heart Mungara knew it was Baba who had blessed him on Thursday morning.

When he reached home he was shocked to see the window panes of his home shattered. Usha, his wife told him that the pressure cooker had exploded on Thursday morning shattering everything and damaging the walls and the roof. She also added that due to Baba's grace at the time of the accident she was in the adjacent room so had been saved from injury and burns. Mungara remembered the fakir who had accepted the bread and blessed him on Thursday morning. He thanked Baba for protecting his family while he was away.

Ref: *Shri Sai Leela* Magazine; Vol. 64, No. 3, June 1985

***

BABA AS A PORTER RECEIVES THE DAKSHINA

On 16 August 1990 the Indore Bhakta Nivas Council gathered together for a meeting in Shirdi. After the meeting was over, the members decided to return home that very day. Gajanan P. Nirke went to take permission from Baba to leave Shirdi and visit his son in Mumbai. At about 9 p.m. he went to the Samadhi Mandir, and bowed on the Samadhi and said, "Baba please can I leave now? I will be going to Mumbai to meet my son; then I will go to Indore." Then he turned to Baba's idol and looked at it with love and devotion. Soon he distinctly heard a voice say, "You bought it? So you will build the Dhramshala. I will come and stay there." He was overwhelmed at hearing Baba's voice, as no one there knew him or his purpose of coming to Shirdi. Then as the temple was getting crowded he exited it.

He had hired a car to take him to Manmad and reached the station in time. On the way he realised he had not put the dakshina of 5.25 rupees in the box. This had never happened to him before and he repented. At the station he heard his train was late by an hour, so he sat on a bench and looked around. On a bench in front of him an old man with a red and white turban was lying down. A few minutes later an old porter came to Nirke and said, "So you are going to Mumbai? I will get you a seat but you will have to give me some money."

Finally the train arrived and the same porter came and told him to stand in a certain place. The train came to a halt and the bogie that he wanted to board stood right in front of him. After the passengers alighted the porter firmly held Nirke's bag and brought him to a vacant seat. Then he asked for payment. Nirke took out the 5 rupee bill that he had and gave it to him. Then the porter said, "Babuji here is your bag. Now why are you keeping the quarter rupee with you? Give it to me so that I can buy tobacco for the old man." Nirke then gave him the quarter rupee and the porter smiled and went away. The train pulled out of the station and Nirke realised that Baba had

273

come all the way to Manmad to seat him in the train and recover his
5.25-rupee dakshina.

Ref: *Sai Chintan* Magazine; September 1990

***

September 18

BABA FOREWARNS HIM OF HIS
IMPENDING DEATH

Baba had forewarned Gurudas S. Hattiangadi of Mumbai a year
earlier but he couldn't grasp its meaning. On 1 November 1992
he was praying in the Dwarka Mai when Gurudas had a vision. He
saw his body covered with a white cloth lying in front of the dhuni.
Baba and an elderly person were doing something to it and then he
got up quite alive.

On 7 January 1993 Gurudas was in Chennai, as the Chairman
of the medical session of the World Vegetarian Conference. After the
conference he and an eminent doctor were leaving when he suddenly
became very breathless. Then he chocked and had difficulty breathing,
with chest pains. The doctor realised that he was having a heart
attack and immediately took him to the hospital. Gurudas felt that his
condition was serious and started praying to Baba. He was admitted
and given treatment by the same elderly doctor who he had seen in
the vision. He kept losing consciousness off and on for 4 days and
so was placed on a ventilator.

Later the doctors told him that when he was admitted he was
dead and revived against all hopes of revival. All the tests showed
that there was severe brain damage. But miraculously he suddenly
recovered fully and was subsequently discharged. He says, "Baba
cannot change what is ordained but he does come to the aid of his
devotees."

In this leela Gurudas was fortunate to climb the steps of the
Dwarka Mai so Baba burnt all his karma's and gave him a second
chance at life. He sees Baba and the elderly doctor actually giving him

chaitanya or life again. Baba not only comes to his devotee's aid and changes what is predestined as he is the 'creator' but also changes their destiny. Just as Jyotindra Tarkhad was given a second chance at life; he should have drowned in Shirdi when he was hit by a wall of water that advanced towards him following a 'cloud burst'. Or when the dead body of the Bhil is resurrected when Das Ganu pleads and sings, *"Sai raham nazar karma bachhon ka palan karana."* Notice how in all the above leelas destiny is changed by Baba's blessings.

Ref: Gurudas S. Hattiangadi; *Saianubhav*

***

September 19

BABA IN THE PHOTOGRAPH REACTS TO EVERY SITUATION

(The next few leelas were experienced by Sashiprabha whose family resides in Madhya Pradesh, while she resides in Pune with her family.)

Sashiprabha S. Vilelker states, "My family is devoted to Baba as my great grandfather started his worship way back in the '20s. Baba has become our family deity, and every family member is devoted to him. In fact no one steps out of the house without first applying Udi. Every situation big or small is placed before Baba and no decision is taken prior to his worship.

Once we heard that my uncle was running fever for some time; my father sent Udi to him. And as soon as the Udi was applied, the fever came down. At that moment the photograph of Baba in Sashiprabha's home started sweating.

My paternal aunt had once gone to draw water from the well and slipped and fell into the well. At that time my maternal aunt was standing before Baba's photograph and looking at him. Suddenly Baba opened his mouth wide and said, *"Aha."* My aunt was extremely frightened and was shrieking with fright and everyone ran to her aid. She related what she had just seen. At that very moment she and the rest of them saw her paternal aunt in the photograph. Then they

275

realised why Baba had opened his mouth round and wide. All the male members ran to the well and rescued her. Although the well was deep, my aunt didn't sustain any serious injury. She had a few bruises that healed with the application of Baba's Udi."

Ref: *Shri Sai Sagar* Magazine; 2004 (*Deepavali* Special Issue)

***

| September 20 |

"YOUR EFFORT HAS REACHED ME"

Every evening in 1987 when Sashiprabha returned home from office, she would wash up and have a cup of tea. She then went down the alley to attend Arati at Vijay Wadeker's home. But every evening she was late for the Arati and regretted that she could never attend the entire Arati on time because of her office hours. Nonetheless one evening as Sashiprabha walked for the Arati she mentally sang, "*Sainath guru maji ayie Maja thava dyava payi*" (Sainath guru my mother, grant me a place at your feet)." That evening though she sang the Arati, she was preoccupied with a certain file at work. Then she looked at Baba's idol and mentally said, "Baba what is the use if I come here and mechanically sing your Aratis while my mind is on that file?" She sat before Baba's idol and thought this. Then Sashiprabha had a wonderful experience. She saw a bright halo spinning behind Baba's head. The halo itself was golden and there were specks of red and white in it. Then the halo disappeared and simultaneously Sashiprabha felt an electric current enter both her big toes traverse up her body and stop at her throat. At that time she was speechless. Then she heard a voice say, "That you take the time and come here every day that is sufficient for me. And that has reached me."

Ref: *Shri Sai Sagar* Magazine; 2004 (*Deepavali* Special Issue)

***

EQUALITY OF RELIGIONS PHILOSOPHICALLY

Vijaykumar Mule now resides in Pune; earlier he resided in Sholapur and in that very building a saint named Shankar Maharaj resided. One Sunday, Mule visited a friend of his who had received *mantra diksha* (iniciation through mantra) from Shankar Maharaj. The conversation turned to the topic of all religions being equal and the same philosophically. Then a heated argument arose, as his friend opposed this very thought of equality.

At that moment someone came to the door. Mule went to see who it was when he saw a tall fakir with a magnetic personality standing at the door holding a bowl before him. Mule asked him how he happened to be at the door when it wasn't Friday. The fakir replied, "Child I am a fakir, and I go where ever and whenever I feel like."

Mule put a coin in his bowl and bending down touched his feet. The fakir then took some Udi from his jholi and applied it on his forehead and blessed him touching his entire body with his peacock feathers. Then he said, "I am fortunate to have had darshan of Lord Datta."

Mule called his friend and his wife and asked them to give some coins to the fakir. He also told them not to send the fakir emptyhanded from their door. But as he was a Muslim they were not inclined to do so. Finally when they went to the door the fakir had gone. Later he told them what the fakir had said, but they couldn't comprehend it or chose not to.

Mule states, "If I see a fakir anywhere I never fail to put a coin in his bowl, with the result that I have been blessed abundantly by them. Also I am never sure in what form Baba may choose to appear." In *Sreepada Sreevallabha Charitaamrutam* chapter 45, it's described how Humaman is absorbed into Shripada and the resultant manifestation is Samartha Sadguru Sainath of Shirdi. In whatever form Baba may appear, he is none other than Lord Datta.

Ref: *Shri Sai Sagar* Magazine; 2004 (*Deepavali* Special Issue)

***

THE LADY GIFTED THEM THE MONEY

A few years ago Pandit K. Naik had gone to Auckland, New Zealand for a stay of 9 months. He was to hold talks on the "Customs and culture of India." There he met many Indians from all states of India. They asked Naik if he could give them discourses on the saints of India as he was well versed in the tradition of saints in India. He obliged them by talking on this subject during his free time and soon the topic turned to Baba. Naik was devoted to Baba so he was more than happy to talk about him.

The group soon decided to build a temple of Baba there. They collected money and an estimated cost of 80,000 dollars was decided on. They formed a trust called *Shirdi Sai Sansthan, Auckland* and Jagdishbhai Mackenzie was the Chairman. They did the Arati and the counting was begun. They found that they fell short of 60,000 dollars. Now where would they get such a large amount from? Everyone was standing around trying to figure out where to get the money from.

Just then a middle-aged lady with a magnetic personality wearing snow white clothes walked up to Mackenzie and said, "I heard that you plan to construct Baba's temple in Auckland and I am very happy. I heard that you need 60,000 dollars so I brought the check with me," and she handed over the check for that amount to them.

Everyone wanted to know about her. She replied, "As Baba has sent me it's not necessary to know my name and address. Your work can be completed now," and saying so she left.

The next week Jagdishbhai and his wife came to Shirdi to thank Baba.

Ref: *Shri Sai Sagar* Magazine; 2004 (*Deepavali* Special Issue)

***

WHO WAS THAT SADHU?

Baba had given Mhalsapathy a pair of his padukas. The *Akhanda Nama Sapta Sapthams* had organised a program at Vijayawada and the padukas were taken to various places in Andhra Pradesh. At Machlipatnam it was decided that the padukas be carried in a palkhi to Vijayawada. The padukas were placed in a heavy wooden palkhi and the destination was about 50 miles away. They carried it without stopping while continuously doing Naam Jaap. After a while they were extremely tired and their shoulders were aching nonetheless they continued walking.

One devotee in the group had broken a coconut before setting out, so he cut pieces of them and gave them to the palkhi bearers. At that time they saw a rather short sadhu standing on the left side and they gave him a piece too. He had four horizontal lines of vibhuti on his forehead with a vermillion dot in the centre. Soon they started running as they had to reach Vijayawada by 5 p.m. After traversing about 5 miles they were surprised to see the same sadhu standing on the left side of the road. How did that sadhu get there before them, as no vehicle had passed by?

Finally they reached their destination and were astonished to see the idol; it was short and its forehead was decorated with four horizontal lines of vibhuti with a vermillion dot in the centre. All the while they were wondering who that sadhu was. They then realised that the short sadhu they had met on the way was Baba himself. At that moment all their tiredness vanished and they were filled with joy.

The next leela was that an old lady had brought tea and biscuits for them. That afternoon while she slept, Baba appeared in her dream and asked her to take some refreshment for his devotees who were coming tired and hungry. She immediately prepared tea, bought some biscuits and came to the temple, as she didn't know where the devotees were. Neither did she know who the devotees were or how many. Enroute she saw the palkhi going towards the temple and realised that she was to give the food to them.

Ref: A. Sambasiva Rao; *Shri Sai Leela* Magazine; April 1987

***

September 24

SUHAS ASKS THE DOCTOR TO GIVE BABA HIS SEAT

Four-year-old Suhas J. Pavar residing in Thane became ill in January of 1981. It was a strange malady as the boy was all right during the day and happily played around. Every night he would go to bed and comfortably sleep for an hour. After that he had difficulty in breathing and would be restless. The X-Rays were normal and various treatments were given but there was no improvement. He was admitted to Dr. Agarawal's hospital in Thane. Numerous investigations were conducted and treatment given without any improvement. To give him relief, oxygen and saline were administered to him regularly.

Dr. Merchant of Wadia Children's Hospital examined him but was unable to discover the cause. He told the parents that because every treatment had been given; as a last resort now bronchopy needed to be done. Suhas was transferred to the ICU in K.E.M. Hospital and the time for the procedure fixed. Dr. Jadav and Dr. Karnik were to perform the procedure the next day. On the previous night they visited Suhas. While Dr. Karnik was examining him, Dr. Jadav sat on the chair near his cot. Suddenly Suhas said, "Doctor Uncle please get up and vacate the chair you are sitting on. Look Sai Baba has come. We should honour him by giving him a seat." Dr. Jadav couldn't see Baba and said, "Where is Baba? I can't see him." Suhas replied, "He is standing beside you, and I can see him clearly. Please offer him the seat."

The bronchoscopy was done successfully and a small piece of tamarind seed was removed. Now Suhas had no further problems.

Ref: S. Maney; *The Eternal Sai*

***

BABA ROCKED THE CRADLE, SO THE MOTHER COULD REST

A devotee states, "My second child gave us a lot of trouble, as it cried incessantly the whole night. The child was given medicines for colic, a warm water bottle, it was cuddled and finally we walked about with it, but to no avail. The child cried the whole night. Thus we had a sleepless night. This continuous crying continued for five nights. On the fifth night we were quite disgusted as the sleepless nights took its toll on us. My wife was quite vexed with the child. In desperation my wife prayed to Baba saying, "Baba you look after our every need then why have you failed to help us now. Why is my child crying incessantly and why are you not helping us?"

As she was exhausted, she fell asleep and the child became quiet. After about an hour later she got up to check the child and was astonished to see Baba standing next to the child swinging the cradle. Delighted at the sight she woke me up and narrated what she saw. With tears of gratitude she said, "I was so harsh with my Baba and he came running to rock my child to sleep. What a lot of trouble I gave him at night."

Ref: *Sai Sudha* Magazine; Vol. 2, No. 3, August 1941

***

THE CONCH SHELLS INDICATE PROTECTION FROM ADVERSITY

In 1957 A. K. Kumtheker worked as a foreman in the Inspectorate of Armaments in the Ordanance Factory Khamaria, Jabalpur. He conscientiously looked after his aged bedridden father and never thought of leaving him in the care of others. One morning his boss informed him that he was to attend an 18-week course of Senior Armament Examiners in Kirkee. Now he was in a quandary; the course would enable him to get a promotion and better pay but that meant he would have to leave his father in the care of someone. If he took his father along with him, the back and forth journey would jeopardise his health. He pondered over the situation and couldn't sleep.

The next morning he discussed his problem with his boss and requested that he be transferred to Kirkee on compassionate grounds. His boss refused the request, nonetheless he asked him to send in an application. That evening Kumtheker went to meet Dr. P. S. Ramaswami an ardent devotee of Baba and told him about his problem. Ramaswami was glad that he had come to him as this was the first seed of faith in Baba, as he had narrated many wonderful leelas to Kumtheker.

A week later he met Kumthekar who was dejected as his request was rejected and he was ordered to proceed a week later. Ramaswami told him that Baba's ways were inscrutable, and he often acts at the last moment when everything else fails. And that is exactly what happened the evening before Kumtheker's departure; he received a letter stating that the order had been cancelled.

The next day just as Kumtheker was about to have lunch, a fakir stood at his door. Kuntheker gave him some money that he refused, but instead asked for some food. Kumtheker happily gave him a meal and the fakir gave him a small packet of Udi. He asked him to place it front of Lord Datta's picture, perform Arati and then open it. Kumthekar did that but when he opened it he found five miniature conch shells instead of Udi. The fakir had disappeared, and then Kumtheker realised that it was Baba who had blessed him. He realised that Baba had bestowed a priceless blessing on him by turning the Udi into conch shells. The conch shell is a symbol of protection from adversity arising from the five basic elements.

Ref: *Shri Sai Leela* Magazine; October 1986

***

HE RECOVERS WITH BABA IN HIS HEART

In November 1997 K. S. Shenoy, a resident of Pune, along with his wife visited their daughter in the United States. He was a diabetic and had bronchitis for which he was treated prior to his departure. One day he got severe chest pains and began to have difficulty in breathing. His wife immediately called her daughter and son-in-law who were at work. To make matters worse it was snowing heavily and the temperature had fallen to below zero. In a short while his daughter and her husband arrived, and immediately called the Emergency Services. There were two doctors on duty that day both of whom examined him and carried out an ECG. As he had suffered a heart attack he was quickly hospitalised. Numerous tests were conducted and an angiogram showed that four of his arteries were blocked. The doctors got the consent to perform an 'open heart bypass surgery'.

Within two hours of his arrival at the hospital all the tests were completed and he was taken to surgery. It took about 5 hours for the surgery to be completed. He says, "I was not aware of anything being performed on my physical body. I was gleefully wandering about in the most beautiful garden with lush green lawns and numerous flowering plants. It was a serene place and I was filled with a blissful calmness. I was aware that I was not alone and Lord Sainath was with me. My wife was constantly praying to Baba for the success of the surgery. Then I became conscious, but I was trying to find me. Suddenly I realised that I was with Baba, and I was walking down from the inside of his heart back to my bed. I didn't understand why I had to leave Baba and that beautiful garden and come to this miserable place. I started looking for him, but I couldn't find him. Now I know one thing for sure, and that is, what has entered my heart now, are not the new veins, but Baba. He is there, and will always be there. And that I will never be alone again, as he is there to protect and look after me at all times."

Death is to the body and not the soul. Baba performs 'bypass' surgery of our hearts and bliss flows without any blockades and this leads to 'self-realization'.

Ref: *Shri Sai Leela* Magazine; May–June 2000

***

BABA'S GRACE RESTORES HER SIGHT

S. Sreenath resided in Nandyal, Andhra Pradesh. His wife was a diabetic, and she was unable to see objects that were very near. She went for a checkup and the doctor said, "Rush to Kurnool Medical College Hospital. You have almost become blind. Why did you wait so long"? Sreenath immediately took his wife to be examined by the specialist. He told them that she would require taking medicines and needed injections in her eyes for at least 6 months. After that she might require surgery.

The couple was devoted to Baba and they sought refuge in him. They were also blessed by their Guruji. His wife took all the necessary treatments, as advised. One night she suddenly woke up around midnight and said, "Open the door, Sai has come." Her husband switched on the light. A small picture of Baba that was kept on the switchboard had fallen on her bed beside her.

Within three weeks of treatment there was dramatic improvement in her condition. The doctor who was also a devotee of Baba exclaimed, "Your progress is unbelievable. It is Baba who is curing you. This amazing progress in such a hopeless case cannot be due to our efforts and medicines." A few days later she dreamt that she had the surgery done. About 2 months later the doctor said that she could stop the treatment as she was completely cured by Baba's grace. She states, "I am eternally grateful to Baba as he gave me the dream of the eye surgery being conducted on me. And Baba cured me through *Swapna Shaktipath* just as he cured Bhimaji Patil of his tuberculosis." Swapna Shaktipath is transference of spiritual energy from the Guru to his devotee via the medium of a dream.

Then some doctors conducted an Eye Camp at Mahandi. They had heard about her miraculous cure and wanted to see the lady that Baba had cured. She also worked as a volunteer in that camp as a gesture of gratitude towards Baba and her Guru.

Baba performs surgery on our "inner" eyes and the blindness caused by maya is removed.

Ref: *Shri Sai Leela* Magazine; September 1986

***

AN ATHEIST TURNED INTO AN ARDENT DEVOTEE

In 1952 D. D. Rege, a staunch devotee of Baba met Mr. Hazare a high ranking officer in the Police Department. Hazare had just returned from Shirdi; Rege asked him how he became devoted to Baba. Rege was curious how a Police Officer was devoted to Baba as that department is notorious for accepting bribes and is rather corrupt. Hazare said, "Years ago I worked as a Sepoy for Mr. Kulkarni a magistrate. Kulkarni was totally devoted to Baba, and visited Shirdi every week; as it was my duty I accompanied him. But when he went into the temple I promptly refused to accompany him, as I was not interested in gods and saints. Week after week I refused to enter the temple.

Once Kulkarni had an overnight stay; in those days Shirdi was a remote village without any amenities. Early next morning I went to the fields for my morning ablutions and returned to the premises. Kulkarni had gone for Kakad Arati and I had to wait for it to finish. I walked around as I had some free time; a few villagers were up and about. When I entered the Sansthan I saw Baba sitting on a square stone. He had on his torn white kafni with a white cloth tied around his head. The spiritual vibrations that he radiated were intensely powerful. His was sitting there serenely and a strange sense of peace and calm filled every cell of my body. He looked at me and said, "Did you recognize me." "Yes," I replied. Then he vanished; I pinched my self and it was real. When I told my boss he said, "You are indeed fortunate. For the past so many years I have been visiting Shirdi, but wasn't fortunate enough to see Baba. And you Hazare an atheist are privileged to see him." My life changed after that and I became devoted to Baba, and now I visit Shirdi as often as I can."

The moment you step on the soil of Shirdi you are enveloped by Baba's spiritual energy.

Ref: *Shri Sai Sagar* Magazine; 1996 (*Deepavali* Issue)

***

SADHU FORCES BABA TO VISIT THE HIMALAYAS

The Kakad Arati was over and S. B. Patawardhan went and sat in the sanctum sanctorum of the Dwarka Mai. He wanted to meditate there, when he saw a young sadhu. The sadhu was dressed in an ochre-coloured robe and was standing next to Baba's portrait. He was gently massaging Baba's feet; Patawardhan watched him for some time. The sadhu then turned towards him and came and sat next to him. He said, "You must be wondering as to what I was doing. I have to tell you it's not just a portrait of Baba, but Baba himself sitting there. You have to have devotion and look at it from your soul and then you will realise what I am saying."

He continued, "Baba's grace and blessings are with me. Thus, I was able to make a pilgrimage to Badrinath, Kedarnath, Gangotri and Yamunotri four times when I didn't have even a single rupee in my pocket. You must have heard that many sages and saints often appear in the Himalayas before their devotees. Once I was wandering through the Himalayas and I thought if other saints and sages can appear there why can't Baba. I devised a plan; I would beg Baba to appear before me within 2 hours of my praying to him. If he appeared within that time well and good, if he failed to appear I would jump into the deep ravine and end my life. I chose my place and sat and prayed for him to come. He didn't appear; as there was still some time left I prayed with more intensity and earnestness. Still he didn't appear. Finally there were only 3 minutes left; I called out loudly to him. This I did three times; and as I didn't see him, I was getting up to end my life when he stood right in front of me. He blessed me and disappeared. Thus I got a glimpse of Baba's eternal omnipresence."

"The message for us in this Leela is that if we call Baba wholeheartedly, he will surely appear. The mere remembrance of him forces him to come running to our aid as he is *Samrthru Gami*, that is, the power to appear when called. And he prevents us from jumping into the ravine of life."

Ref: *Shri Sai Sagar* Magazine; 1993 (*Deepavali* Issue)

***

SUBMERGED PICTURE OF BABA
FOUND INTACT

Bhaskar Maghede a resident of Mumbai states, "Tukaram's wife Jijabai intensely disliked Tukaram's devotion and worship of Lord Vitthal. My wife is like Jijabai. I worshiped Baba every day and on Thursday I would garland him and offer some confectionary that my wife had prepared. Then the next day I would put the old garland and flowers in a bag, and immerse them in the sea at chowpati."

On 7 May 1986, a Friday, my wife and me were talking casually and soon our talk turned into an argument and then into a quarrel. My wife lashed out saying, "I am not going to allow you to pray to Baba anymore. What has he ever done for us. We are not affluent. We live on your salary and face numerous hardships." Then angrily she collected the old garland, flowers, Arati book, *Stavan Manjari* and all the small photographs of Baba and Lord Datta and thrust then into the bag. Then she took the bag and pulled me by the hand and took me to Chowpati. There she threw all the photographs, garland and books into the sea. She made sure that nothing was left behind, so she shook the bag vigorously then turned it inside out to completely empty it, and later we returned home. I, however, continued to pray to Baba.

The next Friday I asked my wife to fetch the bag and place the old garland in it, when I heard her shrieking loudly. I went to see what had happened. There in the bag were all the books and photographs of Baba and Lord Datta intact. She was shaking with fright and she fell at my feet asking for forgiveness. I thought just as Lord Vitthal saved Tukaram's Abhangs from drowning in the Indriyani River, Lord Shri Sai Baba had saved the Stavan Manjari, *Asthothar* and photographs from sinking in the sea at Chowpati. I then asked her to fall at Baba's feet and beg his forgiveness. Then she placed her head at Baba's feet sobbing and begged him to forgive her; needless to say she started praying to Baba from that moment on."

Baba is Parabrahma — one who cannot and will not be destroyed by drowning in the ocean of maya. Neither will he let us drown in that vast ocean of maya.

Ref: *Sai Prasad* Magazine; 1993 (*Deepavali* Issue)

***

October 2

BABA FOREWARNS NALANI OF THE ACCIDENT

It was a vividly frightening dream that Nalani Pai, a resident of Mumbai had wherein she saw a tall, fair man dressed in a long white kurta, with a cloth tied around carrying an unconscious man over his shoulder. He then handed her a bundle saying, "Here is your man, and here are his possessions," and placed both of them in front of her and disappeared. The man on his shoulder looked familiar but she couldn't discern who he was. The next morning she told her husband about her terrifying dream.

Early that morning her son-in-law Suresh Gareshwar had gone to Nasik for a business transaction and was to return home that night. She prayed to Baba for his safe return. She was busy with her household chores when she received a call from the Civil Hospital Nasik stating that her son-in-law was admitted there. Immediately they went to see him; at that time he was unconscious and was being treated for head injuries. When he was stable he told them that when he was returning home, a truck was approaching from the opposite direction at full speed. He made way for it to pass when the accident took place. The windows of his car were shattered and the glass splinters struck him. The force of the impact threw him out of the car and he got injured on his head and started bleeding. Then an old man dressed in a white kurta and a towel around his head picked him up and brought him to the hospital. The description of the accident and the man tallied with Nalini's dream.

288

Her husband went to retrieve Suresh's car and found all his articles intact; there was a bag full of money from the transaction, which lay untouched. Suresh was later shifted to a hospital nearer to their home and subsequently recovered completely.

The moral of this leela is that, in this transient world all of us "meet with accidents," that is, some unavoidable circumstance that envelopes us in sorrow. It's only the grace of the Sadguru that can carry this human being to the hospital — the hospital in which he provides the appropriate treatment for the ailment and relieves us of the sorrow to give us a state of equilibrium. Because no other person can take our karma, the bag of money is left there intact.

Nalani and her husband went to Shirdi and thanked Baba for carrying Suresh like a father on his shoulders all the way to the hospital and got him treated immediately.

Ref: *Sai Prasad* Magazine; 1993 (*Deepavali* Issue)

***

October 3

SAI AND RAM ARE THE SAME

Along with his friends C. V. Naidu entered a coffee shop where he saw a picture of Baba. He was drawn to it and kept gazing at it. His friends finished their coffee and asked him to come along, but he was oblivious of them so they left. After some time when he returned to his normal state he asked the proprietor of the shop who that saint was? He wondered whether he was a Muslim Saint so he asked him about the saint. As the proprietor did not know much about the saint he directed him to ask C. S. Chetty who had given him the picture. Naidu immediately went to meet Chetty who was very pleased and presented him with a small picture of Baba and a packet of Udi, and asked him to pray to it. Naidu started praying to Baba that very evening and on Thursdays he would offer fruits, a coconut and burn incense.

On 13 December 1939 Naidu had a dream vision where he saw Baba's Samadhi and got a whiff of incense; it was the same incense that he used at home. Two days later he again dreamt of Baba who ordered him to come to Shirdi. On the twentieth Naidu had a wonderful dream vision of Shri Ram who was his chosen deity. Shri Ram was standing with his hand raised in a blessing posture; suddenly Shri Ram disappeared and Baba was in his place, who also blessed him.

The next day he and his family made a pilgrimage to Shirdi and stayed there for 4 days. He spent the time in utter bliss and peace and visited all the holy sites. At Shirdi he met Abdul Baba who blessed them, then took them to Baba's Samadhi Mandir. He also took Naidu around Shirdi and told him many leelas of Baba that occurred in his presence. Just before they left Shirdi Abdul Baba said, "Sai Baba will take care of you and look after your interest throughout your entire life." Naidu returned home in a calm and peaceful state of mind. His devotion for Baba increased by leaps and bounds.

The 'Sadguru increases our faith in our chosen deity and by taking his place Baba confirms that he and Lord Ram are the same.

Ref: Ramalingaswami; *Ambrosia in Shirdi*

***

October 4

"JUST WRITE SHIRDIKAR"

Mr. Pathak was the Court Receiver of Shri Sai Baba Sansthan Shirdi. One evening during his tenure he received an urgent message that 600 devotees were arriving in the evening. He was in a quandary as all the money collected for that day had already been deposited in the treasury, and there was no spare money at hand. How was he to arrange food for so many devotees, as he would need about 1200 rupees? He was pondering over his problem, when two villagers entered his office. They told him that they wanted to make a donation of 600 rupees, for Annadan. He asked them to come the next day as that day's collection had already been deposited. They told him that they had to leave immediately so he should accept the donation and make the necessary arrangements or use it for Annadan. The older person agreed and said, "Yes the best option is to use it for

Annadan and feed the numerous devotees that arrive unexpectedly."
Surprised at what they said, he accepted the donation, and made a
receipt. Then he asked them, "Whose name should I make the receipt
on? And what name should I write?" One of them said, "What does
it matter whose name is written?" Then the older gentleman with a
white beard said, "Just write Shirdikar." *Shirdikar* is a term or name
used for a person residing in Shirdi.

Three days later Dr. Gavankar a long-standing devotee of Baba
met Mr. Pathak and said, "I had a dream 3 days ago and I saw Baba
and Abdul Baba entering your office and handing some money to you
for Annadan. Were you in need of money that evening?" With tears
in his eyes Pathak narrated the miracle.

Baba assured us that there would be no dearth of food and
clothing in the home of his devotee. Then will he allow his children
to go hungry in his home, that is, the Sansthan?

Ref: As narrated by Dr. Sainath Gavankar

***

October 5

DESHMUKH MEETS BABA AND ABDUL BABA

Once Balchandra Gagenandre, Ramrao Deshmukh and Vilas Turker
went to Shirdi and had a wonderful experience there. The three
were on the spiritual path, and hoped to have a fulfiling visit. Upon
reaching Shirdi they visited all the holy sites. The next morning at
about 5 a.m., they went to Lendi Baugh. They were eager to worship
the pipal tree. This tree is known as the *Nava Graha* tree, as decades
ago it was dying and Baba brought it back to life by installing the
Nava Graha in it. The Nava Graha are the nine zodiac signs which if
appeased and worshiped, especially the sign Saturn, are said to bestow
health and prosperity. Hence, this tree had nine huge roots and nine
large branches. Unfortunately now they are not clearly discernable as
they have been hacked.

Gagenandre, Deshmukh and Turker saw two men dressed in Muslim attire seated under the tree. One man was old with a white beard and wearing a white kafni. Deshmukh prostrated before them when one of them roared, "Have you come here to test me?" He shouted so loudly that a crowd gathered there. Deshmukh who had gone through numerous spiritual encounters replied with utmost calm, "When you are all one and the same then who should I test?" The fakir was happy to hear this and he blessed Deshmukh by touching a bunch of peacock feathers all over his body. Then he took some Udi from his jholi and applied it to his forehead. The other two friends also prostrated and were blessed by the fakir.

When they returned to their room, Deshmukh asked them about the incident. He said, "And did you see Baba?" They shook their head and said, "No." Then he said, "The older fakir was Baba and the younger man was Abdul Baba." The two friends had failed to recognise them. Then Deshmukh answered their questions in this sentence, "God is not found in temples alone; if you look around you with faith and devotion Baba will definitely appear."

In chapter 18 of *Sreepada Sreevallabha Charitaamrutam* it is stated that Shankara Bhatt along with two Brahmins has the good fortune of meeting Sreepada. Bhatt immediately prostrated before him and received his blessings, while his companions were hesitant to do so. Bhatt introduced them saying that they were Brahmins. The omniscient Sreepada, however, knew that they were Muslims and ate beef. His companions then confessed that they indeed ate the flesh of cows as they were Muslims. Sreepada refused to accept their prostrations and drove them away. But he did bless them as they had the good fortune to meet him. He said, "There shall be no dearth of food or clothing in your life. And both of you were fortunate to have my darshan; you will become famous as Bade Baba and Abdul Baba and be uplifted by my Sadguru incarnation as Samarth Sadguru Shri Sai Baba in the village of Shiladhi in Maharastra."

Ref: *Shri Sai Sagar* Magazine; 1996 (*Deepavali* Issue)

***

THE LEELA OF THE ASH

A young boy went to the Himalayas with his guru and learnt about medicinal plants and cures. When his guru passed away, he came back and visited numerous villages distributing free herbal remedies. Then he went to Mumbai and was befriended by a devotee of Baba, who calls himself "Baba's *Bhakt*" (meaning Baba's devotee) because he probably wishes to remain anonymous. The devotee told him about Baba's divinity and miracles and the *Bramachari* (phase of life — celibate) lad was now eager to visit Shirdi. The Baba's Bhakt invited him on his next visit, but he didn't accompany him as he already had a guru, and his going to Shirdi would be the cause of the wrath of his guru. Nonetheless, he was mentally devoted to Baba.

Once he visited Karmala to give some medicines to a man, when a rich moneylender entreated him to give medicines to his sick son. The Bramachari went there and knew that his medicines would be of no use as the child was at death's door. So he told the father that he wouldn't be able to help his child. The father lashed out in anger and said, "Why have you worn ochre clothes if you can't help." The Bramachari then asked the father to give him a fistful of the ash, which he rubbed on the child's body and put a little in his mouth silently taking Baba's name. Inwardly he said to himself, "When this child recovers I will feed 15 fakirs," and then he silently left for Pune.

At a station ahead of Pune, a man stood on the platform calling, "Who is the Bramachari distributing medicines." Then that man came directly to him and told him that the boy in Karmala had recovered completely. And as per his desire 15 fakirs had been fed.

Then he disappeared and the train pulled out of the station. Upon reaching Pune he wrote to the boy's father asking him about his child. The reply came back that his child was fine and 15 fakirs were also given a hearty meal. To feed 15 fakirs is to feed the Indriyias and ego complex with spiritual food.

Baba's name and Udi has never let his devotee down.

Ref: *Sai Sudha* Magazine; Vol. 7, Part 4, September 1946

***

THE FOOT OF BABA'S IDOL BREAKS AND MEGHA IS CURED

One bleak winter evening, Megha Khakre developed high fever with chills and rigours. She covered herself and tried to sleep, but sleep had forsaken her. It was her habit to apply Udi every night to her forehead and her body and then sleep. She got up and did this routine and chanting Baba's name went to sleep. The next morning she still had fever, and it failed to come down the entire day. Her family was persistently asking her to be checked by a doctor. She had more faith in Baba's Udi than in any doctor on this Earth. Finally she gave in to the wishes of her family and got a checkup done and agreed to take medicines. But she took Udi first followed by the medicines. However, the fever raged on relentlessly.

One night at about 9 p.m., she had excruciating pain in her left leg. She wanted to drink some water as she was extremely thirsty. But she couldn't get out of bed she didn't want to wake anybody so she just went back to sleep. After some time the pain became unbearable so she tried to get up and have a drink of water. As soon as she placed her foot on the floor she couldn't bear any weight on it. Finally she slept soundly.

The next morning she woke up feeling better, she wasn't feverish nor was her foot hurting. Her granddaughter came running to her screaming, "Granny! Look at what has happened to Baba's foot?" Slowly she got out of bed and went to the room where Baba's idol was kept. The left foot of the idol had broken at the knee.

Megha had recovered from the illness and Baba in his compassion had taken her illness on himself. Silently she prayed to that idol for the last time thanking him for his kindness. Then she placed the broken idol in a bag and immersed it in a well in her yard.

Baba the omnipresent and omniscient takes prarabdha of his devotees on himself.

Ref: *Sai Prasad* Magazine; 1993 (*Deepavali* Issue)

***

DONGARJI AND HIS SON-IN-LAW'S LIVES ARE SAVED

On 8 October 1982, Dongarji Jani and his son-in-law were on their way to Rajasthan from Vardha. They travelled up to Ratlam by train. They then went to the bus depot to board the bus to their final destination, Basvada. The bus was empty when they boarded it except for two other passengers, so each one took a whole seat for themselves. The bus had started when some passengers came running; they were about 15 of them. The passengers requested Jani, "Please could both of you sit together at the back. We would like to sit together as we are all members of the same family." Jani agreed and he and his son-in-law moved to the rear of the bus.

The bus proceeded and soon was speeding on the highway. Then at about 9 p.m., the bus entered a village and was crossing a bridge, when it got out of control and fell into a river. It fell 15 feet below the bridge; all the passengers were stunned, not knowing what had happened. Then they were all shrieking, while Jani and his son-in-law were quietly praying to Baba for help. Later the bus was pulled out by the help of the villagers and the police. The passengers were taken to the hospital; Jani and his son-in-law were discharged as they were not injured. The next day he read in the newspaper that all the passengers had died except both of them. Silently he thanked Baba for making them follow the request of the passengers and move to the rear of the bus, and thus had saved their lives. Baba's mercy is a unique universal mantel that saves his children whereever they may be.

Ref: *Sai Prasad* Magazine; 1993 (*Deepavali* Issue)

***

BABA'S PRESENCE IS MARKED BY AN AROMA

Prabhakar Mule had the good fortune of being employed as a teacher in the school in Shirdi. Thus he had the opportunity of living in this blessed village, and participating in all the festivals. And also often washing or bathing the Samadhi during Baba's *Mangal Snan*. During the period of 15 years that he taught in the school, he had numerous experiences some good while others were not so good. This was during the time that the Sansthan was under the Court Receiver during the 1950s.

It is a well-known fact that when Baba wants to make his presence felt he manifests it as an indescribably wonderful aroma. Both he and his wife Usha felt Baba's presence by this aroma that followed them. The aroma was behind her when she went the Chavadi or the Dwarka Mai and often would be present in her room at night. Once Prabhakar was ill and admitted in hospital; Usha went to give him some milk and the aroma was behind her as she walked along and finally Prabhakar's room was filled by this ethereal aroma. She silently thanked Baba for protecting her as she walked alone in the darkness to the hospital.

She was thankful that during Vijay Dassami she had had the good fortune of consuming Baba's Mahaprasad meal for 15 years and in auctioning Baba's shawls during this period.

Once Prabhakar went on a school trip to Mumbai, and as the children clamoured to see a movie, he obliged them. Some time during the movie, one boy went out and got lost. Now Prabhakar was in a dilemma as to where the child could be. The boy knew nothing of Mumbai and nor could he fend for himself. Prabhaker asked all the children to collectively pray to Baba for their friend's safe return. The earnest prayer was heard by Baba and a short while later the child was found. After a wonderful stay in Shirdi Prabhakar retired and went to Pune and lived there.

The Sadguru will always be behind you protecting you. And sincere prayers to him never ever go unanswered.

Ref: *Shri Sai Sagar* Magazine; 1996 (*Deepavali* Issue)

***

October 10

BABA TAKES A PINCH OF UDI FROM HER BOWL

After Prabhakar retired he went to Pune and lived there. On one Datta Jayanthi his wife Usha did a parayan of the *Shri Sai Satcharita* and completed reading it on the seventh day. During this week she had kept a small bowl filled with Udi before Baba's picture. That day she earnestly prayed to Baba saying, "Baba I desire nothing but you. Please assure me that you are always with me, taking care of me and my family and protecting us"

The next morning when she woke up, as was her habit, she stood in front of Baba's picture and prayed. She looked at the bowl for a sign and was delighted when she saw the imprint of Baba's thumb on the surface of the Udi. It was as if Baba had taken a pinch of Udi with his thumb and forefinger to apply on her forehead. Bappaji Ratnaparkhe had once told her that Baba used to apply Udi to the forehead of his devotees with his thumb and forefinger. Immediately she ran and took a photograph of it.

She went to Shirdi to attend the Poets Conference a few months later. At that time she placed the photograph at Baba's feet. Many of the devotees gathered there were glad to see it. Satish Kote saw the photograph and exclaimed that he saw Baba's idol in it. She and her husband were reassured that Baba had come to their home and was with them at all times. She took the photograph home and placed it in her prayer room and venerated it. Thus, her desire was fulfilled by Baba.

Baba reassures her of his eternal presence and protection.

Ref: *Shri Sai Sagar* Magazine; 1996 (*Deepavali* Issue)

***

JAYANTHI MEETS BABA IN HER NEIGHBOUR'S HOME

(The next two leelas occurred in the life of Jayanthi Aarse, who constantly thought of Baba from morning to night.)

One day her neighbour called her saying that "Baba has come and wants to meet you." She went to her home immediately and was astonished to see Baba seated in her living room having lunch. He was about 6 feet tall, fair, an old man and had dressed exactly like Baba and his face had a striking resemblance to the picture that she worshiped. Her neighbour had served him pithla and bhakri.

Jayanthi prostrated and gave him a coconut and 11 rupees as dakshina. She sat next to him and asked where he had come from. He replied, "I've come from Gangapur. I don't stay at Shirdi now as it has become full of pomp and show. Previously I couldn't get a little oil to light the lamps and now they offer flower chaddars, that is, flower garlands perpendicularly strung on a horizontal twine to make a curtain. However, I continue to go and get alms from five houses. Some people are determined to kill me, but I tell them that Arjun has to be born again to do so. What this means is that when *adharma* (unacceptable code of conduct of living) is rampant, *dharma* (righteous way of living) has to annihilate it. Everyone is in a hurry; they can't sit peacefully and have lunch. So I am served food that's leftover. Then someone stole my sheep wool blanket, so I don't stay in Shirdi too long."

In the meantime Jayanti ran home and brought bhakri and curry of fenugreek leaves that she had just prepared and fed him. She asked him if he would also come to her home as she lived next door. He promised to come during the *Ganpathi* festival for a meal. Disappointed she said that it was a month later. He replied, "I will definitely come." Upon completing his meal he left.

Our prayers should be from the bottom of our hearts, and should be done with peace and calmness.

Ref: *Shri Sai Sagar* Magazine; 1996 (*Deepavali* Issue)

***

BABA APPEARS AS A 14-YEAR-OLD LAD

The Ganpathi festival usually occurs in late August; Jayanti looked forward to Baba coming to her home for lunch. In anticipation she prepared pithla and bhakri daily as it was Baba's favourite food. Everyday she was disappointed as he didn't turn up. Then one day he was at her door; he told her he couldn't have lunch that day as he was in a hurry, and after a few minutes he left.

The days rolled by then one Thursday she served herself after offering the food to Baba's photograph. She was about to put the first morsel into her mouth when she felt the presence of someone at her door. There stood a young lad aged about 14 years, wearing a khaki pant and a white shirt. She asked him what he wanted; he said he was very hungry. She asked him to sit as she could serve him lunch. He sat down right there, so she served him lunch. He bent his head and hungrily ate the food. She asked him where he was from and who else was in his family.

He told her he had come from Shirdi and was alone. Immediately she asked him to come inside and eat. He sat close to her and continued eating. She said, "You must be ravenous so have a hearty meal. Don't hesitate to ask for anything that you need. Do have another helping of the meal." She was glad that she had made pithla and bhakri that day — Baba's favourite meal. She went inside the kitchen to get some more food and when she returned the boy had disappeared. Mentally she thanked Baba for keeping his promise to have a meal with her.

In chapter 40 of *Shri Sai Satcharita*, Baba says to Deo, "If he didn't recognise me why did he invite me? I will give up my life just to keep my word. But the words from my mouth will never be untrue." Baba by keeping his promise is teaching us to do the same.

Ref: *Shri Sai Sagar* Magazine; 1996 (*Deepavali* Issue)

***

REKHA FAILS TO RECOGNISE BABA

During the Divali of 1995, Rehka V. Patil was awaiting the return of her husband and Arun Chowadri. They had gone to pick up their new vehicle from the showroom. She had prepared *Shrikhand* (sweetened, flavoured hung curd confectionary) and *puris* (thin fried wheat cakes). It was 12 o' clock and they had not yet returned and she worried for their safe return.

At that moment an elderly man with a red turban, wearing a dhotar with Baba's picture in his hand came asking for alms. She gave him 1.25 rupees. He said, "Mai don't give me only dakshina give me lunch with something sweet to eat, as the new vehicle will soon be arriving at your doorstep." She didn't pay much attention to what he was saying as she was upset. According to tradition the puja of the new vehicle had to be performed first. Then a thanksgiving with Baba's Arati was to be performed. The food that she had prepared was to be first offered to Baba, and then everyone would eat. Now this man was asking for lunch, she consoled her self with the reasoning that feeding a hungry person was akin to offering it to God himself. But she was losing her temper, when it struck her, "How could this man know that the new vehicle was arriving soon?"

Nonetheless she called him inside her home and served him a platter with four puris and shrikhand. She neither asked him if he was satisfied or whether he wanted some more food as she usually did. Her attention was at the door awaiting the return of her husband; the man ate what was served, blessed her and left. She was picking up his empty platter when her husband and Arun arrived. They were late as they had taken the vehicle to Baba's temple and had puja done to it. But they had not given Baba any dakshina or offered him any confectionery.

She told them everything that had taken place in their absence. Arun said, "Baba came here to receive his dakshina and prasad and you didn't recognise him. You could at least have given that man a full and satisfying meal. But you were worried about rituals; Baba often said if you feed the hungry my hunger is appeased, and I am

300

satisfied. Please don't commit this blunder again." Immediately her husband and his friend went outside looking for that man but he had disappeared. The neighbour was seated outside his door but she had neither seen nor heard the man asking for alms. Neither did he stop at her door for alms.

When Baba does appear before us, we should have the "inner vision" to recognise him.

Ref: *Shri Sai Sagar* Magazine; 1996 (*Deepavali* Issue)

***

October 14

THE DYE FLOWED FROM BABA'S PALM

M. Mahalakshmi resided in Chennai; she thought she had no health problems like many of her friends. An ardent devotee of Sai Baba, she often visited his temple at Gowrivakaram. In August 2003 she suddenly fell ill with repeated bouts of dizziness and vomiting and was admitted in Deepa Hospital. On admission she was hypotensive and soon lost consciousness accompanied with convulsions. An MRI and brain scan revealed that she had a clot in her cerebral artery and was placed on anti-coagulants and anti-convulsive medications. Later she felt better so in 2009 she discontinued all her medications.

In 2011 she had severe headaches with giddiness and was admitted in Ramchandra Medical Centre. Prior to getting admitted, she went to the temple and the priest there reassured her that she would be all right and come home. At the hospital she was diagnosed to have an arteriovenous malformation and a cerebral arterial aneurysm. The aneurysm was five times larger than the size of the artery.

They advised her to have a stent placed to prevent its rupture and further cause hemorrhage; the procedure was explained to her in great detail. Mahalakshmi was frightened of the procedure, as there would be a burning sensation all the way to her brain. She requested the doctor to allow her to keep her small statue of Baba in front of her and he agreed. Then she earnestly prayed to Baba to do the procedure himself.

On the day of the procedure she was conscious and could see it on the monitor. They started the procedure and then she saw the statue of Baba next to the doctor. The statue had his right hand lifted and from his hand the medications were flowing to the catheter. She watched fascinated as the medicines flowed out of Baba's palm into the catheter. The procedure went well and she was finally discharged. Now they had to pay a very huge bill; she presented the bill to her manager as she was sure it would be paid, as her dues were regularly deducted from her pay. Unfortunately the dues had not been forwarded to the Insurance Company and now she would have to pay all of it. She went to the Manager of The Insurance Company to plead her case. As soon as she walked into his office she saw Baba's picture on his table and bowed to it. Then she told him everything that had taken place. She returned a few days later and was surprised to find her bill was paid. Thankfully she bowed to Baba for saving her twice. Baba is the "Doctor of Doctors," not only for our worldly ailments but also for our spiritual ailments.

Ref: As narrated by M. Mahalakshmi

***

October 15

SHE SAID "JAI SAI RAM," AND HER LIFE WAS SAVED

Rosy lived in Delhi with her extended family; her children were small at that time. One night she had a vivid dream wherein she was walking along the railway tracks with her mother. Suddenly a man jumped in front of her and tried to strangulate her. His grip tightened on her throat and she couldn't breathe. So with all her might she shouted, "Jai Sai Ram" and the man fled from there. She was very happy that she had called Baba's name even in her sleep and thought nothing of the dream. Little did she realise that the dream was a warning of events that were to follow.

A month later she had served her children their lunch; she had prepared a chicken curry for them. Her children had a hearty meal but they disliked the gizzards so they left it on their plates and went to play. Her husband was at work at that time and only the servant was around. Then she sat to have her meal when the gizzards got stuck in her wind pipe and she couldn't breathe. She was clutching her chest trying to breathe. The servant was there and she signed to him to thump her back but he was terrified and couldn't understand what she was trying to convey. She could see her son crying while her daughter was silently looking at her. She knew she was dying so she called Baba saying, "Jai Sai Ram" and out flew the gizzard.

This experience of taking Baba's name when she was at death's door and being saved turned her into an ardent devotee. O! The power of Baba's name is unfathomable.

Ref: As narrated by Rosy

***

October 16

DEEPA SAVED FROM A WATERY GRAVE

The entire family was devoted to Baba; they never ever stepped out of the house without first applying Udi on their forehead. Everyone kept a packet of Udi in their purse as a "life saver;" a protection against all ills. Deepa Savant resided in Mumbai and worked as a computer operator in an office. This leela occurred during the monsoons; torrents of rain fell when she left work one evening. That day was 15 June 1996; she and her friend walked to the bus stop; the rain water flowed like a river on the road and filled the sidewalk. Deepa saw a bus approaching them; she took a step to her right to make way for the bus to pass, when she fell into a huge pit. The road had been dug up for some repair work and she wasn't aware of it. As Deepa fell, her friend caught hold of her hand but as she too was being dragged into the pit, she let go and Deepa kept descending deeper and deeper.

Somehow Deepa held on to a root of a tree with one finger and shouted for help. Three male colleagues heard her and somehow pulled

303

her out of the pit. Badly shaken she went home and told her mother about it. "The finger that I held the root with had Baba's ring on it, and there was Udi in my purse. So Baba saved me from a watery grave," she said.

A few days later when the water had dried she took a look at the pit she had fallen in; it was about 20 feet deep and at the bottom of it were some spiky steel rods. She imagined what would have happened had she fallen on them. But she escaped with a few minor bruises.

Baba saves her from the watery grave of worldly existence by her ring finger just like Goverdhan Giri was lifted by Krishna with his little finger.

Ref: Shri Sai Sagar Magazine; 1996 (Deepavali Issue)

***

October 17

AN OLD MAN PULLED HER OFF THE TRAIN

Deepa's family had moved to Kurla. To go to work she had to board both the Western and Central Railways. She was running late one morning; she entered Kandivali station and the train was about to leave. She ran and caught the bar of one of the bogies and tried to enter but there were passengers crowding the entrance of the bogie. Nonetheless she ran holding the bar of the bogie but the train had left the platform. If she had taken another step she would have fallen on the side of the track and God only knows what would have happened.

At that moment an old man appeared out of nowhere and pulled her off the train and saved her life. She turned to thank him but he had disappeared. That evening she seriously thought about these freak accidents and realised that they always happened on *Amavasya* the darkest night of the month. That night she prayed to Baba to save her from these freak accidents that always seemed to occur on the darkest night of the month. She offered a coconut to Baba and prayed for help. After that with Baba's grace she was no more accident prone.

On Amavasya the prarabdha karma's arising from *tamo gunas* are stronger and many more in number. That prarabdha is taken up by Baba, hence no further accidents occur. He saves us not only from accidents that happen in the journey of worldly life but also in the journey of spiritual life.

Ref: *Shri Sai Sagar* Magazine; 1996 (*Deepavali* Issue)

***

October 18

A DEVOTEE OF VITTHAL ASKED HIM FOR SOME UDI

Every year Dnyaneshwar's palkhi exits Pune and traverses the Divae Ghat on their way to Pandarpur. This is a difficult path as it is barren without any villages nearby to give them water or render any help if the need arises. A group of volunteers of about 70 young men from the *Sai Das Mandal,* Pune offer them water and jaggery and some snacks every year. They render voluntary services from 9 a.m. to 6 p.m.; they are also joined by a group of volunteers from Bhivandi, Mumbai.

On 30 June 1996 Appasahib R Shivale had gone to Shivaji Nager Baba temple and brought five packets of Udi with him. He was busy giving water when an unknown gentleman came up to him and asked him for some Udi. He inquired, "Why do you need the Udi?" He told him that a 12-yr-old volunteer from the Bhivandi group was very sick. He had intense itching all over his body and was desparate. It was intolerable and he was tearing his clothes off his body. The group wanted to take the boy 10 miles away to Saswada village where they might find a doctor. But because of the crowds of pilgrims walking together they couldn't overtake them on a vehicle. So he took Appasahib to the boy. Appasahib mixed the Udi in a glass of water and made the child drink it; then Appasahib applied Udi on the child's entire body. A short while later the boy was relieved of his agony.

He asked the group if they knew the man who came to get Baba's Udi. But no one seemed to know him. Neither did the young boy know who he was. The man was a total stranger to Appa also. Appa wondered how a devotee of Vitthal should know about the power of the Udi. Just then the Arati "*Shirdi maje Pandarpur*" was heard on the loudspeaker. Wonderstruck Appa sat a while and thought, "How did that man know that I had Udi with me?" He then searched for that man but he had disappeared. It then dawned on him that he was Baba.

Vithal and Baba are one and the same.

Ref: *Shri Sai Sagar* Magazine; 1996 (*Deepavali* Issue)

***

October 19

LORD DATTA'S PICTURE CHANGED INTO THE FAKIR

His guru was Bramananda Saraswati and he was devoted to Lord Dattatreya. He did not know anything about Baba, and had little interest in finding out about him. This statement was given by Shankarrao Baivalli of Santa Cruz, Mumbai, but all that changed in 1936. His sister requested him to accompany her to Shirdi that year. He refused her invitation. A short while later while worshipping Lord Datta, he lovingly gazed at the photograph, and it gradually changed to the figure of a fakir wearing a torn kafni, with a white cloth tied around his head. Shankarrao got up and cleaned the photograph, with the same result. He cleaned it thrice but every time his favourite deity was transformed into the fakir. He had never seen the photograph of Baba; hence he did not know who it was.

That evening he went to Dr. Thakkar's home and saw Baba's photograph. He recognised him as the fakir that Lord Datta picture had transformed into. Eagerly he asked him who the fakir was. Then he received a lot of information about him. He immediately told his sister that he would gladly accompany her to Shirdi. His visit to Shirdi was the turning point of his life; there he experienced a lot of peace and serenity that he had never experienced before.

306

Again and again he visited Shirdi; Baba's effect on him was so great that he visited Shirdi nine times in a span of 6 months. On one of his visits he read the *Guru Chaitra* in 7 days. On the night of the completion he slept in the courtyard in front of the Samadhi Mandir. At midnight he heard footsteps near him. He looked up and found Baba gazing at him. Baba had walked from the Dwarka Mai, to the Samadhi Mandir. He had never seen Baba before and he was overwhelmed by the love and compassion in his eyes.

Then he consented to be on the executive committee, as Mr. Kharkar had resigned. He thus became the secretary of the Shri Sai Baba Sansthan Shirdi. He states, "All this was because of Baba's grace."

Baba shows him that he is none other than Lord Datta.

Ref: *Sai Sudha* Magazine; Vol. 5, No. 8, June 1945

***

October 20

BABA HIMSELF GIVES HER UDI

One evening Radhabai Neelalakshmi a resident of Bangalore went to the Sai Baba temple in Bellari. After the prayer service was over, she sat in a corner and meditated. Then she saw Baba and could not contain her joy; she started shaking and was drenched in perspiration. He walked up to her and said, "Bai take this Udi; I will give you two portions of Udi. The first amount, do not give to anyone; keep it safely in your home as it is for the longevity and welfare of your husband. The second portion distribute to all the devotees assembled here." As he said this, he placed some Udi on a piece of paper and folded it into a small packet and placed it in the palm of her hand. Then he placed a large quantity of Udi on another paper and placed it in front of her and vanished. A short while later she opened her eyes and found the packet in her palm, and right in front of her was a paper with a large amount of Udi.

With astonishment she tied the packet that was placed in her palm, in the fold of her saree. The Udi in front of her she distributed to the devotees. Her happiness and love for Baba knew no bounds.

With tears in her eyes she related the leela to her family and friends and said, "Baba's blessings are there for one and all."

On 2 October 1946 her husband returned from work in the evening. As soon as he entered the house he told her he was feeling very tired so he lay down. An hour later she went to check on him and found that he was running a high temperature. She made him comfortable, but soon he became delirious; her family advised her to call a doctor, but Radhabai refused stating that Baba could take care of him. She went to her prayer room and prayed fervently to Baba to come to her aid. A short while later she saw Baba riding a motorcycle and driving to her home. He then entered the room in which her husband was lying and the following conversation took place between them:

Baba: Why do you call me for such small things?

Radhabai: Baba my husband is running high fever and is delirious. Who else can I call but you?

Baba then laughed heartily and gave her a handful of Udi and said, "Sprinkle this all over his body." Radhabai did as Baba had ordered and within 15 minutes of administering the Udi, her husband started sweating profusely and his fever was gone. She looked for Baba but he was nowhere to be seen.

Baba comes running to the aid of his children.

Ref: *Sai Sudha* Magazine; Vol. 6, Part 4, September and October 1946

***

October 21

HIS GURU ALSO SAW BABA

(The experiences of O. V. Ganpathi Subrahmanyam, a resident of Madurai, during his long stay at Shirdi are given below. He visited Shirdi in October 1951 and stayed there for about 3 months.)

Subrahmanyam was 12 years old when he was given a picture of Baba, and had been praying to it ever since. However, Lord Subramanya was initiated by a renowned guru from Madras as their family deity. After he completed his studies he moved to Madras in search of a job; there he met Narshima Swamiji and Keshevayyia, and his faith was strengthened by them.

His family guru was upset by his devotion to Baba who he considered to be a Muslim charlatan. Through numerous letters he tried to bring Subrahmanyam back into the fold of devotees worshipping Lord Subrahmanya. He replied time and again that Baba was none other than Lord Subrahmanya himself.

One day Subrahmanyam was summoned by his guru to attend an important function of his family deity and he obeyed. His guru was no ordinary person but was endowed with many miraculous powers. During the function when devotional songs were being sung, many devotees danced in ecstasy. His guru asked him how he felt about the ritualistic worship that was performed. Subrahmanyam answered, "I am delighted as I saw Lord Sainath seated on the throne of Lord Subrahamanya pleasing everyone assembled here with his grace." The guru was utterly dismayed with his reply but lo! When he turned to the idol he saw Lord Sainath instead of the idol of Lord Subrahmanya. The guru then hugged him and blessed him generously.

According to the intensity of faith and the simplicity of devotion, Baba will appear in that form. All manifestations are from Parabrahma and Baba is Parabrahma.

Ref: *Sai the Mother, Anusuya the Amma*

***

October 22

BABA WAS SEATED ON THE THRONE

In 1951 Subrahmanyam took leave for a month and went on a pilgrimage, starting with Tirupati, and from Dond he arrived at Shirdi. He was utterly disappointed at what he saw for he had expected Shirdi to be like heaven on earth. His visit was to last for 3 days, but on the very first day he thought of returning home, after visiting all the holy sites. He marvelled at the devotees who worshiped Baba like their personal GOD while he felt they were mere edifices and photographs. Then he met a family from Andhra Pradesh, who spoke kindly to him and asked the purpose of his visit. There was an elderly lady with them who had the power of soothsaying and had told many devotees what experiences they would have during their stay at Shirdi. She also had the rare privilege of seeing Baba, instead of his idol seated on the throne during the Arati. She said that Baba looked like a king dressed in velvet with a crown and jewels.

Then the lady rushed towards Subrahmanyam and spoke in Hindi instead of her mother tongue. She told him he was to stay in Shirdi for 3 months and if he left prior to that the outcome would bring him immense misery. She also assured him that Baba would take care of all his needs and that he would have numerous spiritual experiences. Now Subrahmanyam was in a dilemma as he was still not sure if Baba really wanted him to stay for such a long period in Shirdi. He was concerned about his food arrangements and a room to stay in, but when Baba wanted him to stay would he not provide for him?

Baba's order to stay in Shirdi for 3 months is to do *sadhana* and surpass the three Gunas.

Ref: *Sai the mother, Anusuya the amma*

***

October 23

SUBRAHMANYAM'S LONG STAY IN SHIRDI

That day Subrahmanyam was meditating in the Dwarka Mai when he received the same message from Baba who had asked him to extend his stay at Shirdi for the next 3 months. Subrahmanyam was concerned that he would lose his job because of his extended stay, and he knew how difficult it would be to get it back. He applied to his office for an extension of leave and was informed that his services would be terminated soon. He wondered where he would stay and how he would survive in Shirdi without food and shelter. He was in a quandary as the food was different from what he usually ate. It was very cold and bleak by late evening. The problem of getting a room to stay in for such a long period loomed large before him.

Desperately he went to the Samadhi Mandir and started circumambulating it, praying that Baba would give him some concrete sign that he was to stay on. As he was circumambulating the Samadhi, it struck him that he should place chits before Baba

310

and thus get a definite reply. Then a lady from Chennai joined him, and Subrahmanyam thought he would ask her to pick up one of his chits after they had completed 108 rounds. While they were circumambulating the Samadhi he asked her if she would pick up a chit for her and she readily agreed.

The gentle lady suddenly went to the centre of the temple and stood there laughing hilariously clapping her hands in utter bliss. Subrahmanyam was terrified at the sudden transformation and a large crowd had gathered there to watch her. A young military deserter from the Rayalseema region got bewildered and taking some Udi rubbed it on her forehead thus breaking her trance. The lady then burst out saying, "Why did you do this; I had the rare opportunity of being with Baba. I beheld Baba in dazzling radiant colours on the Samadhi and both of us were playing there. He also told me that the chits were regarding Subrahmanyam's stay in Shirdi. And Baba had not granted him permission to leave, until his period of 3 months was completed." Thus he got his answer specifically from the lady from Chennai who didn't know the purpose of his placing chits on the Samadhi.

Thus Subrahmanyam finally decided to stay on in Shirdi as he had received confirmation from Baba. The rest of his stay was filled with unique experiences and revelations by Baba.

Every happening is in accordance with Baba's orders.

Ref: *Sai the Mother, Anusuya the Amma*

***

October 24

MANSIRAM ORDERED TO LOOK AFTER HIM

During Subrahmanyam's stay at Shirdi, the Sansthan would not give him a room for 3 months. He met Sagunmeru Naik and told him about his plight and succeeded in getting an extension for a week. Then he requested Shri Savant to provide him some accommodation, but he refused saying, "He was not ordered by Baba to do so." Nonetheless he allowed Subrahmanyam to keep his baggage in the cupboard in the Samadhi Mandir and to keep it locked whenever he went out. Thus he faced a lot of difficulties and finally stayed in the palanquin room in the Dwarka Mai. There he was befriended by Ramaswami who was also ordered by Baba not to leave Shirdi until he specifically allowed him to do so.

Then a strange thought took hold of Subrahmanyam; he thought that Baba was preparing him to lead the life of a monk. One day he gave away all his money, warm clothes and blanket to some of the beggars near the Samadhi Mandir. Thus he found himself cold and hungry; in desperation he sought help from his relatives and asked them to send him money. But the very relatives that had scrounged on him, turned a deaf ear to his pleas. Subrahmanyam thus survived by eating some fruits that had fallen from the numerous trees in Lendi Baugh, and quenched his thirst by drinking water from the canal near the Khandoba temple. But Baba had his own unique way of solving Subrahmanyam's problem.

Mansiram worked as a waiter in Bansiram's restaurant, which was adjacent to the Gurusthan. Mansiram was frantically searching for Subrahmanyam, who was sitting in the Dwarka Mai. Mansiram ran and hugged him and entreated him to have his meals in his hotel. Subramanyam refused, but Mansiram was very persistent and insistent. Finally Subramanyam asked him the reason for his persistence. Mansiram told him that the previous night he had dreamt of Baba, who asked him to take care of all his needs. Mansiram said, "Baba asked me to look after you as I would if he himself appeared before me. Hence I am following his orders." Subramanyam agreed on the condition that he would meticulously keep an account of the bills that he would repay once he returned home. Thus Baba in his unique way took care of Subramanyam's meals.

That evening Mansiram took Subramanyam home with him. It was a tiny room in the village, without any amenities. However Mansiram capably looked after Subramanyam's needs. He provided hot water for his bath, washed his clothes and even massaged his head and body with coconut oil. This arrangement suited Subramanyam, as he spent most of his time in the temple premises. Subrahmanyam spent his time meditating or circumambulating the various holy sites. Thus Baba took care of all his needs.

When Baba wants to draw his devotee to him, he reduces them to a state of zero.

Ref: *Sai the Mother, Anusuya the Amma*

***
312

THE "OUT OF BODY" EXPERIENCE

One night Subramanyam had an "out of body" experience wherein he felt that his entire body was bloated and his etheric being came out of it. It was the replica of the body he had just cast aside. Then it became very small and entered the 'castoff body' through the nostril and traversed the whole body starting with his brain. As it travelled along it examined each cell, vein, artery and nerve, making repairs as needed. Simultaneously it cleaned all of them with holy water. He could see all of this clearly as if he was watching it on a television screen in front of him. He felt this cleansing process was necessary to activate and purify him for some better work later. He also realised that both internal and external cleanliness was absolutely necessary.

Next he felt Baba was taking him to the hall of the Samadhi Mandir. In the middle section in front of the Samadhi, some angels had decorated it exquisitely and had made elaborate preparations. The floor was shimmering and had been cleaned with fragrant water. In the centre there was a huge *Yagna Kund* (a pit of fire for sacrificial rites) and in it a fire was burning brightly. Upasani Baba was sitting in front of it, offering oblations, along with the chanting of Vedic Mantras. He was offering many sacred articles that miraculously appeared in the palm of his hand. Upasani asked Subramanyam, to join him and seated him besides him.

Upasani asked him to watch the rituals and participate in the joyous occasion. Subrahmanyam was delighted to see how joyous the Gods were. Upasani then patted him on his back and commanded him to open his palm, facing upwards. And on his palm delectable eatables with fragrant aroma poured forth one after the other. He asked him to distribute it the great souls gathered there. And everyone participated in the celestial banquet.

One has to obey the Sadguru's command then the Sadguru takes up the responsibility to clean the devotee both externally and internally, so that the devotee realises the "self."

Ref: *Sai the Mother, Anusuya the Amma*

***

BABA PRESIDES OVER THE *SHRADA* CEREMONY

Subrahmanyam yearned to perform shrada (ceremony to appease the manes) for his departed ancestors. And it was accomplished by Baba in this unique way. In yet another dream Baba took Subrahmanyam to the banks of a crystal clear flowing river. Baba made him sit under a huge tree with spreading branches, giving shade to a huge area. The river banks had an abundance of these beautiful trees. Many saintly souls were seated under them in peaceful meditation. Baba told him that this was the holiest river feeding the entire cosmos to bloom with eternal life.

After he sat under the tree, Baba ordered numerous delicious confectionaries and savouries to appear before him. Then he presided over the ceremony and invited all the departed ancestors belonging to his lineage to participate in the feast. Baba ordered Subrahmanyam to serve the food to his ancestors. They were fed to their satisfaction. He recognised some of his ancestors, while he couldn't recognise others. The satisfied souls paid obeisance to Baba and blessed Subrahmanyam abundantly.

He turned to Baba disappointed and said, "Baba unfortunately I can't see my blessed father who gave birth to me. Where could he be?" Baba replied, "Your father has already taken rebirth in an affluent family. He has all the qualities for the fulfilment of life and emancipation in that birth." Subrahmanyam had a keen desire to obtain salvation for his ancestors and it was wonderfully fulfiled by Baba.

Baba teaches us that one has to perform shrada with utter faith under the guidance of the guru, and only then the departed souls will be satisfied and bless their clan.

Ref: *Sai the Mother, Anusuya the Amma*

***

314

BABA SHOWS HIM "THE COSMOS"

A festival of Goddess Sapthshringi was being held in Vani about 18 miles away from Shirdi. Subrahmanyam was eager to attend it as he was devoted to the goddess. He asked permission from Baba to attend the festival, but it was denied. Then he shed torrents of tears in front of Baba's photograph in the Dwarka Mai and finally Baba granted it reluctantly.

Delighted Subrahmanyam informed Mansiram about it and Mansiram brought his rickety bicycle and both of them set out before dawn the next morning. The tedious journey was fraught with difficulties, as the bicycle broke down at numerous places. There was a strong gale with thunder and lightening, interspersed with rain so they had to take shelter in various places. Mansiram huffed and puffed as he peddled on carrying Subrahmanyam. Finally they reached the premises; late in the evening and Subrahmanyam recited the *LakshmisahasraNaam* (thousand names of Lakshmi) before the deity.

That night he had a wonderful dream, wherein he was trying to climb a towering mountain. At the foot of the mountain was a beautifully decorated hall that he entered. There he saw seven beautiful ladies wearing exquisite jewelry and dazzling apparels playing the harp and singing melodiously. They invited him to join them and enjoy their company. Although Subrahmanyam was drugged by their beauty, he resisted temptation and proceeded ahead.

He made the arduous journey up the mountain chanting Baba's name and finally reached the summit. He entered a palace which was decorated with fragrant flowers. There he saw the great height of the sky and the world appeared tiny; he watched the sun, moon, the stars and a host of celestial bodies dangling from it. Suddenly Lord Vishnu appeared in his resplendent glory standing before him for a second, and he then turned into Sai Baba wearing his torn kafni. Baba embraced him and blessed him and promised to be with him through thick and thin. And then Subrahmanyam woke up. Immediately he asked Mansiram to take him back to Shirdi, and the journey back was without any difficulties.

315

He ran to the Dwarka Mai; water was trickling from Baba's eyes in the portrait, and he looked like the merciful goddess. He bowed at Baba's feet and told him that he had no other place to seek except his feet.

The entire cosmos is Baba. One has to surrender unconditionally at his feet, and then he will surely make our journey smooth on the bumpy road of life, and take us to our goal.

Ref: *Sai the Mother, Anusuya the Amma*

***

October 28

HE MEETS MOTHER ANUSUYA

Baba continued to shower his grace on Subrahmanyam even after he left Shirdi. Through Baba's grace he gained equality of vision and love for human beings and animals. He managed to get another job that involved a lot of travelling and thus he was able to visit numerous holy places, and also meet many saints during his frequent tours of duty. A colleague of his at work told him about a saintly lady in Andhra Pradesh, and described her divinity in great detail and requested Subrahmanyam to visit her. Subrahmanyam, however, continued to refuse his friend to accompany him as he hadn't received permission from Baba to do so. Yet he yearned to meet the saintly lady but he wondered how he would get permission as Baba had taken Maha Samadhi.

The next day he went to meet a Muslim friend and after 'Namaz' (Muslim prayers), the friend went into a trance and blessed him profusely. The friend in that state spoke Hindi and not Telugu, his mother tongue. Then he said that Subrahmanyam was blessed by the great *Awalia* Sai Baba and he would soon meet the saintly Mother Anusuya. Thus Subrahmanyam received Baba's permission, but he still wasn't sure so he sought permission through chits. Then ten chits were shuffled and reshuffled and every chit that was picked up gave the same answer, that is, permission was granted.

Subrahmanyam then went to meet Mother Anusuya and he was astonished that she looked exactly like Baba. On the very first meeting Mother spoke about Sai Baba so Subrahmanyam frequently visited her. Through her talks and discussions Subrahmanyam was convinced that Baba was universal and omnipresent and his faith for Baba increased manifold.

In this leela Baba gives a glimpse of his "universality and omnipresence."

Ref: *Sai the Mother, Anusuya the Amma*

***

October 29

CHAITANYA SWAMI'S EXPERIENCE

Subrahmanyam visited Shirdi soon after he had met Mother Anusuya. There he continued his routine of circumambulating the Gurusthan and Baba's Samadhi. Then he would go to Lendi Baugh and meditate for some hours. In Lendi Baugh he met a Swami from Kumbakoram, whose name was Chaitanya Swami. They started conversing with each other; the Swami was a Sanskrit scholar and spoke eloquently about God and devotion. A huge crowd followed him whereever he went.

One day Subrahmanyam spoke about the divine Mother and her marvelous philosophy. The next day Chaitanya Swami was seated outside the Samadhi Mandir, in an agonised state of mind shedding tears because he was not fortunate to meet her. Subrahmanyam, however, asked him to join him in his circumambulation of Baba's Samadhi but he refused to join him. Subrahmanyam left him and went on with his routine. While he was circumambulating the Samadhi he prayed to Baba to grace him in achieving his desire.

Subrahmanyam completed his circumambulation and was about to exit the temple when Chaitanya jumped up and embraced him and told him what had happened. When he was in a meditative trance Baba called him inside, and held his hand and both of them climbed on top of the Samadhi. Then Baba showed him many wonderful things. Then Baba asked the Swami to look at him, and lo! Baba was the Mother in a beautiful silk Saree bedecked with beautiful gold bangles. Then Baba patted the Swami gently on his back and assured

317

him that he would soon see the Mother. The Swami was ecstatic and laughed joyously. When Subrahmanyam next visited the Mother she had worn the same apparel that he had described.

Baba the creator is present in every creation of his.

Ref: Sai the Mother, Anusuya the Amma

***

October 30

THE THREAD CEREMONY OF KULKARNI'S SON

Vishun S. Kulkarni, was an ardent devotee of Baba; he was Prabhune's maternal grandfather. Prior to celebrating the thread ceremony of his eldest son Anil, he went to Shirdi and lovingly invited Baba. He placed the first invitation in the Dwarka Mai and humbly asked Baba to grace the occasion with his presence.

The thread ceremony was celebrated in a grand fashion, and the plates were placed for the feast. The guests were about to be seated when his wife noticed a fakir at the door, who was dressed and looked like Baba. Kulkarni went to him and invited him, and then he held his hand and respectfully seated him for the feast. He and his wife served Baba along with the other guests. Kulkarni placed a *pan vida* (rolled betel leaf with tobacco, lime and betel nut contained in it) next to his plate, as he had an intense desire that Baba should accept the Vida. Finally there was only a *boondi laddu* (Indian confectionery) left on Baba's plate. Baba turned to Kulkarni's wife and said, "Mai I am unable to eat this laddu, but I will surely eat the *rava laddu* (semolina confectionary) that you have in your stainless steel box. She went to fetch it and wondered how he knew that she had rava laddus. She served it to him with love and devotion. After the meal was over they took Baba to the bathroom to wash his hands, and waited outside. Kulkarni had the pan vida in his hand while his wife had a towel in hers. Baba didn't come out for quite a while and he had locked the door behind him. Kulkarni then pushed the door which opened but Baba wasn't there. There was no other door or a window for him to get out of the bathroom.

318

Shortly after the ceremony Kulkarni visited Shirdi and placed a pan vida on Baba's Samadhi as he was eager that Baba would accept it and returned home. Upon his return early one morning he dreamt of Baba. Baba said, "You invited me for the thread ceremony and I kept my promise by attending it."

Kulkarni with folded hands said, "You had your meal but didn't accept the pan vida" Then Baba laughed and said, "You respectfully asked me to have the meal, so I had a hearty meal. However, you just kept the vida there. When did you ask me to eat it? And was it necessary for you to come all the way to Shirdi to offer it to me. I don't need any vida; I need just your love. Just continue to love me the way you do, forever." And then the dream ended.

Every act, however small it may turn out to be, should be performed with love and devotion and not as a routine.

Ref: *Shri Sai Sagar* Magazine; 1998 (*Deepavali* Issue)

***

October 31

BABA GIVES HIM TIRTH IN THE ICU

Suddenly Vinayak Prabhune got severe chest pains; he was checked by his physician who advised him to get hospitalised as further investigations were necessary. The doctor then admitted him in the ICU as his condition was serious. His chest pains didn't reduce much with the treatment. After a few days of bed rest he got anxious about his hospitalisation. He chanted Baba's name and prayed saying, "Baba how much time should I spend lying here?"

That night he was restless and couldn't sleep. At midnight it was very quite in the ward, no one was up and about. Then he felt the presence of someone standing next to his bed. He could see a tall man in a kafni standing next to his bed. The man gently slid his hand under his head and helped him to sit. He asked him to cup his hands and from a bottle poured some water into his palm. Then Baba asked him to drink it and Prabhune drank it and recognised it to be the tirth from Baba's Samadhi. He gave him the tirth three times; Prabhune realised that it was Baba, so he tried his utmost to have a good look at his face but couldn't. Then Baba again gently laid him on the bed and walked out of the ICU

Then Prabhune slept peacefully; when he awoke the next morning he was absolutely well. He got up and went to the bathroom brushed his teeth and had a wash. When he was returning to his bed the doctor accosted him and said, "You are in the ICU anything can happen to you at any time. Why are you up and about?" In return Prabhune said, "There is nothing wrong with me? I am fine" The doctor asked him,

"You are so sick. How did you get the strength to get up and go to the bathroom?" Prabhune then related the leela that took place the previous night. Upon hearing this, the doctor joined his palms together and paid obeisance to Baba.

Baba's tirth is ambrosia, and its power is unfathomable.

Ref: *Shri Sagar* Magazine; July–August 2002

***

$$\boxed{\textit{November 1}}$$

SAINATH SENT ME HERE

Chandrashekar Rane's father-in-law (Nana) suffered from a severe heart attack while attending a wedding. He was immediately admitted to Sion Hospital and Rane went to stay overnight with him. After the initial treatment Nana seemed all right but suddenly he had a severe bout of cough. Rane gave his some water and the coughing seemed to abate. Then the ECG monitor showed bizarre tracing, and this was followed by violent coughing. Rane rang the bell again and again to summon a nurse, but no one came. He could see Nana writhe in pain, but was helpless. Then Nana signed to him to go and fetch help.

Rane went to the doctor's office and saw that the entire staff was there and the doctor was giving orders to them about a patient. They all ran hither and thither fetching intravenous fluids and getting their equipment ready. Rane accosted a nurse who told him that a very young patient was being admitted who had suffered a severe heart attack and was in a serious condition. Soon they all proceed to the OT (operation theatre) and Rane was all alone. He had no other option but to go to the OT or Nana would lose his life. Mentally he prayed, "Baba you are my only refuge; please be with me and help me." Stealthily he approached the OT and opened the door; there what he saw was a flurry of activity — the doctors were administrating artificial respiration and thumping the patient's chest, giving IV fluids, etc. Then a doctor noticed him and shouted, "Who sent you here?" Rane replied, "Sainath sent me here," then he told the doctor about Nana's condition and pleaded for help. That doctor happened to be Nana's doctor and he calmly told Rane to give Nana a tablet from a particular bottle, and also asked Rane to place a tablet in Nana's mouth sublingually. Then he assured Rane that he would see Nana in a short while.

Rane ran to the ward and carried out the instructions the doctor had given, and Nana started improving, except for the ECG monitor; it was still showing erratic tracings. Rane thought, "Nana looks better, but he is still at death's door." After some time the doctor arrived along with the nurses and examined Nana and told Rane that a pacemaker would be necessary. They asked him to get a prescription filled at once, and while they were treating Nana, Rane ran and informed the family that Nana's condition was critical and they should come immediately. When they arrived he took them to the OT; he was shocked to see the door was wide open and no one was there. A nurse informed him that the pacemaker had been placed successfully and Nana was resting in another ward. They proceed to that ward and found Nana sleeping peacefully and on the nightstand was a picture of Baba with his hand raised in the ashirwad posture.

Sai Naam Japa is the pacemaker.

Ref: Chandrashekar Rane; *Saianubhav*

***

November 2

BABA SHOWS HIM HIS *VISHVA ROOP*

In November 2002 Prabhune again suffered from severe chest pain. He felt his chest was constricted and the stabbing pain continued, and he didn't know what to do. He went and sat in the balcony to get a breath of fresh air, but that too didn't seem to work. He continued sitting there and inhaled slowly. His wife asked him if she could help ease his pain. Suddenly he had an irresistible urge to visit the temple. But the daunting task of climbing down three flights of stairs seemed to be impossible in his present condition. Finally when he couldn't hold himself back any longer, he told his wife he just had to go to the temple and left.

As he drove he could hardly breathe, but it was 7 p.m. at that time and if he didn't hurry he would miss the Arati. Somehow he reached the temple and drove right up to the entrance. What he saw made his hair stand on end. The central area had been kept vacant so that devotees could see Baba's idol and padukas from outside if they didn't wish to enter the temple. The padukas had Baba's tooth and chillum enshrined in it. On those very padukas he saw Baba standing, wearing a snow-white kafni and smiling benevolently at him. And his snow-white teeth were visible as he smiled. But the most remarkable feature of this vision was that Baba was huge and as he stood his head touched the ceiling of the sanctum sanctorum. Prabhune's eyes opened wide with astonishment as he beheld Baba's glorious *vishva roop* and Baba seemed to fill the entire universe. Indeed Baba did fill the entire universe with his blessed form. Prabhune went into a trance when he saw this. His chest pain disappeared, and a feeling of peace and calm enveloped his entire being.

He went and parked his motorbike in the stand, and when he returned Baba had disappeared. In a daze he entered the temple and sat down;he was unaware of the Arati being performed. When the Arati was over his friend came and shook him and said, "Today you performed Baba's Arati?" Eagerly Prabhune told him what he had beheld and indeed he had mentally performed Arati to Baba's vishva roop.

Baba removes prarabdha in his own unique way. Through this leela he is teaching us that if our prayers are done with *thrikarna shuddi*, that is, through the mind, body and speech then they will reach him undoubtedly resulting in his *sakshatkar* (divine vision).

Ref: *Shri Sagar* Magazine; July–August 2002

***

November 3

HOW BABA BLESSED PRABHUNE

Before he bought his apartment, Prabhune and his family rented a two-room apartment. One night he was sleeping next to the window, while his daughter was sleeping on a cot that was against the opposite wall. On that wall there was a coloured picture of Baba with his hand raised in the ashirwad position. At night his daughter felt thirsty and woke up. What she saw left her mesmerised and she forgot about her thirst. From Baba's raised hand a beam of light was emitting and it traversed the room and touched her father's body. After touching his body it stayed there and didn't go out of the window.

Fascinated she continued watching this phenomenon; it was as if someone had pointed a flashlight on her father's body. But there was no flashlight in that room. The next morning she related what she had seen the night before. Humbly Prabhune said, "You are indeed fortunate to behold the blessings that pour forth from Baba's hand."

In the early '50s the Abhishek puja was conducted on top of the Samadhi. The devotees were seated on wooden seats in front of Baba's idol, and after the puja they were allowed to prostrate at Baba's feet. Nowadays because of the overwhelming crowds, this practice is discontinued.

Prabhune would without fail reach Shirdi in time to buy an Abhishek ticket. He would get up early in the morning and catch a bus to Shirdi at Shivaji Nager. On one such occasion he missed the bus and there was no bus till 10 a.m., so it was impossible for him to reach in time. So he boarded a bus going to Dhule and reached Shirdi. But there were no tickets available for the Abhishek; disappointed he went to the Dwarka Mai. The Dwarka Mai was empty and he sat in front of the padukas and cried, "Baba this is the first time that I am unable to perform your Abhishek, (Abhishek is the ritualistic holy bath). Do something so I am able to perform it." Then with disappointment he banged his head on the padukas. Tears were rolling down his cheeks as he banged his head again and again.

Then he felt someone place his hand on his head with compassion and caress his head twice. He recognised that touch and looked up. No one was there, but there was a smile on Baba's Dwarka Mai picture. Then he looked down and his tears had accumulated on the padukas; he had done Abhishek to them with his tears.

Baba covers his children with his blue light eternally and fulfils their wishes, however trivial they may be.

Ref: *Shri Sagar* Magazine; 2002 (*Deepavali* Issue)

***

"I EXTENDED HER LIFE FOR 15 DAYS"

Prabhune and his wife once went to a small village in Satara to visit his cousin. His young son wouldn't sleep without drinking milk and there wasn't any milk at home. His cousin went to fetch it and got bitten by a snake. He returned home writhing in pain and the leg had turned blue and became cold and pulseless. It was evident that he would lose his limb and in that village there wasn't a doctor to treat him. His relatives started blaming Prabhune for sending his cousin to fetch milk in the dark as there were no street lights.

In desperation he prayed to Baba and taking some Udi he massaged it on the bitten area; then he took a little and rubbed his entire leg with it. Chanting Baba's name he asked his cousin to vigorously thrust and shake his foot. This he did thrice and soon his pulse returned and the foot returned to normal. His relatives asked what mantra he had recited to purge out the venom. He told them that it was the power of Baba's name and the effect of Baba's Udi that cured his cousin.

One day Prabhune's neighbour's son Raghunath came to his home at night. Sobbing he said, "My mother is seriously sick and my brother has got her admitted in the hospital." Both of them went to the hospital thinking they might be of some help. From 9 p.m. till midnight the doctor tried in vain to revive her. Then both her sons started crying on Prabhune's shoulder. He remembered Baba and his Udi, but as he had left home in a hurry he didn't have any with him.

The only alternative was the ash from an incense stick which also wasn't available in the hospital. His only choice was mud from the street as is mentioned in the *Shri Sai Satcharita*. He prayed to Baba and took some mud from the street and placed it on the palm of her son saying, "Think this is Udi and with faith rub some on your mother's forehead and she will feel better." They did that and lo! Their mother sat up as if she had just woken up.

Prabhune returned home late that night and immediately fell asleep. Early next morning he dreamt of Baba's Dwarka Mai portrait. In the dream Baba was physically seated in the portrait and he said,

325

"Last night you called me so I ran to help you. But that mother was to have expired yesterday. Now I have extended her life for 15 more days. This I did so that your faith in me and my Udi would remain unshaken."

The next day Prabhune went to his neighbour's home and privately spoke to the sons. He asked them to inform their dear and near relatives to visit their mother within a fortnight. Exactly on the fifteenth day she passed away peacefully in her sleep.

Through this incident Baba confirmed that one's immense faith in the Udi and in the chanting of his name would remain unshaken forever.

Ref: *Shri Sai Sagar* Magazine; 1998 (*Deepavali* Issue)

***

November 5

BABA GIVES HIM A SON NAMED SAI PRASAD

Prabhune thought, "If only Baba would bless me with a son." He had two daughters and yearned to have a son. "What if the next child is a daughter," he wondered; so he placed his problem at Baba's feet. Once he went to a renowned saint and asked him about it. The saint told him he would definitely get a daughter as he was not destined to have a son. At that moment he felt that it was a challenge to his faith in Baba.

Some time later his wife became pregnant; he told her he would go to Shirdi every month for the next 9 months till she gave birth. Thus he visited Shirdi and got down at Sathe Wada and went to room number 21, where Nana Sahib Rasne resided. He then went to the Samadhi Mandir and performed Abhishek to the Samadhi and prostrated at the feet of Baba's idol. Nana Sahib loved Prabhune like a son, so he asked, "Why are you coming to Shirdi every month? What important work do you have with Baba?" Prabhune gave him an evasive answer.

On his next visit he stayed overnight with Nana Sahib. He woke up early in the morning and found Nana Sahib seated on the floor smiling at him. Then Nana Sahib said, "Just a short while ago Baba came and sat on your cot. I asked him, the reason of your regular visits to Shirdi. And he told me that you come to Shirdi every month because you want a son. Baba said, 'I cannot grant him that as he isn't destined to have a son.' So I told Baba if he so desires then can't you fulfil his desire; just give him a son and be done with it. But Baba stubbornly said, 'No' and when I kept insisting he finally agreed and left."

When Prabhune returned to Pune he was invited to a devotee's home, because a saint named Gautam Maharaj was visiting them that evening. He went there at the scheduled time and sat in a corner as the room was crowded. The saint arrived and looked around the room and beckoned to Prabhune and said he would like to visit his home. They then went home and his wife welcomed them. Then he said, "I was searching for you as I have a message from Baba for you. He told me to tell you that you will get a son and he should be named Sai Prasad."

A month later Prabhune got a vivid dream wherein he saw a lighted lamp outside his home. Then the light from the lamp came towards him and stopped in front of him and he woke up. He realised that the light was an indication of the light of his descendants, that is, a son would be born. And thus it came to pass; his wife delivered a healthy boy who was named Sai Prasad.

Nothing is impossible with Baba, as every happening will occur at his command and his will.

Ref: *Shri Sai Sagar* Magazine; November and December 2003

***

November 6

BABA CHIDES HIM FOR CALLING HIS SON A STONE

When my wife's due date of pregnancy drew near, she got labour pains and was admitted in hospital late one evening. As I had two small daughters to take care of, I was unable to be with her at the hospital. Even at night there was no news of her delivery, and I fell asleep some time after midnight. Early next morning around 5 a.m., I dreamt of Baba. In the dream I was in the Dwarka Mai where Baba was sitting next to the railing. I ran and placed my head on his feet. Then Baba put his hand out and in a stern voice said, "Give me my peda's." Hearing this I woke up and heard someone knocking on my door. Hurriedly I ran and opened it and there was my sister smiling. She said, "Congratulations you have a healthy boy. And his mother is fine." I went to Shirdi as soon as I could and gave peda's to Nana Sahib Rasne. Then after a bath I went to the Samadhi Mandir and offered peda's at Baba's feet.

"According to Gautam Maharaj's order, the child was christened Sai Prasad. Indeed he was the joyful blessing in our lives, and Baba's caring concern for him was very evident. Sai Prasad, however, was a very stubborn child, and when he started going to school he would have his own way. Often times I chided him saying in Marathi, "You are as stubborn as a stone."

One night I dreamt that I was in the Samadhi Mandir and in place of the idol I saw Baba sitting there. And in his lap I saw Sai Prasad sitting happily. Then I looked at the Samadhi and there was a huge boulder on it. In surprise I asked Baba who had kept the boulder there. Then Baba pointed to Sai Prasad and said, "Arre! You often call him a stone. He isn't a stone he is my blessed prasad that I have given you. Don't ever call him a stone again" I took Baba's words seriously and never called my son a stone again.

Thanks to Baba's blessings, Sai Prasad grew up to be an intelligent kind caring young man. Every time my wife and I go to Shirdi our eyes are filled with grateful tears," states Vinayak Prabhune.

Each and every atom is his manifestation, so we should not disrespect the same. Thus, Baba is teaching us not to disrespect his prasad (blessings).

Ref: *Shri Sai Sagar* Magazine; November and December 2003

***

"GIVE ME MY PEDA'S RIGHT NOW," ROARS BABA

Years ago Parachute and family visited Shirdi and he was in the Dwarka Mai when he met a devotee who resided in Pune. Prabhune resided in a neighbourhood close by; while they were conversing, Prabhune asked him how he became devoted to Baba.

Then Parachute said, "When I was young we resided in a village close to Shirdi. My mother was an ardent devotee of Baba and visited Shirdi often, but I wasn't. After I completed my education I looked for a job everywhere but my attempts were futile. Disheartened I finally gave up, and wasted my time playing marbles with the children in my neighbourhood. My mother was very concerned about this and she spoke to me about it. I, however, told her that I had tried earnestly to find a job but didn't succeed. Finally she couldn't bear to see me waste my life away and asked me to make a pilgrimage to Shirdi. She asked me to pray to Baba's Samadhi for a job, and promise Baba that I would offer half a kilo of peda's out of my first pay. Thus I visited Shirdi not out of any faith but merely to please my mother. I did exactly as she had told me to do.

I stood before Baba's Samadhi with folded hands and a strange peace came over me. Upon my return home, things started happening fast. A company in Ahmednagar hired me, so I brought my family and resided there, I did well and I soon forgot all about the vow. Days passed into months and months into years, and Baba lost his patience. Early one morning I dreamt I was in the Dwarka Mai and Baba was sitting next to the railing. As soon as I entered it, Baba put out his hand and roared, "Give me my peda's right now."

My mother advised me to go immediately, so I asked my boss for a leave to go to Shirdi. He said, "Pack your bags and come to work tomorrow." I thought he was unwilling to sanction the leave, though I repeatedly requested him. The next morning I was surprised that he was waiting with his family in a car. He asked me to sit next to him and started driving. I asked him where we were going. He told me that as I wished to go to Shirdi he also decided to accompany me with his family. I was delighted as finally I was able to fulfil my vow comfortably."

Keep your promise. Never ever forget to fulfil any vow that you make.

Ref: *Shri Sai Sagar* Magazine; 2003 (*Deepavali* Issue)

***

November 8

BABA APPEARS AS A COOLIE AND SAVES HIS LIFE

Sithakanth D. Kamath was transferred from Mizoram to Mumbai in August 1971, as his tenure there was over. His colleagues blessed him as the journey was a long, tedious and treacherous one. Kamath set out after praying to his family deity, as the first stage of the journey was to be by bus that had to traverse through mountain terrain. It was full of steep mountains on one side with deep ravines on the other. If the driver lost control of the vehicle for a second the bus would fall into a deep ravine, on the other hand the region was prone to landslides without any warning. Finally he reached Silchar safely.

The second stage of his journey was to be by train; at Silchar Kamath got a ticket and a berth through a Military officer and was on his way to Mumbai. The train traversed through huge tunnels and was on its way to Guwahati. Kamath lay comfortably on his berth and was dozing off when he felt the presence of someone standing close to him. He looked up and saw a fakir who had donned an ochre kafni, and had a long white beard and moustache. He was about 55 years old, and spoke in Hindi, "Babuji, get down here. Go sightseeing in the city and visit the Kamaksha temple," and saying this disappeared. Now Kamath was in a dilemma; if he did alight here he would have to disembark with his entire luggage and then board another train. What if he didn't manage to get a ticket for the rest of his journey?

He was unaware of when the train halted in Guwahati, and a coolie was standing in front of him. The coolie looked exactly like the fakir except he had on a red uniform with a badge. The badge number was 389; the coolie swiftly collected all his belongings and said, "Let's go." In a daze Kamath followed him and the coolie deposited his luggage in the cloak room and disappeared. After Kamath had had a bath and a cup of tea, he heard that the train in which he had been travelling had met with an accident a few miles away. Unfortunately many passengers lost their lives and others were seriously injured. In vain Kamath searched for the coolie who had saved his life. Then he went to the stationmaster and asked for the coolie whose badge number was 389. He learned that there was no such badge number and hence no such coolie.

The next day he reached Nasik, when he had an irresistible urge to visit Shirdi. Following his instinct he went to Shirdi and then went into the Samadhi Mandir. He was so astonished that he stood gaping at the idol, for it resembled the fakir and the coolie who had saved his life.

We commence our worldly journey with our karmas as our luggage. It is only our Sadguru who acts as a coolie and carries the luggage to save us from accidents that occur on our journey.

Ref: *Shri Sai Sagar* Magazine; July–August 2006

***

November 9

"YOU WILL GO TO SHIRDI FOR SURE," SAID THE OLD MAN

S. D. Mahajan, a resident of Nagpur states, "Till 1974 I was an atheist, but all that changed in December that year." Mahajan worked in the State Transport Service Nagpur, and was sent to Bhosari for a course in Computer Training. After the completion of his course he was given 2 days off to go sightseeing in Maharashtra. He had reserved his seat for his return journey when he met a friend, who entreated him to visit Shirdi. Mahajan made every possible excuse to avoid the trip, when he heard an old man who stood before them say, "When he is entreating you to visit Shirdi why are you refusing to go?" Mahajan turned to the old man in anger and said in English, "What right do you have to interfere in a private conversation." Mahajan then looked at the old man intently; he had a pleasant smile on his face, and placing his hand on Mahajan's shoulder said, "You will go to Shirdi for sure," and disappeared. The moment the old man placed his hand on his shoulder an incredible change took place in him and he agreed to go.

His friend then took his ticket and in return gave him his pass to travel to Shirdi not caring that he had committed an offence by doing so. Mahajan boarded the bus to Shirdi while his friend returned to Nagpur. Mahajan knew nothing about Shirdi, but as soon as he alighted from the bus the same old man stood in front of him. He said, "I have bought two meal tickets for us; I have also taken care of your accommodation. Now have a wash as there is no hot water, and let's proceed for lunch." The old man efficiently took care of everything.

The next day the old man again took him for a meal, but behaved strangely making weird actions with his hands and talking continuously. Then he lifted his arms above his head and said, "He is saved. Otherwise he would have died needlessly. You would have also been in trouble as the ticket was on your name." Mahajan couldn't understand a word of what he was saying. After lunch Mahajan pondered on what the old man had said. Then he heard that the bus in which his friend was travelling had met with a terrible accident and there were many fatalities. Mahajan was concerned about his friend's safety. Later he found out that his friend was safe as he had discontinued his journey at the time the old man was saying that he would have died needlessly. At that moment he realised that the old man was Baba, and Baba had saved his friend's life. Mahajan was saved from a serious offence as his friend was travelling on his ticket. Baba had planned his entire journey and taken care of the minutest detail with care, and the atheist turned into an ardent devotee of Sainath.

Baba draws his children to him at his own will.

Ref: *Shri Sai Sagar* Magazine; July–August 2006

***

332

BABA FORCES THE DRIVER TO
RETURN AND PICK UP HIS DEVOTEE

In 1962 Kamal P. Gore was very excited, as her sister had asked Kamal to accompany her to Shirdi. She went to the Dadar bus stand and waited for the bus which was to arrive at 12 noon, but there was no sign of it. Three hours later she was still waiting there as the bus had not arrived; she was so eager to go to Shirdi that she had not moved an inch from there. Finally a bus turned up but it proceeded without stopping there. She inquired at the counter, the reason for the bus not stopping there and was told that as no passenger had reserved a seat on that bus, it had proceeded without stopping. Silently she told Baba, "If you didn't want me to come to Shirdi why did you give the idea to my sister to ask me to accompany her in the first place." Disappointed she thought of returning home as there was no other bus going to Shirdi after that. Just then to her astonishment the same bus that had gone without stopping, returned. The conductor put his head out of the window and said, "Bai don't worry this bus will not proceed without you."

Kamal entered the bus; all the seats were occupied. Two passengers immediately got up and gave her their seat. Some passengers came and touched her feet, while she wondered what was happening. The conductor told her that the bus had gone up to Ruyia College when the driver heard a voice saying, "Take the bus back to Dadar as my devotee is waiting there." This happened twice; the third time the voice clearly said, "If you go any further the bus will meet with a fatal accident." The driver consulted the passengers who unanimously told him to return to Dadar and so the bus had returned to pick her up.

Baba will definitely take us to his "Gurukul", that is, Shirdi at any cost if we are chosen for his admission.

Ref: *Shri Sai Sagar* Magazine; 2005 (*Deepavali* Issue)

***

BABA SAVES HIM FROM BEING KILLED BY A MUSLIM GANG

There was political unrest in the country in 1947; every day there were numerous Hindu–Muslim riots and bloodshed, especially in Mumbai. At that time Dhundiraj Shejwalkar was 17 years old and an ardent devotee of Baba. His elder brother worked in the Chemistry Department of Dharmarsinghi College in Rajkot and was sick at that time; his condition turned from bad to worse, and he and his family were in desperate need of help. Dhundiraj decided to go to Rajkot, so he prayed to Baba, applied Udi and fearlessly set out. He boarded the train at Bombay Central station; Dhundiraj could speak no other language but Marathi.

A Muslim aged about 50 years along with his wife and teenage daughter came and sat next to him. A short while later, the ladies took off their Muslim habit and hung it on a peg and began to converse with Dhundiraj. The mother asked Dundiraj, if he would mind eating some *shira* (semolina cooked with sugar and clarified butter) that she had brought with them? Dundiraj replied, "As I believe in Baba I don't make any distinction between Hindus, Muslims or Christians. As I am a Brahmin I do not eat meat. So I don't have a problem eating your shira." The mother immediately served him and her family the shira.

At Dadar about 30 Muslims entered their bogie armed with knives, swords and sticks. They were covered with blood and some had bleeding wounds. In anger they shouted, "Are there any despicable Hindus here?" The father and mother said in unison, "No. No. Brothers! We are all Muslims here." They looked around and saw all of them eating shira together and left the bogie satisfied. The family disembarked at Varamgaon the next morning; with tears in his eyes Dhundiraj bid them farewell as they had saved his life.

Upon reaching Rajkot he wrote to his family about the incident on the train. His mother, however, knew he was safe, as Baba had appeared in her dream that night and reassured her. He said, "Your son is safe, as I went and sat next to him and saved his life"

Baba teaches us to be united irrespective of religion, that is, *Sab Ka Malik Ek.*

Ref: *Shri Sai Sagar* Magazine; April, May, June 2005

***

November 12

BABA GIVES RAJU HIS MEAL TO EAT

Some years ago a young lad named Raju worked for the maintenance department of the Shri Sai Baba Sansthan Shirdi; his job was to sweep the Samadhi Mandir and keep it clean. Once it was very crowded and he had to sweep it almost continuously, thus he forgot to have his lunch. Just before his duty was over he was extremely tired so he went upstairs and lay down to rest a moment and fell fast asleep. He slept soundly through the Sej Arati and he was locked inside the Samadhi Mandir. Startled he woke up around midnight and looked around; then he realised what had happened. His stomach was growling with hunger; from the balcony he looked down and could see that the mosquito net was put up. He came down and stood before Baba's idol and earnestly prayed. With tears in his eyes he told Baba what had happened and begged for forgiveness.

Suddenly he saw some movement inside the mosquito net and was astonished to see Baba. Baba lifted the net and said in a calm voice, "You are very hungry aren't you? Come on up; see there they have kept a platter of shira puri for me. Sit and eat it calmly, I assure you that nothing will happen to you," and saying this Baba disappeared. Raju had a hearty meal and got down and sat next to the Samadhi in extreme bliss.

The next morning when the Samadhi Mandir was opened for the Kakad Arati, Raju was reprimanded for staying overnight in the temple. He was reported to the officials and severe action was to be taken against him for breaking the rules. He was accused of intent to steal and was threatened with the loss of his job. Raju pleaded with them and told them what had happened, but no one believed him. Finally he was reported in writing to the head office in Mumbai and further action was to be taken on their recommendation.

That night the officer dreamt of Baba who said, "Do not terminate Raju as I gave him my offering of shira puri to eat. It is not his fault; he's an honest lad. I want you to notify the Sansthan to make his job permanent from this very moment," and Baba disappeared. The officer immediately got up and wrote a letter to the officials at Shirdi to that effect. He also told them that he would be coming to Shirdi to meet Raju. The Sansthan Committee was astonished at the turn of events. The next day the officer reached Shirdi and after bowing to the Samadhi he wanted to meet Raju. Raju was engrossed in sweeping at that time; the officer went straight to him and prostrated before him. He said, "You are indeed fortunate that Baba himself came and fed you his offering of shira puri." Then he related his dream to the astounded Sansthan officials.

Baba teaches us to be considerate and treat this body as a temple where he resides. When we work hard and sincerely for its maintenance, then he will make sure we are not hungry. Baba provides a sumptuous meal of spiritual elevation and self-realisation.

Ref: *Shri Sai Sagar* Magazine; 2001 (*Deepavali* Issue)

***

November 13

THEY MEET BABA IN THE DENSE FOREST

K. C. Panth and Renuka, his wife resided in Pune. Panth was an ardent devotee of Baba but his wife wasn't, although she had visited Shirdi a few times. Their paternal families resided in Bakshi-ke-talab a suburb of Lucknow. Once he and his wife went to visit their family and reached Lucknow late at night. It was very dark when they boarded the bus to Bakshi-ke-talab. They were so engrossed in conversing with each other that they missed their stop. They asked the conductor when their stop would come and he told them that they had already passed the stop some time ago. At that time the bus was traversing through dense forest. They requested the conductor to stop the bus and got down.

Panth and Renuka had heard how travellers were looted and killed by dacoits who lived in the forest. They had to walk back about 5 miles to get to their destination with their baggage. As they had no other choice they walked slowly back alone; it was frightening because they were alone. A few trucks carrying cargo did pass by and they made signs for them to stop but the drivers probably thought that they were dacoits and sped away. Soon they were trembling with fear as they heard eerie noises from the forest, when Renuka suddenly shouted, "Baba please save us." At that moment they saw a *rickshaw* approaching them; they begged him to take them home. The driver readily agreed when he heard where they wished to go. He told them he was returning to Bakshi-ke-talab, after delivering some goods and had got delayed.

Quickly they sat in the rickshaw and proceeded. On the way they met an old bearded sadhu and asked him to join them as he was also going to the same place. He agreed at first but when he saw the couple sitting in a cramped position along with their baggage, he refused. He told the driver that he would walk as he didn't wish to trouble the couple.

Finally they reached home; Panth's parents were surprised to see them arrive at such a late hour. As Panth related what had happened he realised the wonderful leela was Baba's doing. And Baba had appeared before them in the form of the sadhu and Panth had failed to recognise him and thus lost an opportunity of touching his feet.

Baba is the guide of our journey in this dense forest of maya.

Ref: *Shri Sai Sagar* Magazine; 2005 (*Deepavali* Issue)

***

November 14

"EACH ONE IS BORN AND DIES ACCORDING TO HIS KARMA"

After meeting their family Renuka and Panth returned to their home in Pune. Renuka was still wavering in her faith in Baba. Then one day she received the shocking news that her father was in the terminal stages of cancer of the throat. Her husband immediately reserved a ticket to go to Lucknow. They were to leave Pune 10 days later; during this time Renuka took a photograph of her father and applied Baba's Udi on it. She also prayed for the longevity of his life, but on the fifth day she received a telegram stating that her father had passed away. Renuka was devastated to hear this. In anger she took her father's photograph, shook it and blew off the Udi, which fell on the ground. Then she wiped the photograph clean.

Panth tried to explain to her that everyone has to leave this earth at some time. Even Baba and God has to pass away some day, but she continued to be angry.

Then they went to Lucknow and her brother told her that her father had passed away peacefully chanting Baba's name.

On 19 July 1991, Baba appeared before Panth and they had this interesting conversation. Baba said, "What does Renuka think of herself that she accuses me of killing her father. Each one is born and dies according to his karma. No one can evade the fruits of his karmas; they have to be borne. The only help that I can render is to decrease the intensity of the pain and suffering of that person. Ask her if I didn't reduce the intensity of pain for her father? Yet she accused me and blew my Udi away. I will not tolerate such a despicable accusation. Now I will bring her father back."

Panth replied, "But Baba her father's body has been cremated how will you bring him back?"

Baba said, "So what if his body is burned and destroyed? I will bring him back as the son of her brother, and thus give him a new life. Tell her this and ask her to never ever accuse me again."

Panth wrote this entire conversation in his diary and kept it in his prayer room. A few months later Renuka's brother was blessed with a son. Panth then asked Renuka to read the diary, and then she became an ardent devotee.

The Sadguru teaches us the complete theory of karma in a simple manner.

Ref: *Shri Sai Sagar* Magazine; 2005 (*Deepavali* Issue)

***

BABA KICKS THE DRUNKARD

In Shivaji Nager, Pune there is an old temple of Baba near Rasne Chawl. This temple is situated in old Thofkhana, behind Mangala Theater. This temple vibrates with spiritual energy as Baba's tooth and chillum is enshrined there, below Baba's padukas. Many devotees have had numerous experiences here.

An alcoholic used to visit the temple regularly in an inebriated state. The other devotees would often warn him not to do so as Baba would not tolerate this behaviour of his much longer, but he didn't pay any heed to their warnings. One day he staggered into the temple and was about to place his head on the padukas when he fell down and rolled thrice on the floor. The devotees picked him up and asked him what happened. In shock he said, "When I was about to place my head on Baba's padukas he kicked me so hard that I fell down," and he hurriedly staggered out of the temple and never returned.

Once a young man came to the temple seeking a job; at that time the temple was in need of a priest. He was dressed in ochre-coloured clothes, had long matted hair, and a long beard and moustache. He looked like a sadhu, so the committee decided to hire him as a priest. They thought that he would provide good service to the temple. They provided him with a room on the temple premises.

A few days later some of the devotees visiting the temple noted that the priest sat outside the temple and smoked marijuana. They warned him not to do so as he would have to face Baba's wrath. However, he didn't pay any heed to their warnings. One morning the devotees came for Kakad Arati but found the temple was locked and the priest was inside. As the time for the Arati was drawing near, they banged on the door for some time. Finally the door opened and the priest came out in a dishevelled state. The devotees asked him what had happened to him. With folded hands he said, "Sir I will not work here anymore. Last night I had smoked marijuana and slept. I was in deep sleep when you arrived for the Arati. Then someone caught hold of my hair and shook me vigorously and awoke me. Forgive me sir I am leaving as I am afraid of staying here any longer," and saying so he left.

Baba will kick us mercilessly if we are intoxicated by our *Indriyas* and *Arishadvargas*.

Ref: *Shri Sai Sagar* Magazine; 2001 (*Deepavali* Issue)

***

November 16

BABA HELPS THE OLD LADY FIND HER GOAT

Many of the devotees claim to have seen Baba in the temple or in the area surrounding the temple late at night.

There was an old lady who lived behind the temple, and she had a goat that she loved very much. The goat used to be tied to a small stump outside her hut. One night she awoke around midnight and looked outside and her beloved goat was missing. She then searched for it diligently and was quite disheartened at the thought of losing her beloved goat. After she had searched for it for quite a while, she went and stood at the entrance of the temple. As the door to the temple was locked, she folded her hands and prayed to Baba to find her goat for her.

She turned around to return to her hut when in the moonlight she saw a fakir seated on the cement parapet near the entrance. He was an old man and wore a white kafni. She said, "Fakir Baba have you by any chance seen a goat around here?" The fakir silently pointed to a tree near the temple. She looked in that direction and saw her beloved goat peacefully standing under the tree. Delighted she ran to the goat and hugged it. She then returned to thank the fakir but he had disappeared. It was then that she realised that the kind fakir was Baba, for she had already searched under the tree for her goat. But she had prayed to him and her goat had appeared under the tree.

When we lose our *Antkarna Chathustaya* (goat) to maya, it is Sadguru Baba who returns it only after we pray from the bottom of our hearts.

Ref: *Shri Sai Sagar* Magazine; April–June 2011

***

340

BABA'S CONCERN FOR YOGESH'S BURNT PALM

Yogesh was a young man who volunteered to do any type of work in the temple, as he was intensely devoted to Baba. Once in his zeal, he placed a few tablets of ignited camphor on his palm and performed Baba's Arati. This resulted in severe third-degree burns of his palm. Yogesh didn't seek any medical aid for his burns and continued working.

A few days later there was a function in the Khakdi Sai Baba temple and Yogesh went there to help. On the conclusion of the function there was Annadan. Yogesh was helping with the cooking, when he remembered he had to make a call to a Sai devotee so he went in search of a telephone booth. There was a huge playground next to the temple and many children were playing there. He thought he would definitely find a telephone there, but his search was in vain. So he turned to return to the temple, when a fakir came and stood before him. The fakir tenderly took his hand and said, "How is your burnt palm now? Don't worry, Allaha will heal it and everything will be all right." Then he compassionately ran his hand over his back and vanished. Yogesh looked for him everywhere but in vain; later he realised that it was Baba who had appeared before him out of compassion. The next day a devotee who had just returned from Shirdi gave him some oil dripping from the Dwarka Mai and some Udi. Yogesh made a paste of them and applied it to his hand and soon the hand healed without a scar.

Every Thursday the temple was washed at night. One Thursday Yogesh and the other devotees finished washing the temple at midnight. That evening Yogesh had forgotten to have his dinner and he felt extremely hungry. It was too late to get a meal from outside at this hour. Yogesh prayed to Baba saying, "Baba do anything, but give me something to eat." In front of Baba's idol was a bowl that was covered; he knew that it would be empty as the food would have been distributed to the devotees. Nonetheless he went and opened it and indeed it was full of shira.

Yogesh immediately started eating it and thought, "Baba you have given such a small bowl of shira to me, will my hunger be satiated with it?" But he was surprised that the bowl was full of shira even after he had continued eating it for almost half an hour. Finally Yogesh begged Baba to forgive him for doubting if his prasad would fill his stomach and the shira stopped filling up the bowl.

Baba not only fulfils our justified materialistic needs, but also heals our burns caused by maya.

Ref: *Shri Sai Sagar* Magazine; 2001 (*Deepavali* Issue)

***

November 18

BABA'S FOOT IMPRINT ETCHED ON THE PLATE

Lakshman Khandalkar, a resident of Ratnagiri, states, "On 21 November 1983, I got up early in the morning to conduct my ritualistic worship of Baba. Then I offered three palms full of water to Lord Surya (Sun) and poured the water into a large copper dish. When I looked at the water I felt that there was an impression of Baba's left foot in it. To make sure that I had indeed seen Baba's foot, I wore my spectacles and took a good look at it again.

And indeed there was an imprint of Baba's foot; it was about 2 inches long and it seemed to be etched on the plate. Then I earnestly prayed to Baba saying, "Baba if that is truly an imprint of your foot please let it remain as such," and surprisingly it remained there, intact. I then took a photograph of it and sent it to my daughter who resided in Pune.

Soon my home was full of devotees as the news spread like wildfire. I live near the rickshaw stand and they told everybody about the miracle. Then friends, neighbours and numerous devotees thronged to see the imprint. So from then on there was such a huge crowd that I thought we would have to call the police to control the crowds.

Then numerous local newspapers came and photographed it and then hundreds of devotees came to worship the imprint.

Finally around 2 a.m. when we were about to go to bed, the door bell rang, I went and opened the door. There Dr. Gore and two South Indian gentlemen were standing. Dr. Gore said, "I know it's very late, but I would like to have darshan of the footprint if it's all right with you?" I invited them to do so. The two gentlemen wore a *lungi* and a white shirt and had white sacred ash on their forehead. I describe their appearance because later I found out that Dr. Gore had come alone that night. And the incident reminded me of the leela where Baba goes to Dev's home along with two others as is described in *Shri Sai Satcharita* chapter 40, "The narration of the Udyapan story." I feel honoured and humble that Baba himself came to my home to see his own leela of the footprint.

Finally after all the devotees had had darshan of the footprint to their heart's content, I got the copper plate framed and hung it in my prayer room. And even to this day the imprint is still intact and looks the same as the very day it had appeared. Any devotee who wishes to have darshan of it is welcome to do so."

On our total unconditional surrendering to our Sadguru Baba, he will etch his sacred foot print on our heart and keep a vigilant watch over our movements.

Ref: *Sai Prasad* Magazine; 1993 (*Deepavali* Issue)

***

November 19

HOW HE GETS BABA'S *SIRVESH*

Lakshman Khandalkar and his family had often prayed to Baba requesting him to give them a small piece of cloth that had either been worn or had even been touched by him. They fervently hoped that they could get such a treasure so that they could venerate and pray to it daily. This indeed was a strange request, but with Baba nothing is impossible. Then Lakshman and his family visited Shirdi and Sakori; at Sakori they met Nana Patankar who was an administrator there and they soon became friends.

A year later Nana came to Ratnagiri on some business, and he informed Khandalkar about his visit. Khandalkar made all the necessary arrangements for his stay there and looked after him in the best possible manner. Then Nana went to Rajapur to pay homage to his family deity and then came to Khandalkar's home. As he was packing his baggage to return to Sakori, Nana gave a white cloth to Khandalkar and asked him to make a dress out of it for his granddaughter. Casually Khandalkar asked him about the cloth and he said, "Its Baba's *sirvesh*." A sirvesh is the white cloth that Baba tied around his head. Hearing this Kandalkar shed tears of joy.

Around 1913, Baba gave Upasani Maharaj the cloth, and Upasani Maharaj in turn gave it to his favourite disciple Godavari Mata. Godavari Mata then gave the cloth to Nana. Nana said, "Khandalkar this was possibly meant to be. And I brought the cloth along with me by mistake in my baggage. Baba most probably ordained this to happen, and he wishes me to hand it over to you." At that time Khandalkar's entire family was there and they were overwhelmed as Baba had fulfilled their earnest desire. Khandalkar reverentially took the cloth and carefully placed it in a plastic cover and kept it in his prayer room. Every day he offers a garland to it along with his daily worship of it.

Ref: *Sai Prasad* Magazine; 1993 (*Deepavali* Issue)

***

November 20

"EAT A FEW LEAVES FROM MY NEEM TREE," SAID BABA

Dr. Anagha L. Palav once contracted a herpes infection of the intercostal nerves. The pain was intense with burning and itching and she couldn't get a wink of sleep. She was treated for it without success; then she applied Udi on the area but the pain continued. She continued to be restless and afraid, and she prayed to Baba to heal her. One night she saw Baba at her bedside; he gently patted her on her head and said, "You are terrified of such a little pain. What will you do if you get some serious disease in the future? How will you face it? Never mind. When you recover come to Shirdi and go to my Gurusthan; eat a few leaves from my neem tree and the disease will not re-occur again." Suddenly Anagha's father woke her up and asked her who she was talking to. Anagha said, "Look Baba has come and is standing next to my bed. Do worship him quickly." Her family of course couldn't see Baba.

A few days later she recovered completely and visited Shirdi. Immediately she went to the Gurusthan and looked for leaves that may have fallen from Baba's neem tree. There were none there, and the branches of the tree were too high for her to pluck any. Just then a fakir stood before her; he said, "Are you looking for neem leaves? Here are some," and he placed five leaves in the palm of her hand. Anagha immediately put them in her mouth; then she thought she ought to give some to her brother but by then the fakir had disappeared. She searched for him in vain.

Anagha's uncle, Manohar Kulkarni was an ardent devotee of Baba; his wife was a physician, so she rendered service to the needy. Then Manohar got sick and passed away. His wife was overcome with grief and in a fit of rage she took the silver idol of Baba and threw it away. But the idol landed on the ground as if it was placed there. She thought about it and then she accepted the fact that death came on everyone, one day or the other, and one had to face the loss of a loved one some time in life.

After this her life changed and she became totally devoted to Baba. Every morning when she attended her office she would pray to Baba and light incense before his picture. If there was a serious or complicated patient she was treating, she would first pray to Baba and then give the treatment. Thus, her patients had immense faith in her. If any of her patients were in severe pain or had a prolonged illness, she would light incense and read chapter 15 of the *Charita*, and the patient would be relieved of their pain and suffering. Often times she would emphasise the power of chapter 15 to other devotees of Baba. She told them about the patients who were relieved of their sufferings by her reading this chapter on their behalf.

A neem tree signifies spirituality. To progress on the path of self-realization Baba instructs us to eat neem leaves, that is, to do Sadhana and get cured of the disease caused by the world of maya.

Ref: *Shri Sai Prasad* Magazine; 1994 (*Deepavali* Issue)

***

BABA THUMPED HER CHEST

Smitha Badgavkar resided in Pune with her husband Vishvanath; her husband she thought was in good health. On 1 July 2002 he started throwing up; the vomiting was accompanied with severe pain in his stomach. She gave him ginger tea but the vomiting persisted. She took him to Sanjeveni Hospital where he was admitted; the doctors suspected that he was having a heart attack. After relieving his pain they did an ECG and performed an angiogram. The angiogram revealed that three of his major arteries were blocked. They advised him to undergo bypass surgery to prevent further heart attacks. Now Smitha was faced with a huge problem; the surgery would cost her over 2 lakhs of rupees. Neither did she have that much of money nor could she get it from anywhere. She cast her burden on Baba and prayed for a solution.

Her husband worked as an Engineer in the M.S.E.B (Electrical Board) so his friends came to her aid. They got the Board to pay half the bill and went and collected the cheque from the Mumbai Head Office and submitted it to the Hospital. The rest of the money was paid from her savings and the money collected by Vishvanath's colleagues.

The date for the surgery was fixed and then one day Baba gave her an indication that the surgery would be successful. She was sitting at Vishvanath's bedside when she saw Baba. He applied some medicine on Vishvanath's chest and gently thumped his chest and vanished. Her husband woke up and asked, "Who is pounding something?" and indeed there was a pounding sound but she couldn't see anyone. Then she related the treatment that Baba had given him. The next day Vishvanath had his bypass surgery and it was successful. Smitha's husband's life was saved by Baba and both of them are eternally grateful to him.

Baba's act of burning karma can only be experienced but cannot be seen.

Ref: *Shri Sai Sagar* Magazine; 2007 (*Deepavali* Issue)

***

SHRI SADGURU SAINATH KRIPA MATT

The famous Shri Sadguru Sainath Kripa Matt, at Swargate, Pune was built in 1954 by Naryan alias Bhau Sahib D. Lombar. This leela is how Baba ordered and guided him to build this wish-fulfilling temple there.

Bhau Sahib was born in 1907 in Nipani near Kholapur; his parents were devoted to Lord Dattreya and goddess Tulja Bhavani. Thus Bhau Sahib grew up in a very spiritual atmosphere and he chose the path of devotion from a very young age. In 1920 when he was just 13 years old, he visited Shirdi and on that very visit he had a vision of Baba in the Dwarka Mai. From then till the day he passed away, that is, on Lakshmi puja day of 1978, he visited Shirdi regularly. He was a jeweller by profession, which he gave up happily so that he could devote his entire time and energy towards Baba. As his faith grew, the intense desire to build a temple took hold of him. He spent ten days fasting, meditating and praying for guidance from Baba at Arenashwar temple. On the tenth day Baba appeared before him and said, "Why are you sitting here? Return to Pune and at that spot where your feet cannot move any further, build my temple." He faithfully followed Baba's orders. Then sat under a tree near that site and mentally saw a temple there. He bought that land and camped in a tent there. The moment he hung a picture of Baba in that tent, the entire tent was filled with an aroma that is associated with Baba.

Then Baba said, "When you dig the foundation for the temple, preserve whatever you find underground." As they were digging they indeed found a 7-foot long wooden casket; in it they found the remains of possibly a saint as he had worn an ochre-coloured *langoti* (loin cloth).

The temple was completed in 1955, and Das Ganu performed the ritualistic ceremony of establishing Baba's padukas there. In 1956 an idol 4½ feet tall that was made of five metals was established in the temple. Directly below the sanctum sanctorum there is a room in the basement about 10 ft by 10 ft where the casket of the saint is preserved.

There are numerous smaller temples around the main Baba temple; there is also a beautiful museum where some of the rare photographs are preserved. Numerous devotees visit the temple regularly, as they strongly believe that their wishes are always granted there.

Baba makes his devotee an instrument to complete his work in a unique way.

Ref: *Shri Sai Sagar* Magazine; 2007 (*Deepavali* Issue)

***

November 23

THE FAKIR LOOKED AT HER INTENTLY AND SHE RECOVERED

His wife Shubhangi got sick and was admitted in the hospital on 14 May 2007. Arun Jogleker a resident of Thane was at his wits' end as Shubhangi was old and frail but was free of any illness. At first her condition wasn't serious but due to some medical negligence her condition became critical. She had a severe cough with expectoration. Then another lady doctor examined her and had her shifted to the ICU where she was given IV fluids, IV antibiotics and placed on a ventilator, as she had severe pneumonia. Arun felt that Baba had heard his plea for help and sent this doctor. But Shubhangi's condition deteriorated steadily and the doctors gave up hope. They asked Arun to call Shubhangi's near and dear relatives as she would not survive much longer. Arun was dejected as his lifelong companion would pass away.

He sat outside the ICU and started reading the *Charita*. It was very quiet and a strange calm prevailed. Just then a fakir appeared there stomping his feet; he was tall, fair and wore a kafni; he entered the ICU and went straight to Shubhangi's bedside. He looked at her intently, gazing at her from head to foot, and left. Astonished Arun asked his daughter Surekha to follow him and then the fakir entered the elevator. Simultaneously he asked his son Girish to follow him via the stairs. Surekha and the fakir both entered the elevator which was empty and when the doors closed the fakir disappeared. Neither could Girish find him anywhere.

348

A short while later the doctor examined Shubhangi and came to Arun and said, "Truly a miracle has taken place. A short while ago I asked you to call her relatives as she would not survive, but now she is conscious and her vital signs are normal. She has defied medical science with her recovery." Arun through tears saw the fakir curing her with his look and mentally he thanked Baba for his compassion.

Baba cures her through *Dristi Shaktipath*.

Ref: *Shri Sai Sagar* Magazine; 2007 (*Deepavali* Issue)

***

November 24

KATHE MAHARAJ'S SAI DURBAR

Madhavrao Dixit of Pune states, "My guru, Kathe Maharaj was ardently devoted to Sai Baba. He was well built and in good health. At the age of 56 he suddenly developed severe diabetes, with a blood glucose level of 600. I firmly believe that he took my diabetes on himself as I was careless about my health. He took Samadhi a day after worshiping Baba on Gurupurnima and saved my life. I feel he and Baba worked in unison because a year later I had severe chest pain and signs of heart disease. That night I had a vivid dream wherein Baba kicked me on my chest and I was thrown on to the street. Then he came and placed his knee on the left side of my chest. This gave intense pain but my heart disease vanished." Kathe Maharaja's Sai Durbar is at Tingre Nager, Lohegaon. A stubborn atheist once came there to test him. He wanted to know if he was a fake or was spiritually enlightened. If his devotion to Baba was real or a façade so that people could call him Maharaj. The atheist stood before Kathe Maharaj and said, "If you have the power and capability to emit smoke from an empty chillum like Swami Samarth, only then you should call yourself Maharaj." With calm poise Maharaj replied, "I am only a devotee of Sai Baba. I don't possess the power nor capability as minute as a speck of dust of his feet. But to come to this Durbar to test me is not right. However, you are welcome to come here and have a meal which is severed after being offered to Baba. And then you may leave in peace."

The atheist did return for the meal but was restless and he couldn't contain his curiosity. He said, "If you can answer my question, I will definitely call you Maharaj. Tell me how many stars are there in the sky?" Maharaj replied, "I will count them the whole night and give you the answer tomorrow." Then the atheist left.

Kathe Maharaj as usual sought refuge in Baba and sat in mediation. Baba could not bear his dear devotee being insulted so he helped him via his Udi. He appeared before Kathe Maharaj and said, "When the man returns for his answer give him a fistful of my Udi and tell him that the answer lies in the Udi. The number of stars in the sky is the same number as the specks of ash in the Udi that you gave him. Ask him to sit and carefully count them," and then Baba disappeared.

Baba strongly emphasises that you shouldn't test any Saint. The power of the Udi is as much as the entire cosmos comprising of stars and innumerable galaxies.

Ref: *Shri Sai Sagar* Magazine; November and December 2003

***

November 25

FROM HIS JHOLI BABA PRODUCED DELECTABLE CONFECTIONERY

For about 50 years Raghunath B. Sandbhor had the good fortune of performing *Bharood* in front of Baba's rath (chariot) at all the festivals in Shirdi. Bharood is singing ballads along with dance steps. In 1944 Das Ganu Maharaj heard his performance with keen interest and evaluated it. Then he gave him a coconut and a rupee and blessed him, and invited him to perform his Bharood in Shirdi at all the festivals. Thus Sandbhor was performing Bharood till he passed away on 14 August 2002. He along with his companions went to various villages singing Ballads. His mother Yamunabai was devoted to Baba since he was just a child, and she wouldn't eat or drink anything without first offering it to Baba.

His mother lived in a small village called Thinevadi, and Raghunath moved to Pune after his marriage. Every year without

350

fail he visited his mother on Lakshmi puja day in Divali, bringing with him delicious confectionery and savouries. For some reason he couldn't visit Thinevadi the year he got married. His mother was unaware of this and waited for him to arrive. It was her habit to light the lamps and offer the delicacies he had brought to Baba first, and then distribute it to all her friends and neighbours.

Her neighbours visited her that year and sarcastically said, "Your son is now too busy with his wife to visit you. As you have not prepared any savouries and confectionery do come over and have some with us." The words stung her and she stood in front of Baba's picture and begged him to forgive her. With tears in her eyes she prepared Zunka Bhakri and offered it to him.

At that very moment she heard someone saying, "Allaha Malik. Today is Lakshmi puja have you prepared any delicacies for me?" She looked towards the door and there stood a fakir wearing a white kafni with a white cloth around his head. She invited him in and told him what had happened that day. He replied "I have come to eat Zunka Bhakri, but first bring a huge empty platter for me then serve me the meal." She did as asked; from his jholi he placed the most delicious confectioneries and savouries on it. He had a satisfying meal, blessed her and left. In a daze she realised what Baba had just done. Then she took the delicacies and distributed them to her neighbours and friends. Then they all remarked that the savouries and the confectioneries were unusually delicious and delectable. Indeed they would be as Baba had given them to her from his jholi.

Baba assured us that there will be no dearth of food in his devotee's home nor would he ever leave them in the lurch.

Ref: *Shri Sai Sagar* Magazine; 1998 (*Deepavali* Issue)

***

November 26

BABA TOLD HER TO GIVE HIS DEVOTEES A MEAL

Sandbhor and his group went to Gadchiroli a small village in Nagpur to perform Bharood. It was extremely hot and they got lost; they searched for the address of the people who had invited them in vain. It was way past lunch time and hunger, thirst and tiredness had taken their toll.

Finally they found a house and they asked the occupants if they could serve them some food on payment, but they refused. So they set out again and asked a passerby where they could find a restaurant. He told them that the nearest place was 3 miles away. They rested under a tree, when his companion sarcastically said, "Sandbhor will your Baba come and give us lunch here?" Sandbhor told them, "Have a little saburi; Baba will definitely come to our aid."

At that very moment a gentleman came hurriedly towards them and said, "Have you seen four devotees of Baba around here." Sandbhor told him that they were the devotees of Baba and that they performed Bharood at Shirdi during the festivals. Delighted the gentleman invited them home to have a meal. All the plates were laid ready to be served and four special plates were laid for the four devotees of Baba.

While serving them the gentleman's wife said, "Every year I do parayan of the *Charita* and invite my friends and neighbours for the meal upon its completion. Early this morning I saw Baba in my dream and he said, "Four of my devotees will be visiting your village today, give them a hearty meal," and then I woke up. As soon as I had finished cooking the meal, I sent my husband in search of you. I am sure that Baba asked me to serve lunch to you. Please have a satisfying hearty meal." Sandbhor looked at his companions who had hung their heads down.

Baba, like a loving mother extends his caring hand that extends beyond one's imagination.

Ref: *Shri Sai Sagar* Magazine; 1998 (*Deepavali* Issue)

***

November 27

BABA SENT A CAR TO TAKE THEM HOME

Meher Baba said, "You will never be able to understand thoroughly how great Sai Baba was. He was the very personification of perfection. If you knew him as I know him you would call him the master of creation." His words were true then and are true even today.

In 1950 Sandbhor and his group were invited to a village in Thane District to perform Bharood. They were engrossed in the performance and they forgot that they had another performance in Badlapur at 5 p.m. It was night when they left the village; they went to the bus stand and found that the only bus going to Badlapur had left 2 hours ago. The bus stand was open and to make matters worse it started raining heavily. As the stand didn't have a roof to protect them they took shelter under a tree but the rain continued to pour with more force. His friend said, "Sandbhor will your Baba send us a bus in this downpour?" Calmly he replied, "Baba cares for us and he surely will provide some transportation for us."

No sooner had he said that, a car from the opposite direction flashed its head lights on their faces and halted before them. The driver was a tall well-dressed gentleman who got out of his car and said, "You are going to Badlapur isn't it? I am also on my way there and I will drop you." They got into the car and started talking about Baba's leelas, and soon the car halted. The gentleman said, "We have reached Badlapur and this is where you want to go isn't it?" Sandbhor got out of the car and realised that in his excitement he had not given him the address. He took out a paper from his pocket and showed it to him, and to his utter amazement he had halted in front of the Sai temple that they were invited to.

Sandbhor thanked him and said, "Sir what's your name and where do you live" The driver had started his car and replied, "People call me Sainath Seth. Everyone knows me," and drove away. His words kept ringing in Sandbhor's ears when he realised that Sainath himself had driven them to their destination and his eyes welled with tears of gratitude.

When we are ready for our spiritual journey, Baba will come running to take us to our destination.

Ref: *Shri Sai Sagar* Magazine; 1998 (*Deepavali* Issue)

***

"I HAD TO BECOME A MILKMAN AND RUN TO YOUR AID"

This incident took place when the suburbs of Pune were still undeveloped. Many entrepreneurs bought land there and set up their companies. Shri Khandekar worked in Yervada at that time. The area was a remote desolate place and the roads were unlit with dense forests on either side. After work he and his colleagues left work together and rode their bicycles back to Pune where they lived.

Once Khandekar had to wait to collect his pay; he was unaware that his friends had left after receiving their pay. Khandekar searched for them and finally he left alone. By then it was dark, and as he rode his bicycle he was shivering with fear. Then he started chanting, "Sai Ram, Sai Ram" loudly; only a few trucks passed by and the road was deserted.

Suddenly he heard a cyclist riding behind him; frightened he turned around and saw a milkman. He had a long white beard a white dhotar and coat and he was merrily singing a devotional song, which was *Ram ka naam bhajle Bhayyia* (brother keep singing Ram's name with devotion). He had his milk cans on the handles of his bicycle. Khandekar slowed his pace and waited for him. The milkman said, "Brother! Why are you afraid? I am with you. I am going to Pune and we will go together," and together they rode to Shivaji Nager. Khandikar thanked him and the milkman rode away.

Early in the morning he dreamt of Baba who said, "Weren't you extremely frightened last night? Then you started chanting my name in desperation, so I had to become a milkman and run to your aid," and there the dream ended. Khandekar woke up and with tears in his eyes he thanked Baba for his compassionate caring.

Baba explicitly propagates the power of Naam Japa as Shri Krishna confirms in the *Bhagavadgita*. In chapter 10, shloka 25, Krishna states that he is *Japa yagna* — the best yagna amongst all yagna's. Baba also confirms that he is Japa yagna so Naam Japa will take us across this worldly ocean.

Ref: *Shri Sai Sagar* Magazine; 1998 (*Deepavali* Issue)

***

BABA BESTOWED A PROTECTIVE ARMOUR AROUND THE GUPTE FAMILY

In 1957, Sumathi A. Gupte decided to do a parayan of the *Charita*. She started reading it on a Thursday. On Sunday, some relatives visited her. It was her practice to abstain from non-vegetarian food during the parayan. Her husband, however, asked her to prepare a fish curry for the guests. She consoled herself saying, "Guests are akin to god and should be welcomed heartily," and prepared it. Everyone had a hearty meal. Around 5 p.m. she hoped they would leave so she could complete reading that day's portion. Finally they left and Sumathi completed her chores and sat down to read at 10 p.m.

At midnight she had accomplished reading the chapters for that day. She looked up at the picture of Baba in front of her when it suddenly lit up with a brilliant light. Fascinated she stared at it; it was so luminous that she couldn't see Baba in it. Then a saffron golden coloured beam emitted from it. And a round pea-sized piece ejected and settled on the open page of the *Charita* below her thumb. It remained there for a short while and she experienced a sought of tingling pain as it settled on the top of her thumb. Then the piece traversed through the air back into Baba's brilliant light and merged with it. After that she could clearly see Baba in the picture again.

"At that time I couldn't understand the significance of it, but later when life took numerous disastrous turns I realised that Baba had placed his protective shield around me and my family." After this incident she had several operations and was at death's door, but Baba saved her time and again. One day she visited the temple of her family goddess. The train she had to travel by was delayed so she boarded another train. Later she heard that a fire had broken out in the ladies *bogie* of that train and many ladies had sustained severe burns. Her daughter, however, was in that bogie but escaped unharmed. Once her husband was going to work and missed his train by a few seconds; that train had a head-on collision with another train at the next station. Many passengers lost their lives in that accident and numerous passengers were severely injured. "Whenever I remember these incidents, I thank Baba for his compassion. I have also realised the power of reading the *Charita*," states Sumathi.

The power of the *Satcharita* is beyond one's comprehension as it is told by Baba himself.

Ref: Shri Sai Sagar Magazine; 2003 (Ram Navami Issue)

***

November 30

BABA APPEARS AS A TALL CAT

Years ago Suhas U. Gangvane was an executive in a multinational Company in Mumbai. His colleagues started ill treating and harassing him. At first he didn't pay much attention to it, but as it continued he lost his peace of mind. Soon it took its toll on his health and he lost his sight. As he had now become visually challenged, he soon lost his job. His mother took him to every possible ophthalmologist and spent vast amounts of money on his treatments, but to no avail. One day a concerned neighbour told his mother about the Rasne's temple at Shivaji Nager, which was a wish-fulfilling temple. So his mother took him there and after that Sushas attended every Arati. One morning while attending Arati he was shocked because he saw Baba's idol quite clearly. As a token of his gratitude he started sweeping and swabbing the temple and with renewed energy started looking for a job.

One morning after the Kakad Arati, he was about to bow his head down to Baba's padukas when he saw them shake. He thought it was his imagination but it happened after every Arati. When he told his family about it, they didn't believe him. One day his sister and mother attended the Arati and as they bowed they saw the padukas shake; only then did they believe him.

Sushas was still jobless after entreating Baba to give him a job, and as time passed by he got upset with him. He decided that he wouldn't attend Kakad Arati henceforth, and he didn't do so for the next 2 days. On the third morning he felt someone awaken him at 4 a.m. He got up and was startled to see the strangest looking cat in his room. He kept staring at the cat as it was rather tall about 2 feet tall, then the strange-looking cat suddenly disappeared. In a daze he went to the temple and attended the Arati. After the Arati he saw the same cat in the temple, he went after it and again it disappeared. He said, "Thank you Baba for appearing in the form of that strange cat and giving me the good sense to attend your Arati."

Baba takes any form to warn his children.

Ref: *Shri Sai Sagar* Magazine; 2008 (*Deepavali* Issue)

***

SUHAS SAW BABA IN NUMEROUS FORMS

Suhas was now devoted to Baba and he didn't miss going to the Kakad Arati even a single day. After the Arati he would sit for a short while in Shambaji Park and then go home. One day a lady about 50 years old came to him and asked for dakshina, and Suhas gave her a rupee. She said, "Everyday without asking you, you give me a rupee. May Allaha bless you." He tried to get a good look at her face but she disappeared. Then he realised that Baba had appeared in the form of this lady because every day he would offer a rupee as dakshina at the temple. Whenever Baba blessed anybody he always said, "May Allaha bless you," so the lady was indeed Baba in that form.

There was a dog named Mogli at the temple who attended the Kakad Arati every morning. He would merrily "sing" along by producing a strange but happy whine. On 4 May 2008 Mogli was "singing" louder than he usually did. The devotees thought that Mogli had more love and devotion for Baba that day. Sushas, however, looked towards the entrance and he saw a fakir in a white kafni standing at the door. As the Arati was going on he thought his mind was wandering and he started gazing at Baba's idol. As soon as the Arati was over, he asked the other devotees who were standing at the door whether they had seen the fakir. They unfortunately hadn't, but Mogli had seen Baba and he welcomed him by singing joyously that day. Mogli passed away peacefully on 13 July 2008.

At home Sushas offered Baba two Bhakris and curry every day and then went out in search of a job. One day his mother was upset with Baba for not giving him a job. When Sushas was about to offer Baba the Bhakris his mother said, "Since Baba hasn't given you a job yet from now on offer him only one Bhakri." Sushas felt like laughing at what she said, nonetheless he offered only one Bhakri to Baba that day. His mother having said that was busy baking the Bhakris. At that moment a kafni-clad hand reached out and took a Bhakri. His mother saw this but couldn't believe her eyes so she asked Suhas whether he had taken another Bhakri from the basket. He replied that he hadn't; then everyone realised that Baba himself had taken his Bhakri. In early 2009 Suhas finally got a job of his choice and in gratitude he walked along with the palkhi from Pune to Shirdi.

Baba guides his devotees by assuming any form, but he will never leave them. Nothing in this entire universe will go unnoticed by him. Baba's omnipresence is depicted here.

Ref: *Shri Sai Sagar* Magazine; 2008 (*Deepavali* Issue)

***

December 2

HOW HER LIFE'S PROBLEMS VANISHED

Probably she wishes to remain anonymous so she calls herself Shri Sai Padankita (roughly translated means one whose final goal is Shri Sai's feet). Padintika was devoted to Baba since the early '50s. She delivered her first child and became seriously ill with pleurisy. Her condition was so pitiable that her relatives didn't want to be near her.

A concerned Gujarati neighbour of hers spoke to her husband and said, "The only way out of all your problems is Baba." He asked Padintika's husband to place a picture of Baba in his home and also gave him some Udi to apply and ingest. Padintika's husband was very sceptical, as he was jobless, his wife was seriously ill and there was a small baby to look after. As there was no other option he followed the neighbour's advice; shortly after that the same neighbour told him about a job in his friend's company. At first the job paid about a fourth of his previous salary but later he did very well.

His wife gradually regained her health. Her young daughter contracted cholera and the treatment was ineffective. Her fever wouldn't come down and soon she stopped urinating. Padinkita prayed to

Baba and along with the medicines applied Udi on the child. One afternoon while she was sitting at the child's bedside she fell asleep. She dreamt that she and her husband had placed their heads on a picture of Baba. When she looked up, Baba was actually sitting before them in the Dwarka Mai. Baba was seated near the railing. His feet were soft and fair like the feet of a baby. Baba asked her to put her hand out and he placed a few fresh Parijatak flowers in her palm. Delighted Padinkita stared at them but soon the flowers wilted and turned into Udi. Then Baba said, "Child I had to give you this for a long time. Here it is. Allaha will bless you and everything will be all right," This he repeated thrice and she woke up startled as she heard bells ringing loudly.

After this her child recovered completely. Her financial conditions improved. She and her child became healthy. She became confident that no matter what problems might befall them, Baba was there to take care of them. So why should she worry needlessly.

The Parijatak flowers are celestial; they signify divinity. Baba bestows devotees with whatever each one deserves. And it requires shradha and saburi.

Ref: *Shri Sai Sagar* Magazine; 2003 (*Deepavali* Issue)

***

December 3

THE MIRACLE OF THE EVER-INCREASING RICE

Swami Sanjayanand of Badrinath states this is a true leela that occurred in May 1972. "Susheelchandra Varma invited me and my wife to attend a function in Lucknow and we accepted the invitation. The program was to sing devotional songs throughout the night on the first day, followed by Annadan the next day. That day being a Sunday a large crowd participated in it. Each devotee was requested to bring a picture of Baba and 100 grams of *Basmati* rice with them. The rice was to be offered to the picture while chanting Baba's name a 1000 times. After the chanting the rice would be collected and used to cook Sweet Rice for the Annadan. The program went well and at the end the rice collected was about 16 kg. The rice thus collected was tied in a saffron-coloured cloth and placed in front of the decorated alter on which Baba's Dwarka Mai photograph was placed.

At noon the next day that rice along with another 16 kg of rice was placed in a huge vessel to cook. My wife and I were turning the rice around while it cooked. Soon the rice started boiling and the bubbles took the shape of Aum. Every bubble became an Aum, and had the colour of Udi. Finally a huge Aum was formed on the surface of the cooked rice, and the entire sweet rice attained the colour of Udi.

As the vessel was filled to the brim and overflowing, half of it was emptied into another huge vessel. But from the Aum vessel the rice again came to its original level and started to overflow. This phenomena of the ever-increasing rice continued non-stop. Numerous huge vessels were obtained and new vessels were bought by the devotees. Then I asked the devotees to pray to Baba to stop the miracle of the ever-increasing rice. After our collective prayers it stopped. Finally numerous cars and vans were brought and the rice was taken to the *Mankameshwar* temple where a fair was being held. Every devotee visiting the fair and every beggar had a satisfying meal.

Before leaving Varma's home, I locked all the doors but left one small window open so that passerbys could see the beautifully decorated picture of Baba. When we returned we saw an aged bearded man resembling Baba seated on the chair that was kept for Baba. How did he manage to enter a locked house? All of us sat on the floor after prostrating before him. Then he came and sat next to me. I started singing devotional songs, to the accompaniment of the harmonium while he beat the drums (tablas). Then he said, "Now I will sing and you accompany me on the tabla. He started to sing but I couldn't accompany him, as the rhythm was in the *Zap Taal* (meter). Though I played the tabla very well this was the only meter that I didn't know. I didn't learn it as I would have had to find and make a guru just to learn one meter. Then Baba patiently said, "Son the rhythm is Zap taal and its meter is a count of 10 beats," and then he showed me how to play it along with the vocal beat and *ragas*. Then I played it while he sang. How incredibly kind of him; my Sadguru taught me the taal. But the message we devotees can learn from this leela is that Baba will also teach us to master this taal of 10 beats. The underlying meaning is that the number 10 represents our 10 *Indriyias* or senses and if we can control them then we too can sing in bliss.

Finally we went to sleep on the floor; when I got up at about 4 a.m., Baba had vanished.

Ref: *Shri Sai Sagar* Magazine; 2003 (*Deepavali* Issue)

***

| **December 4** |

"CHILD THIS WELL IS THE ORIGIN OF ALL THE SACRED RIVERS"

Many years ago Subdhra Chori visited Shirdi; in the afternoon she sat in the Dwarka Mai and chanted Baba's name with utter devotion. She wondered how the sanctum sanctorum must have looked like in the bygone days. How did Baba look at that time? Would Baba ever grace her with a vision of himself as he was then? Then she went and worshiped all the other holy sites. She then went to the Samadhi Mandir to attend Sej Arati, but as there was about half an hour left she thought, "Let me go and see what the Dwarka Mai looks like at night. The Dwarka Mai was lit up by the light from the ever-burning lamps and the blazing Dhuni Mai.

Then she saw Baba wearing a white kafni; he was pacing about with his hands behind his back. In wonder she said, "Baba it's you?" He replied, "Come my child.

I was waiting for you. You wanted to see me and my Dwarka Mai isn't it?" Subdhra prostrated at his feet and he lifted her by her shoulders. He continued, "I'm pleased with your devotion. I want you to know that I am present in every picture in your home. My devotees will come to you and according to their faith I will answer their questions. Whenever someone speaks ill of you keep quiet, because they have dug a hole for themselves. Many spoke ill of me. Have faith in me." Just then the Sej Arati started and he left saying that he would meet her in Lendi Baugh the next day.

The next morning she went to the well in Lendi Baugh and saw Baba sitting on its rim. He said, "Child this well is the origin of all the sacred rivers but no one offers a coconut to it. Then how can I give water to people. After some time the water won't be seen in it, as it will start drying up. Don't ever stop worshiping this pipal tree. Don't forget the Audambar tree it's the resting place of Lord Guru Datta." Then he shared with her many important facts, medicines and remedies and asked her not to reveal them without his consent. Then he asked her to promise that she would keep them a secret.

Then he walked to the Gurusthan and she followed. Finally he said, "You will come after 3 years, along with my prasad." Indeed 3 years later she came to Shirdi with her son named Chandan Prasad and her child was placed at the feet of Baba's idol in the Samadhi Mandir.

Here Baba is confirming the sacredness of Shirdi.

Ref: *Sai Prasad* Magazine; 1990 (*Guru Purnima* Issue)

***

December 5

"WHEN BABA IS PROTECTING US WHAT CAN DEATH DO"

Pushpalata Nachne a resident of Thana states, "My father Vamanrao was an ardent devotee of Sainath. However, none of his children survived after birth, so he built a temple for the goddess *Tungareshwar*. The temple of the goddess is situated on top of a hill, in a small village in Vasai *Taluka*. This temple is well known as the family deity of the *Kholis's* (fishermen). After my father built the temple his children survived. The first born was a son, and then another son and I am the youngest child. Every year we go to pay homage to the goddess. The climb to the temple is steep and treacherous. There is a small footpath leading to the temple and on either side are deep ravines.

Last year my entire family visited the temple, as we trudged up the hill I slipped and fell into the deep ravine. While falling I blacked out but I felt someone cushion my fall and gently lift me and place me next to my family. When I regained consciousness I saw the concerned faces of all my relatives, as they hovered around me. My father was utterly calm. They asked me what had happened when I fell, and I related everything. My father, however, wasn't surprised as he had shouted, "Baba, save my child."

Many devotees on top of the hill had seen me fall and they came and spoke to us. I told them what had occurred and they said with surprise, "You are extremely lucky because every year someone falls to his death." My father however said, "When Baba is there to protect us what can death do."

Baba is Parabrahma so the question of disobeying his order doesn't arise. Even the Lord of death has no choice but to obey him.

Ref: *Sai Prasad* Magazine; 1988 (*Deepavali* Issue)

***

December 6

A CROW APPEARED DAILY TILL THE SURGERY

In 1984 Vinayak Malekar's son fell ill and there was a slight swelling of his entire body. His concerned parents took him to their physician who immediately got him admitted into the hospital. His parents were informed that both his kidneys had failed and he wouldn't survive for long if he didn't receive a kidney transplant. All his family members were willing to donate a kidney to save his son's life. They were all tested for a match, and his mother was finally chosen to donate her kidney and she gladly agreed.

The next hurdle that the family had to face was the huge hospital bill. The parents were told that the bill would be around 1 lakh. His father was rather poor, so how would he pay the hospital bills. Vinayak's friends and family helped as much as they could but it didn't amount to much. One of his friends wrote his story in the local paper and numerous people donated money. The funds ranged from 5 rupees to a thousand rupees. Finally Vinayak had to pay about 5,000 rupees towards the hospital bill. The transplant was done successfully and both his wife and son did well.

Throughout this entire heart-wrenching period, Vinayak prayed to Baba and sought refuge at his feet. He states, "One never knows in what form Baba might appear. During this dark period a black crow would appear daily and whoever was at home at time would feed it. When my wife was hospitalised for the removal of her kidney, it would come and sit on the window sill till it was fed something. After the transplant was successfully conducted it stopped coming. Prior to the removal of the kidney her health was not too good but she steadily improved. Now 4 years later, both mother and son are doing fine"

Baba by assuming the form of a crow has cleared the prarabdha of the devotee that would have occurred by the dissatisfaction of the departed souls.

Ref: Sai Prasad Magazine; 1988 (Deepavali Issue)

***

December 7

"YOU WERE SICK SO I CAME TO SEE YOU"

Avinash Padye, a devotee from Mumbai states, "Even after his *Maha Samadhi* Baba continues to guide his devotees. When he was at Shirdi he appeared in the dreams of numerous devotees and guided them.

In January 1993 I was very sick, and that evening I lay on my cot as I was exhausted. I had chest pain and was extremely restless. I got up and lit the lamp in my prayer room. Then applied Udi on my forehead and prayed. I said, "Baba I am unwell today please take care of me," A short while later I felt better so I started chanting Baba's name, then I fell asleep.

At about 5 a.m., I had this wonderful dream, wherein I heard the neighbours shouting that Baba had come. I got up at once and opened the door. I saw Baba standing before my door. He looked very tired and was being helped by four men. I noticed that his eyes were sunken and so were his cheeks. I prostrated at his feet and said, "Baba you have come all the way from Shirdi; if I had known I would have come there myself" Baba replied, "You were sick so

I came to see you." Hearing this, my eyes filled with tears and my throat chocked. I requested Baba to be seated on my cot, but he sat on the floor so I sat next to him.

Then he said, "You make horoscopes and do palmistry, now read the lines on my palm," and he extended his right palm. I was astounded to see numerous *Trishul's* (tridents) on his palms. Then he said, "Which hand do you read in men and which one in women," by now I was utterly confused. Then he held out his right palm and then his left and then he held out both palms in front of me. I was astounded to see both his palms were full of auspicious markings. Bewildered I closed my eyes and bowed my head. He placed his hand of benediction on my head and blessed me saying, "Don't worry. Whatever you predict that will come to pass. My blessings are always with you," and then my dream ended. I woke up with a start, but my heart was singing with joy.

The hindrance to bestow the Shakti path has been removed by making the devotee sick. Then through Swapna Shakti path Baba has blessed this devotee.

Guru in his own way removes the obstacles to bestow his grace.

Ref: *Sai Prasad* Magazine; 1988 (*Deepavali* Issue)

***

December 8

"WE HAVE TIES FROM MANY PREVIOUS BIRTHS"

Mira Kadilkar and her husband lived in Chadisar a small town in Palanpur Taluka. One evening Mira suddenly became very ill. Her husband informed their neighbour who was a physician, and she was immediately taken to the health centre. Unfortunately the health centre wasn't equipped with necessary medications, and her condition started deteriorating.

The decision was to move her to the Civil Hospital in Palanpur, which was 20 miles away. Her husband tried to make contact with Palanpur but couldn't succeed. At about 10 p.m. he went to the railway station and literally begged the official to make some telephonic contact with the hospital. After an hour of pleading, a contact was made; her case history and condition was described and then an ambulance was sent. Finally she was admitted in the hospital; Dr. Trivedi examined her and said, "Her condition is critical, and if she is not given a blood transfusion immediately she will not survive." Her husband readily agreed to donate blood and showed his donor card. But the doctor wouldn't agree and said, "You are alone with her; if something happens to you following the blood donation, who will be responsible? We will wait till the morning," and then he returned home.

Her husband was reduced to tears and fervently prayed to Baba for help. At that very moment a sadhu came and stood at her bedside. He asked her husband with utter compassion what the problem was. Mira's husband told him every single detail and the sadhu said, "Son don't worry, I will bring the Civil Surgeon and take care of everything." True to his word he brought the doctor and he was also willing to donate blood; fortunately his blood group was compatible with Mira's and the transfusion was done.

The next morning Mira's condition improved and she became conscious. Her husband was so touched by the sadhu's kindness that he brought breakfast for all of them. Then he was about to give him some money when the sadhu cautioned him saying, "You better keep the money, lest you need to buy some medicines later. I live nearby and when her condition is stable I will surely take the money."

Mira's parents arrived and her husband also received money from his job, so he went to look for the sadhu. His searched all over Palanpur but was unable to find him. Four days later Mira was discharged and they were proceeding to the railway station when they saw the sadhu seated on the wall of a garden. They stopped the vehicle and her parents and husband ran to give him some money. Her parents said, "You saved our daughter's life so whatever amount of cash you want we will happily give you." Her husband also thanked him and asked him to accept the money. The sadhu looked at them surprised and said, "I am a sadhu so why will I take money from you. Besides I have never donated blood in my entire life, so why should I accept money for something I have not done." Nonetheless her husband begged him to accept some money but he refused saying, "We have *rinanubandic* ties from many previous births. I will surely ask Allaha to bless you." As it was getting late they prostrated at his feet and left. Disappointed the husband said, "How kind my Baba is. He came running in my time of need and helped me. And in return wouldn't accept any money, but comforted me by saying that he had ties with me from many previous births."

The *rinunabandh* with the guru exists from many births.

Ref: *Sai Prasad* Magazine; 1996 (*Deepavali* Issue)
***

December 9

BABA'S OUT-STRETCHED HAND SUPPORTS AN OLD LADY

Padmavati Vaid a resident of Pune states, "My entire life revolves around Sainath and I can't live a moment without him. A short while ago I had gone to Mumbai to visit my son, and a day later I fell ill. My son got me treated by his physician and 2 days later I was quite all right. During those 2 days I missed going to Baba's temple. As soon as I recovered, I visited a temple nearby and was very happy there.

The next day while I was walking in the passage to enter the hall I slipped and was about to fall, when I saw a hand reach out and hold me by my shoulder. The hand was clad in a white kafni, and it supported me till I sat on the floor. I looked back to see who had assisted me while I fell but no one was there. I would have stretched out my own hand as I fell, but feared I would fracture it as I am 80 years old. A friend of mine who is as old as me fell and both the bones of her wrist were broken and I know how she suffered. And because Baba supported me during my fall I didn't experience the same pain and agony.

Upon my return home I went for a checkup to my doctor. He said I was all right despite the fall. Then he said, "It's a miracle that you didn't have a compound fracture of your wrist, for if you did you would surely have had surgery."

I thanked Baba for his kindness and thought, when Baba is there with me what can destiny do. For when I was destined to fall Baba turned destiny around and saved me. Every day I pray and ask him to take me to his heavenly abode when I pass away, and never leave me alone."

The Sadguru's helping hand prevents us from slipping into the slippery world of maya.

Ref: *Sai Prasad* Magazine; 1996 (*Deepavali* Issue)

***

December 10

"LET'S SEE IF THIS MUSLIM WILL SAVE HIM"

When N. R. Ansurkar was 8 years old, he was fortunate to be blessed by Gadge Maharaj. He had stolen and eaten his Bhakri and was caught; then Gadge Maharaj sat him on his lap and stroked his head and blessed him. His father was an ardent devotee of Lord Vishnu. And throughout the year he was engrossed in religious rituals and worship.

In 1952 he got a job in a British Company; until that time he often heard about Sai Baba but wasn't devoted to him. However, in that company one of his co-workers was an ardent devotee and wouldn't commence any work prior to chanting Baba's name. Before joining this company, Ansurkar worked for a Parsee gentleman; on the last day his boss gave him his due and a picture of Baba. He said, "Son don't forget Baba; pray to him with devotion. He will take care of you in any misfortune that may befall you." Apprehensively Ansurkar accepted the picture, because he was sure his father would vehemently disapprove of a Muslim saint's picture being kept in the home. However, his father didn't oppose it and Baba was placed among the other deities in the small shrine.

Then Ansurkar fell seriously ill; he was diagnosed with typhoid and his health deteriorated over the next 2 years. The physician who came to treat him kept staring at Baba's picture that was kept above his head. He gave him some medicines and before leaving said, "Let us see if this Muslim will save his life, as he doesn't have much time left." At that time though Ansurkar was semiconscious, he could hear what was being said.

Then his family physician, Dr. Trivedi started treating him and he didn't leave Ansurkar's bedside as he had only 48 hours to live. At that time Ansurkar had not passed urine for 24 hours; his abdomen was distended and hovering at death's door. The doctor's assistant tried to catheterise him but couldn't, so Dr. Trivedi took the catheter from him and was successful. Dr. Trivedi looked at Baba's picture and said, "Baba you saved him." Ansurkar states, "Baba saved my life and drove away the disaster. After this terrible ordeal I started saying, *"Jai Sainath"* constantly.

Naam Japa is the catheter that will remove toxic substances and prevent us from being intoxicated by our Indriyas and Arishadvargas.

Ref: *Sai Prasad* Magazine; 1994 (*Deepavali* Issue)

***

December 11

THE FAKIR CURES HIS INTRACTABLE DIARRHEA

Ansurkar states, "In 1971 I was blessed with twins, but Sachin developed diarrhea when he was 6 months old. It was continuous watery stools. He was checked by specialists and admitted in hospital, but the loose stools continued. Finally all the doctors gave up hope and he was brought home. The pediatrician told me that Sachin's condition was so critical that he would not survive more than 48 hours.

I sat in my living room going over the prognosis of my son. Then I wondered if this was the consequence of my own doing. Was it because I had started worshipping *Shri Swami Samarth* of Akkalkot and my faith in Baba had started wavering? I was quite confused as I wondered what I should do now. This was the first time death was hovering in my very home. I had never experienced the death of anyone in my family.

The door bell rang; startled I looked at the clock before I opened the door. A fakir stood at my door, he wore a long white kurta and had a green turban and a bunch of peacock feathers in his hand. With compassionate eyes he looked at me and gently said, "My child, you look distressed; is something wrong? Tell me and I will help you." He coaxed me and said, "Tell me son, what's wrong?" My eyes filled with tears as I told him that Sachin was hovering near death. Impulsively I ran into his room and picked him up and brought him to the fakir; I held him before him in the palms of my hand. He gently touched him with the peacock feather. He moved the feathers gently over his entire body thrice. He then said, "He will recover and be all right." I asked him what I could offer him; he replied that he would take some money when the child recovered. Then he said he would return 2 days later. Miraculously Sachin recovered the very next day and the loose stools didn't reoccur. My wavering mind kept questioning whether the fakir was Baba or Swami Samarth. The fakir came as promised and said, "Give me some money for a meal," he then asked for a rupee and left never to be seen again.

My family visited Shirdi when the twins were a year old. There Rakhyia a vendor gave us everything that we requested. He also gave us a coupon for the Abhishek puja so I didn't have to stand in the queue for it. The other devotees questioned me, "How is your name called out ahead of ours when you weren't in the queue?" I pointed to Baba's idol and replied, "Ask him." We performed the puja on the Samadhi. Then laid the twins at Baba's feet and thanked him. As we were descending from his Samadhi, Sachin had a loose explosive stool and I got my answer. My wife happily washed the floor with immense gratitude. Sachin never ever had a loose stool thereafter."

Swami Samarth and Baba are one and the same.

Ref: *Sai Prasad* Magazine; 1994 (*Deepavali* Issue)

***

THE FAKIR PROTECTED HIM
WHENEVER HE FELL ILL

Sometimes the entire life story of a devotee ought to be written as it is evident that Baba supported and helped him in every step of the way. Such a leela is given below; unfortunately the devotee has not mentioned his name or where he resided.

This devotee states, "My ties with Baba are deep and his grace has been with me since childhood. When I was a child my health was not too good, and frequently I was at death's door. My mother was never sure whether I would survive or not? But my grandmother often told my mother not to worry as she saw a fakir standing behind me every time I was sick. She was convinced that nothing bad would happen to me as this 'guardian angel' was there to protect and take care of me. I believed what my grandmother said because time and again I came out unscathed from many a crises because of Baba's grace.

During my childhood my father was very affluent, later he incurred severe losses in his business and was unable to recover them. I wasn't a good student, and had failed in my final year of school twice. Hence, I had to give up my studies and look for a job; this search took me to various cities. It was during this time I heard about Baba's divinity and thought I should visit Shirdi, but kept postponing it. By then Baba had taken Maha Samadhi. I regret till this day having missed that golden opportunity."

In my childhood I got interested in *Pranayam Yoga*. I started reading about it and attended lectures on it. Once I decided to practice Pranayam without a guru or someone to guide me through the process. I sat down without knowing the correct *asana* or posture and started inhaling and exhaling. Then I took a deep breath and could not regulate it. I inhaled and my breath went up and I fell down. At that time I fell down and stopped breathing. Some time later my mother came into my room. When she saw my condition she thought I was dead and started wailing. The neighbours heard the wailing and a large crowd gathered there. Then a *Nath Panthi Sadhu* made his way through the crowd and stood beside me. He took his tongs and hit me on my head; it started bleeding a little, but I regained consciousness." Then he turned to my mother and said, "*Bai*, your son is naughty, take care of him," and then he left."

Later my mother and the neighbours searched for him but he was not traceable. So who was that sadhu? Later Baba told me that he had appeared that day and saved my life. Time and again I got into difficult situations and Baba was always there to save me."

Baba is emphasising that nothing should be practiced without a guru. The guru is a guide for any and everything.

Ref: *Shri Sai Leela* Magazine; Vol. 17, No. 1, 2, 3, 1940,
Chaitra, Vaishak, Jesth, shake 1862

***

December 13

BABA ENSURES HER SAFE DELIVERY

Years later, this anonymous devotee began to live in Pune as he had found a job there. One day while he was walking past Dube *Mama's* shop he saw a photograph of Baba and was attracted to it. He made inquires about it and Dube told him in detail the glory of Sai Baba. Dube also gifted him a photograph of Baba, and included him in the group of devotees that met regularly for discourses.

At that time his wife was pregnant with their first baby. As her pregnancy progressed he decided to send her to her parental home. As she boarded the train he saw a divine person in a white kafni standing behind her. He did not recognise that fakir, but he remained standing behind her all the time. Even as the train pulled out of the station, he was there behind her. He felt uneasy and thought that something untoward would happen. Four days later he received a letter from his father-in-law in which he had angrily written, "How could you send your wife without checking her date of delivery? She gave birth that afternoon in the train. What is unbelievable is that the compartment was empty and there was no one to help her. This is her first delivery and who was there to take care of her during the delivery, the after birth and the new born?" But during the birth of the baby, his wife did not have any trouble, nor did she remember anything about it. The reason being that Baba was there standing behind her to take care of her.

Upon reading the letter he was overwhelmed by Baba's love and caring, and cried copiously in front of Baba's picture. That night he dreamt of Baba who was laughing heartily and said, "Arre! For people like you I am indebted for so many lifetimes. So I had to take care of the girl and her baby."

"I leave it to the readers to imagine what took place in the empty compartment of the train," he states.

We all are impregnated with good and bad karmas. Baba ensures that we have a safe delivery to reach him.

Ref: Shri Sai Leela Magazine; Vol. 17, No. 1, 2, 3, 1940,
Chaitra, Vaishak, Jesth, shake 1862

***

December 14

"MY DOCTOR IS THE FATHER OF DHANVANTARI"

He visited Shirdi for the first time, a few months after his baby was born, he asked his wife to accompany him but she refused. At Shirdi he met Dixit, Tarkad and other devotees who had been with Baba. He eagerly listened to their experiences, and learnt a lot about Baba. Then he went through some financial difficulties and couldn't get any money from his friends and relatives. As a last resort he thought he would have to pawn his wife's jewellery. By Baba's grace his problem was solved.

By then he had developed intense faith and devotion in Baba, but his wife was sceptical. He visited Shirdi again and just as he set out, his wife sarcastically remarked, "You think your Baba is great?" Her words hurt him terribly and he hoped that one day she would have faith.

Upon his return his wife developed a mass in her abdomen with bouts of severe pain. He consulted all the specialists but none of them could reach a final diagnosis. Finally they decided that exploratory surgery was required for the diagnosis and treatment. But both of them were in a state of panic at the very thought of surgery. Besides the surgery would cost a great deal of money. That night Baba appeared in his dream and said, "Look here, no one from our home will go under the knife. And don't ever think of pawning my daughter's jewellery, is that clear?"

So he continued giving the prescribed medications along with Udi and the pain abated and the mass disappeared. One day his doctor asked him with surprise, "This recovery was not due to the medicines prescribed by me. Tell me which specialist did you consult and what treatment was given to her." He replied under his breath, "My doctor is Baba and he is the father of Dhanvantri." Dhanvantri is the physician of all the deities.

Baba is far superior to Dhanvantri and is an expert in removing ailments caused by prarabdha.

Ref: Shri Sai Leela Magazine; Vol. 17, No. 1, 2, 3, 1940,
Chaitra, Vaishak, Jesth, shake 1862

***

December 15

BABA STITCHES THE CHILD'S ABDOMEN

In 1936 the most incredible leela took place in his home. His son was seriously ill, but he did not give up hope as Baba was there to protect them. On the very first day Baba appeared in his dream and said, "The illness will last for 60 days. There is no need to worry." The condition of the child continued to deteriorate. On the twenty-first day the child perspired profusely, and became cold and clammy and went into shock. He applied Udi and went to get the doctor. The doctor gave him an injection and said, "If you were late by 5 minutes the child would not have survived." His fever shot up twice and was relentlessly high. The father had placed a picture of Baba beside the bed, behind the child's head.

One evening he was sitting at his bedside when he saw Yama the Lord of death. He had a rope in his hand and had climbed up the staircase and stealthily entered the room. Then he saw Baba's picture and hesitated a while. Just as he took a step forward, Baba stepped out of the picture and manifested with his *satka* (staff) in his hand. Seeing Baba Yama retraced his steps and reached the staircase. Baba ran towards him and beat him mercilessly saying, "Will you dare to come again?" Yama replied, "No, never I made a grave mistake." Then Baba flung him down the stairs.

A short while later Baba entered the room with a thread in his hand and then he took a long needle about 6 to 7 inches long from his pocket. He approached his son and deftly like a surgeon stitched his abdomen. Upon completion of the sutures he looked at the devotee and said, "Be worry-free." Then he entered the picture placed at the head of his child. The devotee states, "I just sat and watched mesmerised at the drama unfolding before my eyes." Needless to say his son recovered completely and was healthy thereafter.

"Why fear when I am here," affirms Baba.

Ref: *Shri Sai Leela* Magazine; Vol. 17, No. 1, 2, 3, 1940,
Chaitra, Vaishak, Jesth, shake 1862

***

December 16

YAMA WILL FOLLOW BABA'S ORDER

After Rukhmani got married she resided in Amalnere, where her husband Malhari Bendre worked as a sanitary inspector. Her father Krishnaji Brahma, alias Abha Sahib was devoted to Baba. He lived in Ahmednagar where he worked as a police officer and had the good fortune of meeting Baba several times. Baba blessed him and gave him Udi hence his entire family worshiped Baba and visited Shirdi often. After his retirement he lived with his eldest son Lakshman in Bhadgaon.

Then Lakshman was transferred to Amalnere and they along with Abha moved into a house close by. Abha visited the library daily and on the way visited Rukhmani. One day he failed to visit her; on the second day Rukhmani got worried and went to meet him.

Abha was running a high fever and Rukhmani's mother was giving him a cold compress. He looked at her with affection and his eyes filled with tears. Then he said, "I doubt I will recover from this illness." The doctor was summoned and he administered some injection and advised him bedrest and fluids. The fever continued relentlessly for 8 days, despite the treatment, and soon Abha lost his voice.

On the ninth day his condition took a turn for the worse; at midnight he shrieked loudly in a strange tone of voice. Then half an hour later he shrieked again, so his family gave him a sedative but he continued to be restless. Two days later his fever started decreasing and then returned to normal. He made signs to them that he wanted to write something. Her brother and husband helped him to sit up, and handed him a slate and chalk. Abha then wrote, "Sai Baba was there at the foot of my cot protecting me. I screamed when I saw four hideous-looking men who were about to carry me away. They asked Baba to move away from my bed so that they could take me away. Then Baba menacingly shook his satka at them; at that very moment a lot of dogs started barking loudly. The four men fled for their lives. Then Yama the Lord of death came there; he was more hideous than his messengers; I shrieked again. He was extremely enraged and his red eyes were bloodshot with rage. When he saw Baba he calmed down a little. Baba, however, was calm and said, "This is an ardent devotee of mine, and I am his guru. Let him stay and continue doing my work for some more time." Yama said, "all right if you so desire. Let me know when I am to take him away. I will wait for your orders and follow them." Then he bowed to Baba and left." Abha recovered completely after that dream vision.

Baba is Parabrahma and everything will happen as per his orders.

Ref: Sai Prasad Magazine; 1993 (Deepavali Issue)

***

"I HAVE A LOT OF WORK IN SHIRDI"

Avinash Padhya resided in Mumbai, and he was fortunate to visit Shirdi numerous times in 1991. On 27 February he decided to visit his relatives in Shri Rampur. He went to the bus station and boarded the bus early in the morning at 3:50 a.m. He was glad that there were a few passengers, but when the bus arrived he found that all the seats were occupied. So he had to travel standing, up to Manmad; to help make the journey easier he started chanting Baba's name silently. He had often prayed to Baba saying, "Baba I will be blessed if you at least appear once in my dream." As he was chanting he wondered if Baba would ever appear in his dream.

The bus was now proceeding to Kopergaon when he casually turned and looked towards the door. He couldn't believe his eyes when he saw a fakir standing next to the door. He had on a long white kafni; a cloth tied around his head, a jholi slung on his left shoulder and had a pair of iron tongs in his right hand. He looked exactly like the picture of Baba that he worshiped at home. The fakir looked directly at him and smiled. Mentally he thought if he is indeed Baba he will alight in Kopergaon and go towards Shirdi. The fakir did alight at Kopergaon and Avinash followed him. The fakir took a few steps then turned towards him and said, "My child I will go now as tomorrow is Thursday and I have a lot of work to do in Shirdi." Avinash prostrated before him and the bus started moving.

He jumped into the bus and his mind was buzzing with thoughts. "I got the proof that this fakir is Baba. All along I thought I would consider myself blessed if Baba appeared in my dream. Today I saw Baba in the physical form and he spoke to me; now I am blessed a thousandfold."

When we pray from the bottom of our heart, Baba will certainly answer our prayers.

Ref: *Sai Prasad* Magazine; 1997 (*Deepavali* Issue)

***

BABA'S IDOL RECEIVED THE DAKSHINA

In 1974, Shailla was to appear for the final exams in Home Science; she loved the course and hoped she would pass with distinction. One of her friends borrowed her notes to study, and inadvertently dropped them in a barrel of water. Thus Shailla lost all the work she had done for that year; secondly a percentage of marks were to be given on that work, thirdly she had a severe urinary tract infection during that period. Shailla saw her hopes for a distinction dwindle in front of her. Nonetheless she and her mother sat throughout the night and rewrote the entire notes. Because of the infection Shailla ran a temperature and her stomach hurt so badly that she couldn't sit still and was very restless

On the day of her exam, she dreamt that she had entered a room that had numerous beds and sick people lay on them. And Baba was tenderly nursing them and looking after their needs. She went to the examination hall confidently as she knew that Baba was there to nurse her and look after her. She completed her paper without feeling feverish or ill from the infection. Her results were announced on the day of Swami Samarth's *punyathithi* (anniversary of his passing away) and she had passed with distinction. She also received a cash award for securing the first position.

A few years later she decided to do a *saptha*, that is, to complete reading the *Charita* in a week. That morning she dreamt she was in the Samadhi Mandir and after Baba's holy bath she climbed on the Samadhi. She went forward to offer dakshina, and Baba's idol put out his hand to accept it and then started counting the dakshina. She said, "Baba I am going to do a saptha of your *Charita*; please wake me up early every morning. And also please come to my home." Then she descended from the Samadhi and sat with her family, and Baba himself came and distributed prasad to all of them.

On the first day of the saptha at the time of the Arati a sadhu came to her home. He was a priest of goddess *Tulja Bhavani*; they asked him to stay back for a meal and he readily agreed. After the meal he disappeared; it was then that she realised that Baba had come in the form of a priest and fulfilled her wish.

Here powerful reassurances are given by Baba through dreams, which will be bestowed practically.

Ref: *Shri Sai Sagar* Magazine; July and August 2005

***

December 19

"WHEN I AM HERE WHY DOES HE ASK FOR DEATH?"

In 1964 Narhari Kadam developed tuberculosis and became extremely ill. He was treated by a number of doctors but his condition deteriorated and his disease progressed. One night when he could not bear the progression of the disease any longer, he beseeched Baba to either give him some relief. And if that wasn't possible to give, then because of his bad karmas he begged Baba to give him death. The next morning his wife told him that Baba appeared in her dream and said, "I will cure your husband. Tell your husband that when I am here to look after him why does he ask for death?" Then he pulled a strand of wool from his blanket and tied it around his big toe. Then he assured her that he would definitely recover and the dream ended. Baba possibly tied the strand of wool as a *Kanganam* (bangle) to confirm his promise to love, protect and nurture his devotees. The big toe is where all the nerves start and end, thus it's the lifeline for the entire nervous system.

That day Narhari met a friend who suggested that he should be treated by another doctor and asked him to visit Dr. Patil. Narhari followed his advice; the doctor told him that although he was in the last stage of the disease, nonetheless he would treat him in the best possible way. Surprisingly within a week Narhari felt better and 6 months later he was cured. Many people remarked, "What is so miraculous about that? These days tuberculosis is a curable disease?" Narhari replied, "Undoubtedly medical science has made remarkable advances. In my case it's the relationship between me and Baba that is miraculous, he is my saviour and I am indebted to him for coming to my aid so quickly and saving me from a torturous death. Only a person suffering from any disease can know what that suffering is."

In this leela Baba's confirmation of his promise to love, protect and nurture his devotee is described. Thus he can move forward in calm peaceful manner.

Ref: *Shri Sai Sagar* Magazine; July and August 2005

***

| December 20 |

"WHEN I AM HERE WHY FEAR?"

Rajshri and her husband Sailesh Khedekar resided in Pune and both were ardent devotees of Baba. He loved his sister very much, and then she got married and moved to Satara with her husband. But her husband beat her brutally; at that time she had a 6-month-old son and a few days later she committed suicide. Sailesh was very upset to hear about this and he felt that such a cruel person should be punished for his actions. He sought justice in the court, and as his brother-in-law resided in Satara, so Sailesh had to register the case there. Unfortunately his brother-in-law's name isn't mentioned.

The case was a long process and it went on for 7 years. Sailesh worked in the police department and he managed to continue going to work and also attended the court dates. His brother-in-law resorted to devious means like bribery, being absent at the hearings and destroying the evidence, but Sailesh had faith in Baba.

One day early in the morning, Sailesh became extremely ill. He had difficulty in breathing and his respiration became slow and laboured. He started perspiring profusely; he was unable to wake up. He thought he would soon die. At that moment he started chanting Baba's name. He was staring at the picture of Baba that was hanging on the wall. Sailesh then saw the picture sliding to the floor and from it Baba emerged and stood before him. Baba stood like Lord Vitthal with both his hands on his waist, and in a thundering voice he said, "When I am here, why are you worried? I will see what anyone will do to you. Don't be frightened nothing will happen to you," and disappeared. Immediately Sailesh started feeling better and then he woke up. All his symptoms disappeared and he felt all right.

Ref: *Shri Sai Sagar* Magazine; January–March 2011

***

December 21

UDI BREAKS THE *AGHORI'S* SPELL

Sailesh's brother-in-law tried other devious means of harassing them. He got an *Aghori Tantric* to cast his black magic spell on Rajashri. *Aghoris* are a sect of sadhus who cover their body with ash; the tantrik group resort to cannibalism, drinking liquor and perform black magic spells.

Early that morning she dreamt that an Aghori sadhu had two dolls with him and he was fiercely pricking it with a huge needle. Simultaneously Rajshri felt severe and unbearable pain in her body exactly in the same area that the doll was pricked. Then he threw both the dolls into fire. At that moment Baba appeared; his eyes were red with anger and he looked fierce. He immediately put his hand into the pit of fire and pulled out both the dolls. Rajshri couldn't bear the thought that Baba had burned his hand to save them, and she burst out crying. Finally she woke up crying and she narrated her dream to her husband. Three such episodes occurred and Baba came to their aid everytime and finally the Aghori stopped troubling them.

In this manner numerous Aghori practices of black magic spells were cast on them, but they neither told anyone about it nor tried to seek an antidote for it. They had implicit faith in Baba and his Udi. They ate Udi in the morning and night and were saved from the ill effects of the spells. The brother-in-law had plotted against them and had not submitted all the papers so that the case would be retried. He also failed to appear in court and finally the Judge sent out a warrant for him. Sailesh had utmost faith in Baba and he knew that finally the verdict would be against his sister's husband.

Baba's mercy and kindness is endless and bountiful.

Ref: *Shri Sai Sagar* Magazine; January–March 2011

***

December 22

BABA CAME AND PROMISED JUSTICE

A bout three days before the final hearing, Rajshri was sound asleep. Around midnight someone was pounding on their door; as her husband was sound asleep he didn't get up. Then it happened again, so Rajshri woke him up and asked him to see who it was. He went to the door and looked out through the 'eye piece' but was unable to see anyone so he returned to bed. Then it happened again; Rajshri was sitting on the bed with her eyes closed, but she could see the door quite clearly and saw Baba standing behind it. She told her husband to open the door at once as Baba had come. Rajshri then said, "Look Baba has come and is sitting on my cot." She saw that Baba wore a white kafni and carried a long stick in his hand. He had come with his devotees who waited outside. She could recognise the devotees, as his entourage were of the devotees in the painting of the palkhi procession by Jaykar.

With her eyes still closed Rajshri said, "Why are you behaving like this? Baba is seated on the cot. He has come to check the file of the case, as there is something amiss in the file. He says that the file is kept on the top shelf of the cupboard. And he wants you to take it out and give it to him." Sailesh did as she said but he couldn't see Baba so he kept the file on the bed next to her. Then Baba read each and every paper in the file carefully and said, "You will receive justice." Then Rajshri said, "Baba I am sorry that you had to come all the way from Shirdi for this." To this Baba replied, "This is his last attack on you. So I had to come here. He tried Aghori black magic and spells, but when I am here to protect you none of it will affect you. Do not be afraid, as I have come from Shirdi just to save you. You will get justice and he will be punished."

Rajshri states, "While Baba was telling me all this, the devotees outside were murmuring amongst themselves and I could hear them. They said, "Who has Baba gone to save?" Another devotee said, "He surely must have gone to save someone who is in grave trouble, as he has made us wait outside." Sailesh was standing a little distance away from the cot and was very calm. Rajshri told her husband, "Baba has come to our house at least offer some sugar to him." He brought a bowl of sugar and placed it in front of Baba's picture. Although Sailesh couldn't see Baba he carefully listened to the conversation between them, and was utterly calm as he had intense faith in Baba.

Baba requires only simple, sincere love and implicit faith in him.

Ref: *Shri Sai Sagar* Magazine; January–March 2011

***

THE THREE BLACK SERPENTS

Baba had gone to Khedekar's house a few days before the conclusion and the verdict of the case against Sailesh's brother-in-law was to be pronounced. He went through the entire file and reassured them. The accused had made a mistake in the papers submitted, and he pointed it out to Rajshri. Her husband was astounded to hear Baba say this as only he and his lawyer knew about it. Then Baba said, "I am in a hurry as I have to go and see what new problems the accused is creating for you." Then Baba took out three black serpents from his jholi. And he killed two of them and the third serpent he put back into his jholi and left. His devotees were patiently waiting outside for him. Rajshri could recognise most of them from Jaykar's painting. She was overwhelmed to see Bayja Mai, Tatya her son and Mhalsapati; then Baba along with his entourage of devotees left.

Finally the date for the verdict dawned. The Judge had gone through the files of both the lawyers. Then he pointed out the mistake that the accused had committed to Sailesh's lawyer. His opponent immediately asked for the trial to be retried, so that it would take another 7 to 10 years. But the Judge overruled his plea and said that he had the power to set that right. Second, the accused hadn't appeared in court so he asked the police to carry out the warrant and bring him to court on the next date.

The last date was then set and the accused was present. The Judge sentenced him to life imprisonment and thus by Baba's grace they got justice. It was then that Rajshri realised the meaning of the serpents. The first serpent killed by Baba represented the mistake of the accused that the Judge had corrected with his power. The second serpent killed was the last date set by the judge and the accused being brought to court. And finally the third serpent represented the final verdict that was in their favour; hence it was put back alive into Baba's jholi.

Rajshri states, "With this entire experience of 7 years our faith in Baba grew stronger. People who are faced with insurmountable problems run here and there trying to find relief. They wear different stones and conduct various rituals to appease gods and goddesses. The only prerequisite is that you should have intense faith in Baba, and know that he is always there to help his devotee. And if the need arises he will appear in person or in a dream and show them the solution, or solve the problem himself."

Ref: *Shri Sai Sagar* Magazine; January–March 2011

***

December 24

"MY SADGURU WILL CHANGE YOUR LIFE"

(The next few leelas are about Dada Kadam, a resident of Ratnagiri, and how his life was changed by Baba's doings and how the famous Aum Sai Sidhalaya temple came about in Ratnagiri.)
Dada states, "My father was the physician of Sayyiaji Rao Gaikward of Baroda. And he wanted me to follow in his footsteps, but I was involved in the political upheaval of those times. At a very young age I secretly distributed 'Flyers' with political news and was caught and punished for it twice. The turning point came in 1970 and slowly the spirituality in me was awakened. In 1960 I got married to Sumitra Desai and moved to Mumbai. Soon after my marriage I accompanied my friends to Andheri, Vasorva, to meet a young Yogi named Sarasvati Amma. I had gone there not out of reverence but just to be in the company of my friends.

Sarasvati Amma asked me to come forward and sat me down in front of her. A short while later she said, "Put your hand forward" and

I obeyed. She then paced her right hand on my outstretched open palm and I felt powerful vibrations like electricity pass into my body. The surprising fact was that I actually saw flashes of light like lightening in the sky exit from her palm and enter mine. My friends also saw this strange phenomenon. Then as she removed her palm there was a beautiful, small brass idol of Radha Krishna on my palm. Then she smiled gently at me and asked me to worship the idol everyday. She also said, "Twenty years from now you will meet my Sadguru who will change your entire life." I was inclined towards politics so what she told me about being changed into a spiritual being made no sense to me. Nonetheless I did keep the idol in my prayer room. In 1968 I decided to leave Mumbai and return to Ratnagiri."

Baba moulds his devotees suitably.

Ref: *Sai Prasad* Magazine; 1998 (*Deepavali* Issue)

***

December 25

BABA TAKES DAKSHINA FROM HIM

In 1970 Dada Kadam had gone to Ratnagiri on work regarding the newspaper. A lot of his colleagues were assembled in his home that day. At around 11 a.m. a fakir was at his door chanting "*Guru Dev Datta*." The fakir was dressed in a lungi with a long white shirt over it. He had a jholi slung over his shoulder and had very short hair. Kadam went out to give him one anna. Just as he was about to give it, the fakir held his hand in his and Kadam literally felt electricity pass through his hand. Then the fakir said, "I am going to Ganpatipule; will you give me some money for the pilgrimage?" So Kadam gave him 3 rupees. Then the fakir said, "Is there anyone inside your home? I get the feeling that some people are there." Kadam told him that they were his colleagues. Then the fakir said, "Son will you bring some mud?" Kadam obeyed; then he asked Kadam for a piece of paper to put it in. Kadam went inside and brought a piece of paper. The fakir placed the mud in it and made a neat packet, and then he recited something that Kadam couldn't understand. He then placed the packet in the palm of his hand and closed his palm. At that time

Kadam felt as if his body temperature had risen to 105 degrees. The fakir laughed heartily and it fell to normal. Then he asked him to open it saying, "Don't reveal this to anyone. It will be of use to you later." Kadam was astonished to see that in the place of the packet there was something else that he could not reveal to anyone.

The fakir said, "I have to give some offering to the deity of Gangapur. Will you give it to me?" Kadam went inside and brought 15 rupees as a kilo of pedas cost 15 rupees at that time. The fakir then asked him to make it 21 rupees. So Kadam gave him 6 rupees more. As the fakir was leaving he said, "Will you give me a *chaddar* (bed spread)?" Kadam thought, "This fakir's demands are neverending. The more I give the more he demands." Then he turned and went away. In the evening when his wife returned from work he told her about the fakir. She said, "If he asked for a bedspread he must surely be Baba." Kadan, however, said "He may have been Baba. I can't say for sure if he was."

Baba covers his devotee with his blue light.

Ref: *Sai Prasad* Magazine; 1998 (*Deepavali* Issue)

***

December 26

"SON YOU HAVE THE KEY. THAT'S GOOD."

The next day his wife asked him to go to the bazaar and bring some *Surf* detergent. That day some of his friends turned up and as they were leaving he told them he would accompany them up to the bazaar. He distinctly remembered that he locked the front door and left. He bought some vegetables and was returning when he remembered that he hadn't bought the detergent so went into a grocery shop and bought some other detergent which had the logo of a key on it.

He returned home and entered and was astounded to see the same fakir seated at his dining table waiting for him. The fakir was dressed in a torn tattered kafni but his eyes were full of compassion and love. His mind was whirling with all sorts of thoughts. "May be this fakir has used some evil power on me. Now the best option left for me is surrender to him, and seek refuge in him. In any case I have to die one day or the other." The fakir laughed and pointing to the detergent said, "Son you have already got the key and that's good. Now I should be leaving." Kadam accompanied the fakir to the next room, but he disappeared.

Kadam states, "Following the fakir's visit I started hearing different voices giving me instructions, accompanied with vivid dreams that came to pass. Then I handed my life over to Baba and surrendered to his will. Then I moved to Pune and was there from 1980 to 1985. He asked me to sell my home in Ratnagiri. However, I couldn't find a buyer. Then Baba said, "Hasn't Haseen Mia come yet? I had asked him to come" The very next day a man named Haseenbhai came and purchased my home. Baba also showed me my future home that was in Deccan Gymkhana in my dream where he drove me by car saying, "I will show you your new home," and the transaction took place without my giving any 'earnest' money.

In 1985 Baba initiated me to chant my mantra. The mantra was *"Aum Hrim Shri Sai Aum."* This is a *beej*, and a *Brahma mantra*. This mantra I chanted millions upon a million times. (The beej mantra is the imperishable monosyllable indicating Parabrahaman.)

When the devotee is 'ready' Baba hands him the key to his treasure chest, which is overflowing with spiritual treasures.

Ref: *Sai Prasad* Magazine; 1998 (*Deepavali* Issue)

***

December 27

BABA TAKES HER LEG PAIN ON HIMSELF

Kadam states, "At Pune I started chanting my mantra continuously day and night. This was followed by a lot of physical problems like palpitations and constriction of the chest. I got myself examined by a cardiologist, Dr. Katdhare. He did a full cardiology workup and numerous tests but every single test came back as 'normal'. Finally the doctor said, "Your problem is possibly psychological." Then I told him everything. Then he wrung his hands and said, "This is inexplicable." Then all the symptoms suddenly subsided and I felt calm; again I started my rigorous chanting. Now even when I am talking to someone, the chanting continues.

My wife Mai got severe cramps in her legs and the pain was unbearable so I got her examined by Dr. Choudary an orthopaedic surgeon. He informed us that surgery would be required and that her right foot would be an inch shorter than the left foot. That night Baba appeared in my dream, and stood at the foot of the bed. He lifted his kafni up to his knees and I could clearly see that both his feet were swollen. When Mai got up the next morning her pain had disappeared completely.

I had decided to visit Shirdi, every *Purnima* for nine consecutive Purnimas (full moon nights). After the ninth Purnima we returned home. My wife was about to cook some rice and when she put her hand into the rice container an idol of Lord Datta came along with the rice. Now our lives are totally changed."

Sadguru's grace will be increasing and will be in full bloom on Purnima.

Ref: *Sai Prasad* Magazine; 1998 (*Deepavali* Issue)

***

December 28

HOW *AUM SAI SIDHALAYA* CAME ABOUT

In 1985 he returned to Ratnagiri from Pune. There he again started hearing Baba's commands. Baba said, "Between Shivaji Maharaj and the file you will find your home." Kadam understood that next to the statue of Shivaji Maharaj was the Maruti Mandir, and some distance away was the J. K. Filing Factory. Kadam then started an intensive search in that area. There he found his present home; it had commercial shops in the front of it and the house was in the rear. It belonged to the disciple of Madhavnath Maharaj, Mr. Dinanath Contractor and he agreed to sell it to Kadam. Then Baba said, "I want to see the sun," so the prayer room was added to the house. And the prayer room thus became east facing and so the idol of Baba was placed facing the east.

When they went to live there they hadn't conducted the *Vastu Shanti* Puja. Then he heard Baba say, "Why worry; both of us are here and that's enough" Kadam thus didn't conduct any puja. Then he sold the commercial shops. As time went by people started coming to his prayer room and soon it became a temple. Numerous devotees were granted their wishes there. Some devotees got male offsprings; others were cured of their diseases by Baba's grace. Soon his prayer room became a temple. Then he got a vivid dream in which he saw a full moon and in it *Aum* was visible. And a star in which Sai was seen. So he got the words Aum Sai. He gave the name *Sidhalaya* as Baba had told him that this was the home where wishes are fulfilled or granted. The next day he wrote Aum Sai exactly as he had seen it in his dream and added Sidhalaya. Thus he got the name Aum Sai Sidhalaya for his temple and later a trust was formed. People flock from all over the country to that temple and get their wishes granted.

Ref: *Sai Prasad* Magazine; 1998 (*Deepavali* Issue)

***

December 29

THE DHUNI MAI MANIFESTED

One day early in the morning at about 4 a.m., Baba woke Kadam up. He appeared as Kathkar Maharaj and said, "Look *Agni Dev* has come; look after it." Kadam got up and saw that there were 8–10 pieces of wood with flames emitting from them. His wife also got up and saw this wonderful phenomenon. Only Kadam and his wife were at home. Baba had indeed made his Dhuni Mai there, right in front of his picture. He had faith in Baba but he wondered what was happening in his home. He said to his wife, "Let us go back to sleep and see how long this fire keeps burning." They got up at 6 a.m. and the fire was still burning and the wood wasn't any shorter than it was earlier. He didn't know what to do so it was left as such the entire day. That day was Buddha Purnima and he heard Baba say, "Lord *Agni* has come don't let it get extinguished. Or I will break both your feet." Kadam hurriedly went and got some firewood and he offered it to the dhuni. He thought, "If I don't follow his instructions he really will break my feet."

Baba instructed him to build a separate room for his dhuni and Kadam obeyed. Then different devotees at different times were instructed by Baba in visions to put their hand in it and pull out sacred articles. Mr. Jadav of Kelva, Thana pulled out a silver Trident and his hand wasn't burnt. Then Rasal Bhabi pulled out a black *Shiva Lingam* and Baba said, "This is *Gurneshvar Shiva Lingam*. Mai pulled out a silver *Nag* (idol of a serpent) and a brass *Nandi* (the sacred bull that Lord Shiva rode on; it's always placed in front of the Shiv Linga). These sacred articles are placed before Baba and worshipped daily. The Udi from the dhuni is distributed to the devotees.

Ref: *Sai Prasad* Magazine; 1998 (*Deepavali* Issue)

***

December 30

BABA'S PADUKAS WERE FOUND UNDER THE TAMARIND TREE

Regarding all the idols in the temple Kadam states, "I didn't buy a single idol they just came to me." The Hanuman idol arrived on *Hanuman Jayanthi*. A gentleman came and gifted the idol, and on top of the idol was a 5-rupee bill on which *Maruti Kadam* was inscribed. One day it was raining in torrents when an old man dressed in a thin towel with a shirt, a jacket and a cap came to my door. He then took out this idol from a bag and handed it to me. Saying, "I have come from Ajmer to give you this idol. He is Lord Vishnu take care of him," and left. I followed him and asked him, "where is your umbrella," as he was totally dry while it was pouring outside. He pointed to the sky and said, "Everything up there is mine. It's also my umbrella." And he disappeared.

Once Baba told my wife he would give her an idol of Lord Rama. My wife stubbornly insisted that he give her the idol of *Kodhanddhari Ram*, that is, that idol that is embellished with his armament.

391

The next day when she was cleaning the prayer room she found the idol on Baba's lap. From that year we celebrated Ram Navami in a grand fashion. At that time the construction of some rooms had been undertaken. One day a truck full of silt came to the site. And in it was this idol of *Shani Maharaj,* which is identical to the idol in Shani Signapur. The wonderful fact was that it was covered with oil, embellished with black gram and ochre. And though it was embedded in the silt it wasn't covered by even a grain of silt.

The padukas of Baba were found under the tamarind tree near the dhuni on Gurupurnima. They are definitely Baba's as Baba's right hand was longer than his left, and so was his right foot. The right paduka is slightly longer that the left so I am confident that it's Baba's padukas.

Many saints visited the temple thereafter; Kethkar Maharaj visited the temple twice. When he came here he said, "So Lord Agni Dev has come." So I realised that his first visitation was when the Agni first manifested. On this visit he came along with a gentleman who was concerned about his son, who had absconded from home. Baba said, "Do not try to find him as he is on the right path." This was a confirmation to what Kethkar Maharaj had already told the anxious father.

Then Rahul Maharaj arrived; he pointed to the sky and said, "Don't forget *Dinkar.*" As I didn't understand what he said so he explained, "He comes from here and goes there." This he said pointing first to the East and then moving his hand to the West. So I understood that he wanted me to continue doing *Surya Namaskar* (praying to the Sun God). Then he took the 5-rupee bill and offered it to Baba and left."

This is the story of Kadam who was inclined towards politics and how Baba changed his life to make him a highly spiritual person. His life revolves around his temple and a trust has also been formed.

Ref: *Sai Prasad* Magazine; 1998 (*Deepavali* Issue)

***

392

WHY DIDN'T SWAMI SAMARTH APPEAR?

Moreshwar Joshi lived in Thana, and his friend told him about Swami Samarth and he was attracted towards him. This was in 1960; then one day his father's friend came over to his home and handed him the *Charita* of Swami Samarth and said, "I brought this book for you, as I want you to read it and learn about the divinity of this great saint. Read it in 7 days and then return it." About 2 days later he started reading it so that he could complete it in 7 days. On the seventh day just as he had completed it, the door bell rang. When he went and opened it, he was astonished to see Baba standing at his door.

Baba smiled and said, "Have you finished reading chapter 21, that is, the last chapter of my *Charita*?" He thought the *Charita* was Swami Samarth's and Baba standing in front of me was saying it's his *Charita*. His mind was in turmoil, and he stood there silently looking at him. Then Baba said, "I have come from so far; won't you let me sit for a few minutes in your home?" Then Joshi took him and seated him, and asked if he would like to have some tea or coffee. Baba refused so Joshi brought some sugar and gave it to him. The moment he placed the sugar in his hand, the entire house was filled with a fragrant aroma. Then Baba blessed him saying, "Let this aroma fill your home forever." Baba's presence is often preceded by an aroma. Then he left walking slowly down the stairs. There is an *Audumbar* (holy fig) tree in front of the building, and he seemed to disappear into it. Joshi still wasn't sure of the relationship between Baba and Swami.

Some days later he had gone to the Vitthal Mandir and was chatting with his friend there. There a lad of about 5 years, wearing a yellow pair of shorts entered the temple and laid his head on the idol's feet for a long time. Joshi asked the lad what his name was and where he resided. He replied, "My name is Gaganan Pradhan, and I am devoted to Baba, but whenever I have a vision of Baba, he appears as Swami Samarth." Then the lad disappeared and Joshi got his answer and his mind was calm.

Ref: *Sai Prasad* Magazine; 1992 (*Deepavali* Issue)

***

GLOSSARY

A
Abhishek: ritualistic bathing of an idol or padukas
Arati: circulatory waving of wicks along with singing of praises of deity
Arishad Vargas: lust, anger, covetousness, delusion, pride and envy

B
Bhil: tribal people
Brahma: supreme Hindu deity; the creator of the universe

D
Darshan: divine vision
Dakshina: offering of money as gift to god
Dhoti or dhotar: a long cloth extending from the waist to the ankles
worn in a particular way by men
Dhuni: sacred fire

G
Gunna: qualities

I
Indriyias: sense organs

J
Jholi: a bag for receiving alms slung over the shoulder

K
Kafni: ankle-length loose robe
Kirtankar: a person who sings praises of God or saints

L
Leela: a divine sport
Lungi: a long cloth tied around the waist extending to the ankles

M

Mangal Snan: bathing Baba's idol after Kakad Arati in the Samadhi Mandir

N

Naam Jap: continually chanting the Lord's name
Nanda Deep: an ever-burning lamp in Lendi Baugh

P

Padukas: holy footwear
Parabrahma: the unmanifested Brahma
Parayan: reading a sacred text with religious observances
Pradakshina: to circumambulate an idol, a holy tree or a holy place

S

Sabha Mandap: the courtyard of the Dwarka Mai
Saburi: patience with fortitude
Sansthan: a trust that looks after a temple, ashram or holy building
Saptha: 7 days or a week
Shrada: appeasing the holy manes
Shradha: unconditional faith

T

Tamo Gunna: quality of inertia
Tirth: holy water

U

Udi: holy ash from the dhuni

V

Vaid: a physician of indigenous medicines

W

Wada: a dwelling

Z

Zunka: a dry curry made of gram flour with onions and green chilies

•••

Our Books on SHIRDI SAI BABA

Shirdi Sai Baba is a household name in India as well as in many parts of the World today. These books offer fascinating glimpses into the life and miracles of Shirdi Sai Baba and other Perfect Masters. These books will provide you with an experience that is bound to transform one's sense of perspective and bring about perceptible and meaningful spiritual growth.

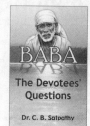

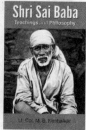

SHIRDI SAI BABA

Baba's Divine Symphony
Vinny Chitluri
ISBN 978 81 207 8485 7
₹ 250

Sai Baba an Incarnation
Bela Sharma
ISBN 978 81 207 8833 6
₹ 200

**Shirdi Sai Baba:
The Perfect Master**
*Suresh Chandra Panda &
Smita Panda*
ISBN 978 81 207 8113 9
₹ 200

**The Eternal Sai
Phenomenon**
A R Nanda
ISBN 978 81 207 6086 8
₹ 200

**Baba's Rinanubandh
Leelas during His Sojourn in Shirdi**
Compiled by Vinny Chitluri
ISBN 978 81 207 3403 6
₹ 200

**Baba's Gurukul
SHIRDI**
Vinny Chitluri
ISBN 978 81 207 4770 8
₹ 200

**Baba's Anurag
Love for His Devotees**
Compiled by Vinny Chitluri
ISBN 978 81 207 5447 8
₹ 125

**Baba's Vaani: His Sayings and
Teachings**
Compiled by Vinny Chitluri
ISBN 978 81 207 3859 1
₹ 200

**The Gospel of Shri Shirdi Sai
Baba: A Holy Spiritual Path**
Dr Durai Arulneyam
ISBN 978 81 207 3997 0
₹ 150

**Jagat Guru: Shri Shirdi
Sai Baba**
Prasada Jagannadha Rao
ISBN 978 81 207 8175 7
₹ 100

Spotlight on the Sai Story
Chakor Ajgaonker
ISBN 978 81 207 4399 1
₹ 125

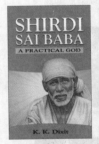

**Shirdi Sai Baba
A Practical God**
K. K. Dixit
ISBN 978 81 207 5918 3
₹ 75

STERLING

Sab Ka Malik Ek

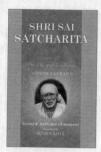

Shri Sai Satcharita
The Life and Teachings of Shirdi
Sai Baba
Translated by Indira Kher
ISBN 978 81 207 2211 8 ₹ 550(HB)
ISBN 978 81 207 2153 1 ₹ 450(PB)

Shirdi Sai Baba
The Divine Healer
Raj Chopra
ISBN 978 81 207 4766 1
₹ 100

Shirdi Sai Baba and
other Perfect Masters
C B Satpathy
ISBN 978 81 207 2384 9
₹ 150

Sai Hari Katha
Dasganu Maharaj Translated by
Dr. Rabinder Nath Kakarya
ISBN 978 81 207 3324 4
₹ 100

Unravelling the Enigma:
Shirdi Sai Baba in the
light of Sufism
Marianne Warren
ISBN 978 81 207 2147 0
₹ 400

I am always with you
Lorraine Walshe-Ryan
ISBN 978 81 207 3192 9
₹ 150

BABA- May I Answer
C.B. Satpathy
ISBN 978 81 207 4594 0
₹ 150

Ek An English Musical on
the Life of Shirdi Sai Baba
Usha Akella
ISBN 978 81 207 6842 0
₹ 75

Sri Sai Baba
Sai Sharan Anand
Translated by V.B Kher
ISBN 978 81 207 1950 7
₹ 200

Sai Baba: His Divine Glimpses
V B Kher
ISBN 978 81 207 2291 0
₹ 95

A Diamond Necklace To:
Shirdi Sai Baba
Giridhar Ari
ISBN 978 81 207 5868 1
₹ 200

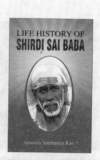

Life History of Shirdi
Sai Baba
Ammula Sambasiva Rao
ISBN 978 81 207 7722 4
₹ 200

SHIRDI SAI BABA

Shri Sai Baba- The Saviour
Dr. Rabinder Nath Kakarya
ISBN 978 81 207 4701 2
₹ 100

Sai Baba's 261 Leelas
Balkrishna Panday
ISBN 978 81 207 2727 4
₹ 125

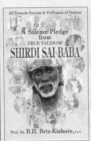

**A Solemn Pledge from
True Tales of
Shirdi Sai Baba**
Dr B H Briz-Kishore
ISBN 978 81 207 2240 8
₹ 95

God Who Walked on Earth:
The Life & Times of Shirdi
Sai Baba
Rangaswami Parthasarathy
ISBN 978 81 207 1809 8
₹ 150

**Shri Shirdi Sai Baba: His
Life and Miracles**
ISBN 978 81 207 2877 6
₹ 30

The Miracles of Sai Baba
ISBN 978 81 207 5433 1 (HB)
₹ 250

**The Thousand Names of
Shirdi Sai Baba**
Sri B.V. Narasimha Swami Ji
Hindi translation by
Dr. Rabinder Nath Kakarya
ISBN 978 81 207 3738 9
₹ 75

**108 Names of
Shirdi Sai Baba**
ISBN 978 81 207 3074 8
₹ 50

Shirdi Sai Baba Aratis
ISBN 978 81 207 8456 7
(English)   ₹ 10

**Shirdi Sai Speaks...
Sab Ka Malik Ek**
Quotes for the Day
ISBN 978 81 207 3101 1
₹ 200

Divine Gurus

Guru Charitra
Shree Swami Samarth
ISBN 978 81 207 3348 0
₹ 200

**Sri Swami Samarth
Maharaj of Akkalkot**
N.S. Karandikar
ISBN 978 81 207 3445 6
₹ 200

Hazrat Babajan:
A Pathan Sufi of Poona
Kevin R. D. Shepherd
ISBN 978 81 207 8698 1
₹ 200

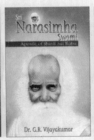

**Sri Narasimha Swami
Apostle of Shirdi Sai Baba**
Dr. G.R. Vijayakumar
ISBN 978 81 207 4432 5
₹ 90

**Lord Sri Dattatreya
The Trinity**
Dwarika Mohan Mishra
ISBN 978 81 207 5417 1
₹ 200

STERLING

श्री शिरडी साई बाबा

जेल में साई साक्षात्कार
राकेश जुनेजा
978 81 207 9507 5
₹ 150

श्री साई चरित्र दर्शन
मोहन जगन्नाथ यादव
978 81 207 8350 8
₹ 200

श्री साई सच्चरित्र
श्री शिरडी साई बाबा की अद्भुत
जीवनी तथा उनके अमूल्य उपदेश
गोविंद रघुनाथ दाभोलकर (हेमाडपंत)
978 81 207 2500 3   ₹ 300 (HB)

शिरडी अंत: से अनंत
डॉ. रबिन्द्रनाथ ककरिया
978 81 207 8191 7
₹ 750

साई सुमिरन
अंजु टंडन
978 81 207 8706 3
₹ 90

बाबा की वाणी-उनके वचन तथा आदेश
बेला शर्मा
978 81 207 4745 6
₹ 100

बाबा का अनुराग
विनी चितलुरी
978 81 207 6699 0
₹ 100

बाबा का ऋणानुबंध
विनी चितलुरी
978 81 207 5998 5
₹ 150

बाबा का गुरुकुल-शिरडी
विनी चितलुरी
978 81 207 6698 3
₹ 125

साई की आत्मकथा
विकास कपूर
978 81 207 7719 4
₹ 200

बाबा-आध्यात्मिक विचार
चन्द्रभानु सतपथी
978 81 207 4627 5
₹ 150

पृथ्वी पर अवतरित भगवान शिरडी के साई बाबा
रंगास्वामी पार्थसारथी
978 81 207 2101 2
₹ 150

स्टर्लिंग

श्री शिरडी साई बाबा

श्री शिरडी साई बाबा एवं अन्य सद्गुरु
चन्द्रभानु सतपथी
978 81 207 4401 1
₹ 90

साई शरण में
चन्द्रभानु सतपथी
978 81 207 2802 8
₹ 150

साई – सबका मालिक
कल्पना भाकुनी
978 81 207 9886 1
₹ 200

साई बाबा एक अवतार
बेला शर्मा
978 81 207 6706 5
₹ 100

साई सत् चरित का प्रकाश
बेला शर्मा
978 81 207 7804 7
₹ 200

श्री साई बाबा के परम भक्त
डॉ. रबिन्द्रनाथ ककरिया
978 81 207 2779 3
₹ 75

श्री साई बाबा के उपदेश व तत्त्वज्ञान
लेफ्टिनेंट कर्नल
एम. बी. निंबालकर
978 81 207 5971 8   ₹ 100

साई भक्तानुभव
डॉ. रबिन्द्रनाथ ककरिया
978 81 207 3052 6
₹ 125

श्री साई बाबा के अनन्य भक्त
डॉ. रबिन्द्र नाथ ककरिया
978 81 207 2705 2
₹ 100

साई का संदेश
डॉ. रबिन्द्र नाथ ककरिया
978 81 207 2879 0
₹ 125

शिरडी संपूर्ण दर्शन
डॉ. रबिन्द्रनाथ ककरिया
978 81 207 2312 2
₹ 50

मुक्तिदाता – श्री साई बाबा
डॉ. रबिन्द्रनाथ ककरिया
978 81 207 2778 6
₹ 65

स्टर्लिंग

सबका मालिक एक

साई दत्तावधूता
राजेन्द्र भण्डारी
978 81 207 4400 4
₹ 75

साई हरि कथा
दासगणु महाराज
978 81 207 3323 7
₹ 65

श्री नरसिम्हा स्वामी
शिरडी साई बाबा के
दिव्य प्रचारक
डॉ. रबिन्द्र नाथ ककरिया
978 81 207 4437 0   ₹ 75

**शिरडी साई बाबा - की सत्य
कथाओं से प्राप्त - एक पावन
प्रतिज्ञा**
प्रो. डॉ. बी.एच. ब्रिज-किशोर
978 81 207 2346 7   ₹ 80

**शिरडी साई बाबा की दिव्य
लीलाएँ**
डॉ. रबिन्द्र नाथ ककरिया
978 81 207 6376 0   ₹ 150

श्री साई चालीसा
978 81 207 4773 9
₹ 50

शिरडी साई बाबा आरती
978 81 207 8195 5
₹ 10

आरती संग्रह (Boardbook)
ISBN 978 81 207 9057 5
Size: 10.70 cm x 15.45 cm
₹ 100

शिरडी साई के दिव्य वचन-सब का मालिक एक
प्रतिदिन का विचार
978 81 207 3533 0
₹ 180

स्टर्लिंग

श्री शिरडी साई बाबा

Oriya Language

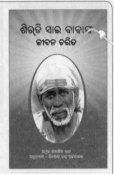

ଶ୍ରୀ ସାଇ ସଚ୍ଚରିତ୍ (Oriya)
ଶ୍ରୀ ଗୋବିନ୍ଦରାଓ ରଘୁନାଥ ଦାଭୋଳକର
(ହେମାଦପନ୍ତ)
978 81 207 8332 4 ₹ 300

ଶ୍ରୀ ଶିରିଡ଼ି ସାଇବାବା କଥାମୃତ
ପ୍ରଫେସର ଜ. ବି. ଏଚ୍, ବ୍ରିଜ୍‌କିଶୋର (Oriya)
978 81 207 7774 3
₹ 80

ଶିରୁଡ଼ି ସାଇ ବାବାଙ୍କ
ଜୀବନ ଚରିତ (Oriya)
ଅନୁକ ଶାରଭିକ ରାଓ
ଅନୁବାଦକ - କିଶୋର ଚନ୍ଦ୍ର ପଟ୍ଟନାୟକ
978 81 207 7417 9 ₹125

Other Indian Languages

ಶಿರಡಿಸಾಯಿಬಾಬಾ (Telugu)
ಪ್ರೊ. ಡಾ. ಬಿ.ಎಚ್. ಬ್ರಿಜ್–ಕಿಶೋರ್
978 81 207 2294 1
₹ 80

ಫ್ರೊಫೆಸ್ರ್ ಏರಡಿ ಸಾಯಬಾಬಾ ಅವರ
(Kannada)
ಪ್ರೊ. ಡಾ. ಬಿ.ಎಚ್. ಬ್ರಿಜ್–ಕಿಶೋರ್
978 81 207 2873 8
₹ 80

ஶ்ரீ ஸாயிபாபாவின் (Tamil)
உன்னமைக்கதைகளிலிருந்து
பெருநிதிமான நூல்கள்
ப்ரொ. டா. பி.எச். ப்ரிஜ்–கிஶோர்
978 81 207 2876 9
₹80

978 81 207 8930 2
₹225

Shirdi Sai Baba Aratis
(Tamil) ₹ 10

Shirdi Sai Baba Aratis
(Telugu) ₹ 10

Shirdi Sai Baba Aratis
(Kannada) ₹ 10

शिर्डी साईबाबांची दिव्य वचने (Marathi)
सबका मालिक एक
दैनंदिन विचार
978 81 207 7518 3 ₹ 180

STERLING PUBLISHERS PVT. LTD.
Regd. Office: A-59, Okhla Industrial Area, Phase-II, New Delhi-110020, CIN: U22110PB1964PTC002569
For Online order & detailed Catalogue visit our website:
www.sterlingpublishers.com, E-mail : mail@sterlingpublishers.com, Tel. 91-11-26386165, 26387070